T0221111

THE VHDL REFERENCE

THE VHDL REFERENCE

A Practical Guide to Computer-Aided Integrated Circuit Design including VHDL-AMS

Ulrich Heinkel
Lucent Technologies, Nuremberg, Germany

Martin Padeffke
Werner Haas
Thomas Buerner
Herbert Braisz
Thomas Gentner
Alexander Grassmann
Friedrich Alexander University of Erlangen-Nuremberg, Germany

JOHN WILEY & SONS, LTD
Chichester • Weinheim • New York • Brisbane • Singapore • Toronto

Copyright © 2000   U Heinkel , M Padeffke, W Haas, T Buerner, H Braisz, T Gentner, A Grassmann,
Friedrich Alexander University of Erlangen-Nuremberg

Published by   John Wiley & Sons, Ltd
Baffins Lane, Chichester,
West Sussex, PO 19 1UD, England

National 01243 779777
International (+44) 1243 779777
e-mail (for orders and customer service enquiries): cs-books@wiley.co.uk

Visit our Home Page on http://www.wiley.co.uk or http://www.wiley.com

Reprinted January 2002

Other Wiley Editorial Offices

John Wiley & Sons, Inc., 605 Third Avenue,
New York, NY 10158-0012, USA

WILEY-VCH Verlag GmbH
Pappelallee 3, D-69469 Weinheim, Germany

Jacaranda Wiley Ltd, 33 Park Road, Milton,
Queensland 4064, Australia

John Wiley & Sons (Canada) Ltd, 22 Worcester Road
Rexdale, Ontario, M9W 1L1, Canada

John Wiley & Sons (Asia) Pte Ltd, 2 Clementi Loop #02-01,
Jin Xing Distripark, Singapore 129809

British Library Cataloguing in Publication Data

A catalogue record for this book is available from the British Library

ISBN 0 471899720

Printed and bound by CPI Antony Rowe, Eastbourne

CONTENTS

VHDL TUTORIAL

VHDL-AMS TUTORIAL

VHDL WORKSHOP

REFERENCE

Preface

The hardware description language VHDL has been established as a means for digital integrated circuit design capture for some time. We find it in use for standard ASIC design as well as in advanced design flows for high-performance products. The reasons for this remarkable development from a DoD documentation language to an international design workhorse are quite complex, but the main driving force has been the continuous struggle for more design efficiency. In the past two decades the development methods for integrated circuits have had to be optimized to handle rapidly increasing complexities in a short time. The manufacturing technology is able to put about $30-60\%$ more transistors on a chip every year, but the design productivity is improving only about 20 % per year. After the introduction of Low Level Synthesis no substantial break-through in Design Automation has been achieved. Major improvements are expected from the extended 're-use' of large digital functions, essentially in the form of verified hardware-description-language code, to be instantiated, perhaps in a parameterized form. This is a very complex business' however, and the description using, for example, VHDL is only a part of it. Many issues, such as verification, test, and the trade with Intellectual Property, are still not fully understood.

A second major development is the rapidly growing use of programmable logic for low volume applications, which forces many smaller design groups to use a hardware description language.

Finally, a language extension suitable for the description of Analogue and Mixed-Signal systems has recently been defined (VHDL-AMS). We expect a quick utilization of the emerging language by system engineers, provided that usable simulation software becomes available in the market. In contrast to the use of VHDL in the digital domain, synthesis for analogue circuits, not to speak of systems, is not available. So there will be an interest in VHDL-AMS only after robust and powerful simulation software has become available. As a simulator for testing VHDL-AMS models is not available at this time, the chapter on VHDL-AMS is limited to a short description of the new syntax elements and basic mechanisms of a mixed-signal simulator.

One of the major market forces that will enforce the use of all-round hardware description languages in the design community is the trend to use executable specifications in business relations, for example between a subsystem vendor and a system integrator.

We may now safely conclude that the fluency in hardware description languages such as VHDL and VHDL-AMS will be a stringent requirement for most electronic design engineers in the future.

In the Institute for Computer Aided Circuit Design we have been teaching the use of VHDL for several years – not only the language as such, but emphasizing its efficient use for the synthesis of digital circuits. The courses were taught not only accompanying a digital design project class in the university, but also for engineers working in the industry, then in a modified form in three or five days.

This book assumes that readers have a basic understanding of computer science fundamentals. The tutorial section is tailored to VHDL beginners and should help in becoming familiar with the language concepts and syntax. Some chapters might also be of interest for the experienced user to refresh his or her knowledge of a specific topic. Yet, the reference section will be more important for actual designers' as it provides in depth coverage of the VHDL standard. The book is accompanied by a CD-ROM, which holds an electronic version of the reference, suitable for online use (see also **http://www.vhdl-online.de**). A design workshop is also included to allow the beginner to practice his or her VHDL skills. The exercises start out from simple logical functions and evolve towards a larger design example. Emphasis is put on synthesis, using commercial tools, which cannot be included on the CD-ROM.

Here I have to thank many former and current PhD students and scientific assistants of the institute, and also the students who were exposed to our efforts to learn how to teach, and who did much to debug the material.

The activity was started under my predecessor, Prof. Müller-Glaser, now in Karlsruhe, by some of his co-workers, and continued in my time by the authors of this book. Especially for this effort I would like to thank Ulrich Heinkel, who was the leading spirit behind the book.

Wolfram H. Glauert
Erlangen, October 1999

The accompanying CDs referenced in this book are no longer available. The material can now be found at the following website:
http://www.tu-chemnitz.de/etit/sse/VHDL-Buch/.

VHDL TUTORIAL

1 VHDL : Overview and Application Field

1.1 Application Field of HDLs

- **What is hardware?**

- **What kind of description?**

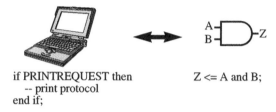

    if PRINTREQUEST then   Z <= A and B;
    -- print protocol
    end if;

- **Hardware Description Language (HDL) =
  'Programming'-language for modelling of (digital) hardware**

VHDL is a hardware description language. The word 'hardware', however, is used in a wide variety of contexts, which range from complete systems such as personal computers on the one hand side to the small logical gates on their internal integrated circuits on the other.

This is why different descriptions exist for the hardware functionality. Complex systems are often described by the behaviour that is observable from the outside. Abstract behavioural models are used in this case that hide all the implementation details. In this example the print protocol will be executed whenever a PRINTREQUEST occurs. This can be either a pressed key or a software command, etc. The description of a basic logic gate, on the other hand, may consist of only one boolean equation. This is a very short and precise description.

The language VHDL covers the complete range of applications and can be used to model (digital) hardware in a general way.

1.1.1   Application of HDLs (1)

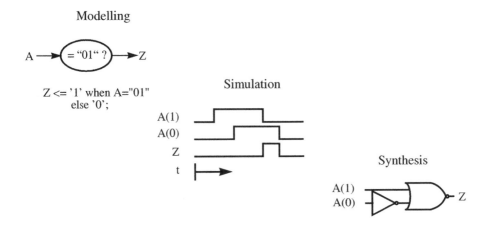

Let us have a look at the field of application for a hardware description language:

The most evident application is probably the development of a formal model of the behaviour of a system. With formality, misunderstandings and misinterpretations can be avoided. Because of the self-documenting character of VHDL, a VHDL model can even serve as system documentation to a certain degree.

The big advantage of hardware description languages is the possibility to actually execute the code. In principle, they are nothing else than specialized programming languages. Coding errors of the formal model or conceptual errors of the system can be found by running simulations. There, the response of the model on stimulation with different input values can be observed and analysed.

During the development cycle the description has to become more and more precise until it is actually possible to manufacture the product. The (automatic) transformation of a less detailed description into a more elaborated one is called synthesis. Existing synthesis tools are capable of mapping specific constructs of hardware description languages directly to the standard components of integrated circuits. This way, a formal model of the hardware system can be used from the early design studies to the final netlist. Software support is available for the necessary refinement steps.

1.1.2 Application of HDLs (2)

Reuse:

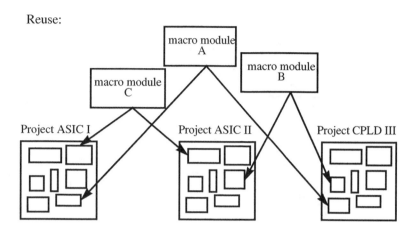

Additionally, hardware description languages offer so-called design reuse capabilities. Similar to simple electronic components, such as, for example, a resistor, the corresponding HDL model can be reused in several designs/projects. It is common use that frequently needed function blocks (macros) are collected in model libraries. The selection of an existing module is not only restricted to the design engineer but can sometimes be performed by a synthesis tool.

1.2   Range of Use

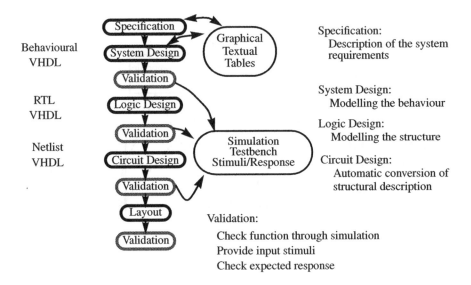

The design process always starts with a specification phase: the component that is to be designed is defined with respect to function, size, interfaces, etc. Despite the complexity of the final product, mainly simple methods, based on paper and pencil most of the time, are being used.

After that, self-contained modules have to be defined on the system level. Their interaction is described very precisely and interfaces (inputs, outputs, data formats), clock speed and reset mechanism are specified. With that information at hand, pure simulation models of the circuit can be developed. Behavioural models of standard components can be integrated into the system from libraries of commercial model developers. The overall system can already be simulated.

On the logic level, the models that have to be designed are described with all the synthesis aspects in view. As long as only a certain subset of VHDL constructs is used, commercial synthesis programs can derive the boolean functions from this abstract model description and map them to the elements of an ASIC gate library or the configurable logic blocks of FPGAs. The result is a netlist of the circuit or of the module on the gate level.

Finally, the circuit layout for a specific ASIC technology can be created by means of other tools from the netlist description.

Every transition to a lower abstraction level must be proven by functional validation. For this purpose, the description is simulated in such a way that for all stimuli (= input signals for the simulation) the module's responses are compared.

VHDL is suitable for the design phases from system level to gate level.

1.3   VHDL : Overview

- **Very High Speed Integrated Circuit Hardware Description Language**
  - Modelling of digital systems
  - Concurrent and sequential statements
  - Machine-readable specification
  - Design lifetime > designer lifetime
  - Man- and machine-readable documentation
- **International Standards**
  - IEEE Std 1076-1987
  - IEEE Std 1076-1993
- **Analogue- and mixed-signal extension: VHDL-AMS**
  - IEEE Std 1076.1-1999
- **Pure definition of language in the LRM (Language Reference Manual)**
  - No standards for application or methodology

VHDL development was initiated originally from the US Department of Defense (DoD). They requested a language for describing a hardware, which had to be readable for machines and humans at the same time and to strictly force the developer to write structured and comprehensible code, so that the source code itself can serve as a kind of specification document. Most important was the concept of concurrency to cope with the parallelism of digital hardware. Sequential statements to model very complex functions in a compact form were also allowed.

In 1987, VHDL was standardized by the US Institute of Electrical and Electronics Engineers (IEEE) for the first time with the first official update in 1993. Apart from the file handling procedures these two versions of the standard are compatible. The standard of the language is described in the Language Reference Manual (LRM).

A new and difficult stage was entered with the effort to upgrade VHDL with analogue and mixed-signal language elements. The upgrade is called VHDL-AMS (**a**nalogue-**m**ixed-**s**ignal) and it is a superset of VHDL. The digital mechanisms and methods have not been altered by the extension.

For the time being, only simulation is feasible for the analogue part because analogue synthesis is a very complex problem affected by many boundary conditions. The mixed signal simulation has to deal with the problems of synchronizing the digital and analogue simulators and finding solution algorithms for all kinds of nonlinear differential equations.

1.3.1   VHDL : History

- **early '70s**   :   **Initial discussions**
- **late '70s**   :   **Definition of requirements**
- **mid -'82**   :   **Contract of development with IBM, Intermetrics and TI**
- **mid -'84**   :   **Version 7.2**
- **mid -'86**   :   **IEEE-Standard**
- **1987**   :   **DoD adopts the standard -> IEEE.1076**
- **mid -'88**   :   **Increasing support by CAE manufacturers**
- **late '91**   :   **Revision**
- **1993**   :   **New standard**
- **1999**   :   **VHDL-AMS extension**

VHDL is a language that is permanently being extended and revised. The original standard itself needed more than 16 years from the initial concept to the final, official IEEE standard. When the document passed the committee it was agreed that the standard should be revised every 5 years. The first revision phase resulted in the updated standard of the year 1993.

Independently of this revision agreement, additional effort is made to standardize 'extensions' of the pure language reference. These extensions cover, for example, packages (std_logic_1164, numeric_bit, numeric_std, ...) containing widely needed data types and subprograms, or the definition of special VHDL subsets such as the synthesis subset IEEE 1076.6.

The latest extension is the addition of analogue description mechanisms to the standard, which results in a VHDL superset called VHDL-AMS.

1.3.2   VHDL : Application Field

- **Hardware design**
  - ASIC: technology mapping
  - FPGA: CLB mapping
  - PLD: smaller structures, hardly any use of VHDL
  - Standard solutions, models, behavioural description, ...
- **Software design**
  - VHDL – C interface (tool-specific)
  - Main focus of research (hardware/software co-design)

VHDL is used mainly for the development of Application Specific Integrated Circuits (ASICs). Tools for the automatic transformation of VHDL code into a gate-level netlist were developed already at an early point of time. This transformation is called synthesis and is an integral part of current design flows.

For use with Field Programmable Gate Arrays (FPGAs) several problems exist. In the first step, boolean equations are derived from the VHDL description, no matter whether an ASIC or an FPGA is the target technology. But now, this boolean code has to be partitioned into the Configurable Logic Blocks (CLB) of the FPGA. This is more difficult than the mapping onto an ASIC library. Another big problem is the routing of the CLBs, as the available resources for interconnections are the bottleneck of current FPGAs.

While synthesis tools cope pretty well with complex designs, they usually obtain only suboptimal results. Therefore, VHDL is hardly used for the design of low-complexity Programmable Logic Devices (PLDs).

VHDL can be applied to model system behaviour independently from the target technology. This can be useful to provide standard solutions, for example for micro controllers, error correction (de-)coders, etc., or behavioural models of microprocessors and RAM devices can be used to simulate a new device in its target environment.

An ongoing field of research is the hardware/software co-design. The most interesting question is which part of the system should be implemented in software and which part in hardware. The decisive constraints are the costs and the resulting performance.

1.3.3 ASIC Development

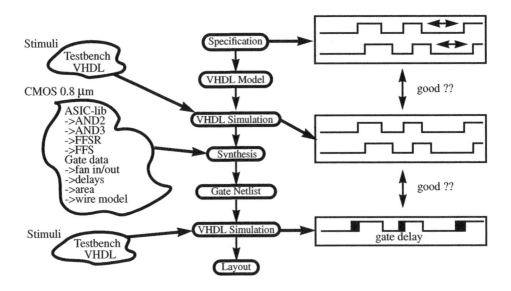

The development of VHDL models starts with their specification, which covers functional aspects and the timing behaviour. Sometimes a behavioural VHDL model is derived from here, yet synthesizable code is frequently requested right from the beginning. VHDL code can be simulated and checked for the proper functionality.

If the model shows the desired behaviour, the VHDL description will be synthesized. A synthesis tool selects the appropriate gates and flip flops from the specified ASIC library in order to reproduce the functional description. It is essential for the synthesis procedure that the sum of the resulting gate delays along the longest paths (from the output to the input of every flip flop) is less than the clock period.

As soon as a model built of ASIC library elements is available, a simulation on gate level can be performed. Now gate and propagation delays have to be taken into account. Delay values can be included in each VHDL model description, i.e. the designer receives the first clues about maximum clock frequency and critical paths already after synthesis.

The propagation delay along the signal wires have to be estimated first because the actual values are available after the layout is finished. The process of feeding these values back into the VHDL model is called back annotation. Once again it must be checked whether the circuit fulfils the specified timing constraints.

1.4 Concepts of VHDL

- **Execution of assignments:**
  - Sequential
  - Concurrent

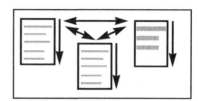

- **Methodologies:**
  - Abstraction
  - Modularity
  - Hierarchy

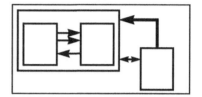

VHDL distinguishes itself from other languages in the way assignments are executed because two basic types of statements are known:

Sequential statements are executed one after another, as in software programming languages. Subsequent statements can override the effects of previous statements this way. The order of the assignment must be considered when sequential statements are used.

Concurrent statements are active continuously. So the order of the statements is not relevant. Concurrent statements are especially suited to model the parallelism of hardware.

VHDL also features three important modelling techniques:

Abstraction allows for the description of different parts of a system with different amounts of detail. Modules that are needed only for the simulation do not have to be described in as much detail as modules that might be synthesized.

Modularity enables the designer(s) to split big functional blocks and to write a model for each part.

Hierarchy lets the designer build a design out of submodules, which themselves may consist of several submodules. Each level of hierarchy may contain modules of different abstraction levels. The submodules of these models are present in the next lower hierarchical level.

1.4.1   Abstraction

- **Abstraction is hiding of details:**
  Differentiation between essential and non-essential information

- **Creation of abstraction levels:**
  On every abstraction level only the essential information is considered,
  non-essential information is left out

- **Equability of the abstraction:**
  All information of a model on one abstraction level contains the same degree of
  abstraction

Abstraction is defined as the hiding of information that is too detailed. It is therefore necessary to differentiate between essential and non-essential information. Information that is not important for the current view of the problem will be left out from the description. Abstraction levels are characterized by the kind of information that is common to all models of this level.

A model is said to be of a certain abstraction level if every module has the same degree of abstraction. If this is not the case then the model will be a mixture of different abstraction levels.

1.4.2 Abstraction Levels in IC Design

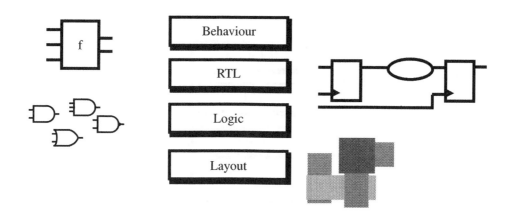

The four abstraction levels of a digital circuit design are shown in the figure. The functional description of the model is outlined in the behavioural level. There is no system clock and signal transitions are asynchronous with respect to the switching time. Usually, such descriptions are simulatable only, but not synthesizable.

In the next step, the design is divided into combinational logic and storage elements. This is called the Register Transfer Level (RTL). The storage elements (flip flops (FFs), latches) are controlled by a system clock. In synchronous designs, FFs should be used (driven by the edge of the clock signal) exclusively, because transparent latches (driven by the level of a control signal) are not spike-proof. For the description on RT level, only 10–20% of all VHDL language constructs are needed and a strict methodology has to be followed. This description on RT level is called synthesizable description.

On the logic level, the design is represented as a netlist with logic gates (AND, OR, NOT, ...) and storage elements. The final layout is at the bottom of the hierarchy. The different cells of the target technology are placed on the chip and the connections are routed. After the layout has been verified, the circuit is ready for the production process.

1.4.3 Abstraction Levels and VHDL

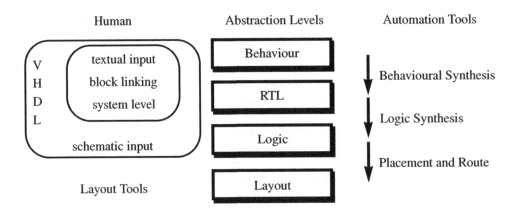

VHDL is applicable to the upper three abstraction levels shown in the figure. It is not suitable to describe a layout. The design entry in behavioural and RT levels is usually done by text editors. Graphical tools are also available, but experienced users often find it easier to write the code by hand. On the gate level, a schematic is modified, as VHDL netlist descriptions tend to become too complex pretty soon.

The transition from an upper abstraction level to a lower one is supported more or less efficiently by software.

Behavioural synthesis is still a dream of many researchers, as only very simple behaviour models are synthesizable. A common application is the design of RAM cells for the target technology, where only the generic parameters (width, depth, number of ports, (a)synchronous, ...) need to be specified.

Logic synthesis, however, has been perfected in recent years. As long as the designer confines himself or herself to certain simple VHDL constructs that are sufficient for RT level descriptions, the synthesis tools will be able to reproduce the behaviour in the logic level.

As a result of the ongoing research into efficient place and route algorithms, the step from the logic level to the final layout has been widely automated for digital standard cell designs.

1.4.4   Description of Abstraction Levels

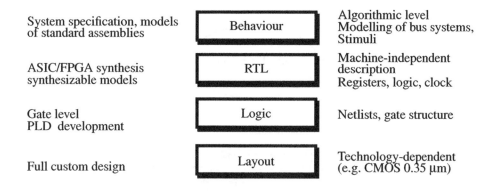

System specification, models
of standard assemblies

Behaviour

Algorithmic level
Modelling of bus systems,
Stimuli

ASIC/FPGA synthesis
synthesizable models

RTL

Machine-independent
description
Registers, logic, clock

Gate level
PLD development

Logic

Netlists, gate structure

Full custom design

Layout

Technology-dependent
(e.g. CMOS 0.35 μm)

In the behaviour level, complete systems can be modelled. Bus systems or complex algorithms are described without considering synthesizability. The stimuli for simulation of RTL models are described in the behaviour level, for example. Stimuli are signal values of the input ports of the model and are described in the testbench, sometimes called the validation bench.

The designer has to take great care to find a consistent set of input stimuli that do not contradict the specification. The responses of the model have to be compared with the expected values, which, in the simplest case, can be done with the help of a waveform diagram that shows the simulated signal values.

On the RT level, the system is described in terms of registers and logic that calculates the next value of the storage elements. It is possible to split the code into two blocks (cf. process statement) that contain either purely combinational logic or registers. The registers are connected to the clock signal and provide for synchronous behaviour. In practice, the strict separation of Flip Flops from combinational logic is often annulated, and clocked processes describe the registers and the corresponding update functions.

The gate netlist is generated from the RT description with the help of a synthesis tool. For this task, a cell library for the target technology that holds the information about all available gates and their parameters (fan-in, fan-out, delay) is needed.

Based upon this gate netlist, the circuit layout is generated. The resulting wire lengths can be converted into propagation delays, which can be fed back into the gate level model (back annotation). This allows for thorough timing simulations without the need for additional simulator software.

1.4.5 Behavioural Description in VHDL

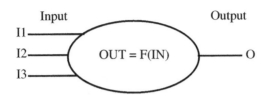

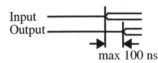

```
O <= transport I1 + I2 * I3 after 100 ns;
```

A simple specification of the function of a module is shown above. The output O depends upon the three input values I1, I2 and I3. Furthermore, it is specified that a new output value must be stable at the latest 100 ns after the input values have changed.

In a behavioural VHDL description, the function can be modelled as a simple equation (e.g. I1 + I2 * I3) plus a delay of 100 ns. The worst case, i.e. that 100 ns are needed to calculate a new output value, is assumed here.

1.4.6   RT Level in VHDL

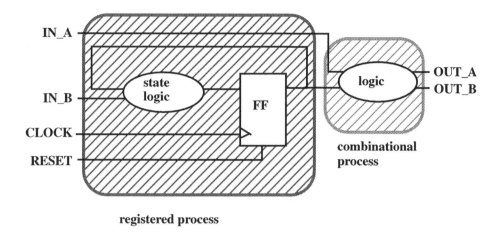

registered process

In VHDL functional behaviour is modelled with so-called processes. Two different types of processes exist in RT level descriptions: the pure combinational process and the clocked process. All clocked processes infer flip flops and can be described in terms of state machine syntax.

In addition to the data input and data output signals, the control signals such as the module clock (CLOCK) and reset (RESET) for asynchronously resetable flip flops have to be considered in modelling on RT level. When a synchronous reset strategy is employed, the reset input is treated like an ordinary data input.

It follows that RT-level VHDL code also contains some sort of structural information in addition to the functional behaviour as storing and non-storing elements are separated. Timing issues in the form of when signal values may be updated (e.g. synchronously to the clock signal) are also considered.

1.4.7   Gate Level in VHDL

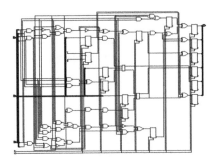

```
U86 : ND2 port map(A => n192, B => n191, Z => n188);sss
U87 : ND2 port map(A => I3_2, B => I2_0, Z => n175);
U88 : ND2 port map(A => I2_2, B => I3_0, Z => n173);
U89 : NR2 port map(A => mul_36_PROD_not_0, B => n174, Z => n185);
U90 : EN  port map(A => n181, B => n182, Z => n180);
U91 : ND2 port map(A => I3_2, B => I2_1, Z => n181);
U92 : ND2 port map(A => I2_2, B => I3_1, Z => n182);
U93 : IVP port map(A => n180, Z => n192);
U94 : AO6 port map(A => n173, B => n174, C => n175, Z => n172);
U95 : NR2 port map(A => n174, B => n173, Z => n176);
U96 : ND2 port map(A => I3_1, B => I2_1, Z => n174);
U97 : EN  port map(A => n183, B => n178, Z => product64_4);
U98 : ND3 port map(A => I2_2, B => I3_2, C => n174, Z => n183);
```

A VHDL gate-level description contains a list of the gates (components) that are used in the design. Another part holds the actual instantiation of the components and lists their interconnection.

A schematic of the gate structure of a digital circuit can be seen on the top side of the above figure. The bottom side shows a part of the corresponding VHDL description. Each single element of the circuit (e.g. U86) is instantiated as a component (e.g. ND2) and connected to the corresponding signals (n192, n191, n188). All used gates are part of the selected technology library where additional information like area, propagation delay, capacity, etc. is stored.

1.4.8   Information Content of Abstraction Levels

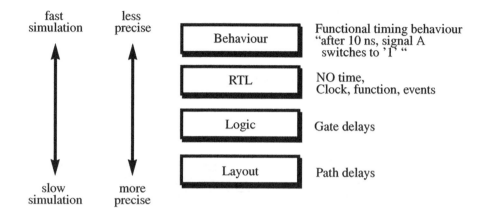

The behavioural model is a simple way to describe the behaviour of a circuit, similar to usual software programming languages, such as PASCAL or C. With this description, only the functional behaviour can be simulated by a VHDL simulator.

The clock pulse is the distinguishing mark for the RT-level description. All operations are related to the clock signal. RT-level simulations give no information about the real timing behaviour, which means that is impossible to tell whether or not all signals have actually settled to stable values within one clock period.

When the model is described on the logic level, delays can be applied to the used gates for simulation. The timing information is part of the synthesis library. This enables a rough validation of the timing behaviour. The uncertainty stems from the propagation delay along the signal wires, which has not yet been considered. These delays may very well make up the main part of the entire delay in larger designs.

If the layout is completed, the wire lengths and thus the propagation delays will be known. The design can be simulated on gate level with the additional delay values, and consequently the timing behaviour of the entire circuit can be validated. However, the simulation time grows considerably with the increased amount of information about the circuit, which restricts timing simulation to small parts of complex designs.

1.4.9 Modularity and Hierarchy

- **Partitioning in several partial designs**
- **Restrict complexity**
- **Enable teamwork**
- **Study of alternative implementations**
- **Soft macros**
- **Simulation models**

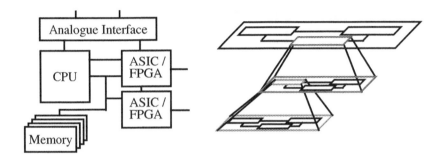

Modularity allows the partitioning of big functional blocks into smaller units and the grouping closely related parts in self-contained subblocks, so-called modules. In this way, a complex system can be divided into manageable subsystems. The guidelines for partitioning can differ from design to design. Most of the time, functional aspects are considered as partitioning constraint. The existence of well-defined subsystems allows several designers to work in parallel on the same project, as each designer will view his or her part as a new, complete system.

Hierarchy allows one to build a design out of modules which themselves may be built out of (sub-) modules. One level of a hierarchical description contains one or more modules that can even have different degrees of abstraction. Possibly, existing submodules are present in the next lower hierarchical level.

Modularity and hierarchy help to simplify and organize a design project. Additional advantages are that different implementation alternatives can be examined for the modules, e.g. in a simulation. Only the corresponding component instantiation needs to be changed for this in the overall model. Also, analogue interfaces can be modelled in VHDL and added to the system model for simulation. Sometimes, simulation models of the devices that will be connected to the new design exist and can be used for a simulation of the design under test in its real working environment.

1.5   Summary

- **Hardware and software concepts**
- **Hardware is part of the system design**
- **Behavioural and RTL style**
- **Structure**
- **Concurrency (simultaneity)**
- **Sequential statements**
- **Description of timing behaviour is possible**
- **One language for model development and verification**
- **VHDL extension towards analogue modelling (VHDL-AMS)**

Hardware and software concepts are present in VHDL to model a digital system. There is a clear distinction between a pure behavioural model and RT-level modelling for synthesis.

VHDL permits a structural (modular) and hierarchical description of a digital system.

Concurrency is an important concept in VHDL: concurrent statements are executed virtually in parallel. The simulation is event-driven. If a certain event occurs (e.g. initiated by the stimulus), processes that depend on this event are triggered. These processes contain sequential statements, which are evaluated one after ancother. Each process as a whole can be viewed as a concurrent statement. In this way, the changes of signal values caused by the execution of several processes occur at the same time in the simulation.

Furthermore, it is possible to describe timing behaviour in VHDL. This eliminates the need for other languages for stimuli generation for test purposes or timing verification of the final design.

2   VHDL Language and Syntax

2.1   General

```
---------------------------------
-- Example VHDL Code --
---------------------------------

signal mySignal: bit; -- an example signal

MYsignal<= '0',              -- start with '0'
           '1' AFTER 10 ns,  -- and toggle after
           '0' after 10 ns,  -- every 10 ns
           '1' afTer 10 ns;
```

- **Case-insensitive**
- **Comments: '--' until end of line**
- **Statements are terminated by ';'** (may span multiple lines)
- **List delimiter: ','**
- **Signal assignment: '<='**
- **User-defined names:**
  - letters, numbers, underscores
  - start with a letter

VHDL is generally case-insensitive which means that lower case and upper case letters are not distinguished. This can be exploited to define one's own rules for formatting the VHDL source code. VHDL keywords could for example be written in lower case letters and self-defined identifiers in upper case letters. This convention is valid for the following figures.

Comments can be inserted after two consecutive hyphens. From this point forward to the end of the current line everything will be considered as comment.

Statements are terminated in VHDL with a semicolon. That means as many line breaks or other constructs as wanted can be inserted or left out. Only the semicolons are considered by the VHDL compiler.

Lists are normally separated by commas. Signal assignments are notated with the composite assignment operator '<='.

Self-defined identifier as defined by the VHDL'87 standard may contain letters, numbers and underscores and must begin with a letter. Further, no VHDL keywords may be used. The VHDL'93 standard allows one to define identifiers more flexibly, as the next figure will show.

2.1.1 Identifier

```
mySignal_23       -- normal identifier

rdy, RDY, Rdy     -- identical identifiers

vector_&_vector   -- X: special character

last of Zout      -- X: white spaces

idle__state       -- X: consecutive underscores

24th_signal       -- X: begins with a numeral

open, register    -- X: VHDL keywords
```

```
\mySignal_23\            -- extended identifier

\rdy\, \RDY\, \Rdy\ -- different identifiers

\vector_&_vector\    -- legal

\last of Zout\       -- legal

\idle__state\        -- legal

\24th_signal\        -- legal

\open\, \register\  -- legal
```

- **(Normal) Identifier**
  - Letters, numerals, underscores
  - Case-insensitive
  - No two consecutive underscores
  - Must begin with a letter
  - No VHDL keyword

- **Extended Identifier (VHDL'93)**
  - Enclosed in back slashes
  - Case-sensitive
  - Graphical characters allowed
  - May contain spaces and consecutive underscores
  - VHDL keywords allowed

Simple identifiers as defined by the VHDL'87 standard may contain letters, numbers and underscores. So 'mySignal_23' is a valid simple identifier. Further, VHDL is case-insensitive, which means 'rdy', 'RDY' and 'Rdy' are identical. In particular, the identifier has to begin with a letter, so '24th_signal' is not a valid identifier. Also not allowed are graphical characters, white spaces, consecutive underscores and VHDL keywords.

In the VHDL'93 standard a new type of identifier is defined. These identifiers are called extended identifiers and are enclosed in back slashes. Within these back slashes nearly every combination of characters, numbers, white spaces and underscores is allowed. The only thing to consider is that extended identifiers are now case-sensitive. So '/rdy/', '/RDY/' and '/Rdy/' are now three different identifiers.

2.1.2 Naming Convention

architecture CONVENTION of NOTATION is

end **architecture** CONVENTION;

`93` The keyword 'architecture' may be
repeated after the keyword 'end'

△ Output port modes have to match

⊡ Not generally synthesizable

Ọ The direction of arrays should
always be defined the same way

- **VHDL keywords are written
  in lower case letters**

- **Important parts are written in
  bold letters**

- **Explains syntax of the
  VHDL'93 standard**

- **Pointing out particular issues
  to watch out for**

- **Pointing out synthesis
  aspects**

- **Gives a tip in using the
  language effectively**

The naming convention for this book is that VHDL keywords are written in lower case letters
while user-defined identifiers are written in upper case letters. If something has to be
highlighted, this is done by writing it in bold letters.

There are several self-explanatory icons. They mark special issues about the VHDL'93
syntax (compared to that of VHDL'87), things to remark, synthesis aspects and special tips.

2.2   VHDL Structural Elements

- **Entity:**   **Interface**
- **Architecture:**   **Implementation, behaviour, function**
- **Configuration:**   **Model chaining, structure, hierarchy**
- **Process:**   **Concurrency, event-controlled**
- **Package:**   **Modular design, standard solution, data types, constants**
- **Library:**   **Compilation, object code**

The main units in VHDL are entities, architectures, configurations and packages (together with package bodies).

While an entity describes an interface consisting of the port list most of the time, an architecture contains the description of the function of the corresponding module. In general, a configuration is used for simulation purposes only. In fact, the configuration is the only simulatable object in VHDL, as it explicitly selects the entity/architecture pairs to build the complete model. Packages hold the definition of commonly used data types, constants and subprograms. By referencing a package, its content can be accessed and used.

Another important construct is the process. While statements in VHDL are generally concurrent in nature, this construct allows for a sequential execution of the assignments. The process itself, when viewed as a whole object, is concurrent. In reality, the process code is not always executed. Instead, it waits for certain events to occur and is suspended most of the time.

A library in VHDL is the logical name of a collection of compiled VHDL units (object code). This logical name has to be mapped by the corresponding simulation or synthesis tool to a physical path on the file system of the computer.

2.2.1   Declaration of VHDL Objects

	Entity	Architecture	Process/ Subprogram	Package
Subprogram	x	x	x	x
Component		x		x
Configuration		x		
Constant	x	x	x	x
Data type	x	x	x	x
Port	x			
Signal		x	x[a]	x
Variable			x[b]	

a. Signals may not be declared in functions

b. Global variables (VHDL'93) may also be declared in entities, architectures and
    packages

The above table lists the legal places for the declaration of different objects:

A subprogram is similar to a function in C and can be called many times in a VHDL design. It can be declared in the declarative part of an entity, architecture, process or even another subprogram, and in packages. As a subprogam is thought to be used in several places (architectures), it is useful to declare it in a package, always.

Components are necessary to include entity/architecture pairs in the architecture of the next higher hierarchy level. These components can only be declared in an architecture or a package. This is useful if an entity/architecture pair might be used in several architectures as only one declaration is necessary in this case.

Configurations themselves are complete VHDL design units. But it is possible to declare configuration statements in the declarative part of an architecture. This possibility is only rarely used, however, as it is better to create an independent configuration for the whole model.

Constants and data types can be declared within all available objects.

Port declarations are allowed in entities only. They list those architecture signals that are available as interface to other modules. Additional internal signals can be declared in architectures, processes, subprograms and packages. Note that signals cannot be declared in functions, a special type of a subprogram.

Generally, variables can only be declared in processes and subprograms. In VHDL'93, global variables are defined that can be declared in entities, architectures and packages.

2.2.2 Entity

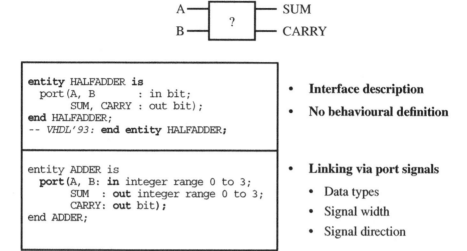

```
entity HALFADDER is
   port(A, B     : in bit;
        SUM, CARRY : out bit);
end HALFADDER;
-- VHDL'93: end entity HALFADDER;
```

- • **Interface description**
- • **No behavioural definition**

```
entity ADDER is
   port(A, B: in integer range 0 to 3;
        SUM  : out integer range 0 to 3;
        CARRY: out bit);
end ADDER;
```

- • **Linking via port signals**
  - • Data types
  - • Signal width
  - • Signal direction

'93   **The keyword 'entity' may be repeated after the keyword 'end'**

On the following pages, a fulladder consisting of two halfadders and an OR gate will be created step by step. We confine ourselves to a purely structural design, i.e. we are using gate-level descriptions and do not need any synthesis tools. The idea is to demonstrate the interaction of the different VHDL objects in a straightforward manner.

The interface between a module and its environment is described within the entity declaration which is initiated by the keyword '**entity**'. It is followed by a user-defined (hopefully) descriptive name, in this case HALFADDER. The interface description is placed between the keyword '**is**' and the termination of the entity statement, which consists of the keyword '**end**' and the name of the entity. In the new VHDL'93 standard the keyword '**entity**' may be repeated after the keyword '**end**' for consistency reasons.

The input and output signal names and their data types are defined in the port statement which is initiated by the keyword '**port**'. The list of ports is enclosed in a '(' ')' pair. For each list element the port name(s) is given first, followed by a ':', the port mode and the data type. Within the list, the ';' symbol is used to separate elements, not to terminate a statement. Consequently, the last list element is not followed by a ';'!

Several ports with the same mode and data type can be declared by a single port statement when the port names are separated by ','. The port mode defines the data flow (in: input, i.e. the signal influences the module behaviour; out: output, i.e. the signal value is generated by the module) while the data type determines the value range for the signals during simulation.

2.2.3 Architecture

```
entity HALFADDER is
    port(A,B       : in bit;
         SUM, CARRY : out bit);
end HALFADDER;

architecture RTL of HALFADDER is

begin

    SUM    <= A xor B;
    CARRY <= A and B;

end RTL;
-- VHDL'93: end architecture RTL;
```

- **Implementation of the design**
- **Always connected with a specific entity**
  - One entity can have several architecures
  - Entity ports are available as signals within the architecture
- **Contains concurrent statements**

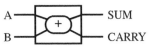

A —————— SUM
B —————— CARRY

93 **The keyword 'architecture' may be repeated after the keyword 'end'**

The architecture contains the implementation for an entity which may be either a behavioural description (behavioural level or, if synthesizable, RT level) or a structural netlist or a mixture of those alternatives.

An architecture is strictly linked to a certain entity. An entity, however, may very well have several architectures underneath, e.g. different implementations of the same algorithm or different abstraction levels. Architectures of the same entity have to be named differently in order to be distinguishable. The name is placed after the keyword '**architecture**', which initiates an architecture statement. 'RTL' was chosen in this case.

It is followed by the keyword '**of**' and the name of entity that is used as interface ('HALFADDER'). The architecture header is terminated by the keyword '**is**', as in entity statements. In this case, however, the keyword '**begin**' must be placed somewhere before the statement is terminated. This is done the same way as in entity statements: the keyword '**end**', followed by the architecture name. Once again, the keyword '**architecture**' may be repeated after the keyword '**end**' in VHDL'93.

As the VHDL code is synthesizable, RTL was chosen as architecture name. In the case of this simple function, however, there is no difference from the behavioural (algorithmic) description. We will use 'BEHAVE', 'RTL', 'GATE', 'STRUCT' and 'TEST' to indicate the abstraction level and the implemented behaviour, respectively. The name 'EXAMPLE' will be used whenever the architecture shows the application of new VHDL elements and is not associated with a specific entity.

2.2.4 Architecture Structure

```
architecture EXAMPLE of STRUCTURE is

  subtype DIGIT is integer range 0 to 9;

  constant BASE: integer := 10;

  signal DIGIT_A, DIGIT_B: DIGIT;
  signal CARRY          : DIGIT;


begin

  DIGIT_A <= 3;

  SUM <= DIGIT_A + DIGIT_B;

  DIGIT_B <= 7;

  CARRY <= 0 when SUM < BASE else
           1;

end EXAMPLE;
```

- **Declarative part:**
  - Data types
  - Constants
  - Additional signals ('actual' signals)
  - Components
  - ...
- **Definition part (after 'begin'):**
  - Signal assignments
  - Processes
  - Component instantiations
  - Concurrent statements: order not important

Each architecture is split into an optional declarative part and the definition part.

The declarative part is located between the keywords '**is**' and '**begin**'. New objects that are needed only within the architecture constants, data types, signals, subprograms, etc. can be declared here.

The definition part is initiated by the keyword '**begin**' and holds concurrent statements. These can be simple signal assignments, process statements, which group together sequential statements, and component instantiations. Concurrency means that the order in which they appear in the VHDL code is not important. The signal SUM, for example, always gets the result of $(3 + 7)$, independently of the location of the two assignments to the signals DIGIT_A and DIGIT_B.

Signal assignments are carried out by the signal assignment operator '<='. The symbol represents the data flow, i.e. the target signal whose value will be updated is placed on the left side of the operator. The right side holds an expression that evaluates to the new signal value. The data types on the left and on the right side have to be identical. Remember that the signals that are used in this example were defined implicitly by the port declaration of the entity.

2.2.5   Entity Port Modes

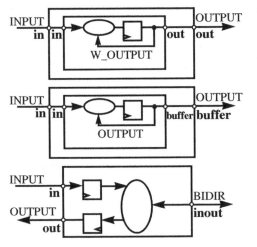

- **in:**
  - signal values are read-only
- **out:**
  - signal values are write-only
  - multiple drivers
- **buffer:**
  - comparable to out
  - signal values may be read, as well
  - only 1 driver
- **inout:**
  - bidirectional port

⚠ **Output port modes have to match**

The mode of an entity port restricts the direction of the data flow. The port mode '**in**' is used to classify those signals that are only read in the underlying architecture. It is not possible to update their values.

Likewise, the port mode '**out**' denotes signals whose values are generated by the architecture. Their values cannot be used to influence the behaviour in any form. If the current output value has to be used to calculate the next signal value, e.g. within a counter module, an intermediate signal must be declared. Internal signals do not have a data flow direction associated with them!

Alternatively it is possible to use the port mode '**buffer**'. This eliminates the need for an additional signal declaration. However, there is just a single source allowed for these signals.

In order to model busses, where multiple units have access to the same data lines, either the port mode '**out**' has to be used, if each unit is only writing to this data bus, or the port mode '**inout**', which allows a bidirectional data flow.

Note that the port modes have to match if the output port of a submodule is connected directly to the output port of the entity on a higher hierarchy level. At the worst, intermediate signals have to be declared to avoid compilation errors.

2.2.6 Hierarchical Model Layout

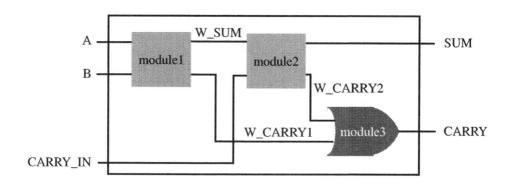

Fulladder: 2 halfadders + 1 OR-gate

VHDL allows for a hierarchical model layout, which means that a module can be assembled out of several submodules. The connections between these submodules are defined within the architecture of a top module. As you can see, a fulladder can be built with the help of two halfadders (module1, module2) and an OR gate (module3).

A purely structural architecture does not describe any functionality, and contains just a list of components, their instantiation and the definition of their interconnections.

2.2.7 Component Declaration

```
entity FULLADDER is
  port (A,B, CARRY_IN : in bit;
          SUM, CARRY    : out bit);
end FULLADDER;

architecture STRUCT of FULLADDER is
  signal W_SUM : bit;
  signal W_CARRY1, W_CARRY2 : bit;

  component HALFADDER
    port (A, B       : in bit;
           SUM, CARRY : out bit);
  end component;

  component ORGATE
    port (A, B : in bit;
           RES  : out bit);
  end component;

begin
. . .
```

- **In declarative part of architecture**
- **Comparable to a 'socket' type**

 The component port list does not replace the declaration of connecting signals (local objects only)

The entity of the fulladder can be derived directly from the block diagram. The inputs A and B, as well as a CARRY_IN input, are required, together with the SUM and the CARRY signals that serve as outputs.

As the fulladder consists of several submodules, they have to be 'introduced' first. In a component declaration all module types which will be used are declared. This declaration has to occur before the '**begin**' keyword of the architecture statement. Note that just the interface of the modules is given here and their use still remains unspecified. The component declaration is therefore comparable with a socket definition, which can be used once or several times and into which the appropriate entity is inserted later on. The **port list elements of the component** are called local elements, which means that they **are not signals**!

In this case, only two different sockets, namely the socket HALFADDER and the socket ORGATE, are needed. Arbitrary names may be chosen for the components, but it is advisable to use the name of the entity that will be used later on. Additionally, the port declaration should also be identical. This is absolutely necessary when the design is to be synthesized, as the software ignores VHDL configuration statements and applies the default rules.

2.2.8   Component Instantiation

```
architecture STRUCT of FULLADDER is
  component HALFADDER
    port (A, B       : in bit;
          SUM, CARRY : out bit);
  end component;
  component ORGATE
    port (A, B : in bit;
          RES  : out bit);
  end component;
  signal W_SUM, W_CARRY1, W_CARRY2: bit;

begin

  MODULE1: HALFADDER
  port map(A, B, W_SUM, W_CARRY1);

  MODULE2: HALFADDER
  port map (W_SUM, CARRY_IN,
            SUM, W_CARRY2);

  MODULE3: ORGATE
  port map (W_CARRY2, W_CARRY1,CARRY);

end STRUCT;
```

- **Socket generation**

- **How many do I need?**

- **Instantiation in definition part of architecture (after 'begin')**

- **Places socket on PCB**

- **Wires signals:**

  - default: positional association

If a component has been declared, that means that the socket type is fixed, it can be used as often as necessary. This is done in form of component instantiations, where the actual socket is generated. This is comparable to the placement of sockets on a printed circuit board (PCB). The entity/architecture pair that provides the functionality of the component is inserted into the socket at a later time when the configuration of a VHDL design is built.

Each component instance is given a unique name (label) by the designer, together with the name of the component itself. Component instantiations occur in the definition part of an architecture (after the keyword '**begin**'). The choice of components is restricted to those that are already declared, either in the declarative part of the architecture or in a package.

As the component ports or socket pins have to be connected to the rest of the circuit, a port map statement is necessary. It has to list the names of the architecture signals that will be used. As default, the so-called positional association rules apply, i.e. the first signal of the port map list is connected to the first port from the component declaration, etc.

2.2.9   Component Instantiation: Named Signal Association

```
entity FULLADDER is
  port (A,B, CARRY_IN : in bit;
        SUM, CARRY    : out bit);
end FULLADDER;

architecture STRUCT of FULLADDER is

  component HALFADDER
    port (A, B       : in bit;
          SUM, CARRY : out bit);
  end component;
  . . .
  signal W_SUM : bit;
  signal W_CARRY1, W_CARRY2 : bit;

begin
  MODULE1: HALFADDER
    port map(A     => A,
             SUM   => W_SUM,
             B     => B,
             CARRY => W_CARRY1);
  . . .
end STRUCT;
```

- **Named association:**

  - left side: 'formals'
    (port names from component declaration)

  - right side: 'actuals'
    (architecture signals)

- **Independent of order in component declaration**

Instead of the positional association that was used in the previous example, it is also possible to connect architecture signals directly to specific ports. This is done by the so-called named association where the order of the signals is not restricted. The port names from the component declaration, also called 'formals', are associated with an arrow '=>' with the signals of the entity ('actuals').

In the example, the output port SUM is declared third in the component declaration. In the port map statement, however, this port is connected to the signal W_SUM in the second place. Note that the list elements are separated by ',' symbols in the port map statement, unlike the ';' symbols that are used in port declarations.

2.2.10 Configuration

```
entity HALFADDER is
  port(A, B       : in bit;
       SUM, CARRY : out bit);
end HALFADDER;

. . .

  component HALFADDER
    port(A, B       : in bit;
         SUM, CARRY : out bit);
  end HALFADDER;

  signal W_SUM : bit;
  signal W_CARRY1, W_CARRY2: bit;
. . .

  MODULE1: HALFADDER
    port map(A, B, W_SUM, W_CARRY1);
```

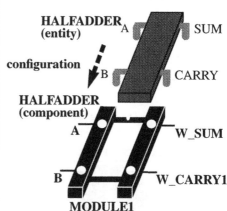

'93   **Entities may be instantiated directly without a preceding component declaration**

Component declaration and instantiation are independent of VHDL models that are actually available. It is the task of the VHDL configuration to link the components to entity/architecture pairs in order to build the complete design. In summary: a component declaration provides a certain kind of socket that can be placed on the circuit as often as necessary with component instantiations. The actual insertion of a device into the instantiated sockets is done by the configuration.

In VHDL'93 it is possible to omit the component declaration and to instantiate entities directly (see the examples in 9.6 Component Instantiation, in the Reference).

2.2.11 Configuration: Task and Application

```
entity FULLADDER is
. . .
end FULLADDER;
architecture STRUCT of FULLADDER is
. . .
end STRUCT;

configuration CFG_FULLADDER of
                       FULLADDER is
   for STRUCT
   -- select architecture STRUCT
   -- use default configuration rules
   end for;
end configuration CFG_FULLADDER;
```

- **Selects architecture for top-level entity**

- **Selects entity/architecture pairs for instantiated components**

- **Generates the hierarchy**

- **Creates a simulatable object**

- **Default binding rules:**

  - selects entity with same name as component

  - signals are associated by name

  - last compiled architecture is used

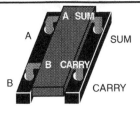

'93 **The keyword 'configuration' may be repeated after the keyword 'end'**

The connection between the entity and the architecture that is supposed to be used for the current simulation is established in the configuration, i.e. it creates the final design hierarchy. This includes the selection of the architecture for the top-level entity. The configuration is the only VHDL object that can be simulated or synthesized. While it is possible to control the configuration process manually for simulation purposes, synthesis tools always apply the default rule set. So synthesis tools are not able to read configurations but build them implicitly by themselves.

For this to succeed, the component names have to match the names of existing entities. Additionally, the port names, modes and data types have to coincide – the order of the ports in the component declaration is ignored. The most recently analysed architecture for the specific entity will be selected as corresponding architecture.

The example shows the default configuration for a structural architecture. Some simulators require an explicit configuration definition of this kind for the top-level entity. A configuration refers to a specific entity, which is FULLADDER in this case. The architecture STRUCT is selected with the first 'for' statement. As no additional configuration commands are given, the default rules apply for all other components.

2.2.12 Configuration: Example (1)

```
                                         entity FULLADDER is
                                           port(A, B, CARRY_IN : in bit;
entity HA1 is                                    SUM, CARRY    : out bit);
  port(A, B        : in bit;              end FULLADDER;
       SUM, CARRY : out bit);
end HA1;                                  architecture STRUCT of FULLADDER is

architecture RTL of HA1 is                  component HALFADDER
. . .                                         port(A, B        : in bit;
end RTL;                                            SUM, CARRY : out bit);
                                            . . .

                                            signal W_SUM, W_CARRY1, W_CARRY2: bit;
entity HA2is
  port(U, V : in bit;                     begin
       X, Y : out bit);                     MODULE1: HALFADDER
end HA2;                                      port map (A, B, W_SUM, W_CARRY1);

architecture GATE of HA2 is                 MODULE2: HALFADDER
. . .                                         port map(W_SUM, CARRY_IN, SUM, W_CARRY2);
end GATE;                                    . . .

                                         end STRUCT;
```

Examine the VHDL code fragments in order to understand a more elaborate configuration example:

In the end, a fulladder will be simulated again. The structure of this fulladder is the same as in the example before, i.e. two halfadders are used. Each halfadder is declared to have two signals of data type '**bit**' as input and output, respectively. The component ports are connected to the architecture's signals by position, i.e. the first signal is connected to the first port.

An entity named HALFADDER shall not be available, however, and the two entities HA1 and HA2, which also have different architectures named RTL and GATE, respectively, are to be used. Both entities match the ports from the component declaration.

2.2.13 Configuration: Example (2)

```
configuration CFG_FULLADDER of FULLADDER
                                     is
  for STRUCT
    for MODULE2: HALFADDER
      use entity work.HA2(GATE);
      port map (U => A,
                V => B,
                X => SUM,
                Y => CARRY);
    end for;

    for others: HALFADDER
      use entity work.HA1(RTL);
    end for;
  end for;
end CFG_FULLADDER;
```

- **Entity/architecture pairs may be selected by use of**
  - instance names
  - 'all': all instances of the specified component
  - 'others': all instances not explicitly mentioned
- **If the port names differ => port map clause**
- **Possible to reference an existing configuration of a submodule**

Again, the architecture STRUCT is selected for the FULLADDER entity. Within this for loop, however, the entities and architectures for the subordinated components are selected.

For this, the for statement is used again. The first name after the keyword '**for**' names the component instantiation, followed by a ':' and the component name. The keyword '**all**' can be used if all instances of a component are to be addressed. Within the for loop, the use statement selects the entity by specifying the absolute path to that object. Unless explicitly changed, all VHDL objects are compiled into the library work. The architecture for the selected entity is enclosed in a '(' ')' pair.

As the port names of the entity HA2 do not match the port names from the component declaration, a port map statement is again necessary. Again, it is possible to map the names by positional association, but an explicit named association should always be used to enhance readability. In this case, the formal parameters are the port names of the entity, while the component port names are used as actuals.

It is also possible to address all those components that have not yet been configured with the keyword '**others**'. This is necessary in this case, as there does not exist an entity named HALFADDER. Instead, the entity A and the corresponding architecture RTL is used for all HALFADDER instantiations other than MODULE2. A port map clause is not necessary, as the entity port names are equivalent to the names of the component.

All other components that might exist are treated according to the default configuration rules.

In order to simplify the hierarchy definition of large designs, it is often useful to define the configuration for the submodules and to reference these configurations from the top level.

2.2.14 Process

```
entity AND_OR_XOR is
  port(A, B        : in bit;
       Z_OR, Z_AND : out bit;
       Z_XOR       : out bit);
end AND_OR_XOR;

architecture RTL of AND_OR_XOR is
begin
                        ←sensitivity list
  A_O_X: process (A,B)
  begin
    Z_OR   <= A or B;
    Z_AND  <= A and B;
    Z_XOR  <= A xor B;
  end process A_O_X;

end RTL;
```

- **Contains sequentially executed statements**
- **Exist within an architecture only**
- **Several processes run concurrently**
- **Execution is controlled either via**
  - sensitivity list (contains trigger signals), or
  - wait statements
- **The process label is optional**

Because the statements within an architecture operate concurrently, another VHDL construct is necessary to achieve sequential behaviour. A process, as a whole, is treated concurrently like any other statement in an architecture and contains statements that are executed one after another as in conventional programming languages. In fact it is possible to use the process statement as the only concurrent VHDL statement.

The execution of a process is triggered by events. Either the possible event sources are listed in the sensitivity list or explicit wait statements are used to control the flow of execution. These two options are mutually exclusive, i.e. no wait statements are allowed in a process with sensitivity list. While the sensitivity list is usually ignored by synthesis tools, a VHDL simulator will invoke the process code whenever the value of at least one of the listed signals changes. Consequently, all signals that are read in a purely combinational process, i.e. that influence the behaviour, have to be mentioned in the sensitivity list if the simulation is to produce the same results as the synthesized hardware. Of course the same is true for clocked processes, but new register values are to be calculated with every active clock edge only. Therefore the sensitivity list contains the clock signal and asynchronous control signals (e.g. reset).

A process statement starts with an optional label and a ':' symbol, followed by the '**process**' keyword. The sensitivity list is also optional and is enclosed in a '(' ')' pair. Similar to the architecture statement, a declarative part exists between the header code and the keyword '**begin**'. The sequential statements are enclosed between '**begin**' and '**end process**'. The keyword '**process**' has to be repeated! If a label was chosen for the process, it should be repeated in the end statement as well.

2.2.15 VHDL Communication Model

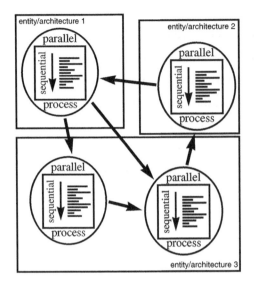

- **Processes are concurrent statements**
- **Several processes**
  - run parallel
  - linked by signals in the sensitivity list
  - sequential execution of statements
- **Link to processes of other entity/architecture pairs via entity interface**

Process statements are concurrent statements while the instructions within each process are executed sequentially, i.e. one after another. All processes of a VHDL design run in parallel, no matter in which entity or hierarchy level they are located. They communicate with each other via signals. These signals need to be ports of the entities if processes from different architectures depend on one another.

2.2.16 Signals

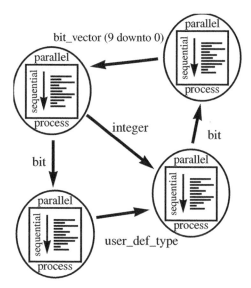

- **Every signal has a specific data type**
  - number of possible values

- **Predefined data types**
  - bit, bit_vector, integer, real, ...
- **User-defined data types**
  - more accurate hardware model
  - enhanced readability
  - improved error detection

Each signal has a predetermined data type that limits the amount of possible values for this signal. Synthesizable data types offer only a limited number of values, i.e. it is possible to map these values to a certain number of wires. Only the most basic data types are already predefined in VHDL, such as bit, bit vectors and integer.

The user can define his or her own data types that might become necessary to enhance the accuracy of the model (tristate drivers, for example, may be set to high impedance instead of a low or high voltage level), for better readability (e.g. a signal value called 'IDLE' tells more about its function than "00101" or "17") and to allow for automatic error detection (e.g. by restricting the range of legal values).

2.2.17 Package

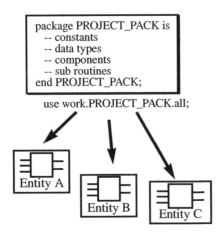

package PROJECT_PACK is
-- constants
-- data types
-- components
-- sub routines
end PROJECT_PACK;

use work.PROJECT_PACK.all;

Entity A
Entity B
Entity C

- **Collection of definitions, data types, subprograms**
- **Reference made by the design team**
- **Any changes are known to the team immediately**
  - Same data types ("downto vs. to")
  - Extended functions for all
  - Clearing errors for all

A package is a collection of definitions of data types, subprograms, constants, etc. This is especially useful in teamwork situations where everyone should work with the same data types, e.g. the same orientation of a vector range. This simplifies the connection of the modules of different designers to the complete VHDL model later on. Necessary changes are also circularized immediately to all persons concerned.

It is possible to split a package into a header and a body section. The package header contains prototype declarations of functions or procedures, the definition of all required data types and so on. The actual implementation of the subprograms can be placed in the body section. This simplifies the compilation process, because only the usually rather short package header must be read in order to decide whether the current VHDL code conforms to the previous declarations/definitions.

A package is referenced by a use clause. After the keyword 'use' follows the so-called "selected name". This name consists of the library name where the compiled package has been placed, the package name itself and the object name which will be referenced. Usually, the keyword 'all' is used to reference all visible objects of the package.

2.2.18 Library

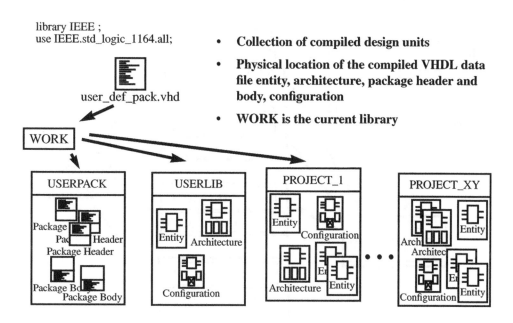

library IEEE ;
use IEEE.std_logic_1164.all;

user_def_pack.vhd

- **Collection of compiled design units**

- **Physical location of the compiled VHDL data file entity, architecture, package header and body, configuration**

- **WORK is the current library**

All analysed objects such as packages, package bodies, entities, architectures and configurations can be found in a library. In VHDL, the library is a logical name with which compiled objects can be grouped and referenced. The default library is called "work". This logical name can be mapped to another logical library name as shown in the figure, but it has to be mapped to a physical path on a storing device eventually.

Usually, every designer operates within his or her own work library. However, he or she can use units from other libraries, which might hold data from former projects (PROJEKT_1 and PROJEKT_XY) or the current project packages (USERPACK). If a library other than WORK is to be used, it will have to be made visible to the VHDL compiler. This is done with the library statement, which starts with the keyword '**library**', followed by the logical name of the library. For example, the library IEEE is commonly used because it contains standardized packages.

2.2.19 Design Structure: Example

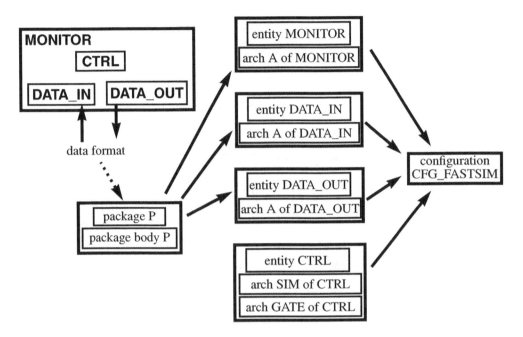

In the example the design consists of four modules. The top level is the module MONITOR which uses three other submodules. These other modules are called CTRL, DATA_IN and DATA_OUT.

The data types for the data format that will be monitored are defined in a package P, as the data types might be used in other designs that communicate with this one. A separate package body has also been written. The package P is referenced by the entities MONITOR, DATA_IN and DATA_OUT, as these three modules will use the new data types. The CTRL module will process control signals only, which can be modelled with the predefined data types. The entities MONITOR, DATA_IN and DATA_OUT each have a architecture A. Two different architectures (SIM and GATE) exist for the entity CTRL. A configuration is necessary for the simulation.

Secondary units such as package bodies and architectures are linked automatically to their primary units (package and entities). Other links have to be made explicitly. Therefore the package P needs to be referenced with a use clause before the entities are declared, while this is not necessary for the corresponding architectures. The assembly of the final design is made by the configuration, i.e. hierarchy errors such as incompatible interfaces will be reported when the configuration is analysed. If several architectures exist for one entity, the configuration will also select the architecture that is to be used for the current simulation.

2.2.20 Sequence of Compilation

- **Primary units are analysed before secondary units**
  - entity before architecture
  - package before package body
- **All units that are referred to have to be analysed first**
  - entity after package
  - configuration after entity/architecture

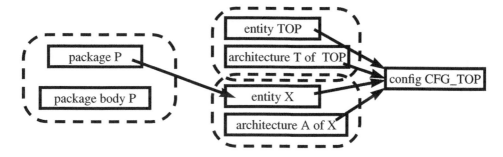

The sequence of compilation is predetermined by the dependency of model parts. If a dependency tree was built, one would have to compile from the lowest level of hierarchy to the top.

As secondary units rely on information given in their primary units (e.g. the interface signals have to be known for an architecture), they can only be compiled when the corresponding primary unit has already been compiled. Consequently, primary units have to be analysed before their secondary units (entity before architecture, package header before package body).

The same applies for references. A package, for example, has to be analysed before an entity that references this package can be compiled, because the entity or its architecture(s) need the information about the data types, etc. The second rule is to compile modules that are referenced by others before the modules that are actually referencing it. Therefore the configuration, which builds up the design hierarchy, has to be analysed last.

2.2.21 Outlook: Testbench

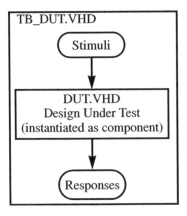

- **VHDL code for top level**
- **No interface signals**
- **Instantiation of design**
- **Statements for stimuli generation**
- **Simple testbenches: response analysis by waveform inspection**
- **Sophisticated testbenches may need >50% of complete project resources**

The most commonly used method to verify a design is simulation. As VHDL was developed for the simulation of digital hardware in the first place, this is well supported by the language.

A new top level, usually called testbench, is created that instantiates the Design Under Test (DUT) and models its environment. Therefore, the entity of this top level has no interface signals. The architecture will also contain some processes or submodules that generate the stimuli for the DUT and sometimes additional processes or submodules that simplify the analysis of the responses of the DUT.

The effort invested in the creation of a testbench varies considerably and can cost the same amount of the time as the modelling of the DUT. It depends on the type of testbench, i.e. how much functionality (stimuli generation, response analysis, file I/O, etc.) has to be supplied.

2.2.22 Simple Testbench Example

```
                                    entity TB_ADDER IS
                                    end TB_ADDER;
                                    architecture TEST of TB_ADDER is
entity ADDER IS                       component ADDER
  port(A,B : in   bit;                  port(A, B      : in   bit;
       CARRY,SUM : out bit);                 CARRY, SUM : out bit);
end ADDER;                            end component;
                                      signal A_I, B_I, CARRY_I, SUM_I : bit;
architecture RTL of ADDER is        begin
begin
  ADD: process (A,B)                  DUT: ADDER port map(A_I, B_I, CARRY_I, SUM_I);
  begin
    SUM <= A xor B;                   STIMULUS: process
    CARRY <= A and B;                 begin
  end process ADD;                      A_I <= ´1´; B_I <= ´0´;
end RTL;                                 wait for 10 ns;
                                         A_I <= ´1´; B_I <= ´1´;
                                         wait for 10 ns;
                                         -- and so on ...
                                        end process STIMULUS;
                                    end TEST;
                                    configuration CFG_TB_ADDER of TB_ADDER is
                                      for TEST
                                      end for;
                                    end CFG_TB_ADDER;
```

The example shows the VHDL code for a simple design and its corresponding testbench. The design to be tested is the ADDER, which implements a halfadder. The architecture RTL contains one pure combinational process, which calculates the results for the SUM and CARRY signals whenever the input signals A or B change.

The testbench is shown on the right side. First the empty entity TB_ADDER is defined. There is no need for an interface, so no port list is present. In the architecture TEST of the testbench the component ADDER and the intermediate signals are declared. The intermediate signals (*_I) are connected to the component in the port map of the component instantiation. The signals that are connected to the input ports of the component ADDER get their values assigned in the process STIMULUS. New values are set every 10 ns. The reaction of the DUT can be observed in a waveform display of the simulator.

At the bottom of the VHDL source code, the configuration is listed. Only the architecture TEST for the TB_ADDER entity is specified, and the rest is left to the default rules as the name of the component and the entity are identical.

2.2.23 Summary

- **VHDL is a very precise language**
  - Signal types and directions have to match
  - All objects have to be declared
  - One language for design and validation

- **Validation by means of a TESTBENCH**
  - Provides stimuli and expected response
  - Top hierarchy level
  - No in-/output ports

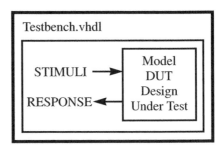

VHDL is a very strict language in which a cryptic programming style is hardly possible (as is the case with the programming language C). Every signal, for example, has to possess a certain data type, it has to be declared at a certain position, and it only accepts assignments from the same data type.

To make a functional test of a VHDL model, a testbench can also be written in VHDL, which delivers the verification environment for the model. In it, stimuli are described as input signals for the model, and furthermore the expected model responses can be checked. The testbench appears as the top hierarchy level, and therefore has neither input- nor output ports.

2.3   Sequential Statements

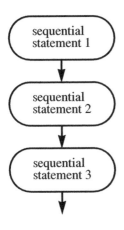

- **Executed according to the order in which they appear**
- **Permitted only within processes and subprograms**
- **Used to describe algorithms**

2.3.1   IF Statement

```
if CONDITION then
   -- sequential statements
end if;

if CONDITION then
   -- sequential statements
else
   -- sequential statements
end if;

if CONDITION then
   -- sequential statements
elsif CONDITION then
   -- sequential statements
. . .
else
   -- sequential statements
end if;
```

- **Condition is a boolean expression**
- **Optional elsif sequence**
  - Conditions may overlap
  - Priority
- **Optional else path**
  - Executed if all conditions evaluate to false

 Attention: elsif but end if

2.3.2   IF Statement: Example

```
                    entity IF_STATEMENT is
                      port (A, B, C, X : in bit_vector (3 downto 0);
                            Z         : out bit_vector (3 downto 0));
                    end IF_STATEMENT;
```

```
architecture EXAMPLE1 of IF_STATEMENT i
s
begin
  process (A, B, C, X)
  begin
    Z <= A;
    if (X = "1111") then
      Z <= B;
    elsif (X > "1000") then
      Z <= C;


    end if;
  end process;
end EXAMPLE1;
```
```
architecture EXAMPLE2 of IF_STATEMENT i
s
begin
  process (A, B, C, X)
  begin

    if (X = "1111") then
      Z <= B;
    elsif (X > "1000") then
      Z <= C;
    else
      Z <= A;
    end if;
  end process;
end EXAMPLE2;
```

All statements in processes or subprograms are processed sequentially, i.e. one after another. As in ordinary programming languages, there exist a variety of constructs to control the flow of execution. The if clause is probably the most obvious and most frequently used.

The if condition must evaluate to a boolean value ('**true**' or '**false**'). After the first if condition, any number of elsif conditions may follow. Overlaps may occur within different conditions. An else branch, which combines all cases that have not been covered before, can optionally be inserted last. The if statement is terminated with '**end if**'.

The first if condition has top priority: if this condition is fulfilled, the corresponding statements will be carried out and the rest of the '**if – end if**' block will be skipped.

The example code shows two different implementations of equivalent behaviour. The signal assignment to the signal Z in the first line of the left process (architecture EXAMPLE1) is called a default assignment, as its effects will only be visible if it is not overwritten by another assignment to Z. Note that the two conditions of the '**if**' and '**elsif**' part overlap, because X="1111" is also true when X>"1000". As a result of the priority mechanism of this if construct, Z will receive the value of B if X="1111".

2.3.3   CASE Statement

```
case EXPRESSION is

  when VALUE_1 =>
        -- sequential statements

  when VALUE_2 | VALUE_3  =>
        -- sequential statements

  when VALUE_4 to VALUE_N =>
        -- sequential statements

  when others =>
        -- sequential statements

end case;
```

- **Choice options must not overlap**
- **All choice options have to be covered**
  - Single values
  - Value range
  - Selection of values ("|" means "or")
  - "when others" covers all remaining choice options

2.3.4   CASE Statement: Example

```
entity CASE_STATEMENT is
  port (A, B, C, X : in integer range 0 to 15;
        Z          : out integer range 0 to 15;
end CASE_STATEMENT;

architecture EXAMPLE of CASE_STATEMENT is
begin
  process (A, B, C, X)
  begin
    case X is
      when 0 =>
        Z <= A;
      when 7 | 9 =>
        Z <= B;
      when 1 to 5 =>
        Z <= C;
      when others =>
        Z <= 0;
    end case;
  end process;
end EXAMPLE;
```

2.3.5 Defining Ranges

```
entity RANGE_1 is                        entity RANGE_2 is
port (A, B : in integer range 0 to 15;   port(A, B : in bit_vector(3 downto 0);
     C, X : in integer range 0 to 15;        C, X : in bit_vector(3 downto 0);
     Z    : out integer range 0 to 15;       Z    : out bit_vector(3 downto 0);
end RANGE_1;                             end RANGE_2;

architecture EXAMPLE of RANGE_1 is       architecture EXAMPLE of RANGE_2 is
begin                                    begin
   process (A, B, C, X)                     process (A, B, C, X)
   begin                                    begin
      case X is                               case X is
         when 0 =>                               when "0000" =>
            Z <= A;                                 Z <= A;
         when 7 | 9 =>                           when "0111" | "1001" =>
            Z <= B;                                 Z <= B;
         when 1 to 5 =>                          when "0001" to "0101"=>-- wrong
            Z <= C;                                 Z <= C;
         when others =>                          when others =>
            Z <= 0;                                 Z <= 0;
      end case;                               end case;
   end process;                             end process;
end EXAMPLE;                              end EXAMPLE;
```

⚠ **The sequence of values is undefined for arrays**

While the priority of each branch is set by means of the query's order in the if case, all branches are equal in priority when using a case statement. Therefore it is obvious that there must not be any overlaps. On the other hand, all possible values of the case expression must be covered. For covering all remaining, i.e. not yet covered, cases, the keyword '**others**' may be used.

The type of the expression in the head of the case statement has to match the type of the query values. Single values of expression can be grouped together with the '|' symbol if the consecutive action is the same. Value ranges allow to cover even more choice options with relatively simple VHDL code.

Ranges can be defined for data types with a fixed order only, e.g. user-defined enumerated types or integer values. In this way, it can be decided whether one value is less than, equal to or greater than another value. For array types (e.g. a '**bit_vector**') there is no such order, i.e. the '**range** "0000" **to** "0100" ' is undefined and therefore not admissible.

2.3.6   FOR Loops

```
entity FOR_LOOP is
  port(A : in integer range 0 to 3;
       Z : out bit_vector (3 downto 0));
end FOR_LOOP;

architecture EXAMPLE of FOR_LOOP is
begin
  process (A)
  begin
    Z <= "0000";
    for I in 0 to 3 loop
      if (A = I) then
        Z(I) <= '1';
      end if;
    end loop;
  end process;
end EXAMPLE;
```

- **Loop parameter is implicitly declared**
  - Cannot be declared externally
  - Read-only access
- **The loop parameter adopts all values from the range definition**
  - Integer ranges
  - Enumerated types

2.3.7   Loop Syntax

```
[LOOP_LABEL :]
for IDENTIFIER in DISCRETE_RANGE loop
  -- sequential statements
end loop [LOOP_LABEL];


[LOOP_LABEL :]
while CONDITION loop
  -- sequential statements
end loop [LOOP_LABEL];
```

- **Optional label**
- **FOR loop identifier**
  - Not declared
  - Read-only
  - Not visible outside the loop
- **Range attributes**
  - 'low
  - 'high
  - 'range

 Synthesis requirements:
  - **Loops must have a fixed range**
  - **'while' constructs usually cannot be synthesized**

2.3.8 Loop Examples

```
                    entity CONV_INT is
                      port(DIN     : in  bit_vector(7 downto 0);
                           RESULT  : out integer);
                    end CONV_INT;
```

-- Example 1	-- Example 2	-- Example 3
...	...	...
process(DIN)	process(DIN)	process(DIN)
variable TMP: integer;	variable TMP: integer;	variable TMP : integer;
		variable I : integer;
begin	begin	begin
TMP := 0;	TMP := 0;	TMP := 0;
		I := DIN'high;
for I in 7 downto 0 loop	for I in DIN'range loop	while (I >= DIN'low) loop
if (DIN(I)='1') then	if (DIN(I)='1') then	if (DIN(I)='1') then
TMP := TMP + 2**I;	TMP := TMP + 2**I;	TMP := TMP + 2**I;
end if;	end if;	end if;
end loop;	end loop;	I := I - 1;
		end loop;
RESULT <= TMP;	RESULT <= TMP;	RESULT <= TMP;
end process;	end process;	end process;
...	...	...

Loops operate in the usual way, i.e. they are used to execute the same VHDL code a couple of times. Loop labels may be used to enhance readability, especially when loops are nested or the code block executed within the loop is rather long. The loop variable is the only object in VHDL which is implicitly defined. The loop variable cannot be declared externally and is only visible within the loop. Its value is read-only, i.e. the number of cycles is fixed when the execution of the for loop begins.

If a for loop is to be synthesized, the range of the loop variable must not depend on signal or variable values (i.e. it has to be locally static). By means of the range assignment, both the direction and the range of the loop variable are determined. If a variable number of cycles is needed, the while statement will have to be used, as while loops are executed as long as condition evaluates to a '**true**' value. Therefore this construct is usually not synthesizable.

The three loop example architectures are functionally equivalent. The difference lies in the specification of the loop range. Examples 1 and 2 use the for statement. Instead of a hard coded range specification, signal attributes that are dependent on the signal type and are therefore fixed during runtime in example 2. Example 3 shows an equivalent implementation using a while construct. Note that an additional loop variable I has to be declared in this case.

Range attributes are used to make the same VHDL code applicable to a number of signals, independent of their width. They are especially useful when dealing with integer or array types. The following code fragments represent equal functionality, provided that Z's range is from 0 to 3:

"for I in 0 to 3 loop – for I in Z'low to Z'high loop – for I in Z'range loop"

2.3.9 WAIT Statement

- **'wait' statements stop the process execution**
  - The process is continued when the instruction is fulfilled
- **Different types of wait statements:**

  - wait for a specific time

wait for SPECIFIC_TIME;

  - wait for a signal event

wait on SIGNAL_LIST;

  - wait for a true condition (requires an event)

wait until CONDITION;

  - indefinite (process is never reactivated)

wait;

 Wait statements must not be used in processes with sensitivity list

2.3.10 WAIT Statement: Examples

- **Flip flop model**   • **Testbench: stimuli generation**

```
entity FF is
  port(D, CLK : in bit;
       Q     : out bit);
end FF;
```

```
architecture BEH_1 of FF is
begin
  process
  begin
    wait on CLK;
    if (CLK = '1') then
      Q <= D;
    end if;
  end process;
end BEH_1;
```

```
architecture BEH_2 of FF is
begin
  process
  begin
    wait until CLK = '1';

    Q <= D;

  end process;
end BEH_2;
```

```
STIMULUS: process
begin
  SEL    <= '0';
  BUS_B  <= "0000";
  BUS_A  <= "1111";
  wait for 10 ns;

  SEL    <= '1';
  wait for 10 ns;

  SEL    <= '0';
  wait for 10 ns;

  wait;
end process STIMULUS;
```

2.3.11 WAIT Statements and Behavioural Modelling

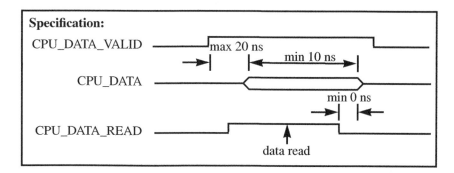

- **Timing behaviour from specification**

- **Translation into VHDL**

- **Based on time**

```
READ_CPU : process
begin
    wait until CPU_DATA_VALID = '1';
    CPU_DATA_READ <= '1';
    wait for 20 ns;
    LOCAL_BUFFER <= CPU_DATA;
    wait for 10 ns;
    CPU_DATA_READ <= '0';
end process READ_CPU;
```

As mentioned before, processes may be coded in two flavours. If the sensitivity list is omitted, another method will be needed to stop process execution. Wait statements put the process execution on hold until the specified condition is fulfilled. If no condition is given, the process will never be reactivated again.

Processes without sensitivity list are executed until a wait statement is reached. In the example architecture BEH_1 of a flip flop, the execution resumes as soon as an event is detected on the CLK signal ('**wait on CLK**'). The following if statement checks the level of the clock signal and a new output value is assigned in case of a rising edge. In BEH_2, both checks are combined in a single '**wait until**' statement. The evaluation of the condition is triggered by signal events, i.e. the behaviour is the same. Via '**wait for**' constructs it is very easy to generate simple input patterns for design verification purposes.

Wait constructs, in general, are an excellent tool for describing timing specifications. For example it is easy to implement a bus protocol for simulation. The timing specification can directly be translated to simulatable VHDL code. But keep in mind that this behavioural modelling can only be used for simulation purposes as it is definitely not synthesizable.

Wait statements must not be combined with a sensitivity list, independent of the application field.

2.3.12 Variables

```
architecture RTL of XYZ is
  signal A, B, C : integer range 0 to 7;
  signal Y, Z    : integer range 0 to 15;
begin
  process (A, B, C)
    variable M, N : integer range 0 to 7;
  begin
   M := A;
   N := B;
   Z <= M + N;
   M := C;
   Y <= M + N;
  end process;
end RTL;
```

- **Variables are available within processes only**
  - Named within process declarations
  - Known only in this process
- **VHDL'93: shared variables**
- **Immediate assignment**
- **Keep the last value**
- **Possible assignments**
  - Signal-to-variable
  - Variable-to-signal
  - Types have to match

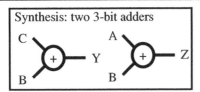

Synthesis: two 3-bit adders

2.3.13 Variables vs. Signals

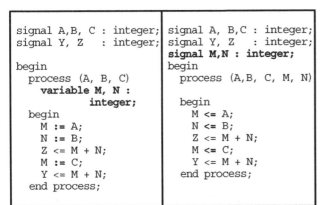

```
signal A,B, C : integer;
signal Y, Z   : integer;

begin
  process (A, B, C)
    variable M, N :
              integer;
  begin
   M := A;
   N := B;
   Z <= M + N;
   M := C;
   Y <= M + N;
  end process;
```

```
signal A, B,C : integer;
signal Y, Z  : integer;
signal M,N : integer;
begin
  process (A,B, C, M, N)

  begin
   M <= A;
   N <= B;
   Z <= M + N;
   M <= C;
   Y <= M + N;
  end process;
```

- **Signal values are assigned after the process execution**
- **Only the last signal assignment is carried out**
- **M <= A;
  is overwritten by
  M <= C;**
- **The 2nd adder input is connected to C**

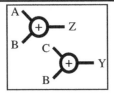

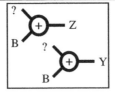

2.3.14 Use of Variables

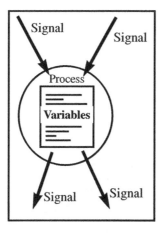

- **Intermediate results of algorithm implementations**
  - signal-to-variable assignment
  - execution of algorithm
  - variable-to-signal assignment
- **No access to variable values outside their process**
- **Variables store their value until the next process call**

Variables can only be defined in a process and they are only accessible within this process.

Variables and signals show fundamentally different behaviours. In a process the last signal assignment to a signal is carried out when the process execution is suspended. Value assignments to variables, however, are carried out immediately. To distinguish between a signal and a variable assignment different symbols are used: '<=' indicates a signal assignment and ':=' indicates a variable assignment.

The two processes shown in the example implement different behaviour as both outputs X and Y will be set to the result of B+C when signals are used instead of variables. Note that the intermediate signals have to added to the sensitivity list, as they are read during process execution.

Variables are especially suited for the implementation of algorithms. Usually, the signal values are copied into variables before the algorithm is carried out. The result is assigned to a signal again afterwards. Variables keep their value from one process call to the next, i.e. if a variable is read before a value has been assigned, the variable will have to show storage behaviour. That means it will have to be synthesized to a latch or flip flop respectively.

2.3.15 Variables: Example

- **Parity calculation**

```
entity PARITY is
  port (DATA: in bit_vector (3 downto 0);
        ODD : out bit);
end PARITY;

architecture RTL of PARITY is
begin
  process (DATA)
    variable TMP : bit;
  begin
    TMP := '0';

    for I in DATA'low to DATA'high loop
      TMP := TMP xor DATA(I);
    end loop;

    ODD <= TMP;
  end process;
end RTL;
```

- **Synthesis result:**

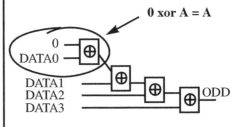

2.3.16 Global Variables (VHDL'93)

```
architecture BEHAVE of SHARED is
  shared variable S : integer;
begin
  process (A, B)
  begin
    S := A + B;
  end process;

  process (A, B)
  begin
    S := A - B;
  end process;
end BEHAVE;
```

- **Accessible by all processes of an architecture**
  (shared variables)

- **Can introduce non-determinism**

 Not to be used in synthesizable code

In VHDL'93, global variables are allowed. These variables are not only visible within a process but within the entire architecture. The problem may occur that two processes assign a different value to a global variable at the same time. It is not clear then which of these processes assigns the value to the variable last. This can lead to non-deterministic behaviour!

In synthesizable VHDL code global variables must not be used.

2.4   Concurrent Statements

- **Concurrent statements are executed at the same time, independent of the order in which they appear**

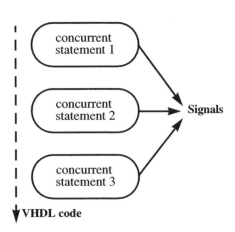

2.4.1   Conditional Signal Assignment

```
TARGET <= VALUE;


TARGET <= VALUE_1 when CONDITION_1 else
          VALUE_2 when CONDITION_2 else
          . . .
          VALUE_n;
```

- **Condition is a boolean expression**
- **Mandatory else path, unless unconditional assignment**
  - Conditions may overlap
  - Priority
- **Equivalent of if ..., elsif ..., else constructs**

2.4.2   Conditional Signal Assignment: Example

```
entity CONDITIONAL_ASSIGNMENT is
   port (A, B, C, X : in bit_vector (3 downto 0);
            Z_CONC     : out bit_vector (3 downto 0);
            Z_SEQ      : out bit_vector (3 downto 0));
end CONDITIONAL_ASSIGNMENT;

architecture EXAMPLE of CONDITIONAL_ASSIGNMENT is
begin
   -- Concurrent version of conditional signal assignment
   Z_CONC <= B when X = "1111" else
             C when X > "1000" else
             A;

   -- Equivalent sequential statements
   process (A, B, C, X)
   begin
      if (X = "1111") then
         Z_SEQ <= B
      elsif (X > "1000") then
         Z_SEQ <= C;
      else
         Z_SEQ <= A;
      end if;
   end process;
end EXAMPLE;
```

All statements within architectures are executed concurrently. While it is possible to use VHDL processes as the only concurrent statement, the necessary overhead (process, begin, end, sensitivity list) lets designer look for alternatives when the sequential behaviour of processes is not needed.

The signal assignment statement was the first VHDL statement to be introduced. The signal on the left side of the assignment operator '<=' receives a new value whenever a signal on the right side changes. The new value stems from another signal in the simplest case (i.e. when an intermediate signal is necessary to match different port modes) or can be calculated from a number of signals.

The signal assignment can be extended by the specification of conditions. The condition is appended after the new value and is introduced by the keyword '**when**'. The keyword '**else**' is also strictly necessary after each condition, as an unconditional signal assignment has to be present. Consequently, it is not possible to generate storage elements with an conditional signal assignment. Otherwise the behaviour is equivalent to the if ..., elsif ..., else ... construct that is used within processes.

In the example, two equivalent descriptions of a simple multiplexer are given. Note that all signals appearing on the right side of the signal assignment operator are entered into the process's sensitivity list. The unconditional else path could be replaced by an unconditional signal assignment in front of the if statement. This assignments would be overwritten if any of the conditions were true.

2.4.3   Selected Signal Assignment

- **Choice options must not overlap**
- **All choice options have to be covered**

```
with EXPRESSION select

   TARGET <= VALUE_1 when CHOICE_1,
             VALUE_2 when CHOICE_2 | CHOICE_3,
             VALUE_3 when CHOICE_4 to CHOICE_5,
             . . .
             VALUE_n when others;
```

  - Single values
  - Value range
  - Selection of values ("|" means "or")
  - "when others" covers all remaining choice options

- **Equivalent of case ..., when ... constructs**

2.4.4   Selected Signal Assignment: Example

```
entity SELECTED_ASSIGNMENT is
  port (A, B, C, X : in integer range 0 to 15;
        Z_CONC     : out integer range 0 to 15;
        Z_SEQ      : out integer range 0 to 15);
end SELECTED_ASSIGNMENT;

architecture EXAMPLE of SELECTED_ASSIGNMENT is
begin
  -- Concurrent version of selected signal assignment
  with X select
    Z_CONC <= A when 0,
              B when 7 | 9,
              C when 1 to 5,
              0 when others;

  -- Equivalent sequential statements
  process (A, B, C, X)
  begin
    case X is
      when 0      => Z_SEQ <= A;
      when 7 | 9  => Z_SEQ <= B;
      when 1 to 5 => Z_SEQ <= C;
      when others => Z_SEQ <= 0;
    end case;
  end process;
end EXAMPLE;
```

2.4.5   Concurrent Statements: Summary

- **Modelling of multiplexers**
    - Conditional signal assignment: decision based upon several signals
    - Selected signal assignment: decision based upon values of a single signal
- **"Shortcuts" for sequential statements**
    - Conditional signal assignment <=> if ..., elsif ..., else ..., end if
    - Selected signal assignment <=> case ..., when ..., end case

 Unconditional else path is mandatory in conditional signal assignments

The behaviour of the so-called selected signal assignment is similar to the case statement. It suffers from the same restrictions as its sequential counterpart, namely that all possible choice options have to be covered and none of the choice options may overlap with another.

As with conditional signal assignments, the signal assignment operator '<=' can be seen as the core of the construct. Again, the choice options are appended after the keyword '**when**', but the different assignment alternatives are separated by ',' symbols. The equivalent of the '**case** EXPRESSION **is**' construct from the case statement must be placed as header line in front of the actual assignment specification. The keywords have to be translated, however, to '**with** EXPRESSION **select**'.

All concurrent statements describe the functionality of multiplexer structures. It is impossible to model storage elements like flip flops with concurrent statements only. Consequently, the unconditional else path is necessary in conditional signal assignments. Every concurrent signal assignment, whether conditional or selected, can be modelled with a process construct, however. As sequentially executed code is easier comprehensible, the concurrent versions should be used as a shortcut only when simple functionality would be obfuscated by the process overhead.

2.5   Data Types

```
entity FULLADDER is
  port(A, B, CARRY_IN : in bit;
       SUM, CARRY      : out bit);
end FULLADDER;

architecture MIX of FULLADDER is
  component HALFADDER
    port(A, B      : in bit;
         SUM, CARRY : out bit);

  signal W_SUM, W_CARRY1, W_CARRY2 : bit;

begin
  HA1: HALFADDER
    port map(A, B, W_SUM, W_CARRY1);
  HA2: HALFADDER
    port map(CARRY_IN, W_SUM, SUM,
             W_CARRY2);

  CARRY <= W_CARRY1 or W_CARRY2;

end MIX;
```

- **Every signal has a type**
- **Type specifies possible values**
- **Type has to be defined at signal declaration...**
- **...either in**
  - entity: port declaration, or in
  - architecture: signal declaration
- **Types have to match**

2.5.1   Standard Data Types

```
package STANDARD is
   type BOOLEAN is (FALSE,TRUE);
   type BIT is ('0','1');
   type CHARACTER is (-- ascii set);
   type INTEGER is range
        -- implementation_defined
   type REAL is range
        -- implementation_defined
   -- BIT_VECTOR, STRING, TIME
end STANDARD;
```

- **Every type has a number of possible values**
- **Standard types are defined by the language**
- **User can define his or her own types**

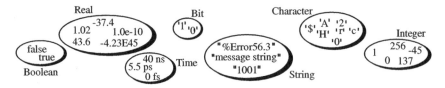

'93 New types added to the 'standard' package, e.g. umlauts

2.5.2   Data type 'time'

```
architecture EXAMPLE of TIME_TYPE is
  signal CLK : bit := '0';
  constant PERIOD : time := 50 ns;

begin
  process
  begin
    wait for 50 ns;
    . . .
    wait for PERIOD;
    . . .
    wait for 5 * PERIOD;
    . . .
    wait for PERIOD * 5.5;
  end process;

  . . .


  -- concurrent signal assignment
  CLK <= not CLK after 0.025 us;
  -- or with constant time
  -- CLK <= not CLK after PERIOD/2;
end EXAMPLE;
```

- **Usage**
  - Testbenches
  - Gate delays
- **Multiplication/division**
  - Multiplied/divided by integer/real
  - Returns TIME type
  - Internally in smallest unit (fs)
- **Available time units**
  'fs', 'ps', 'ns', 'us', 'ms', 'sec', 'min', 'hr'

In VHDL, signals must have a data type associated with them that limits the number of possible values. This type has to be fixed when the signal is declared, either as entity port or an internal architecture signal, and cannot be changed during runtime. Whenever signal values are updated, the data types on both sides of the assignment operator '<=' have to match.

A number of data types are already defined in the standard package, which is always implicitly referenced. '**boolean**' is usually used to control the flow of the VHDL execution while '**bit**' uses level values ('**0**', '**1**') instead of truth values ('**false**', '**true**') and is therefore better suited to model wires. Number values can be communicated via signals of type '**integer**' or '**real**'. The actual range and accuracy depends on the platform implementation, and only lower bounds are defined, e.g. integers are guaranteed to be at least 32 bits wide. Floating-point operations cannot yet be synthesized automatically, i.e. the use of '**real**' data types is restricted to testbench applications. The same applies to '**character**' and '**time**'.

'time' is a special data type, as it consists out of a numerical value and a physical unit. It is used to delay the execution of statements for a certain amount of time, e.g. in testbenches or to model gate and propagation delays. Signals of data type '**time**' can be multiplied or divided by '**integer**' and '**real**' values. The result of these operations remains of data type '**time**'. The internal resolution of VHDL simulators is set to femtoseconds (fs).

2.5.3 Definition of Arrays

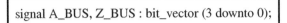

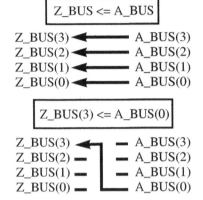

- **Collection of signals of the same type**
- **Predefined arrays**
  - bit_vector (array of bit)
  - string (array of character)
- **Unconstrained arrays: definition of actual size during signal/port declaration**

2.5.4 'integer' and 'bit' Types

```
architecture EXAMPLE_1 of DATATYPES
                                 is

  signal SEL :      bit;
  signal A, B, Z :
        integer range 0 to 3;

begin
  A <= 2;
  B <= 3;

  process(SEL,A,B)
  begin
    if SEL = '1' then
      Z <= A;
    else
      Z <= B;
    end if;
  end process;
end EXAMPLE_1;
```

OR:

```
architecture EXAMPLE_2 of DATATYPES
                                 is

  signal SEL : bit;
  signal A, B, Z :
        bit_vector(1 downto 0);

begin
  A <= "10";
  B <= "11";

  process(SEL,A,B)
  begin
    if SEL = '1' then
      Z <= A;
    else
      Z <= B;
    end if;
  end process;
end EXAMPLE_2;
```

- **Example for using 'bit' and 'integer'**

2.5.5   Assignments with Array Types

```
architecture EXAMPLE of ARRAYS is
   signal Z_BUS : bit_vector (3 downto 0);
   signal C_BUS : bit_vector (0 to 3);
begin
   Z_BUS <= C_BUS;
end EXAMPLE;
```

Z_BUS(3) ◀━━━━━ C_BUS(0)
Z_BUS(2) ◀━━━━━ C_BUS(1)
Z_BUS(1) ◀━━━━━ C_BUS(2)
Z_BUS(0) ◀━━━━━ C_BUS(3)

 Elements are assigned according to their position, not their number

 The direction of arrays should always be defined in the same way

Arrays are useful to group signals of the same type and meaning. Two unconstrained array data types, i.e. whose range is not limited, are predefined in VHDL: '**bit_vector**' and '**string**' are arrays of '**bit**' and '**character**' values, respectively. Note that the array boundaries have to be fixed during signal declarations, e.g. '**bit_vector**(3 **downto** 0)'. Only constrained arrays may be used as entity ports or architecture signals.

Integer signals will be mapped to a number of wires during synthesis. These wires could be modelled via bit vectors as well, but '**bit_vector**' signals do not have a numerical interpretation associated with them. Therefore the synthesis result for the two example architectures would be the same. The process models a simple multiplexer that selects the input A as source for its output Z when the select signal SEL is '1' and the input B otherwise. Note that the multiplexer process is exactly the same for both data types!

Special care is necessary when signal assignments with arrays are carried out. Although the data type and the width of the signals have to match, this is not true for the order of the array elements. The values are assigned according to their position within the array, not according to their index. Therefore it is strongly recommended to use only one direction (usually '**downto**' in hardware applications) throughout one's designs.

2.5.6   Bit String Literals

```
architecture EXAMPLE of ASSIGNMENT is

  signal Z_BUS : bit_vector (3 downto 0);
  signal BIG_BUS :bit_vector (15 downt 0);

begin

  -- legal assignments:
  Z_BUS(3)   <= '1';
  Z_BUS      <= "1100";

  Z_BUS      <= b"1100";
  Z_BUS      <= x"C";
  Z_BUS      <= X"C";
  BIG_BUS    <= B"0000_0001_0010_0011";

end EXAMPLE;
```

- **Single bit values are enclosed in '.'**
- **Vector values are enclosed in "..."**
  - optional base specification (default: binary)
  - values may be separated by underscores to improve readability

 Different specification of single bits and bit vectors

 Valid assignments for the data type 'bit' are also valid for all character arrays, e.g. 'std_(u)logic_vector'

The specification of signal values is different for the base types '**character**' and '**bit**' and their corresponding array types '**string**' and '**bit_vector**'. Single values are always enclosed in single quotation marks (' '), while double quotation marks (" ") are used to specify array values.

As bit vectors are often used to represent numerical values, VHDL offers several possibilities to increase the readability of bit vector assignments. First, a base for the following number may be specified. Per default binary data consisting of '0's and '1's is assumed. Note that the values have to enclosed in double quotation marks even though only a single symbol might be necessary when another base is used! Additionally, underscores (_) may be inserted at will to split long chains of numbers into smaller groups in order to improve readability.

Since VHDL'93, the same rules also apply to the enhanced bit vector types 'std_(u)logic_vector', which will be discussed later on.

2.5.7 Concatenation

- **Concatenation operator: &**

- **Resulting signal assignment:**

```
architecture EXAMPLE_1 of CONCATENATION is
  signal BYTE : bit_vector (7 downto 0);
  signal A_BUS, B_BUS :
               bit_vector (3 downto 0);
begin

   BYTE   <= A_BUS & B_BUS;

end EXAMPLE;
```

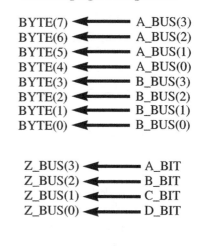

BYTE(7) ◄────── A_BUS(3)
BYTE(6) ◄────── A_BUS(2)
BYTE(5) ◄────── A_BUS(1)
BYTE(4) ◄────── A_BUS(0)
BYTE(3) ◄────── B_BUS(3)
BYTE(2) ◄────── B_BUS(2)
BYTE(1) ◄────── B_BUS(1)
BYTE(0) ◄────── B_BUS(0)

```
architecture EXAMPLE_2 of CONCATENATION is
  signal Z_BUS : bit_vector (3 downto 0);
  signal A_BIT, B_BIT, C_BIT, D_BIT : bit;
begin

   Z_BUS <= A_BIT & B_BIT & C_BIT & D_BIT;

end EXAMPLE;
```

Z_BUS(3) ◄────── A_BIT
Z_BUS(2) ◄────── B_BIT
Z_BUS(1) ◄────── C_BIT
Z_BUS(0) ◄────── D_BIT

 The concatenation operator '&' is allowed on the right side of the signal assignment operator '<=', only

As signal assignments require matching data types on both sides of the operator, it is sometimes necessary to assemble an array in the VHDL code. The concatenation operator '&' groups together the elements on its sides which normally have to be of the same data type, only. Again, the array indices are ignored and only the position of the elements within the arrays is used. The concatenation operator may be used on the right side of signal assignments only!

2.5.8 Aggregates

```
architecture EXAMPLE of AGGREGATES is
   signal BYTE  : bit_vector (7 downto 0);
   signal Z_BUS : bit_vector (3 downto 0);
   signal A_BIT, B_BIT, C_BIT, D_BIT : bit;
begin
   Z_BUS <= (A_BIT, B_BIT, C_BIT, D_BIT);
   A_BIT, B_BIT, C_BIT, D_BIT) <= bit_vector'("1011");
   (A_BIT, B_BIT, C_BIT, D_BIT) <= BYTE(3 downto 0);

   BYTE <= (7 => '1', 5 downto 1 => '1', 6 => B_BIT,
            others => '0');
end EXAMPLE;
```

- **Aggregates bundle signals together**

- **May be used on both sides of an assignment**

- **Keyword 'other' selects all remaining elements**

 Some aggregate constructs may not be supported by your synthesis tool

 Assignment of '0' to all bits of a vector regardless of the width: VECTOR <= (others => '0');

Another way of assigning signals which does not suffer from this limitation, is via the aggregate construct. Here, the signals that are to build the final array are enclosed in a '( )' pair and separated by ','. Instead of a simple concatenation, it is also possible to address the array elements explicitly by their corresponding index, as shown in the last signal assignment statement of the aggregate example. The keyword '**others**' may be used to select those indices that have not yet been addressed.

2.5.9   Slices of Arrays

```
architecture EXAMPLE of SLICES is
  signal BYTE  : bit_vector (7 downto 0);
  signal A_BUS : bit_vector (3 downto 0);
  signal Z_BUS : bit_vector (3 downto 0);
  signal A_BIT : bit;
begin
  BYTE (5 downto 2) <= A_BUS;
  BYTE (5 downto 0) <= A_BUS;          -- wrong

  Z_BUS (1 downto 0) <= '0' & A_BIT;
  Z_BUS <= BYTE (6 downto 3);
  Z_BUS (0 to 1) <=  '0' & A_BIT;    -- wrong

  A_BIT   <= A_BUS (0);
end EXAMPLE;
```

- **Slices select elements of arrays**

  The directions of the 'slice' and of the array must match

The inverse operation of concatenation and aggregation is the selection of slices of arrays, i.e. only a part of an array is to be used. The range of the desired array slice is specified in parentheses and must match the range declaration of the signal! Of course, it is possible to select only single array elements.

2.6   Extended Data Types

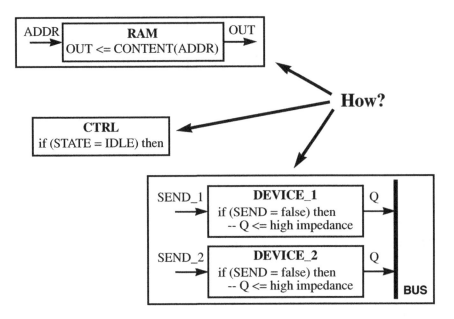

The standard data types are of limited use for practical modelling tasks. Of course, it would be possible to implement the behaviour of RAM or ROM cells via case constructs, but the resulting VHDL would look pretty awkward. Coding would be much easier if arrays of other data types were available.

Another case for additional types is based on readability issues. VHDL code should be usable as documentation as well. Symbolic, descriptive names for signal values usually lead to self-documenting code. This does not mean that comments are no longer necessary, though!

While relatively easy workarounds exist for these two problems, the modelling of bus systems is a nightmare when only predefined data types are to be used. The main characteristic of a data bus is the existence of multiple bus participants, i.e. the same signal wires are used by multiple modules. If such a device does not transmit anything, its output driver must be set to a value that does not destroy other data values.

2.6.1 Type Classification

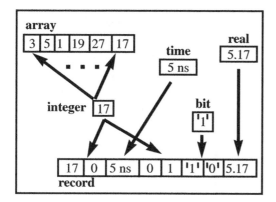

- **Scalar types:**
  - Contain exactly one value
  - Integer, real, bit, enumerated, physical

- **Composite types:**
  - May contain more than one value
  - **Array**: values of one type, only
  - **Record**: values of different types

- **Other types:**
  - 'file'
  - 'access'

In VHDL, data types are classified into three categories: scalar types, composite types and other types. Scalar types have exactly one value. Examples are the predefined integer, real and bit values. Physical data types (e.g. time) also fall into this category, as do user-defined data types whose range of values is declared via an enumeration. Scalar types do not have distinguishable elements. Composite types, on the other hand, usually hold a collection of values. This collection is called an array if all values are of the same type; different data types may be present in records.

FILE and ACCESS types are data types that provide access to other objects. The FILE type is used to read or store data in a file; ACCESS types are comparable to pointers.

2.6.2   Enumeration Types

```
architecture EXAMPLE of ENUMERATION is

   type T_STATE is
       (RESET, START, EXECUTE, FINISH);

   signal CURRENT_STATE : T_STATE;
   signal NEXT_STATE    : T_STATE;
   signal TWO_BIT_VEC : bit_vector(1 downto 0);

begin

   -- valid signal assignments
   NEXT_STATE      <= CURRENT_STATE;
   CURRENT_STATE <= RESET;

   -- invalid signal assignments
   CURRENT_STATE <= "00";
   CURRENT_STATE <= TWO_BIT_VEC;

end EXAMPLE;
```

- **Designers may define their own types**

  - Enhanced readability (commonly used to describe the states of a state machine)
  - Limited legal values

   Synthesis tools map enumerations onto a suitable bit pattern automatically

It is possible to define new scalar data types in VHDL. They are called enumeration types because all possible object (constant, signal, variable) values have to be specified in a list at type declaration. User-defined data types are frequently used to enhance readability when dealing with so-called state machines, i.e. modules that behave differently depending on the state of internal storage elements. Instead of fixed bit patterns, the symbolic names of the data type values are used, which will be mapped to a bit-level representation automatically during synthesis.

In the example a new data type with values denoting four different states (RESET, START, EXECUTE, FINISH) is defined. This type is used for the two signals CURRENT_STATE and NEXT_STATE, and the four declared type values can be assigned directly. Of course, after synthesis, there will be two bits for each signal, but a direct assignment of a two-bit vector is not allowed. In a signal assignment only those values may be used which are enumerated in the type declaration.

Some synthesis tools allow the designer to map the different values onto specific bit patterns.

2.6.3   Enumeration Types : Example

```
architecture RTL of TRAFFIC_LIGHT is
   type  T_STATE is
     (INIT,RED,REDYELLOW,GREEN,YELLOW);
   signal STATE, NEXT_STATE : T_STATE;

   signal COUNTER: integer;
   constant END_RED   : integer := 10000;
   constant END_GREEN : integer := 20000;

begin
   LOGIC : process (STATE, COUNTER)
   begin
     NEXT_STATE <= STATE;
       case STATE is
         when RED  =>
           if COUNTER = END_RED then
             NEXT_STATE <= REDYELLOW;
           end if;
         when REDYELLOW => -- statements
         when GREEN     => -- statements
         when YELLOW    => -- statements
         when INIT      => -- statements
     end case;
   end process LOGIC;
end RTL;
```

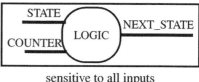

sensitive to all inputs

The example demonstrates the impact of user-defined data types on code readability. The LOGIC block will implement the behaviour of a traffic light controller. The data type T_STATE is defined in the declarative part of the architecture and is used for the signals STATE and NEXT_STATE. The functional behaviour of the algorithm should be pretty obvious as only symbolic names are used. For this purpose, additional constants were defined for the specific counter values that are checked within the code.

2.6.4   BIT Type Issues

• **Values '0' and '1', only**

  • Default value '0'

```
type bit is ('0', '1');
```

• **Additional requirements for simulation and synthesis**

  • Uninitialized

  • High impedance

  • Undefined

  • 'don't care'

  • Different driver strengths

2.6.5   Multivalued Types

• **Multivalued logic systems are declared via new data types**

  • Uninitialized

  • Unknown

  • High impedance

  • ...

• **Manufacturer-dependent implementation**

  • mvl4, mvl7, mvl9, ..., mvl46

• **No common standard before 1992**

• **IEEE standard**

  • 9-valued logic system defined and accepted by the IEEE

  • Standard IEEE 1164 (STD_LOGIC_1164)

2.6.6 IEEE Standard Logic Type

```
type STD_ULOGIC is (
    'U',    -- uninitialized
    'X',    -- strong 0 or 1 (= unknown)
    '0',    -- strong 0
    '1',    -- strong 1
    'Z',    -- high impedance
    'W',    -- weak 0 or 1 (= unknown)
    'L',    -- weak 0
    'H',    -- weak 1
    '-',    -- don't care);
```

- **9 different signal states**
- **Superior simulation results**
- **Bus modelling**
- **'ASCII-characters'**

- **Defined in package 'IEEE.std_logic_1164'**
- **Similar data type 'std_logic' with the same values**
- **Array types available: 'std_(u)logic_vector', similar to 'bit_vector'**
- **All 'bit' operators available**

 The IEEE standard should be used in VHDL designs

The '**bit**' type has only the two values '0' and '1'. While this is enough to model simple logic where the wires are driven either high or low level, further options are desirable, especially for simulation purposes. VHDL objects are initialized with their default value, which is the leftmost value from the type declaration. Therefore every variable/signal of type '**bit**' would be set to '0' at the beginning of each simulation. This makes it impossible to verify the proper reset behaviour of a design if the reset value of a register is also '0'.

Additional legal wire conditions are necessary if different driver strengths or high-impedance outputs of real hardware drivers are to be modelled. It depends on the synthesis tool whether these additional logic values can be mapped to the corresponding hardware cells. In order to avoid hardware overhead, one might think of designating bit positions that may safely be ignored during synthesis ('don't care').

For simulation, the opposite is desirable, i.e. a value which indicates that something went wrong and needs to be inspected ('undefined'). In the beginning, several incompatible multivalued logic systems were defined by the different software companies. In order to solve the resulting problems, a standardized 9-valued logic system was defined and accepted by the IEEE in 1992.

The new data type is called '**std_ulogic**' and is defined in the package '**std_logic_1164**', which is placed in the library IEEE (i.e. it is included by the following statement: '**use IEEE.std_logic_1164.all**'. The new type is implemented as enumerated type by extending the existing '0' and '1' symbols with additional ASCII characters. The most important ones are probably 'u' (uninitialized) and 'x' (unknown value). The 'u' symbol is the leftmost symbol of the declaration, i.e. it will be used as initial value during simulation.

2.6.7   Resolved and Unresolved Types

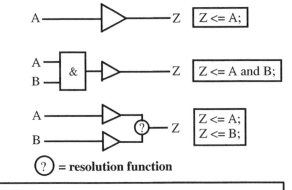

- **Signal assignments are represented by drivers**

- **Unresolved data type: only one driver**

- **Resolved data type: possibly several drivers per signal**

(?) = resolution function

```
architecture EXAMPLE of ASSIGNMENT is
  signal A, B, Z : bit;
  signal INT     : integer;
begin
  Z <= A;
  Z <= B;
  Z <= INT;   -- wrong
end EXAMPLE;
```

- **Conditions for valid assignments**

  - Types have to match

  - Resolved type, if more than 1 concurrent assignment

2.6.8   Std_Logic_1164 Package

```
PACKAGE std_logic_1164 IS

  --------------------------------
  -- logic state system (unresolved)
  --------------------------------
  TYPE STD_ULOGIC IS (
    'U',     -- uninitialized
    'X',     -- Forcing  Unknown
    '0',     -- Forcing  0
    '1',     -- Forcing  1
    'Z',     -- High Impedance
    'W',     -- Weak Unknown
    'L',     -- Weak 0
    'H',     -- Weak 1
    '-',     -- don't care);
  --------------------------------
  --
  unconstrained array of std_ulogic
  -- for use with the resolution
  -- function
  --------------------------------
  TYPE std_ulogic_vector IS
    ARRAY(NATURAL RANGE <>) OF
    std_ulogic;
```

```
  --------------------------------
  -- resolution function
  --------------------------------
  FUNCTION resolved
    (s : std_ulogic_vector )
    RETURN std_ulogic;
  --------------------------------
  -- ** industry standard logic type **
  --------------------------------
  SUBTYPE std_logic IS resolved
    std_ulogic;
  --------------------------------
  -- unconstrained array of std_logic
  -- for use in declaring signal arrays
  --------------------------------
  TYPE std_logic_vector IS
    ARRAY(NATURAL RANGE <>) OF std_logic;

END std_logic_1164;
```

2.6.9 Resolution Function

```
FUNCTION resolved(s : std_ulogic_vector )
                         RETURN std_ulogic IS
  CONSTANT resolution_table : std_logic_table :=(
  --  U   X   0   1   Z   W   L   H   -   ------
  -- -------------------------------------------
    ('U','U','U','U','U','U','U','U','U'),  -- U
    ('U','X','X','X','X','X','X','X','X'),  -- X
    ('U','X','0','X','0','0','0','0','X'),  -- 0
    ('U','X','X','1','1','1','1','1','X'),  -- 1
    ('U','X','0','1','Z','W','L','H','X'),  -- Z
    ('U','X','0','1','W','W','W','W','X'),  -- W
    ('U','X','0','1','L','W','L','W','X'),  -- L
    ('U','X','0','1','H','W','W','H','X'),  -- H
    ('U','X','X','X','X','X','X','X','X')); -- -
  VARIABLE result : std_ulogic := 'Z';  -- weakest
                                  -- state default
BEGIN
  IF (s'LENGTH = 1) THEN
    RETURN s(s'LOW);
  ELSE
    FOR i IN s'RANGE LOOP
      result := resolution_table(result, s(i));
    END LOOP;
  END IF;
  RETURN result;
END resolved;
```

- **All driving values are collected in a vector**

- **The result is calculated element by element according to the table**

- **Resolution function is called whenever signal assignments involving resolved types are carried out**

Besides the type definition of '**std_ulogic**' the '**std_logic_1164**' package also contains the definition of a similar type called '**std_logic**', which has the same value set as '**std_ulogic**'. Like '**bit_vector**', array data types '**std_(u)logic_vector**' are also available. Additionally, all operators that are defined for the standard type '**bit**' are overloaded to handle the new replacement type.

As mentioned before, the '**bit**' data type cannot be used to model bus architectures. This is because all signal assignments are represented by drivers in VHDL. If more than one driver tries to force the value of a signal a resolution will be needed to solve the conflict. Consequently, the existence of a resolution function is necessary for legal signal assignments. Note that resolution conflicts are detected at run time and not during compilation!

Predefined VHDL data types do not possess a resolution function, because the effects of multiple signal drivers depend on the actual hardware realization. The '**std_ulogic**' data type ('u' = 'unresolved') is the basis for the resolved data type '**std_logic**'. The 'resolved' function that is also defined in the '**std_logic_1164**' package is called whenever signal assignments involving '**std_logic**' based data types are carried out.

The conflict resolution process itself, i.e. the decision about the final signal value in case of multiple drivers, is based upon a resolution table. All driving values are collected in an array and handed to the resolution function, even if only a single driver is present! The result is calculated element by element: the current result selects the row of the resolution table, and the value of the next signal driver selects the column of the resulting signal value.

2.6.10 STD_LOGIC vs. STD_ULOGIC

	Benefit
STD_ULOGIC **STD_ULOGIC_VECTOR**	• **Error messages in case of multiple concurrent signal assignments**

	Benefit

STD_LOGIC
STD_LOGIC_VECTOR
	• **Common industry standard**
	  • Gate-level netlists
	  • Mathematical functions
	• **Required for tristate busses**

 STD_LOGIC(_VECTOR) is recommended for RT level designs

 Use port mode 'buffer' to avoid multiple signal assignments

By far most of the connections in a design, either as abstract signals or later on as real wires, are from one point to another, i.e. multiple signal drivers would indicate an error. This kind of error will be easily detected if just unresolved data types are used.

However, the resolved counterpart '**std_logic**' has been established as de facto industry standard despite some shortcomings. As all kind of hardware structures, including bus systems, can be modelled with this data type, it is used by synthesis tools for the resulting gate-level description of a design. Even a workaround exists, so that multiple signal assignments can still be detected: the port mode '**buffer**' allows for a single signal driver only. According to the VHDL language definition, however, the resolution function has to be called when resolved signals are assigned. The impact on simulation performance depends on the compiler/simulator implementation.

The last, but certainly not the least, advantage of '**std_logic**' based designs is the existence of standard packages defining arithmetical operations on vectors. This eliminates the need for complex type conversion functions and thus enhances the readability of the code.

2.6.11 The NUMERIC_STD Package

- **Provides numerical interpretation for 'std_logic' based vectors**
  - Signed: 2-complement (sign+absolute value)
  - Unsigned: binary representation of positive integers
- **Overloaded mathematical operators**
  - Allow mixture of vector and integer values (vector <= vector + 1)
- **Overloaded relational operators**
  - Avoid problems when dealing with different vector lengths
  - Comparison of vector with integer values
- **NUMERIC_BIT package with 'bit' as basis data type**

 The use of 'bit' and 'bit_vector' is not recommended

The '**numeric_std**' package is located in the library IEEE and provides two numerical interpretations of the bit vector, either as signed or as unsigned integer value. Overloaded operators to mix vectors and integers in expressions are also available.

Note that it is impossible to overload the signal assignment operator, i.e. a function must be called in this case. Conversion functions '**to_integer**' and '**to_(un)signed**' are also defined in the package.

The equivalent of '**numeric_std**' for '**bit**' based operations is called '**numeric_bit**'. The use of '**bit**' based signals is not recommended, however, due to the disadvantages of a 2-valued logic system.

2.6.12 Arrays

```
type STD_ULOGIC_VECTOR is
  array (natural range <>) of STD_ULOGIC;
type MY_BYTE is array(7 downto 0) of STD_ULOGIC;


signal BYTE_BUS : STD_ULOGIC_VECTOR(7 downto 0);
signal TYPE_BUS : MY_BYTE;
```

```
architecture EXAMPLE of ARRAY is
  type CLOCK_DIGITS is
    (HOUR10,HOUR1,MINUTES10,MINUTES1);
  type T_TIME is array(CLOCK_DIGITS)
    of integer range 0 to 9;
  signal ALARM_TIME : T_TIME := (0,7,3,0);

begin
  ALARM_TIME(HOUR1)                   <= 0;
  ALARM_TIME(HOUR10 to MINUTES10) <= (0,7,0);
end EXAMPLE;
```

- **Definition of an array type**
  - Constrained or unconstrained size
- **Declaration of a signal of that type**
  - Range specification necessary
- **The index set can be of any type**

  Only integer index sets are supported by all synthesis tools

2.6.13 Multidimensional Arrays

```
architecture EXAMPLE of ARRAY is

  type INTEGER_VECTOR is
      array (1 to 8) of integer;

  -- 1 --
  type MATRIX_A is array(1 to 3) of
      INTEGER_VECTOR;

  -- 2 --
  type MATRIX_B is array(1 to 4, 1 to 8)
      of integer;

  signal MATRIX3x8 : MATRIX_A;
  signal MATRIX4x8 : MATRIX_B;

begin

  MATRIX3x8(3)(5)  <= 10;  -- array of array

  MATRIX4x8(4, 5)  <= 17;  -- 2 dim array

end EXAMPLE;
```

- **2 possibilities**
  - Array of array
  - Multidimensional array
- **Different referencing**
- **Barely supported by synthesis tools**

2.6.14 Aggregates and Multidimensional Arrays

```
architecture EXAMPLE of AGGREGATE is
   type INTEGER_VECTOR is
      array (1 to 8) of integer;
   type MATRIX_A is
      array(1 to 3) of INTEGER_VECTOR;
   type MATRIX_B is
      array(1 to 4, 1 to 8) of integer;

   signal MATRIX3x8 : MATRIX_A;
   signal MATRIX4x8 : MATRIX_B;
   signal VEC0, VEC1 : INTEGER_VECTOR;
   signal VEC2, VEC3 : INTEGER_VECTOR;
begin

   MATRIX3x8 <= (VEC0, VEC1, VEC2);
   MATRIX4x8 <= (VEC0, VEC1, VEC2, VEC3);

   MATRIX3x8 <= (others => VEC3);
   MATRIX4x8 <= (others => VEC3);

   MATRIX3x8 <= (others => (others => 5));
   MATRIX4x8 <= (others => (others => 5));

end EXAMPLE;
```

- **Aggregates may be nested**
- **Aggregates can be used to make assignments to all elements of a multidimensional array**

Arrays are a collection of a number of values of a single data type and are represented as a new data type in VHDL. It is possible to leave the range of array indices open at the time of definition. These so-called unconstrained arrays cannot be used as signals, however, i.e. the index range then has to be specified in the signal declaration. The advantage of unconstrained arrays is the possibility to concatenate objects of different lengths, for example, because they are still of the same data type. This would not be allowed if each array length was declared as separate data type. VHDL does not put any restrictions on the index set of arrays, as long it is a discrete range of values. It is even legal to use enumeration types, as shown in the code example, although this version is not generally synthesizable.

Multidimensional arrays can simply be obtained by defining a new data type as an array of another array data type (1). When accessing its array elements, the selections are processed from left to right, i.e. the leftmost pair of brackets selects the index range for the 'outermost' array. Thus 'MATRIX_3x8(2)' selects the second 'INTEGER_VECTOR' of 'MATRIX_A'. The range enclosed in the next pair applies to the array that is returned by the previous slice selection, i.e. 'MATRIX_3x8(2)(4)' returns the fourth integer value of this 'INTEGER_VECTOR'.

Multiple dimensions can also be specified directly within a new array definition (2). The ranges of the different dimensions are separated by ',' symbols. If a whole row or column is to be selected, the range has to be provided in the slice selection. Multidimensional arrays are generally synthesizable up to dimension 2 only. The most convenient way to assign values to multiple array elements is via the aggregate mechanism. Aggregates can also be nested for this purpose.

2.6.15 Records

```
architecture EXAMPLE of AGGREGATE is
  type MONTH_NAME is (JAN, FEB, MAR, APR,
                      MAY, JUN, JUL, AUG,
                      SEP, OCT, NOV, DEC);
  type DATE is record
    DAY   :   integer range 1 to 31;
    MONTH :   MONTH_NAME;
    YEAR  :   integer range 0 to 4000;
  end record;

  type PERSON is record
    NAME     : string (0 to 8);
    BIRTHDAY : DATE;
  end record;

  signal TODAY     : DATE;
  signal STUDENT_1 : PERSON;
  signal STUDENT_2 : PERSON;
begin
  TODAY      <= (26, JUL, 1988);
  STUDENT_1  <= ("Franziska", TODAY);

  STUDENT_2 <= STUDENT_1;
  STUDENT_2.BIRTHDAY.YEAR <= 1974;
end EXAMPLE;
```

- **Elements of different type**

- **Possible assignments**

  - record   <= record
  - record   <= aggregate
  - record.element <= value

In contrast to array types, records admit different data types within the newly created structure. Three choices exist for value assignments: The most obvious method is to assign one record to another ('STUDENT_2 <= STUDENT_1'). This does not allow one to set individual values, however. Again, aggregates are commonly used for this purpose, i.e. the different element values are grouped together (e.g. 'TODAY <= (26, JUL, 1988)'). The single elements are addressed via RECORD.ELEMENT constructs, such as 'STUDENT_2.BIRTHDAY. YEAR <= 1974'. As can be seen, this syntax applies also to nested records.

2.6.16 Type Conversion

```
architecture EXAMPLE of CONVERSION is
  type MY_BYTE is array (7 downto 0) of
      std_logic;

  signal VECTOR: std_logic_vector(7 downto 0);
  signal SOME_BITS : bit_vector(7 downto 0);
  signal BYTE       : MY_BYTE;
begin

  SOME_BITS <= VECTOR;                      -- wrong
  SOME_BITS <= Convert_to_Bit(VECTOR);

  BYTE <= VECTOR;                           -- wrong
  BYTE <= MY_BYTE(VECTOR);

end EXAMPLE;
```

- **Data types have to match for assignments**
  - Type conversion functions
  - Type cast
- **Closely related types**
  - integer <-> real
  - Arrays with the same length, index set and element types

Matching data types are a strict language requirement in assignment operations. This can always be achieved via type conversion functions that have to be defined by the user for all necessary pairs of data types.

If the data types in question are so-called 'closely related', the call of a conversion function can be replaced by a simpler type cast. '**integer**' and '**real**' are closely related, for example, i.e. the following code line represents legal VHDL:

REAL_SIGNAL <= real(INTEGER_SIGNAL);

The syntax is similar to a function call, except that the desired data type is used directly as prefix.

Arrays are also called closely related when they are built of the same data type for their elements and coincide in their length and index set. Consequently, type casts occur frequently when dealing with vector operations, as bit vectors ('**bit_vector**', '**std_(u)logic_vector**') themselves do not have a numerical interpretation associated with them. The arithmetic and relational operators for bit vectors operate with '**signed**' or '**unsigned**' data types that interpret the bit values as 2-complement (sign bit + absolute value) of an arbitrary integer number or binary representation of a positive integer value, respectively. These new data types are built of the same basic types ('**bit**', '**std_logic**'), i.e. whenever numerical operations are to be carried out with vectors, their interpretation is provided via the corresponding type cast expression. Of course, the type and operator definitions must be made available first ('**use IEEE.numeric_bit/std.all**').

2.6.17 Subtypes

```
architecture EXAMPLE of SUBTYPES is
  type MY_WORD is array(15 downto 0) of
      std_logic;
  subtype SUB_WORD is
      std_logic_vector(15 downto 0);

  subtype MS_BYTE is integer range 15 downto 8;
  subtype LS_BYTE is integer range 7 downto 0;

  signal VECTOR :
      std_logic_vector(15 downto 0);
  signal SOME_BITS : bit_vector(15 downto 0);
  signal WORD_1 : MY_WORD;
  signal WORD_2 : SUB_WORD;

begin
  SOME_BITS <= VECTOR;                    -- wrong
  SOME_BITS <= Convert_to_Bit(VECTOR);

  WORD_1 <= VECTOR;                       -- wrong
  WORD_1 <= MY_WORD(VECTOR);

  WORD_2 <= VECTOR;                       -- correct!

  WORD_2(LS_BYTE) <= "11110000";
end EXAMPLE;
```

- **Subsets of existing types**
- **Same type as the original type**
- **More readable signal assignments**
  - Eliminates type casts and type conversions
  - Symbolic names for array ranges

2.6.18 Aliases

```
architecture EXAMPLE of ALIAS is
  signal DATA is bit_vector(9 downto 0);

  alias STARTBIT: bit is DATA(9);
  alias MESSAGE: bit_vector(6 downto 0) is
      DATA(8 downto 2);

  alias PARITY:   bit is DATA(1);
  alias STOPBIT:  bit is DATA(0);
  alias REVERSE:  bit_vector(1 to 10) is DATA;

  function CALC_PARITY(data: bit_vector)
      return bit is
    . . .

begin
  STARTBIT    <= '0';
  MESSAGE     <= "1100011";
  PARITY      <= CALC_PARITY(MESSAGE);
  REVERSE(10) <= '1';

end EXAMPLE;
```

- **Give new names to already existing objects**
- **Make it easier to handle complex data structures**

 Aliases are not always supported by synthesis tools

Instead of declaring a completely new data type, it is possible to declare so-called 'subtypes' if the new type that is required is just a somewhat restricted version of another type. Subtypes have the same type as their original type and are therefore compatible with the basic type without the need for type casts or conversion functions. Subtypes can also be used to create symbolic names for array ranges. This is synthesizable alternative to the **'alias'** construct in VHDL. Aliases are used to give another name to already existing objects. In this way, it is possible to break down complex data structures into simpler parts that can be accessed directly.

2.7   Operators

logical	and	or	nand	nor	xor	xnor
	not					
relational	=	/=	<	<=	>=	>
shift	sll	srl	sla	sra	rol	ror
arithmetic	+	-				
	*	/	mod	rem		
	**	abs				

sorted in order of increasing precedence (top -> down)

 New operators: xnor, shift operators

2.7.1   Logical Operators

```
entity LOGIC_OP is
  port (A, B, C, D : in bit;
        Z1          : out bit;
        EQUAL       : out boolean);
end LOGIC_OP;

architecture EXAMPLE of LOGIC_OP is
begin

  Z1 <= A and (B or (not C xor D)));

  EQUAL <= A xor B;    -- wrong

end EXAMPLE;
```

- **Priority**
  - not (top priority)
  - and, or, nand, nor, xor, xnor (equal priority)
- **Predefined for**
  - bit, bit_vector
  - boolean
- **Data types have to match**

 Parentheses must be used to define the order of evaluation

2.7.2 Logical Operations with Arrays

```
architecture EXAMPLE of LOGICAL_OP is
  signal A_BUS : bit_vector (3 downto 0);
  signal B_BUS : bit_vector (3 downto 0);
  signal Z_BUS : bit_vector (4 to 7);
begin
  Z_BUS <= A_BUS and B_BUS;
end EXAMPLE;
```

- **Operands of the same length and type**

- **Assignment via the position of the elements (according to range definition)**

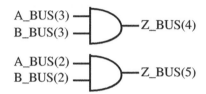

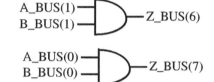

2.7.3 Shift Operators: Examples

Defined only for one-dimensional arrays of bit or boolean!

 signal A_BUS, B_BUS, Z_BUS : bit_vector (3 downto 0);

Z_BUS <= A_BUS sll 2; ◄── At the end, the first value of the
Z_BUS <= B_BUS sra 1;   type is used for filling up
Z_BUS <= A_BUS ror 3;

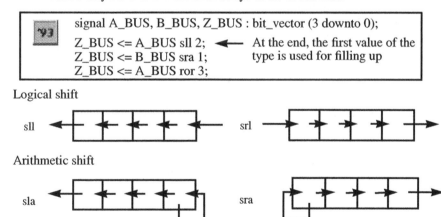

Logical shift

sll   srl

Arithmetic shift

sla   sra

Rotation

rol   ror

2.7.4 Relational Operators

```
architecture EXAMPLE of RELATIONAL_OP
                                   is

  signal NR_A, NR_B: integer;

  signal A_EQ_B1, A_EQ_B2:  bit;
  signal A_LT_B : boolean;

begin
  -- A,B may be of any standard data
type
  process (A, B)
  begin
    if (A = B) then
      A_EQ_B1 <= '1';
    else
      A_EQ_B1 <= '0';
    end if;
  end process;

  A_EQ_B2 <= A = B;     -- wrong

  A_LT_B <= B <= A;
end EXAMPLE;
```

- **Predefined for all standard data types**
- **Result: boolean type (true, false)**

<
less than

<=
less or equal

=
equal

/=
unequal

>=
greater or equal

>
greater

2.7.5 Comparison Operations with Arrays

```
architecture EXAMPLE of COMPARISON is
  signal NIBBLE : bit_vector(3 downto 0);
  signal BYTE   : bit_vector(0 to 7);
begin
  NIBBLE <= "1001";
  BYTE   <= "00001111";

  COMPARE: process (NIBBLE, BYTE)
  begin
    if (NIBBLE < BYTE) then
      -- evaluated as:
      -- if (NIBBLE(3) < BYTE(0))   or
      --    ((NIBBLE(3) = BYTE(0)) and
      --     (NIBBLE(2) < BYTE(1))) or
      --    ((NIBBLE(3) = BYTE(0)) and
      --     (NIBBLE(2) = BYTE(1)) and
      --     (NIBBLE(1) < BYTE(2))) or
      ...
      -- better:
      if (("0000"&NIBBLE) <= BYTE) then
      ...
  end process COMPARE;
end EXAMPLE;
```

- **Operands of the same type**
- **Arrays:**
  - May differ in length
  - Left-alignment prior to comparison
  - Are compared element after element
- **No numerical interpretation (unsigned, 2-complement, etc.)**

 Adjust the length of arrays prior to comparison

2.7.6   Arithmetic Operators

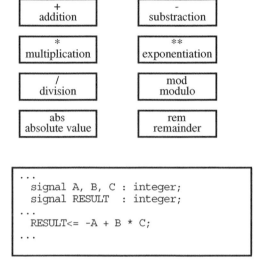

+ addition
- substraction
* multiplication
** exponentiation
/ division
mod modulo
abs absolute value
rem remainder

```
...
  signal A, B, C : integer;
  signal RESULT  : integer;
...
  RESULT<= -A + B * C;
...
```

- **Operands of the same type**
- **Predefined for**
  - integer
  - real (except mod and rem)
  - physical types (e.g. time)
- **Not defined for bit_vector (undefined number format: unsigned, 2-complement, etc.)**
- **Conventional mathematical meaning and priority**
- **'+' and '-' may also be used as unary operators**

The VHDL operators are rather self-explanatory. While relational operators are available for all predefined data types, the logical, shift and arithmetical operators may only be used with bit and numerical values, respectively.

Logical operations with arrays require operands of the same length. The operation is then carried out element by element. This requirement does not exist for comparison operations with arrays. The arrays are left-aligned prior to comparison instead. Therefore it is recommended to adjust the length of the operands with the help of the concatenation operator.

Shift and rotation operations on arrays were introduced with the VHDL'93 standard. Rotation means that none of the element values is lost, as the value that is rotated out of the array on one side will be used for the vacant spot on the other side. This is different from the shift operations, where the value is discarded. During so-called arithmetic shift operations the vacant spot receives its previous value; in the case of logical shift operations the default value of the signal, i.e. the leftmost value from the type declaration, will be used.

Note that two operations to calculate the remainder of an integer division are defined. The signs of the results of '**rem**' and '**mod**' operations are equal to the signs of the first and second operands, respectively.

Examples:
```
 5   rem   3  =  2,    5  mod   3  =  2 ( 5 =    1 *  3  +   2  )
(-5)  rem   3  = -2,  (-5) mod   3  =  1 (-5 =  (-1)*  3  + (-2)
                                       = (-2)*  3  +   1) )
(-5)  rem (-3) = -2,  (-5) mod (-3) = -2 (-5 =    1 *(-3) + (-2) )
 5   rem (-3) =  2,    5  mod (-3) = -1 ( 5 =  (-1)*(-3) +   2
                                       = (-2) *(-3) + (-1) )
```

2.8   Subprograms

- **Functions**
  - Function name can be an operator
  - Arbitrary number of input parameters
  - Exactly one return value
  - No WAIT statement allowed
  - Function call <=> VHDL expression
- **Procedures**
  - Arbitrary number of parameters of any possible direction (input/output/inout)
  - RETURN statement optional (no return value!)
  - Procedure call <=> VHDL statement
- **Subprograms can be overloaded**
- **Parameters can be constants, signals, variables or files**

 'impure' functions are allowed in VHDL'93

The term subprogram is used as collective name for functions, procedures and operators. Operator definitions are treated as a special case of function definitions where the name is replaced by the operator symbol, enclosed by quotation marks (" "). Note that it is not permitted to declare new operators, i.e. it is just possible to provide a function with a different set of input parameters. This feature is called overloading (different subprograms differ by their parameters, only) and may be applied to all subprograms.

Subprogram definitions consist of the subprogram declaration, where the identifier and parameter list are defined, and the subprogram body, defining the behaviour. The statements in the subprogram body are executed sequentially.

A function call is an expression (such as 'a + b') that can exist within a statement only. A procedure call, on the other hand, is a statement (such as 'c := a + b;') and therefore it can be placed inside a process, where it is executed sequentially, or inside an architecture, where it acts like any other concurrent statement. The return value is given after the keyword '**return**', which may be placed several times within a subprogram body. Note that procedures do not have a return value!

IMPURE functions can have access to external objects outside their scope. This allows returning different values, even when called with the same parameters. If, for example, a function call was used to read input values from a file, the file would have to be declared inside the function in VHDL'87. Consequently, the file would be opened with each function call and closed whenever at the end of the execution of the function. Therefore always the first character would be read! It was impossible to read character after character via a function call in VHDL'87, unless the file itself was provided with each function call.

2.8.1 Parameters and Modes

	Function	Procedure	
mode:	in	in	out/inout
class:	**constant** signal	**constant** signal variable	**variable** signal
no mode:	file	file	file

- **Formal parameters (parameter declaration)**
  - Default mode: IN
  - Default parameter class for mode IN: constant, for mode OUT/INOUT: variable
  - File parameters have no mode
- **Actual parameters (subprogram call)**
  - Must match classes of formal parameter
  - Class constant matches actual constants, signals or variables

 Function parameters are always of mode IN and can not be declared as variables

The IMPURE mechanism and the existence of global objects in VHDL'93 allows one to open the file somewhere in the VHDL code and to read character after character by a function call. Another good example is the implementation of a random number generator, which returns a different value each time it is called. Of course, the random numbers could then be read from a file.

Analogous to entity ports, subprogram parameters have a certain mode associated with them. The default mode is IN, i.e. these objects can be read only. Signal attributes ('**event**', 'last_value', etc.) are only available if the formal parameter (i.e. in the declaration part of the subprogram) has been declared as signal. Note that use of the signal attributes '**stable**', '**quiet**', '**transaction**' and '**delayed**' is forbidden.

Actual parameters are those used in the subprogram call and are treated as constants by default. The classes of the formal and actual parameters must match. So it is an error if a parameter is declared as signal and a variable is used as actual parameter in the call. Parameters of type '**constant**' are an exception as they match all possible types.

2.8.2   Functions

```
architecture EXAMPLE of FUNCTIONS is
  [(im)pure] function COUNT_ZEROS (A :
               bit_vector) return integer is
    variable ZEROS : integer;
  begin
    ZEROS := 0;
    for I in A'range loop
      if A(I) = '0' then
        ZEROS := ZEROS + 1;
      end if;
    end loop;
    return ZEROS;
  end COUNT_ZEROS;
  signal WORD: bit_vector(15  downto 0);
  signal WORD_0: integer;
begin
  WORD_0 <= COUNT_ZEROS("01101001");
  process(...)
  begin
    if COUNT_ZEROS(WORD) > 0 then
        . . .
    end if;
    . . .
  end process;
end EXAMPLE;
```

- **(Im)pure declaration optional (default: 'pure' = VHDL'87)**

- **Body split into declarative and definition part (cf. process)**

- **Unconstrained parameters possible (array size remains unspecified)**

- **Are used as expression in other VHDL statements (concurrent or sequential)**

The keyword '**pure**' can be used for "oldstyled" functions, the keyword '**impure**' declares the new VHDL'93 function type. By default, i.e. if no keyword is given, functions are declared as PURE. A PURE function does not have access to a shared variable, because shared variables are declared in the declarative part of an architecture and PURE functions do not have access to objects outside their scope.

The code example shows a function that counts the number of '0's in a bit vector. Only parameters of mode '**in**' are allowed in function calls, and are treated as '**constant**' by default. The size of the bit vector is not declared, i.e. a so-called unconstrained formal parameter is used. Consequently, the subprogram code has to be written independently of the actual vector width. This can be done with the help of predefined attributes, such as the attribute '**range**' in the example. In this way, the FOR loop works for any vector size passed to the function. If a constrained array is used instead (e.g. bit_vector(15 downto 0)), the actual parameter will have to be of the same type, i.e. the types of the array elements and the size of the array must match. The directions of the array ranges may differ.

Functions may be used wherever an expression is necessary within a VHDL statement. Subprograms themselves, however, are executed sequentially like processes. Similar to a process, it is also possible to declare local variables. These variables are initialized with every function call with the leftmost element of the type declaration (boolean: false, bit: '0'). The leftmost value of integers is guaranteed to be at least $-(2^{31})-1$, i.e. ZEROS must be initialized to 0 at the beginning of the function body. It is recommended to initialize all variables in order to enhance the clarity of the code.

2.8.3 Procedures

```
architecture EXAMPLE of PROCEDURES is
  procedure COUNT_ZEROS(A: in bit_vector;
             variable Q: out integer) is
    variable ZEROS : integer;
  begin
    ZEROS := 0;
    for I in A'range loop
      if A(I) = '0' then
        ZEROS := ZEROS + 1;
      end if;
    end loop;
    Q := ZEROS;
  end COUNT_ZEROS;

  signal WORD: bit_vector(15  downto 0);
begin
  process(WORD)
    variable COUNT : integer;
  begin
    COUNT_ZEROS(WORD, COUNT);
    if COUNT > 0 then
      . . .
    end if;
    . . .
  end process;
end EXAMPLE;
```

- **No return value**

- **Parameter values may be updated (mode out/inout)**

- **Body split into declarative and definition part (cf. process)**

- **Unconstrained parameters possible (array size remains unspecified)**

- **Are used as VHDL statements (concurrent or sequential)**

Procedures, in contrast to functions, are used like any other statement in VHDL. Consequently, they do not have a return value, although the keyword '**return**' may be used to indicate the termination of the subprogram. Depending on their position within the VHDL code, either in an architecture or in a process, the procedure as a whole is executed concurrently or sequentially, respectively. The code within all subprograms is always executed sequentially.

Procedures can feed back results to their environment via an arbitrary number of output parameters. As the default mode of a parameter is '**in**', the keyword '**out**' or '**inout**' is necessary to declare output signals/variables. By default, output parameters are of the class variable. The VHDL compiler will report an error message if a function declared with a signal as parameter is called with a variable and vice versa.

Since the class of the parameters have to match, one might think of overloading a procedure, i.e. by writing procedures that differ in the class declaration of the parameters and the corresponding assignment operators, only. However this is **not** possible, because the parameter class is ignored when the appropriate subprogram is selected!

The example procedure is the equivalent of the previously presented function for counting the '0' elements within a bit_vector. Again, all internal variables should be initialized because subprograms do not store variable values and initialize them with type'left at each call instead.

2.9 Subprogram Declaration and Overloading

- **Subprograms may be declared/defined in any declaration part**
  - Package
  - Entity
  - Architecture
  - Process
  - Subprogram
- **Overloading of subprograms possible**
  - Identical name
  - Different parameters
  - Works with any kind of subprogram
- **During compilation/runtime that subprogram is called whose formal parameters match the provided actuals**

Subprograms may be declared/defined in any declarative part of a VHDL object. The actual definition of the behaviour may also be separated from the declaration, which is often the case when packages are split into package and package body. The usual object visibility rules apply, e.g. a subprogram that is declared in a package may be used in all units that reference this package. Subprograms that are declared within another subprogram are available within this 'parent' subprogram only.

It is legal to declare subprograms with identical names, as long as they are distinguishable by the compiler. Thus, if the two subprogram names match, the parameter set/return values have to differ. This is called overloading and is allowed for all subprograms. It is especially useful when applied to operators, which can be seen as functions with a special name. This allows one, for example, to use the conventional '+' symbol for the addition of integer values and, likewise, with bit vectors that should be interpreted as numbers.

During compilation, that procedure is chosen whose formal parameters match the actual parameters in the procedure call.

2.9.1   Overloading Example

```
procedure READ(L      : inout line;
              VALUE : out character;
              GOOD  : out boolean);

procedure READ(L      : inout line;
              VALUE : out character);

procedure READ(L      : inout line;
              VALUE : out integer;
              GOOD  : out boolean );

procedure READ(L      : inout line;
              VALUE : out integer );

. . .
```

- **Input routines from TEXTIO package**

  - Extract different data types from a line
  - Identical names
  - Different number of parameters
  - Different parameter types

2.9.2   Overloading : Illegal Redeclarations

```
package P_EXAMPLE is
  -- 1 --
  procedure TEST(A : bit;
    variable X_VAR : out integer);
  -- 2 --
  procedure TEST(B : bit;
    variable X_VAR : out integer);
  -- 3 --
  procedure TEST(A : bit;
    variable X_VAR : in integer);
  -- 4 --
  procedure TEST(A : bit;
      signal X_SIG : out integer);
  -- 5 --
  procedure TEST(A : bit;
      signal X_SIG : out integer;
             FOO : boolean := false);
end P_EXAMPLE;
```

- **Relevant information for overloading:**

  - Number of formal parameters
  - Types of the formal parameters
  - Order of the parameter types

- **The following will be ignored when overloading a subprogram:**

  - Names of formal parameters (2)
  - Modes of formal parameters (3)
  - Classes of formal parameters (4)

 Default parameters should not be used in synthesizable code

2.9.3 Overloading : Ambiguity

```
-- Declarations 2-4 need to be removed from the
-- package P_EXAMPLE in order to compile!
use work.P_EXAMPLE.all;

entity AMBIGUITY is
end AMBIGUITY;

architecture EXAMPLE of AMBIGUITY is
  signal A:        bit;
  signal X_SIG: integer;
begin
  process
    variable X_VAR: integer;
  begin
    -- 1 --
    TEST(A, X_VAR);
    -- 2 --
    TEST(A, X_SIG);
    -- 3 --
    TEST(A => A, X_SIG => X_SIG);
    -- 4 --
    TEST(A => A, X_VAR => X_VAR);
    wait;
  end process;
end EXAMPLE;
```

- **Ambiguous calls occur if it is not possible to find a unique subprogram by**
  - name
  - number of formal parameters
  - types and order of actual parameters (1/2)
  - names of formal parameters (named association only)

The file I/O procedures read, write, readline, writeline and the line types are predefined in the standard TEXTIO package. Several overloaded read/write procedures for the standard data types are declared. They extract a value of the desired type from a file line. The line itself is modified, as indicated by the mode declaration '**inout**', i.e. several values may be read from a single line.

It is not possible to declare two subprograms which have the same number of parameters and the same types but different names, modes or classes. The compiler will report an error message similar to 'illegal redeclaration'. The example package P_EXAMPLE will not compile successfully unless the declarations (2)–(4) are removed, e.g. by marking them as comments. These four procedures have the same name as the first, and all need a bit and an integer parameter. If a subprogram is necessary to deal with signal and variable parameters, it is possible to declare an additional dummy input parameter and assign it a default value. In this way, the declared subprograms differ in the number of parameters and a redeclaration error is avoided. Additionally, it is necessary to use the named association mechanism to map the actual parameters to the formal ones. Otherwise, the compiler will try to find an unique subprogram of the given name which has the same number and type of parameters as in the call. If this fails, an error message about an ambiguous expression will be generated (TEST statements 1, 2). Input parameters with a default value assigned to them need not be present in the subprogram call. Their use is not recommended, however, as some synthesis tools map absent parameters to the default value of the data type (type'left), which may lead to different behaviour if the parameter is actually used in the body.

2.9.4   Operator Overloading

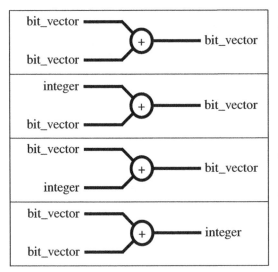

- **Similar to function declarations**
  - Name = existing operator symbol, enclosed in quotation marks
  - Operand left/right of operator are mapped to first/second parameter
- **Extends operator functionality to new data types**
- **Operator call according to the individual context**
- **Definition of new operators is not allowed**

⚠ **Arithmetic operations with 'bit_vector' are not defined**

2.9.5   Operator Overloading : Example

```
package P_BIT_ARITH is
   function "+" (L: bit_vector; R: bit_vector) return bit_vector; -- 1
   function "+" (L: integer; R: bit_vector) return bit_vector;    -- 2
   function "+" (L: bit_vector; R: integer) return bit_vector;    -- 3
   function "+" (L: bit_vector; R: bit_vector) return integer;    -- 4
end P_BIT_ARITH;
use work.P_BIT_ARITH.all;
entity OVERLOADED is
   port(A_VEC, B_VEC : in bit_vector(3 downto 0);
        A_INT, B_INT : in integer range 0 to 15;
        Q_VEC        : out bit_vector(3 downto 0);
        Q_INT        : out integer range 0 to 15);
end OVERLOADED;
architecture EXAMPLE of OVERLOADED is
begin
   Q_VEC <= A_VEC + B_VEC; -- a
   Q_VEC <= A_INT + B_VEC; -- b
   Q_VEC <= A_VEC + B_INT; -- c
   Q_VEC <= A_INT + B_INT; -- d
   Q_INT <= A_VEC + B_VEC; -- e
   Q_INT <= A_INT + B_INT; -- f
end EXAMPLE;
```

All standard VHDL operators can be overloaded but is not allowed to define new operators. Operator declarations are equivalent to function declarations apart from the name which must be placed in quotation marks (" "). The number of parameters is also fixed and cannot be modified. In case of binary operators, i.e. operators with two operands, the left/right operands are mapped to the leftmost/rightmost parameters, respectively.

The code example shows just the operator declarations and their use. The behaviour has to be defined in a package body if the design is to be simulated. During compilation, the VHDL compiler searches its list of operator declarations for a parameter list with matching data types. In this way, the function bodies of the operator declarations (1)–(3) will be used in the signal assignments (a)–(c). Signal assignment (d) will result in an error message as the addition of two integer values to obtain a bit_vector has not yet been defined. Assignment (e) matches the parameter list of declaration (4), and the last assignment will use the standard VHDL operator.

Arithmetic operations based on the data type '**bit**' are defined in the standard package '**numeric_bit**' (library IEEE). In practice, this data type should be avoided, however, as standard packages are available that define more powerful bit vector types and the corresponding operations.

3   Synthesis

3.1   What is Synthesis?

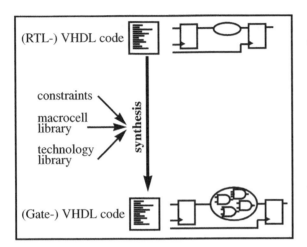

- **Transformation of an abstract description into a more detailed description**

  - '+' operator is transformed into a gate netlist
  - 'if (VEC_A = VEC_B) then' is realized as a comparator that controls a multiplexer

- **Transformation depends on several factors**

3.1.1   Synthesizability

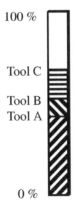

- **Only a subset of VHDL is synthesizable**
- **Different tools support different subsets**

  - Records?
  - Arrays of integers?
  - Clock edge detection?
  - Sensitivity list?
  - ...

3.1.2 Different Language Support for Synthesis

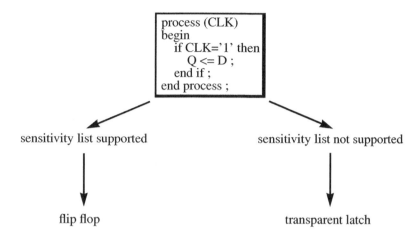

In general, the term 'synthesis' is used for the automated transformation of RT-level descriptions into gate-level representations. This transformation is mainly influenced by the set of basic cells that is available in the target technology. While simple operations such as comparisons and either/or decisions are easily mapped to boolean functions, more complex constructs such as mathematical operators are mapped to a tool-specific macrocell library first. This means that a number of adder, multiplier, etc. architectures are known to the synthesis tool and these designs are treated as if they were designed by the user.

The macrocell library is just one distinguishing feature of synthesis software. VHDL itself is not fully synthesizable and the available tools differ in the language subset that is supported. Complex user-defined data structures such as records and multidimensional arrays (e.g. simple arrays of integers) turn out to be the most problematic cases.

The consequences of different language support on the resulting hardware are demonstrated at the example of a clocked process. In the case where the synthesis tool supports sensitivity lists the result is a flip flop because the process is triggered with every event at CLK and the value of D will be assigned to Q, if CLK='1' as a result of this event. Thus the behaviour of a rising-edge-triggered flip flop is modelled here.

Even if synthesis tools do not support sensitivity lists in general, they often look for templates that describe the behaviour of registers. Usually, the check for the CLK event has to be part of the if condition as well. If the sensitivity list is ignored and the code cannot be matched to a register template, a level-triggered latch will be generated!

3.1.3   How to Do?

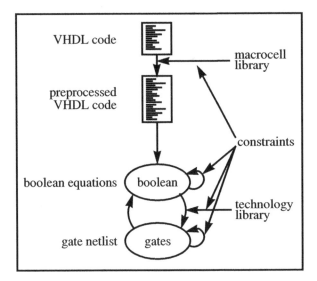

- **Contraints**
  - Speed
  - Area
  - Power

- **Macrocells**
  - Adder
  - Comparator
  - Businterface

- **Optimizations**
  - Boolean: mathematical
  - Gate: technological

3.1.4   Essential Information for Synthesis

- **Load values**
- **Path delays**
- **Driver strengths**
- **Timing**
- **Operating conditions**

3.1.5 Synthesis Process in Practice

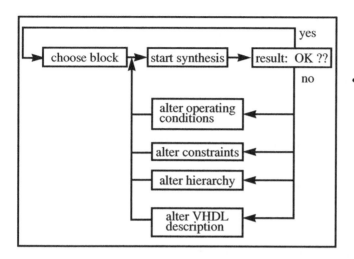

• **In most cases synthesis has to be carried out several times in order to achieve an optimal synthesis result**

Besides the fixed synthesis constraints set by the target technology and the tool capabilities, 'soft' constraints that are imposed by the designer have to be considered as well. Maximum operating speed and required hardware resources are usually the main targets for netlist optimization. This is possible either on a purely abstract mathematical model or by different mappings of the boolean functions on the available technology cells. Due to the complexity, the optimization phase requires quite a lot of iterations before the software reports its final result.

Even after extensive optimizations by the synthesis tool, the result is pretty often not compliant with the system requirements. In this case, the input to the software has to be modified. Several parameters may be modified by the designer: the block operating conditions includes environmental conditions such as operating temperature as well as settings such as necessary driver strength (fan-out) or capacitance of wire connections. They have a direct impact on the actual wire delays.

Hierarchy alterations can simply be performed by selecting a bigger block and allowing the tool to break up the hierarchy definitions from the VHDL source code. If the repeated attempts still fail to produce the desired result, modifications of the original VHDL code become the last way out.

3.1.6   Problems with Synthesis Tools

- **Timing issues**
  - Layout information is missing during the synthesis process
  - Clock tree must be generated afterwards
- **Complex clocking schemes**
  (inverted clocks, multiple clocks, gated clocks)
- **Memory**
  - Synthesis tools are not able to replace register arrays with memory macrocells
- **Macro cells**
  - No standardized way for instantiation of existing technology macrocells
- **IO pads**
  - ASIC libraries have several different IO pads
  - Selection by hand, either within the synthesis tool or in the top-level entity

While algorithms have matured considerably, there still exist a number of problems and pitfalls for the users of synthesis tools. Many issues are related to the separation of netlist and layout generation. Therefore the length of the interconnections can only be estimated during synthesis, and critical nets have to modified by hand afterwards. The clock tree, for example, requires extensive buffering in order to distribute the clock signal evenly on the chip and has to be generated by hand.

While synthesis of synchronous designs with a single clock source is fairly simple, practical systems unfortunately often require additional clock signals. This introduces asynchronous behaviour, which is very complex to handle as long as the exact propagation delays are unknown. Macrocells that are available in the target technology are also hard to use. This is especially true for memory cells that cannot used by synthesis tools automatically. The same applies to the I/O cells of ASIC libraries that have to chosen by hand.

3.1.7   Synthesis Strategy

- **Consider the effects of different coding styles on the inferred hardware structures**
- **Appropriate design partitioning**
    - Critical paths should not be distributed to several synthesis blocks
    - Automatic synthesis performs best at module sizes of several 1000 gates
    - Different optimization constraints may be used for separate blocks

The VHDL coding style itself has a rather big impact on the synthesis result. Therefore it is necessary to keep this in mind even if the model is to be synthesized at the last step of the development cycle.

The design partitioning should be reviewed prior to the synthesis runs. This is mainly due to the fact that the algorithms perform best at module sizes of several thousand gates. It is not necessary to rewrite the RTL description, as submodules can be grouped together during synthesis. This allows for different optimization settings, i.e. high-speed parts can be synthesized with very stringent timing constraints, while non-critical parts should consume the least amount of resources (area) possible.

3.2 RTL Style

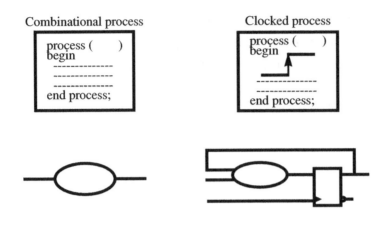

Combinational process   Clocked process

In RTL (Register Transfer Level)-style modelling, the design is split up into storing elements, i.e. flip flops or often simply called registers, and combinational logic, which constitutes the transfer function from one register to the succeeding register. A process is required for each of them: a combinational process, which describes the functionality, and a clocked process, which generates all storing elements. Of course, it is possible to combine these two processes into a single clocked one that models the complete functionality.

3.2.1 Combinational Process: Sensitivity List

```
process (A, B, SELECT)
begin
  if (SELECT = '1') then
    OUT <= A;
  else
    OUT <= B;
  end if;
end process;
```

- **Sensitivity list is usually ignored during synthesis**

- **Equivalent behaviour of simulation model and hardware:**

  sensitivity list has to contain all signals that are read by the process

 What kind of hardware is modelled?

 What will be the simulation result if SELECT is missing in the sensitivity list?

The sensitivity list of a combinational process consists of all signals which will be read within the process. It is especially important not to forget any signals, because synthesis tools generally ignore sensitivity lists in contrast to simulation tools. During simulation, a process will only be executed if there an event occurs on at least one of the signals of the sensitivity list. During synthesis, VHDL code is simply mapped to logic elements. Consequently a forgotten signal in the sensitivity list will most probably lead to a difference in behaviour between the simulated VHDL model and the synthesized design. Superfluous signals in the sensitivity list will only slow down simulation speed.

The code example models a multiplexer. If the signal SELECT were missing, synthesis would create exactly the same result, namely a multiplexer, but simulation would show a completely different behaviour. The multiplexer would work properly as long as an event on SELECT coincided with events on A or B. But without an event on A or B the process would not be activated and thus an event exclusively on SELECT would be ignored in simulation. Consequently, during simulation, the output value OUT would only change if the input signals A or B were modified.

3.2.2   WAIT Statement <-> Sensitivity List

```
process
begin
    if SEL = '1' then
        Z <= A;
    else
        Z <= B;
    end if;
    wait on A, B, SEL;
end process;
```

```
process (A, B, SEL)
begin
    if SEL = '1' then
        Z <= A;
    else
        Z <= B;
    end if;

end process;
```

- **Equivalent processes**
- **Mutually exclusive:**
  - Either sensitivity list
  - Or wait statements

Instead of using a sensitivity list, it is possible to model the same behaviour by the use of a WAIT ON statement. It should be placed as last statement in the process and should quote the same signals, of course.

In the case of a sensitivity list, the process is started whenever an event occurs on one of the signals in the list. All sequential statements are executed and after the last sequential statement the process is suspended until the next event. In the case of a wait statement, the process runs through the sequential statements to the wait statement and suspends until the condition of the wait statement is fulfilled. Process execution must be interrupted via wait statements if no sensitivity list is present, as the simulator would be stuck in an endless loop otherwise.

Remember again that it is not permitted to use a sensitivity list and a wait statement simultaneously in the same process.

3.2.3 Combinational Process: Incomplete Assignments

```
                    entity MUX is
                       port (A, B, SELECT : in std_logic;
                             Z             : out std_logic);
                    end MUX;
```

architecture NO of MUX is	architecture OK1 of MUX is	architecture OK2 of MUX is
| ```
begin
  process (A, B, SELECT)
  begin

    if SELECT = '1' then
      Z <= A;
    end if;
  end process;
end NO;
``` | ```
begin
  process (A, B, SELECT)
  begin
    Z <= B;
    if SELECT = '1' then
      Z <= A;
    end if;
  end process;
end OK1;
``` | ```
begin
  process (A, B, SELECT)
  begin

    if SELECT = '1' then
      Z <= A;
    else
      Z <= B;
    end if;
  end process;
end OK2;
``` |

 What is the value of Z if SELECT = '0'?

 What hardware would be generated during synthesis?

Special care is necessary when modelling combinational hardware in order to avoid the generation of latches. The leftmost code example lacks an unconditional else branch. Therefore the value of Z is preserved in the case of SELECT='0', even if the input signals change. Synthesis would have to generate an adequate storing element, i.e. a latch that is transparent whenever the level of SELECT is '1'.

This kind of storing elements is **not** recommended for synchronous designs. Edge-triggered flip flops are preferred because possibly illegal intermediate signal values are filtered out as long as the combinational logic settles to its final state before the next active clock edge. Additionally latches cannot be tested by a scan test. In scan test mode all flip flops are combined to a single shift register, the so-called scan path. They are all supplied with the same clock signal. This makes it possible to set all registers to specific values by shifting them into the chip using an additional input pin (scan_in). After one system clock period the registers contain new values, which are shifted out using an additional output pin (scan_out). In this way, scan test provides access to otherwise invisible internal states. Scan test is current state of the art technology to improve testability for production tests.

The two coding alternatives are functionally identical and are mapped to purely combinational logic (multiplexer) by synthesis tools. The difference lies in the implementation of the default assignment. Remember that signal values are updated at the end of the process execution only! In this way the default assignment of B to Z in the architecture OK1 will be overwritten if the IF condition is true.
```

3.2.4   Clocked Process: Clock Edge Detection

- **New standard for synthesis: IEEE 1076.6**

- if
  - *clock_signal_name*'EVENT and *clock_signal_name*='1'
  - *clock_signal_name*='1' and *clock_signal_name*'EVENT
  - not *clock_signal_name*'STABLE and *clock_signal_name*='1'
  - *clock_signal_name*='1' and not *clock_signal_name*'STABLE
  - RISING_EDGE (*clock_signal_name*)

- wait until
  - *clock_signal_name*'EVENT and *clock_signal_name*='1'
  - *clock_signal_name*='1' and *clock_signal_name*'EVENT
  - not *clock_signal_name*'STABLE and *clock_signal_name*='1'
  - *clock_signal_name*='1' and not *clock_signal_name*'STABLE
  - RISING_EDGE (*clock_signal_name*)
  - *clock_signal_name*='1'

 IEEE 1076.6 is not yet fully supported by all tools

As the sensitivity list is usually ignored by synthesis tools and wait statements are not synthesizable in general, a solution to the problem of modelling storage elements has to be found. Synthesis tools solved this issue by looking for certain templates in the VHDL code, namely the first option ('**if/wait until X'event and X='1' then**') of the two process styles. All alternatives show the same behaviour during simulation, however. Note that the event detection in the '**wait until**' statement is redundant as an event is implicitly required by the '**wait until**' construct.

In the meantime, the IEEE standard 1076.6 has been passed that lists the VHDL constructs that should infer register generation. As this standard is not yet fully supported by synthesis tools, the first option is still the most common way of describing a rising/falling clock edge for synthesis. When asynchronous set or reset signals are present, only the IF variant is applicable.

The RISING_EDGE function is just mentioned for sake of completeness, as it is not supported by synthesis tools. Nevertheless, it may be useful for simulation.

```
function RISING_EDGE (signal CLK : std_ulogic) return boolean is
begin
  if (CLK'event and CLK = '1' and CLK'last_value = '0') then
    return true;
  else
    return false;
  end if;
end RISING_EDGE;
```

3.2.5 Register Inference

```
library IEEE;
use IEEE.std_logic_1164.all;

entity COUNTER is
  port (CLK:  in std_logic;
        Q : out integer range 0 to 15);
end COUNTER;

architecture RTL of COUNTER is
  signal COUNT : integer range 0 to 15;
begin
  process (CLK)
  begin
    if CLK'event and CLK = '1' then
      if (COUNT >= 9) then
        COUNT <= 0;
      else
        COUNT <= COUNT +1;
      end if;
    end if;
  end process;

  Q <= COUNT;
end RTL;
```

- **Storage elements are synthesized for all signals that are driven within a clocked process**

- COUNT: 4 flip flops

- Q: not used in clocked process

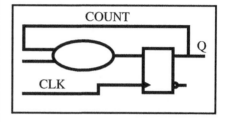

The example shows the VHDL model of a simple 1-digit decimal counter. Several things are worth mentioning:

First, the design is not resetable. This is not a problem for simulation, as initial values can be assigned to the signals. Real-world hardware does not behave this nicely, however, and the state of internal storage elements is unknown after power up. In order to avoid strange and inexplicable behaviour, it is recommended to provide a reset feature that brings the design into a well-defined state.

Second, the range of the integer signals has been restricted. Synthesis tools have to map all data types onto a bit pattern that can be transported via wires. Without explicit range definition, the range for integers would be from -2,147,483,647 to +2,147,483,647, which equals 32 bits. As the maximum counter value is 9, it would be natural to specify a valid range for signal values from 0 to 9. During synthesis, however, 4 bits will be needed to represent the number 9, i.e. the theoretical maximum value of the signal would be 15. In order to avoid possible shortcomings of synthesis tools and to make sure that the counter restarts with 0, indeed, the range is set to match the synthesized hardware.

Third, the internal signal COUNT has been declared in addition to the output port Q. This is due to the fact that Q is declared with port mode '**out**', i.e. its value cannot be read within the architecture. As its next value depends on the previous one, however, it is necessary to declare the intermediate signal COUNT, which is used within the counter process. The process itself is a clocked process without any asynchronous control signals, and thus the CLK signal is the only signal in the sensitivity list.

3.2.6 Asynchronous Set/Reset

```
library IEEE;
use IEEE.std_logic_1164.all;

entity ASYNC_FF is
  port (D, CLK, SET, RST : in std_logic;
        Q               : out std_logic);
end ASYNC_FF;

architecture RTL of ASYNC_FF is
begin
  process  (CLK, RST, SET)
  begin
    if (RST = '1') then
      Q <= '0';
    elsif SET ='1' then
      Q <= '1';
    elsif (CLK'event and CLK = '1') then
      Q <= D;
    end if;
  end process;
end RTL;
```

- **Only possible in processes with sensitivity list**
- **If/elsif structure**
  - Clock edge detection as last condition
  - No unconditional else branch

Flip flops are inferred by clocked processes only. Every signal that might be updated in a clocked process receives a register. Therefore four storage elements will be created for the COUNT signal. The assignment of the output value is done concurrently, i.e. the outputs of the flip flops will be connected directly to the outputs of the COUNTER module.

As noted before, it is advisable to provide each clocked design with a reset capability. If a synchronous reset strategy is employed, the reset signal is treated just like any other control signal, i.e. the clock signal will be still the only signal in the process's sensitivity list.

While purely synchronous clocked processes can also be described with the '**wait until**' construct, asynchronous control signals can only be modelled with processes with sensitivity list. All signals that might trigger the process execution have to be listed again, i.e. the asynchronous signals (usually reset, only) are added. The process itself consists of an IF construct, where the asynchronous signals are checked first, followed by the detection of the active clock edge.

The condition for synchronous actions has to be the last condition of the IF structure because asynchronous control signals are usually treated with higher priority by the underlying hardware cells. An unconditional else path is strictly forbidden, as statements that have to be processed whenever the active clock edge is not present do not have a physical representation.

It is very important not to forget any of these asynchronous signals. Otherwise simulation will differ from synthesis results, as simulation tools base their simulation on the sensitivity list and synthesis tools usually ignore the sensitivity list completely.

3.2.7   Summary: Combinational Process (Rules)

- **Complete sensitivity list**
  - RTL behaviour identical with hardware realization
  - Incomplete sensitivity lists can cause warnings or errors
- **No incomplete if statements**
  - Inference of transparent latches

3.2.8   Summary: Clocked Process (Rules)

```
process
begin
  wait until CLK'event and CLK='1';
  if RESET = '1' then
    -- synchronous register reset
  else
    -- combinational
  end if;
end process;
```

- **WAIT form:**
  no sensitivity list

- **Synchronous reset**

```
process(CLK, RST)
begin
  if (RST = '1') then
    -- asynchronous register reset
  elsif (CLK'event and CLK='1') then
    -- combinational
  end if;
end process;
```

- **IF form:**
  **only clock and asynchronous signals
  (reset) in sensitivity list**

- **Synchronous and asynchronous reset**

 Registers for all driven signals

 All registers should be resetable

3.3   Combinational Logic

3.3.1   Feedback Loops

```
architecture EXAMPLE of FEEDBACK is
   signal B,X : integer range 0 to 99;
begin

   process (X, B)
   begin
    X <= X + B;
   end process;

   . . .
end EXAMPLE;
```

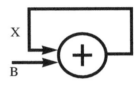

⚠ **Do not create combinational feedback loops!**

3.3.2   Coding Style Influence

Direct implementation

```
EXAMPLE1:
process (SEL,A,B)
begin
   if SEL = '1' then
      Z <= A + B;
   else
      Z <= A + C;
   end if;
end process EXAMPLE1;
```

Hardware realization

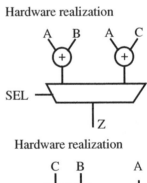

Manual resource sharing

```
EXAMPLE2:
process (SEL,A,B,C)
   variable TMP : bit;
begin
   if SEL = '1' then
      TMP := B;
   else
      TMP := C;
   end if;
   Z <= A + TMP;
end process EXAMPLE2;
```

Hardware realization

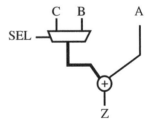

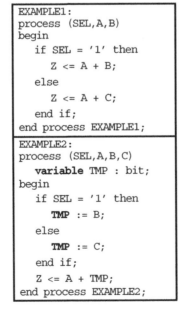

3.3.3 Source Code Optimization

- **An operation can be described very efficiently for synthesis, e.g.:**

OUT1 <= IN1+IN2+IN3+IN4+IN5+IN6   OUT2 <= ((IN1+IN2) (IN3+IN4))+(IN5+IN6)

- **In one description the longest path goes via five, in the other description via three addition components – some optimization tools automatically change the description according to the given constraints.**

When modelling purely combinational logic, it is necessary to avoid combinational feedback loops. A feedback loop triggers itself all the time, i.e. the corresponding process is always active. In the example, this results in a perpetual addition, i.e. X is increased to its maximum value. So simulation quits at time 0 ns with an error message because X exceeds its range. In general, synthesis is possible, but the hardware is not useable.

An IF statement is synthesized to a multiplexer with eventual additional logic. That is why the direct implementation of example 1 results in two adders, as this is exactly what the VHDL code describes. But it is obvious that one adder is sufficient to implement the desired functionality and good synthesis tools will detect this during their optimization cycles. In example 2 a temporal variable is used to implement a functionally equivalent description that requires only one adder. Manual resource sharing is recommended as it leads to a better starting point for the synthesis process.

The structure of the generated hardware, at least in the first synthesis iteration, is determined by the VHDL code itself. Consequently, the coding style has a rather big impact on the optimization algorithms. As not all synthesis tools are able to optimize the design structure itself, it is reasonable to ease their task, e.g. by structuring the code for minimum critical paths.

3.3.4 Example of a Multiplier

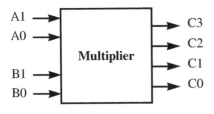

- **2 x 2 bit multiplier**

  - Inputs:
    A1, A0, B1, B0 : 2 bit

  - Outputs:
    C3, C2, C1, C0 : 4 bit

```
entity MULTIPLIER is
  port(A0 : in  bit;
       A1 : in  bit;
       B0 : in  bit;
       B1 : in  bit;
       C0 : out bit;
       C1 : out bit;
       C2 : out bit;
       C3 : out bit);
end MULTIPLIER;
```

- **3 different VHDL implementations**

  - Function table

  - Synthesis 'by hand'
    (boolean functions for the outputs)

  - Use of VHDL integer types and
    operators

Multiplier Function Table

a1	a0	b1	b0	c3	c2	c1	c0
0	0	0	0	0	0	0	0
0	0	0	1	0	0	0	0
0	0	1	0	0	0	0	0
0	0	1	1	0	0	0	0
0	1	0	0	0	0	0	0
0	1	0	1	0	0	0	1
0	1	1	0	0	0	1	0
0	1	1	1	0	0	1	1
1	0	0	0	0	0	0	0
1	0	0	1	0	0	1	0
1	0	1	0	0	1	0	0
1	0	1	1	0	1	1	0
1	1	0	0	0	0	0	0
1	1	0	1	0	0	1	1
1	1	1	0	0	1	1	0
1	1	1	1	1	0	0	1

Multiplier Minterms: Karnaugh Diagram

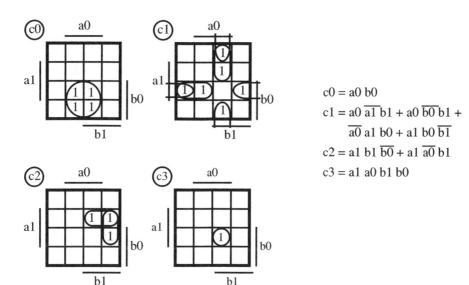

$$c0 = a0 \, b0$$
$$c1 = a0 \, \overline{a1} \, b1 + a0 \, \overline{b0} \, b1 +$$
$$\overline{a0} \, a1 \, b0 + a1 \, b0 \, \overline{b1}$$
$$c2 = a1 \, b1 \, \overline{b0} + a1 \, \overline{a0} \, b1$$
$$c3 = a1 \, a0 \, b1 \, b0$$

Different VHDL coding styles will be demonstrated with a simple module that has to calculate the result of the multiplication of two 2-bit numbers. The maximum value of each input is 3, i.e. the maximum output value is 9, which needs 4 bits in a binary code. Therefore four input ports and four output ports of data type '**bit**' are required. The same entity will be used for all different implementations.

The most direct approach is via the function table of the multiplications. The behaviour of a combinational logic block is completely defined by listing the results for all possible input values. Of course, the function table is usually no the most compact representation.

The function table of this 2x2 bit multiplier leads directly to the four Karnaugh diagrams of the output signals. The bars on the side of the squares indicate those regions where the corresponding input bit is '1'. All '1's of the output signals are marked in the corresponding diagrams. By combining adjacent '1's, the minimal output function can be derived.

Multiplier: VHDL Code Using the Function Table

```
architecture RTL_TABLE of MULTIPLIER is
  signal A_B : bit_vector (3 downto 0);
begin
  A_B <=  A1 & A0 & B1 & B0;
  MULTIPLY : process (A_B)
  begin
    case A_B is
      when "0000" => (C3,C2,C1,C0) <= "0000";
      when "0001" => (C3,C2,C1,C0) <= "0000";
      when "0010" => (C3,C2,C1,C0) <= "0000";
      when "0011" => (C3,C2,C1,C0) <= "0000";
      when "0100" => (C3,C2,C1,C0) <= "0000";
      when "0101" => (C3,C2,C1,C0) <= "0001";
      when "0110" => (C3,C2,C1,C0) <= "0010";
      when "0111" => (C3,C2,C1,C0) <= "0011";

      . . .
      when "1100" => (C3,C2,C1,C0) <= "0000";
      when "1101" => (C3,C2,C1,C0) <= "0011";
      when "1110" => (C3,C2,C1,C0) <= "0110";
      when "1111" => (C3,C2,C1,C0) <= "1001";
    end case;
  end process MULTIPLY;
end RTL_TABLE;
```

- **An internal signal is used that combines all input signals**

- **The internal signal is generated concurrently, i.e. it is updated whenever the input changes**

- **The function table is realized as case statement and thus has to placed within a process. The internal signal is the only signal that controls the behaviour**

Multiplier: VHDL Code Using the Minterm Functions

```
architecture RTL_MINTERM of MULTIPLIER is
begin

  C0 <= A0 and B0;

  C1 <= (A0 and not A1 and B1) or
        (A0 and not B0 and B1) or
        (not A0 and A1 and B0) or
        (A1 and B0 and not B1);

  C2 <= (A1 and B1 and not B0) or
        (A1 and not A0 and B1);

  C3 <= A1 and A0 and B1 and B0;

end RTL_MINTERM;
```

- **The minterm functions are realized directly as concurrent statements**

Multiplier: Integer Realization

```
library IEEE;
use IEEE.NUMERIC_BIT.all;

architecture RTL_INTEGER of MULTIPLIER is
  signal A_VEC : unsigned(1 downto 0);
  signal B_VEC : unsigned(1 downto 0);
  signal A_INT : integer range 0 to 3;
  signal B_INT : integer range 0 to 3;
  signal C_VEC : unsigned (3 downto 0);
  signal C_INT : integer range 0 to 9;
begin

  A_VEC <= A1 & A0;
  A_INT <= TO_INTEGER(A_VEC);
  B_VEC <= B1 & B0;
  B_INT <= TO_INTEGER(B_VEC);

  C_INT <= A_INT * B_INT;


  C_VEC <= TO_UNSIGNED(C_INT, 4);


  (C3, C2, C1, C0) <= C_VEC;
end RTL_INTEGER;
```

- The NUMERIC_BIT package provides all necessary functions to convert bit vectors to integer values and vice versa
- Internal signals are used to generate bit vectors and integer representations of the port signals. The bit vectors will be treated as unsigned binary values
- The single-bit input signals are concatenated to vectors and converted to integer data types
- The multiplication is realized via the standard VHDL operator
- The size of the target vector must be specified when converting integers back to bit vectors
- Finally, the bit vector elements are assigned to the output ports

The conversion of the function table into VHDL is straightforward. An intermediate signal is used to combine the four input signals, which facilitates the coding. Every row is now represented by a different signal value. As all possibilities are covered in the table, a case structure can be used for the implementation.

Because the minterms are rather simple logical functions, they are realized with concurrent statements. This way, it is just a matter of replacing the mathematical symbols with their corresponding VHDL operators.

The most obvious solution via the multiplication operator '*' is not directly applicable because only single bits are provided by the entity. Thus bits belonging together are combined in bit vectors, which are converted to integer values afterwards. The inverse procedure is necessary to assign the integer result to the output ports.

The minterm realization is very tedious and is performed by the synthesis tool automatically when the function table is parsed. The most elegant solution is the integer implementation, as the function of the code is clearly visible and not hidden in boolean functions or in hardcoded values like in the other examples. The use of 'bit' type ports, however, is very awkward. It is better style to use 'unsigned' bit vectors or 'integer'. Note that the conversion of the bit vectors to 'integer' is not necessary, as the arithmetic operators, including '*' are overloaded in the NUMERIC_BIT package. Vector arithmetic is provided for signed and unsigned binary representations

The synthesis result should be identical in all three cases.

3.3.5   Synthesis of Operators

- **Operator structure**
  - Discrete gates
  - Macrocell from the library
- **Operator architecture (e.g. ripple-carry, carry-look-ahead, etc.)**
  - Specific comments for the synthesis tool contained in the VHDL code
  - Optimization based on time/surface defaults

Based on the operator symbol, the synthesis knows about the desired functionality. Depending on the target technology and the corresponding library elements, either a sort of submodule which performs the necessary operations is created out of standard cells, or a macrocell that has already been optimized by the manufacturer is instantiated in the netlist. If alternative implementations exist, e.g. ripple-carry or carry-look-ahead, the decision will be made according to the given speed and area constraints. Sometimes, the user may influence the synthesis process via tool options or special VHDL comments that are evaluated by the software.

3.3.6 IF Structure <-> CASE Structure

- **Different descriptions are synthesized differently**

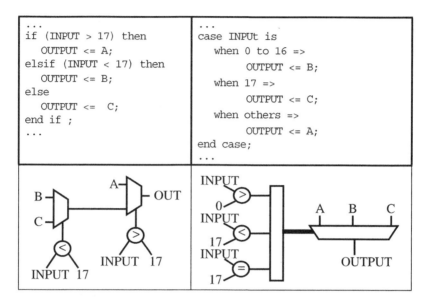

While algorithms can take care of some clumsy VHDL constructs, other model aspects cannot be changed during synthesis. The use of IF constructs, for example, implies different levels of priority, i.e. they infer a hierarchical structure of multiplexers. In CASE statements, however, the different choice options do not overlap and a parallel structure with a single switching stage is the result.

3.3.7   Implementation of a Data Bus

```
entity TRISTATE is
  port(DATA1, DATA2: in std_ulogic;
       EN1, EN2    : in std_ulogic;
       DATA_BUS    : out std_logic);
end TRISTATE;
```

DATA1 ──▷ EN1

DATA2 ──▷ EN2

──── DATA_BUS

```
architecture RTL1 of TRISTATE is
begin
  process (DATA1, EN1)
  begin
    if EN1 = '1' then
      DATA_BUS <= DATA1;
    else
      DATA_BUS <= 'Z';
    end if;
  end process;
  process (DATA2, EN2)
  begin
    if EN2 = '1' then
      DATA_BUS <= DATA2;
    else
      DATA_BUS <= 'Z';
    end if;
  end process;
end RTL1;
```

```
architecture RTL2 of TRISTATE is
begin
  DATA_BUS <= DATA1 when EN1 = '1' else 'Z';
  DATA_BUS <= DATA2 when EN2 = '1' else 'Z';
end RTL2;
```

Problems with Internal Bus Structures

Bus with tristate drivers

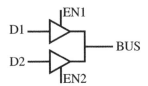

Waveform

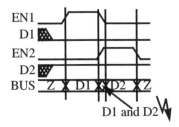

D1 and D2

- **Different propagation delays**

- **A bus controller has to guarantee that at most one driver is active on the bus**

- **Technology dependence**

Portable and Safe Bus Structure

- **Multiplexer instead of tristate driver eliminates internal bus**
- **Three internal signals (DIN, DOUT, DOUT_EN)**

- **Bidirectional I/O pad**
- **Benefit**
  - Safe circuit
  - Portable and testable

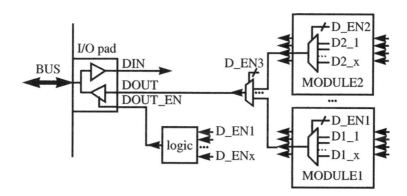

In order to implement a proper internal bus system, it must be guaranteed that only one driver is active while all others are set to high impedance, i.e. driving 'Z'. Otherwise, if one bus member drives a logic '1' and another drives a logic '0', the current might, depending on the actual technology, increase beyond acceptable levels and probably result in permanent damage to the device. This overlap of active drivers may be caused by different propagation delays, which means that the deactivation of one driver takes more time than the activation of another one. As a consequence two drivers are active. Even if the delays are balanced so that everything works properly, a change to another technology will likely induce problems with the delays.

An alternative design structure avoids the problems associated with tristate signals: Multiplexers, driven by the enable signals, guarantee that only one driver exists per signal. Bidirectional signals are eliminated internally by splitting the original bus into two parts. The bidirectional communication with the outside world is done by special I/O pads, i.e. the core structure represents a safe circuit that is fully testable and easily ported to other technologies.

3.4   Sequential Logic

3.4.1   Initialization

- **A reset mechanism is required in hardware to initialize all registers**

- **Asynchronous reset behaviour can only be modelled with processes with sensitivity list**

```
process
begin
  wait until CLK'event and CLK='1'; -- not
                             -- recommended
  DATA <= INPUT ;
end process ;
```

```
process(CLK,RESET)
begin
  if (RESET = '1') then
    DATA <= '0' ;
  elsif (CLK'event and CLK='1') then -- correct
  DATA <= INPUT ;
  end if ;
end process ;
```

INPUT ── [ ] ── DATA
CLK ──▶

INPUT ── [ ] ── DATA
CLK ──▶
RESET ──

3.4.2   RTL: Combinational Logic and Registers

```
LOGIC_A: process
begin

wait until CLK'event and CLK='1';
    -- logic A
end process LOGIC_A;

LOGIC_B: process (ST)
begin
    -- logic B
end process LOGIC_B;

LOGIC_AB: process
begin

wait until CLK'event and CLK='1' ;
    -- logic A and logic B
end process LOGIC_AB;
```

- **Signal assignments in clocked processes infer flip flops**

  - LOGIC_A: logic + flip flops

  - LOGIC_B: purely combinational logic

  - LOGIC_AB: flip flops at the outputs of 'logic A' and 'logic B'
    => wrong implementation

3.4.3   Variables in Clocked Processes

```
VAR_1: process(CLK)
   variable TEMP : integer;
begin

   if (CLK'event and CLK = '1') then
      TEMP := INPUT * 2;
      OUTPUT_A <= TEMP + 1;
      OUTPUT_B <= TEMP + 2;
   end if;
end process VAR_1;
```

- **Registers are generated for all variables that might be read before they are updated**

```
VAR_2: process(CLK)
   variable TEMP : integer;
begin

   if (CLK'event and CLK = '1') then
      OUTPUT <= TEMP + 1;
      TEMP := INPUT * 2;
   end if;
end process VAR_2;
```

- **How many registers are generated?**

Sequential logic is the general term for designs containing storing elements, especially flip flops. While all signals can be initialized prior to simulation by specifying default values, an explicit reset mechanism is necessary to guarantee that the design behaves the same way whenever it is powered up. Usually, a dedicated reset signal is used for this purpose. Note that asynchronous behaviour can only be modelled with processes with sensitivity list, i.e. the process has to react upon the clock and the reset signal.

Additionally, all signals that may receive new values within a clocked process infer flip flops. Though it is recommended from a theoretical point of view that registers and combinational logic are modelled with separate processes, it is often convenient to place the calculation of new flip flop values in the same process. Postprocessing of register values, however, has to be performed within another process or with concurrent statements.

The hardware implementation of variables depends on their use in the process. The VHDL language guarantees that variables still hold their old values when a process is executed again. If this value is not used, however, because it is always updated prior to its use, a storing element will become redundant. Consequently, flip flops are inferred for variables in clocked processes only if they are read before they will be updated.

In the VAR_1 process, the variable is always set to INPUT*2 whenever an active clock edge is detected. Thus TEMP is treated as shortcut for the expression and is not visible in the final netlist. In VAR_2, however, the value of TEMP is used to calculate the new value of the OUTPUT signal, i.e. a register bank (integer: at least 32-bit) will be generated.

3.5   Finite State Machines and VHDL

- **State Processes**
- **State Coding**
- **FSM (Finite State Machine) Types**
  - Medvedev
  - Moore
  - Mealy
  - Registered Output

In this section, the different types of finite state machines, their graphical representation and ways to model them with VHDL will be shown. Furthermore, only synchronous automatons are assumed.

Generally every finite state machine can be described either by one single or by two separated processes. Implementation guidelines and advantages or drawbacks of the different variants will be given.

The actual states of a state machine should generally be described by descriptive names. This can be achieved by use of an enumeration type whose values are these names. Later in the synthesis process, these names have to be mapped to a binary representation. This step is called state encoding.

There are several versions of finite state machines. The standard versions known in theory are Medvedev, Moore and Mealy machines. However, there are far more versions than these three. It is, for example, recommended for several reasons to place storing elements (registers, flip flops) at the module outputs. By doing this, additional versions of finite state machines can be built, which will be shown later.

3.5.1   One 'State' Process

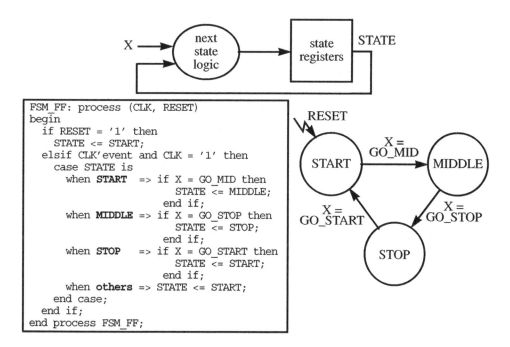

```
FSM_FF: process (CLK, RESET)
begin
  if RESET = '1' then
    STATE <= START;
  elsif CLK'event and CLK = '1' then
    case STATE is
      when START  => if X = GO_MID then
                        STATE <= MIDDLE;
                     end if;
      when MIDDLE => if X = GO_STOP then
                        STATE <= STOP;
                     end if;
      when STOP   => if X = GO_START then
                        STATE <= START;
                     end if;
      when others => STATE <= START;
    end case;
  end if;
end process FSM_FF;
```

Three different notations for a simple state machine are shown in the figure.

The graphic on the top depicts the automaton as an abstract block diagram that contains only the relevant blocks and signals of interest. The first block (oval) represents the logic of the automaton and the second block (rectangle) the storing elements.

In the bottom right graphic, the automaton is described by a so-called bubble diagram. The circles mark the different states of the automaton. If the condition connected to the corresponding transition (arrow) evaluates to 'true' at the time the active clock edge occurs, the automaton will change its state. This is synchronous behaviour. Here the asynchronous reset is the only exception to this behaviour. At the time the reset signal becomes active, the automaton changes to the reset state START immediately.

In the bottom left graphic, the corresponding part of the VHDL source code is shown. The automaton is described in one clocked process. The first IF branch contains the reset sequence. In the second branch, the ELSE branch, the rest of the automaton is described. In the CASE statement that models the state transitions, the current state of the automaton is detected and it is examined whether input values are present that lead to a change of the state.

3.5.2   Two 'State' Processes

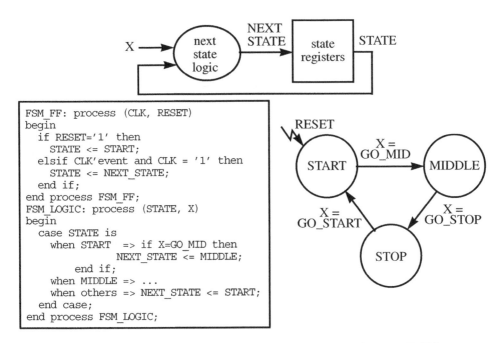

```
FSM_FF: process (CLK, RESET)
begin
  if RESET='1' then
    STATE <= START;
  elsif CLK'event and CLK = '1' then
    STATE <= NEXT_STATE;
  end if;
end process FSM_FF;
FSM_LOGIC: process (STATE, X)
begin
  case STATE is
    when START  => if X=GO_MID then
            NEXT_STATE <= MIDDLE;
        end if;
    when MIDDLE => ...
    when others => NEXT_STATE <= START;
  end case;
end process FSM_LOGIC;
```

Now, the same automaton is used to show an implementation based on two VHDL processes.

The signal NEXT_STATE is examined explicitly this time. It is inserted in the block diagram between the logic and the storing elements. In the bubble diagram no changes have to be made at this point, as the behaviour remains the same.

The VHDL source code contains two processes. The logic for the NEXT_STATE calculation is described in a separate process. The result is a clocked process describing the storing elements and another purely combinational process describing the logic. In the CASE statement, again, the current state is checked and the input values are examined. If the state has to change then NEXT_STATE and STATE will differ. With the next occurrence of the active clock edge, this new state will be taken over as the current state.

3.5.3 How Many Processes?

- **Structure and Readability**

  - Asynchronous combinatoric ≠ synchronous storing elements
    => 2 processes
  - FSM states change with special input changes
    => 1 process more comprehensible
  - Graphical FSM (without output equations) resembles one state process
    => 1 process

- **Simulation**

  - Error detection easier with 2 state processes
    => 2 processes

- **Synthesis**

  - 2 state processes can lead to smaller generic net list
    and therefore to better synthesis results
    => 2 processes

Automaton descriptions with either one or two separated processes were shown previously. Depending on their own liking and experiences, either one of the two versions is preferred by desingers. Generally there are different advantages and disadvantages:

Structure and readability: the VHDL model should represent in some way the hardware which has to be created out of the VHDL source code. So the structure should be mirrored in the VHDL code. As purely combinational logic and storing elements are two different structural elements, these should be separated, i.e. the VHDL source code should be split into two processes. But one is normally only interested in the actual changes of the states of the automaton. These changes can then be observed from the outside of the module. The one-process description is more appropriate for this view. Additionally, the graphical description, which is often used as a specification for the VHDL model, resembles more a one-process than a two-process description.

Simulation: it will be easier to detect possible errors of the VHDL model in the waveform if one has access to the intermediate signal NEXT_STATE. So the time and location where the error occurs for the first time can be determined exactly and with that the source of the error. The two process version is therefore better.

Synthesis: the synthesis algorithms are based on heuristics. Therefore it is impossible to give universally valid statements. But several synthesis tools tend to produce better results (no sophisticated synthesis script assumed), in the sense of fever gate equivalents, when two processes are used to describe the automaton, because they are more closely related to the hardware structure.

3.5.4   State Encoding

```
type STATE_TYPE is (START, MIDDLE, STOP);
signal STATE : STATE_TYPE ;
```

- **State encoding responsible for safety of FSM**

```
START     -> "00"
MIDDLE    -> "01"
STOP      -> "10"
```

- **Default encoding: binary**

```
START     -> "001"
MIDDLE    -> "010"
STOP      -> "100"
```

- **Speed optimized default encoding: one hot**

 if {ld(# of states) ≠ ENTIER[ld(# of states)] } => unsafe FSM!

A finite state machine is an abstract description of digital hardware. It is a synthesis requirement that the states of the automaton are described as binary values or the synthesis tool itself will transform the state names into a binary description on its own. This transformation is called state encoding.

Most synthesis tools select a binary code by default, except that the designer specifies another code explicitly. The states of the automaton above could be encoded by a synthesis tool with the values "00", "01" and "10". However, other possibilities for state encoding exist. A frequently used code that is needed for speed-optimized circuits is the 'one-out-of-n' code, which is also called the one hot code. Here, one bit is used for every state of the automaton. For example, if the automaton has 11 states then the state vector contains 11 bits. The bit of the vector that is set to '1' represents the current state of the automaton.

A problem arises for the encoding of the states that cannot be ignored: if the automaton has n states, one needs ENTIER[ld(n)] flip flops for a binary code. This is the smallest integer value greater than or equal to the result of the binary logarithm of n. In the example above, two flip flops are needed for a binary code. As the automaton consists of only 3 states and two flip flops can represent up to 4 states ("00", "01", "10", "11"), there is one invalid state, which leads to an unsafe state machine, i.e. the behaviour of the design when accidentally entering this state is not determined.

Usually, a mechanism has to be provided that corrects the erroneous entering of an invalid state.

3.5.5   Extension of CASE Statement

```
type STATE_TYPE is (START, MIDDLE, STOP);
signal STATE : STATE_TYPE;
   • • •
   case STATE is
       when START       => • • •
       when MIDDLE      => • • •
       when STOP        => • • •

       when others    => • • •

   end case ;
```

•   **Adding the 'when others' choice**

 Not simulatable; in RTL there exist no other values for STATE

 Not necessarily safe;
some synthesis tools will ignore 'when others' choice

The most obvious method to intercept invalid states is to insert a '**when others**' branch in the CASE statement. With this branch, all values of the examined expression (here: STATE) that are not included in the other branches of the CASE statement are covered. The intention is to intercept all illegal states and to restart the automaton with its reset state (here: START).

VHDL is a very strict language. Therefore, during simulation, only the values defined by the type definition of a signal can be accessed. For this reason, invalid states do not exist in the simulation and consequently cannot be simulated. Furthermore, the synthesized circuit is also not necessarily safe. Some synthesis tools ignore the '**when others**' branch as, by definition, there are no values to cover in this branch.

Inserting a '**when others**' branch into the case statement is not a good solution for creating a safe state machine.

3.5.6   Extension of Type Declaration

```
type STATE_TYPE is (START, MIDDLE,STOP, DUMMY);
signal STATE : STATE_TYPE;
  •••
  case STATE is
      when START    => •••
      when MIDDLE   => •••
      when STOP     => •••

      when DUMMY  => •••  -- or when others

  end case ;
```

- **Adding dummy values**

- **Advantages:**
  - Now simulatable
  - Safe FSM after synthesis

 $\{2^{**}(ENTIER\ [ld(n)]) -n\}$ **dummy states (n=20 => 12 dummy states)**

 Changing to one hot coding => unnecessary hardware
(n=20 => 12 unnecessary flip flops)

The second way is to define additional values for the enumeration type. A sufficient number of values have to be added such that, after state encoding, invalid values can no longer occur. If an automaton contains, for example, 20 states then 5 flip flops are needed with a binary code. With 5 flip flops, one can distinguish 32 values (2^5=32). Thus 12 additional values have to be added to the enumeration type of the state machine.

By adding additional values to the enumeration type, one gets a state machine whose behaviour in the case of errors can now be simulated. The synthesis also results in a safe circuit representing the original state machine. However, this method is somewhat awkward as one has to insert many so-called dummy states eventually. Furthermore, this method is only suitable when binary coding for the states of the automaton is used. If one has added, for example, these 12 additional values for a safe state machine, there will be 12 redundant flip flops when the state encoding is switched to the one hot code, as an extra bit is needed for every state.

It is impossible to make a state machine safe by inserting additional values for dummy states if a one hot code is used. Every new value would lead to an additional flip flop and therefore would only increase the amount of invalid state values after synthesis.

Therefore the method of inserting additional values into the enumeration type is not a good solution, either, as it is applicable only to binary state encoding.

3.5.7 Hand Coding

```
subtype STATE_TYPE is std_ulogic_vector (1 downto 0);
signal STATE : STATE_TYPE;

constant START   : STATE_TYPE := "01";
constant MIDDLE  : STATE_TYPE := "11";
constant STOP    : STATE_TYPE := "00";
•••
  case STATE is
    when START    => •••
    when MIDDLE   => •••
    when STOP     => •••
    when others   => •••
    end case;
```

- **Defining constants**

- **Control of encoding**

- **Safe FSM**

- **Simulatable**

- **Portable design**

- **More effort**

The best method of state encoding is hand coding, i.e. the designer decides by himself or herself which code will be used.

This is done by using a vector type instead of an enumeration type. This vector type can be based upon the '**std_(u)logic_vector**' type for example. The width of this vector depends on the code chosen. The state signal is now of this vector type, which is the reason for the term 'state vector'.

In the next step, constants are defined which represent the corresponding states of the automaton. These constants are set to the state vector values according to the selected code. With these constants, the code can be fixed by the designer and cannot be altered by the synthesis tool. This VHDL model is also 100 % portable. The behaviour in the case of errors can be verified in a simulation, as the state vector can now assume all values that might occur in real hardware.

The only drawback to mention is a little more effort in writing the VHDL code. This is especially true when the code is changed. The hand coding alternative is the best method to design a safe finite state machine, and furthermore is portable among different synthesis tools.

3.5.8   FSM: Medvedev

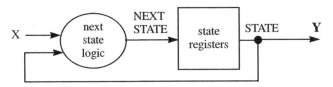

- **The output vector resembles the state vector: Y = S**

```
-- Two Processes                          -- One Process
architecture RTL of MEDVEDEV is           architecture RTL of MEDVEDEV is
   ...                                        ...
begin                                     begin
  REG: process (CLK, RESET)
  begin                                     REG: process (CLK, RESET)
    -- State Registers Inference            begin
  end process REG;                            -- State Registers Inference
                                              -- with Logic Block
  CMB: process (X, STATE)                     end process REG;
  begin
    -- Next State Logic                     Y <= S;
  end process CMB;
                                          end RTL;
  Y <= S;
end RTL;
```

3.5.9   Medvedev Example

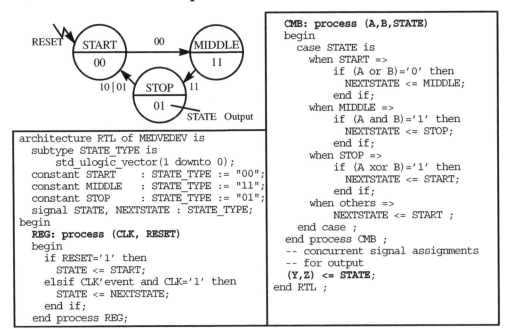

3.5.10 Waveform Medvedev Example

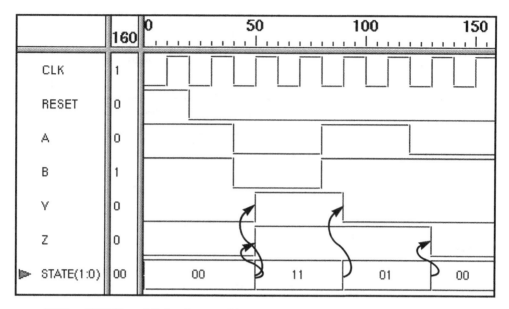

- **(Y,Z) = STATE => Medvedev machine**

The difference between the three types of state machines known in theory (Medvedev, Moore and Mealy machines) is the way the output is generated. In the Medvedev machine the value of the output is identical with the state vector of the finite state machine. That means that the logic for the output consists only of wires, namely the connections from the state vector registers to the output ports. This is done in VHDL by a simple signal assignment, which is shown in the example above. Concurrent assignments are used here.

Here an example of a Medvedev machine is shown. The bubble diagram contains the states of the machine (START, MIDDLE, STOP), the state encoding ("00", "11", "01"; see also the constant declarations) and the state transitions. The so-called weights (labels) of the transitions (arrows) determine the value of the input vector (here the signals A and B) for which the corresponding state transition will be executed. For '10 | 01', the state transition is executed when the input vector has either the value "10" or the value "01". The functionality of the state machine is described in the VHDL source code on the left side. The version with two processes was selected. One can see that the output vector is wired with the state vector by a concurrent signal assignment.

In the waveform one can see the progression over time of the signal values of the design during simulation. It is apparent that it must be a Medvedev automaton, because the values of the output vector (represented by the two singals Y and Z) change synchronously with the state vector.

3.5.11 FSM: Moore

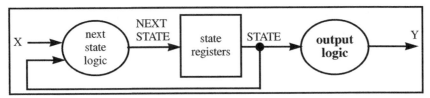

- **The output vector is a function of the state vector: Y = f(S)**

```
-- Three Processes                     -- Two Processes
architecture RTL of MOORE is           architecture RTL of MOORE is
  ...                                    ...
begin                                  begin
  REG: -- Clocked Process                REG: process (CLK, RESET)
                                         begin
  CMB: -- Combinational Process            -- State Registers Inference with
                                           -- Next State Logic
  OUTPUT: process (STATE)                end process REG;
    begin
       -- Output Logic                   OUTPUT: process (STATE)
    end process OUTPUT;                  begin
                                            -- Output Logic
end RTL ;                                end process OUTPUT;
                                       end RTL ;
```

3.5.12 Moore Example

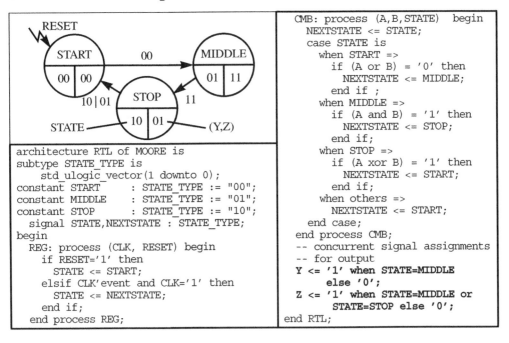

```
                                       CMB: process (A,B,STATE)  begin
                                         NEXTSTATE <= STATE;
                                         case STATE is
                                           when START =>
                                             if (A or B) = '0' then
                                               NEXTSTATE <= MIDDLE;
                                             end if ;
                                           when MIDDLE =>
                                             if (A and B) = '1' then
                                               NEXTSTATE <= STOP;
                                             end if;
                                           when STOP =>
                                             if (A xor B) = '1' then
architecture RTL of MOORE is                 NEXTSTATE <= START;
subtype STATE_TYPE is                        end if;
    std_ulogic_vector(1 downto 0);         when others =>
constant START    : STATE_TYPE := "00";      NEXTSTATE <= START;
constant MIDDLE   : STATE_TYPE := "01";    end case;
constant STOP     : STATE_TYPE := "10";  end process CMB;
  signal STATE,NEXTSTATE : STATE_TYPE;   -- concurrent signal assignments
begin                                    -- for output
  REG: process (CLK, RESET) begin        Y <= '1' when STATE=MIDDLE
    if RESET='1' then                        else '0';
      STATE <= START;                    Z <= '1' when STATE=MIDDLE or
    elsif CLK'event and CLK='1' then         STATE=STOP else '0';
      STATE <= NEXTSTATE;              end RTL;
    end if;
  end process REG;
```

3.5.13 Waveform Moore Example

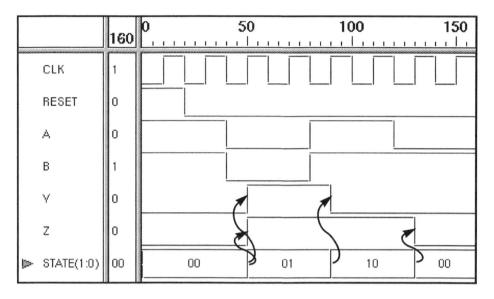

- **(Y,Z) changes simultaneously with STATE => Moore machine**

Here an example of a Moore machine is shown. The value of the output vector is a function of the current state. This is the reason for the second logic block in the block diagram, located after the storing elements. This logic block holds the hardware that is needed to calculate the output values out of the current state of the automaton. In the VHDL source code this logic is implemented with an own combinational process. As the value of the output vector depends on the current value of the state vector only, no other signals appear in the sensitivity list of the process.

Again, the bubble diagram and the corresponding VHDL code are shown; this time for a Moore automaton. The difference from the Medvedev automaton can be recognized in the difference between the state encoding and the corresponding values for the output vector. Both values are specified in the bubbles. The values for the output vector (Y, Z) are the same as in the Medvedev automaton. However, the state encoding is now based upon a binary code. In the VHDL source code the output logic is not contained in a combinational process because of space limitation. Instead, it is implemented via separate concurrent signal assignments. One can see that the output values are calculated out of the state vector values.

Again, the characteristics of the Moore automaton can be seen clearly in the waveform. The values of the output vector change simultaneously with the values of the state vector. But this time the values of the output vector differ from those of the state vector.

3.5.14 FSM: Mealy

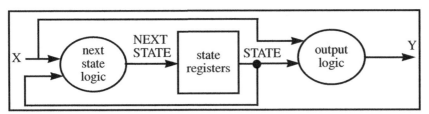

- **The output vector is a function of the state vector and the input vector: $Y = f(X,S)$**

-- **Three Processes**	-- **Two Processes**
architecture RTL of MEALY is	architecture RTL of MEALY is
...	...
begin	begin
REG: -- Clocked Process	MED: process (CLK, RESET)
CMB: -- Combinational	begin
Process	-- State Registers Inference with
	-- Next State Logic
OUTPUT: process (STATE, X)	end process MED;
begin	**OUTPUT: process (STATE, X)**
-- Output Logic	**begin**
end process OUTPUT;	-- Output Logic
end RTL;	**end process OUTPUT;**
	end RTL;

3.5.15 Mealy Example

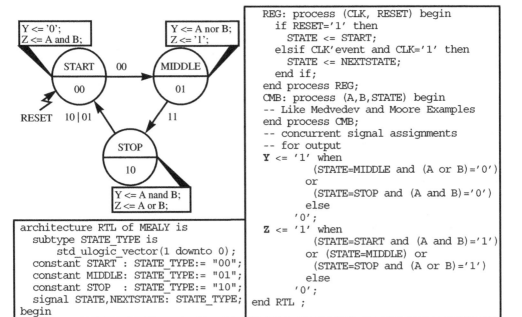

```
REG: process (CLK, RESET) begin
   if RESET='1' then
     STATE <= START;
   elsif CLK'event and CLK='1' then
     STATE <= NEXTSTATE;
   end if;
end process REG;
CMB: process (A,B,STATE) begin
-- Like Medvedev and Moore Examples
end process CMB;
-- concurrent signal assignments
-- for output
Y <= '1' when
        (STATE=MIDDLE and (A or B)='0')
      or
        (STATE=STOP and (A and B)='0')
      else
      '0';
Z <= '1' when
        (STATE=START and (A and B)='1')
     or (STATE=MIDDLE) or
        (STATE=STOP and (A or B)='1')
       else
       '0';
end RTL ;
```

```
architecture RTL of MEALY is
  subtype STATE_TYPE is
     std_ulogic_vector(1 downto 0);
  constant START  : STATE_TYPE:= "00";
  constant MIDDLE : STATE_TYPE:= "01";
  constant STOP   : STATE_TYPE:= "10";
  signal STATE,NEXTSTATE: STATE_TYPE;
begin
```

3.5.16 Waveform Mealy Example

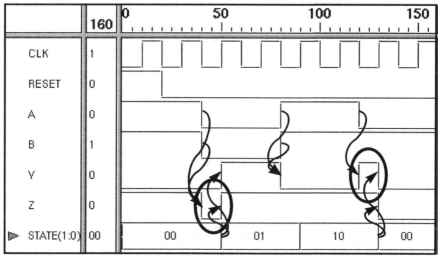

- **(Y,Z) changes with input => Mealy machine**

- **Note the 'spikes' of Y and Z in the waveform**
  FSM has to be modelled carefully in order to avoid spikes in normal operation.

Here a Mealy automaton is shown. The value of the output vector is a function of the current values of the state vector and of the input vector. This is why a line is drawn in the block diagram from the input vector to the logic block calculating the output vector. In the VHDL source code the input vector is now listed in the sensitivity list of the corresponding process.

In contrast to the other two types of automatons described before, the output values cannot be simply written into the corresponding state bubble here. Complete functions have to be written down which differ from state to state. These functions are often 'hidden' behind the state bubble, instead of being displayed explicitly in the graphic. In the VHDL source code the calculation of the output values is described with concurrent signal assignments, again. One can see that the input signals appear on the right side of the assignments and are therefore now part of the output function.

Again, one can see the characteristics of the Mealy automaton clearly in the waveform. The most remarkable feature is the fact that the output values change sometimes together with the values of the input vector. Furthermore, they change together with changes of the state vector values, of course. As one can see, this can lead to so-called spikes, i.e. signal pulses with a smaller width than the clock period. This can lead to misbehaviour in the blocks following thereafter. Of course, this has to be avoided and the designer must take special care when modelling a Mealy automaton in a form similar to the one described here.

3.5.17 Modelling Aspects

- **Medvedev is too inflexible**
- **Moore is preferred because of safe operation**
- **Mealy is more flexible, but there is a danger of**
    - Spikes
    - Unnecessary long paths (maximum clock period)
    - Combinational feedback loops

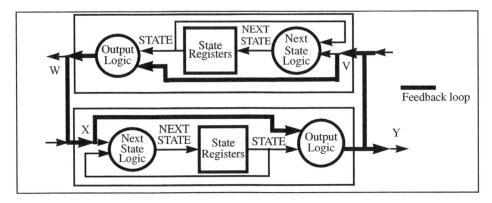

There are different reasons for a designer to use one or another version of the three different automatons. The advantage of the Medvedev automaton is the reduced amount of hardware needed. As the output values are identical with the state vector, no additional combinational logic is needed and the values of the output vector are changed together with the active clock edge. But the designer has to select the code for the state vector by himself or herself. This means that the designer has to put more effort into the design, and a complete redesign is necessary if the code for the state machine has to be changed. The Moore automaton is frequently used because this type of automaton is more flexible than the Medvedev automaton and the output calculation still depends only on the state vector. By this pure dependence on the state vector, the output values are calculated in a relatively safe manner, which means that the new values are stable long before the next active clock edge occurs and spikes are avoided. A disadvantage that sometimes becomes relevant is that a change of the input vector needs one complete clock cycle to affect the output vector (first, the state vector has to change before the output vector can change). Sometimes, this time delay is unacceptable and consequently the Moore automaton cannot be used. The Mealy automaton is the most flexible of the automatons presented. As the output vector depends on the state vector and the input vector, it can react on every change of a value. But there are also some disadvantages, such as the occurrence of spikes as shown before. If two Mealy automatons are connected in a row, there is the danger of combinational feedback loops, as demonstrated in the figure above.

3.5.18 Registered Output

- **Avoiding long paths and uncertain timing**
- **With one additional clock period**

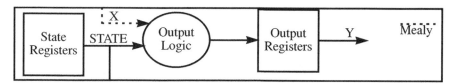

- **Without additional clock period (Mealy)**

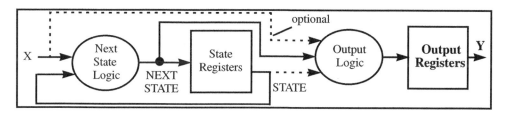

Additionally, long paths are created: two logic blocks are connected in a row, so a change of a value needs a relatively long time to propagate through the logic to the next flip flop. Hence, the clocking frequency is severely limited.

Combinational feedback loops can be avoided if the outputs are 'clocked', i.e. if the outputs are connected to flip flops. Generally, clocked outputs are used to break up combinational loops and long paths. Thus they assure safe timing behaviour. By clocking all outputs, the output logic is separated from the next logic block of the subsequent module, and thus, the path through logic elements is shortened and higher clock frequencies are possible. Furthermore, synthesis tools often have problems when optimizing logic paths that pass module boundaries for speed. By clocking the outputs, these problems can be avoided. Another advantage is that the successive module can work with 'safe' input data. Safe means that the data changes with the active clock edge, only, and thus spikes are ruled out. This allows the designer of the successive module more design flexibility. Two versions are known for clocking the output. In the first version, flip flops are inserted between the output logic and the state machine outputs, which leads to an additional delay of one clock period. However, this delay sometimes cannot be accepted. In the second version, flip flops are present at the state machine output and the output logic uses the NEXT_STATE signal in addition to the state vector. For bigger state machines, this can lead to incomprehensible dependences and relatively long paths, as two logic blocks are again connected in a row. But this version of a state machine is the most flexible and the fastest (in terms of latency) that provides safe (clocked) output signals.

3.5.19 Registered Output Example (1)

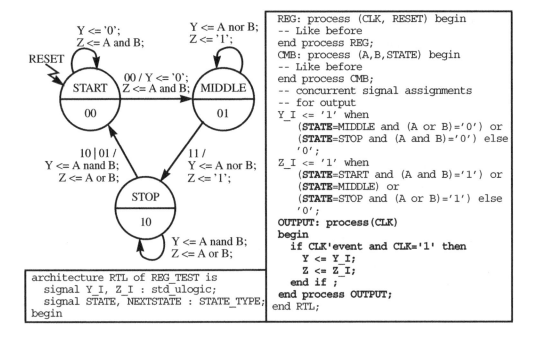

```
architecture RTL of REG_TEST is
  signal Y_I, Z_I : std_ulogic;
  signal STATE, NEXTSTATE : STATE_TYPE;
begin
```

```
REG: process (CLK, RESET) begin
-- Like before
end process REG;
CMB: process (A,B,STATE) begin
-- Like before
end process CMB;
-- concurrent signal assignments
-- for output
Y_I <= '1' when
       (STATE=MIDDLE and (A or B)='0') or
       (STATE=STOP and (A and B)='0') else
       '0';
Z_I <= '1' when
       (STATE=START and (A and B)='1') or
       (STATE=MIDDLE) or
       (STATE=STOP and (A or B)='1') else
       '0';
OUTPUT: process(CLK)
begin
  if CLK'event and CLK='1' then
     Y <= Y_I;
     Z <= Z_I;
  end if ;
end process OUTPUT;
end RTL;
```

3.5.20 Waveform Registered Output Example (1)

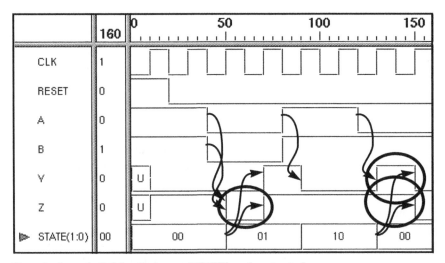

- **One clock period delay between STATE and output changes.**
- **Input changes with clock edge result in an output change.**

  (Danger of unmeant values ⬤)

3.5.21 Registered Output Example (2)

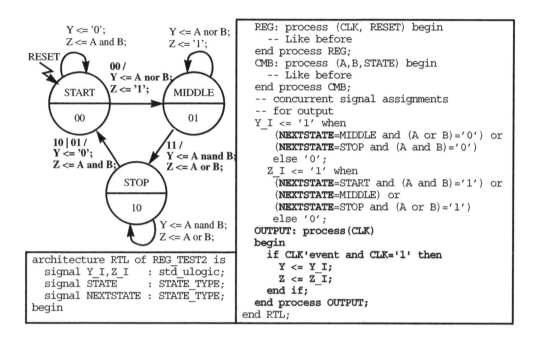

In this figure, the example of the Mealy automaton is shown again. In the bubble diagram the assignments that were hidden behind the states before are now explicitly connected to self-loops. Furthermore, the transitions between states also have signal assignments for the output signals. As transitions take place only when an active clock edge occurs, it is clear that a value is assigned to the output signals with every active clock edge, i.e. flip flops have to be provided for the outputs. As the signal assignments of the old state (which will be exited) are connected to the transitions, the output values depend only on the current (old) state (STATE) but not on the new state (NEXT_STATE). Generally, the signal assignments can be hidden again behind the states in the graphical diagram. For this, so-called in-state actions for the self-loops and exit actions for the transitions are used. In the VHDL source code, intermediate signals (Y_I, Z_I) are evaluated. The values of these signals depend on the input values and the current state. In the following clocked process, the intermediate signals are connected to flip flops.

The waveform depicts the simulation results of the clocked Mealy automaton. It can be seen clearly that the output values change one clock period after the change of the state vector. Furthermore, it can be seen that changes of the input values affect the output values just when the next active clock edge occurs. All value changes of intermediate signals occur only synchronously to the clock, so that the state machine has a fixed and well-known behaviour. Still, the modelling has to be carried out carefully. It is essential to consider the delay of one clock period between the changes of the state vector and the output signals. If it is ignored, the values marked in the waveform can lead to undesired behaviour in the subsequent modules.

3.5.22 Waveform Registered Output Example (2)

- **No delay between STATE and output changes.**
- **'Spikes' of original Mealy machine are gone!**

Again, the Mealy automaton from the previous examples is used. Besides the self-loops that have already been introduced, signal assignments for the state machine outputs are connected to the state transitions. By this, assignments to output signals appear only on clocked transitions, and flip flops have to be provided for the outputs. The assignments connected to the transitions, however, are equivalent to the assignment that leads to a new target state. Therefore the output values depend on the current input values and on the new state (NEXTSTATE). This affects the VHDL sourcecode: the values of the intermediate signals are calculated from the values of the current inputs and the current successor state. Again, flip flops are inferred for the intermediate signals with another process.

The waveform shows the simulation results of the second version of the clocked Mealy automaton. The output values now change synchronously with the state changes and undesired temporary values are eliminated.

3.6   Advanced Synthesis

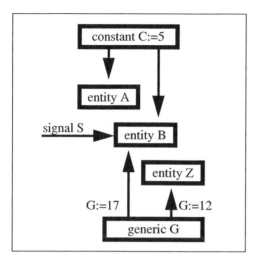

- **Constant C identical in all referencing units**
- **Generic G different but constant within each entity**
- **Input signal S set/changed in operation (different operation modes)**

Once one has finished a design, one hopes that it will be possible to use at least parts of the VHDL code in other designs as well. This is certainly possible as long as one can adopt the VHDL code via copy/paste. But if the function has to be changed slightly, the designer will have to adapt the VHDL code. To make this adaption easier and less error-prone, VHDL provides several ways of parameterizing a design or a module, which means that the behaviour description depends on some parameters. The value of these parameters can then be set differently in different implementations or even on the fly during operation. The intention is that by changing the parameter the behaviour will change accordingly.

3.6.1   Parameterization via Constants

```
package T_PACK is
  constant MAX_VALUE:integer := 15;
end T_PACK;
```

```
use WORK.T_PACK.all;
entity COUNTER_C is
  port(...,
        COUNT : buffer integer
               range 0 to MAX_VALUE);
end COUNTER_C;
architecture RTL of COUNTER_C is
begin
  process(CLK) begin
    if CLK'event and CLK='1' then
      if RESET='1' then
        COUNT <= 0;
      elsif ENABLE='1' then
        if COUNT < MAX_VALUE then
          COUNT <= COUNT + 1;
        else
          COUNT <= 0;
        end if;
      end if;
    end if;
  end process;
end RTL;
```

- **Constants are fixed for the complete design**
- **Instantiations of COUNTER_C produce exactly the same counter**
- **Parametric signals in port map**

3.6.2   Parameterization via Generics (1)

```
entity COUNTER_G is
  generic (MAX_VALUE: integer := 15);
  port(...              -- default value
        COUNT : buffer integer
               range 0 to MAX_VALUE);
end COUNTER_G;

architecture RTL of COUNTER_G is
begin
  process(CLK)
  begin
    if CLK'event and CLK='1' then
      if RESET='1' then
        COUNT <= 0;
      elsif ENABLE='1' then
        if COUNT < MAX_VALUE then
          COUNT <= COUNT + 1;
        else
          COUNT <= 0 ;
        end if;
      end if;
    end if;
  end process;
end RTL;
```

- **Generics are defined in the entity declaration**
- **Treated as constants in the architecture**
- **Default values**
- **Parametric signals in port map**

3.6.3 Parameterization via Generics (2)

```
entity TWO_COUNTERS IS
port(...);
end entity;

architecture RTL of TWO_COUNTERS is
  component COUNTER_G
    generic (MAX_VALUE:integer := 15);
    port(...);
  end component;

begin
  COUNTER1 : COUNTER_G
    port map (...); -- MAX_VALUE with
                    -- default value

  COUNTER2 : COUNTER_G
    generic map (MAX_VALUE => 31)
    port map (...);
...
end RTL;
```

- **Different values for different instantiations**

  - Instantiation with default value

  - Instantiation with generic map

 Every instantiation needs a label

 Only generics of type integer are supported by synthesis tools

One way to parameterize a design is to use constants. The example shows a counter with reset and enable. The counter is freewheeling when enabled. The maximum value (MAX_VALUE) is set by a constant that is defined and given a value in the package T_PACK. Wherever COUNTER_C is built in (by use of a component declaration and component instantiation) the counter range is fixed (from 0 to the value specified in the package).

If one wants to instantiate counters with different counter ranges in one design, it is necessary to switch to generics. Generics are defined like the ports in the entity definition and receive their values during the step of component instantiation. Therefore, in addition to the port map, a generic map is required to provide these values. Generics may be given a default value in the generic clause, which will be used if the generic is not explicitly assigned a value.

The component declaration is as usual except that one must not forget the generic clause. But how does the instantiation of COUNTER_G work? If default values were defined for the generics, the component instantiation does not need a generic map (cf. COUNTER1). Of course, the default value can be overwritten by setting the generic to an explicit value in the generic map of the component instantiation (cf. COUNTER2). The most useful feature is that entities using generics can be instantiated with different values for the generics within the same module. However, only integer-type generics are synthesizable!

3.6.4 GENERATE Statement

```
entity GENERATE_COUNTER IS
   port(...);
end entity;

architecture RTL of GENERATE_COUNTER is
   component COUNTER_G
     generic (MAX_VALUE:integer := 15);
     port(...);
   end component;

begin
  GEN: for K in 2 to 5 generate
    COUNTER : COUNTER_G
      generic map (MAX_VALUE => 2**K-1)
      port map (...);
    end generate;

    . . .
end RTL;
```

- **'for generate' needs a label**
- **'loop' for concurrent statements (component instantiations, signal assignments)**
  - Several instantiations of the same component
  - Different values for generics
  - Loop variable implicitly declared

3.6.5 Conditional GENERATE Statement

```
entity GENERATE_COUNTER IS
   port(...);
end entity;

architecture RTL of GENERATE_COUNTER is
   component COUNTER_G
     generic (MAX_VALUE:integer := 15);
     port(...);
   end component;

begin
  GEN: for K in 1to 8 generate
    COND1: if K<=5 generate
      COUNTER : COUNTER_G
        generic map (MAX_VALUE => 2**K-1);
        port map (...);
    end generate;

    COND2: if K>5 and FLAG generate
      MAX : COUNTER_G
        generic map (MAX_VALUE => 31);
        port map (...);
    end generate;
  end generate;
  . . .
end RTL;
```

- **If condition is true then generate ...**
- **No elsif / else paths**
- **Each generate needs a label**

3.6.6   'Parameterization' via Signals

```
entity COUNTER_S is
  port(MAX_VALUE : in integer range 0 to 1023
      . . .);
end COUNTER_S;

architecture RTL of COUNTER_S is
begin
  process(CLK)
  begin
    if CLK'event and CLK='1' then
      if RESET='1' then
        COUNT <= 0;
      elsif ENABLE='1' then
        if COUNT < MAX_VALUE then
          COUNT <= COUNT+1;
        else
          COUNT <= 0 ;
        end if;
      end if;
    end if;
  end process;
end RTL;
```

- **Set different modes in operation (cf. MAX_VALUE)**

- **No parametric signals in port map**

When a component has to be instantiated several times, the way described above would be exhaustive. The generate statement provides a shortcut to this problem. Within a **'for ... generate ...'** loop, concurrent statements can be iterated. This applies not only to repeated component instantiations but also to concurrent signal assignments. The loop variable is declared implicitly, again, and can only be read, e.g. as generic value. Value assignments will lead to an error.

To make the generate statement even more powerful, one can use an if-generate statement, which allows one to execute the concurrent statements subject to the value of a boolean expression. In contrast to conditional signal assignments or the sequential if statement, elsif and else paths are not permitted. In the example, 8 counters are instantiated. For K=1...5 the maximum counter value is calculated according to the formula 2^K-1, i.e. 1, 3, 7, 15, 31. For higher index values the maximum counter values remains 31. It is also possible to evaluate constants or generics of its own entity in the expression of the if condition.

Constants and generics are very profitable when configuring a module before synthesizing. If it is necessary to switch parameters during operation, the only solution is to feed these parameters via signals into the module. The counter range in the example above can be set to values between 1 and 1023 during operation. For that reason, an overhead of hardware is generated to provide this flexibility in functionality. The signal MAX_VALUE must be stable when the active clock edge occurs. If this cannot be guaranteed, storing elements will have to be created, which hold the current value of MAX_VALUE and are updated at certain times only.

4   Simulation

4.1   Testbenches

Example of a testbench

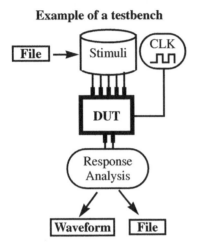

- **Stimuli transmitter to DUT (testvectors)**

- **Need not be synthesizable**

- **No ports to the outside**

- **Environment for DUT**

- **Verification and validation of the design**

- **Several output methods**

- **Several input methods**

A testbench is used to verify the specified functionality of a design. It provides the stimuli for the Device Under Test (DUT) and analyses the DUT's responses or stores them in a file. Information necessary for generating the stimuli can be integrated directly in the testbench or can be loaded from an external file. Simulation tools visualize signals by means of a waveform, which the designer compares with the expected response. In the case where the waveform does not match the expected response, the designer has to correct the source code. When dealing with bigger designs, this way of verification proofs impractical and will likely become a source of errors. The only way out would be a widely automated verification, but this is still a dream for the future.

4.1.1 Structure of a VHDL Testbench

```
entity TB_TEST is
end TB_TEST;
```
• **Empty entity**

```
architecture BEH of TB_TEST is
   -- component declaration of the DUT
   -- internal signal definition
begin
   -- component instantiation of the DUT
   -- clock generation
   -- stimuli generation
end BEH;
```
• **Declaration of the DUT**
• **Connection of the DUT with testbench signals**
• **Stimuli and clock generation (behavioural modelling)**
• **Response analysis**

```
configuration CFG_TB_TEST of TB_TEST is
   for BEH;
      -- customized configuration
   end for;
end CFG_TB_TEST;
```
• **Default or customized configuration to simulate the testbench**

The entity of a testbench is completely empty, because all necessary stimuli are created standalone. Otherwise a testbench for the testbench would be needed. As the DUT's inputs cannot be stimulated directly, internal temporary signals have to be defined. In order to distinguish between port names and internal signals, prefixes can be employed, for instance 'W_' to indicate a wire.

The declaration part of the testbench's architecture consists of the definition of the internal signals, a component declaration of the DUT or DUTs and perhaps some constant definitions e.g to set the clock period duration. A stimuli process provides the values for the DUT's input ports, in which behavioural modelling can be employed as there is no need to synthesize it. Sometimes, models of external components are available (probably behavioural description only) and can be used similar to create a whole system.

A configuration is used to pick the desired components for the simulation.

4.1.2 Example

```
entity TB_TEST is
end TB_TEST;
architecture BEH of TB_TEST is
  component TEST
    port(CLK, RESET : in std_logic;
         A       : in integer range 0 to 15;
         B       : in std_logic;
         C       : out integer range 0 to 15);
  end component;
  constant PERIOD  : time := 10 ns;
  signal W_CLK     : std_logic  := '0';
  signal W_A, W_C  : integer range 0 to 15;
  signal W_B       : std_logic;
  signal W_RESET   : std_logic;
begin
  DUT : TEST
    port map(CLK    => W_CLK,
             RESET  => W_RESET,
             A      => W_A,
             B      => W_B,
             C      => W_C);
  ...
```

- **Declaration part of the architecture**

  - Component
  - Internal signals
  - Subprograms
  - Constants

- **Instantiation of the DUT**
- **Connecting internal signals with the module ports**

 Initial clock signal value set to '0'

Clock and Reset Generation

```
  W_CLK <= not W_CLK after PERIOD/2;

-- complex version

  W_CLK <= '0' after PERIOD/4 when W_CLK='1'
           else
           '1' after 3*PERIOD/4 when W_CLK='0'
           else
           '0';
```

- **Simple signal assignment**
  - Endless loop
  - W_CLK must be initialized to '0' or '1' (not 'u' = 'u')
  - Symmetric clock only
- **Conditional signal assignment**
  - Complex clocking schemes
- **Realization as process introduces huge overhead**

```
  W_RESET <= '0',
             '1' after 20 ns,
             '0' after 40 ns;
```

- **Reset generation**

```
  assert now<100*PERIOD
      report "End of simulation"
      severity failure;
```

- **Simulation termination via assert**

Stimuli Generation

```
...
  STIMULI : process
  begin
    W_A    <= 10;
    W_B    <= '0';
    wait for 5*PERIOD;
    W_B <= '1';
    wait for PERIOD;
    ...
    wait;
  end process STIMULI;
...
```

• **Simple stimuli generation**

```
...
  process(W_C)
  begin
    case W_C is
      when 3 =>
        W_B <= '1' after 10 ns;
      when others =>
        W_B <= '0' after 10 ns;
    end case;
  end process;
...
```

• **Dynamically generated stimuli from DUT response**

The example shows a VHDL testbench for the design TEST. The design is declared as component in the declaration part of the architecture BEH. A constant PERIOD is defined to set the clock period. Internal signals that are needed as connections to the DUT are also declared. It is important to initialize the clock signal either to '0' or '1' instead of its default value 'u' because of the clock generation construct that is used later on. The clock stimulus is the most important one for synchronous designs. It can be created either with a concurrent signal assignment or within a clock generation process. As a process requires a lot of 'overhead' when compared with the implemented functionality, the concurrent version is recommended. In the simplest form shown on top, the clock runs forever and is symmetric. As the signal value is inverted after half of the clock period, the initial signal value must not be 'u', i.e. its start value has to be explicitly declared. The more elaborated example below shows the generation of an asymmetric clock with 25 % duty cycle via conditional signal assignments. Note that the default signal value need not be specified, because of the unconditional else path that is required by the conditional signal assignment. The complete simulation is stopped after 100 clock cycles via the ASSERT statement. Of course, the time check can be included in a conditional signal assignment as well. Clocks with a fixed phase relationship are modelled best with the '**delayed**' attribute similar to the following VHDL statement: 'CLK_DELAYED <= W_CLK'delayed(5 ns);'. The reset realization is straightforward: it is initialized with '0' at the beginning of the simulation, activated, i.e. set to '1', after 20 ns and returns to '0' (inactive) after an additional 20 ns for the remainder of the simulation.

Response Analysis

```
...
  process(W_C)
  begin
    assert W_C > 5 -- message, if false
    report "WRONG RESULT!!"
    severity ERROR;
  end process;
...
```

- **Assertion with severity level**
  - Note
  - Warning
  - Error (default)
  - Failure

```
...
process(W_C)
begin
  assert W_C > 5
  report "WRONG RESULT in " &
         W_C'path_name &
         "Value: " &
         integer'image(W_C)
  severity error;
...
```

- **Additional attributes in VHDL'93**
  - 'path_name
  - 'inst_name
  - 'image

```
WRONG RESULT in TB_TEST:W_C Value: 2
```

- **Report in simulator**

93 Additional attributes for debugging purposes

93 Report without assert statement

All other DUT inputs can be stimulated the same way. However the pattern generation via processes is usually preferred because of its sequential nature. Note that a wait statement is required to suspend a process, as otherwise it would restart. More complex testbenches will show dynamic behaviour, i.e. the input stimuli will react upon DUT behaviour. This may lead eventually to a complete behavioural model of the DUT environment.

The '**assert**' statement is suited best for performing automatic response analysis. An assertion checks a condition and will report a message if the condition is false. Depending on the chosen severity level and the settings in the simulation tool, the simulation either resumes (e.g. note, warning) or stops (e.g. error, failure) after reporting that the assertion fails. The default severity level is '**error**'.

The message that is reported is defined by the designer. In order to achieve dynamic reports that offer more detailed debugging information in the case of errors, several new attributes were defined in VHDL'93. They provide additional information about the circumstances that lead to the failing assertion: '**instance_name**' and '**path_name**' may be used to locate the erroneous module. The path information is necessary when one component is instantiated at various places within a complex design. The '**image**' attribute looks like a function call. Its argument is returned as string representation and the data type is the prefix of the attribute.

As a report is generated whenever the assertion condition evaluates to '**false**', it can be forced by setting this condition to the fixed value '**false**'. This construction is no longer necessary in VHDL'93, i.e. the '**report**' keyword may be used without a preceding assertion.

4.2 Sequence of Compilation

- **Main components are analysed before side- or sub-components**
  - Entity before architecture
  - Package before package body
- **The component which is referred to another one has to be analysed first**
  - Package before entity/architecture
  - Configuration after entity/architecture

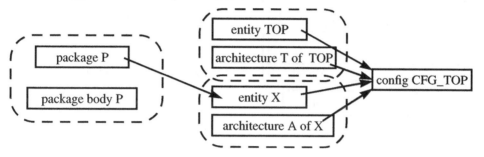

The sequence of compilation is determined by the interdependence of the single parts. Primary units have to be compiled before secondary ones, because secondary units need some information from their corresponding primary unit for the compilation process (e.g. entity ports are available as architecture signals). Thus the entity is compiled before its architecture(s), a package header before the package body and the configuration at the end.

General rule: When a module is referenced, it must have previously been compiled.

Example

Structure of a design

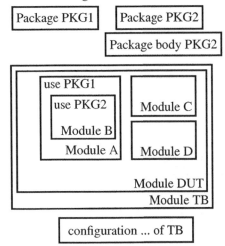

- **Which files will have to be recompiled if there is a change in the following files?**
  (only minor changes, i.e. comments)

  - Entity of module C
  - Architecture of module D
  - Package PKG1
  - Package PKG2
  - Package body PKG2
  - Architecture of TB
  - Configuration of TB

The design DUT which is to be simulated consists of several modules (A,B,C,D). The packages PKG1 and PKG2 are referenced in modules A and B, respectively. The package PKG1 is split into the package header containing declarations of subprograms, data types and constants, and a package body with the corresponding definitions.

The following order is suitable for the initial compilation: PKG1, PKG2, body of PKG2, module D, C, B, A, DUT, TB (entity first) and finally the testbench configuration. As the configuration creates the simulatable object, is has to recompiled whenever something is changed.

If entity C is changed, the corresponding architecture and the configuation have to be recompiled. A modification of D's architecture does not require any additional recompilations apart from the configuration. A recompilation of PKG1 leads to recompilations of the complete module A and the configuration.

Changes in PKG2 imply that the package body and module B have to be recompiled. If the changes are restricted to the package body, only the configuration, as always, remains to be updated. The same applies to modified testbench (TB) architectures and changes to the configuration itself.

Note that only minor modifications, for example in the VHDL comments, were considered here. If entity ports are changed, for example, a simple recompilation is not enough, and the VHDL code of the modules on all hierarchy levels might have to be adjusted accordingly. The interface mismatch is detected when compiling the configuration.

4.3   File I/O

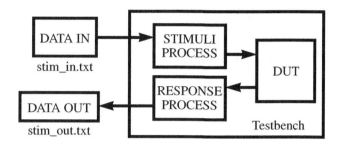

- **Package TEXTIO of STD library**
- **Important functions and procedures:**
  - readline(...), read(...),
  - writeline(...), write(...),
  - endfile(...)
- **Additional data types (text, line)**

- **READ / WRITE overloaded for all predefined data types:**
  - bit, bit_vector
  - boolean
  - character, string
  - integer, real
  - time

In VHDL, the designer is allowed to load data from or save data to a file. To do this, it is necessary to include the TEXTIO package of the STD library, which contains basic functions and procedures. These subprograms (write, writeline, read, readline, ...) facilitate the file I/O mechanism and are defined for the predefined VHDL data types. The main application of file I/O is simulation flexibility. This means that simulation stimuli and response analysis are left to specialized software, which is often easier than writing the corresponding VHDL models.

To get the information from a file, the user reads it line by line (READLINE procedure) and stores the data in a variable of the data type '**line**'. Afterwards it is possible to access the data from this line with the READ command. Usually a line contains information of different data types. To interpret the data in a correct way, i.e. a string as a string and an integer value as an integer, one has to employ actual parameters of the same data type. This fact will become clearer in the following example. Besides it is necessary to read the space character between the information in a separate read statement!

The file output works in a similar way, i.e. a line is assembled first via WRITE commands and is finally written to the file with a WRITELINE statement.

4.3.1 Example for File I/O (1/4)

```
library IEEE;
use IEEE.std_logic_1164.all;
use IEEE.std_logic_unsigned.all;
entity ADDER is
  port(VALUE_1: in std_logic_vector(7 downto 0);
       VALUE_2: in std_logic_vector(7 downto 0);
       OVERFLOW: out std_logic;
       RESULT: out std_logic_vector(7 downto 0));
end ADDER;
architecture RTL of ADDER is
  signal INT_RES: std_logic_vector(8 downto 0);
  signal INT_VAL_1: std_logic_vector(8 downto 0);
  signal INT_VAL_2: std_logic_vector(8 downto 0);
begin
  INT_VAL_1  <= '0' & VALUE_1;
  INT_VAL_2  <= '0' & VALUE_2;
  INT_RES    <= INT_VAL_1 + INT_VAL_2;
  RESULT     <= INT_RES(7 downto 0);
  OVERFLOW   <= INT_RES(8);
end RTL;
```

- **ADDER module**
  - Adds two 8-bit vectors and provides an 8-bit result vector
  - Generates an overflow signal
- **Entity and architecture of the ADDER module**
- **std_logic_unsigned package**
  - Copyright by Synopsys (EDA software company)
  - Not standardized by IEEE
  - Overloaded mathematical operators where std_logic_vector is treated as unsigned number

The first part of the file I/O example shows a design of an adder (entity and architecture). Note the use of the STD_LOGIC_UNSIGNED package. Although this package is located in the IEEE library, it is not standardized by the institute. The package was created by Synopsys Inc., an EDA software company. Their packages, however, have achieved the level of a quasi-standard in industry.

In the architecture, the operands are extended to 9 bits in order to avoid an overflow during the actual addition. The most significant bit of the resulting vector is then used as OVERFLOW signal and the lower 8 bits represent the result of the addition.

Example (2/4)

```
library IEEE;
use IEEE.std_logic_1164.all;
use IEEE.std_logic_unsigned.all;
use IEEE.std_logic_textio.all;
use STD.textio.all;

entity TB_ADDER is
end TB_ADDER;

architecture BEH of TB_ADDER is
  component ADDER
    port(VALUE_1: in std_logic_vector(7 downto 0);
         VALUE_2: in std_logic_vector(7 downto 0);
         OVERFLOW: out std_logic;
         RESULT: out std_logic_vector(7 downto 0));
  end component;

  signal W_VALUE_1: std_logic_vector(7 downto 0);
  signal W_VALUE_2: std_logic_vector(7 downto 0);
  signal W_OVERFLOW : std_logic;
  signal W_RESULT: std_logic_vector(7 downto 0);
begin
  DUT : ADDER
    port map(VALUE_1       => W_VALUE_1,
             VALUE_2       => W_VALUE_2,
             OVERFLOW      => W_OVERFLOW,
             RESULT        => W_RESULT);
```

- **Add package std.textio and IEEE.std_logic_textio for file I/O functions and procedures**

- **Common testbench structure**

  - Empty entity; no external interface
  - Component declaration and instantiation
  - Definition of internal signals to connect the input/output ports with the stimuli/response analysis processes

The testbench for the ADDER design follows the usual structure. The entity remains empty, as no higher hierarchy level exists and in the declarative part of the architecture the design under test and signals for its interface ports are declared. In the component instantiation statement these signals are connected to the DUT ports.

Note that two additional packages are used to handle the file I/O. The standard TEXTIO package provides the basic functionality. The STD_LOGIC_TEXTIO, again a Synopsys package that is not standardized by the IEEE, provides overloaded subprograms to handle '**std_ulogic**' based data types.

Example (3/4)

```
STIMULI : process
  variable L_IN : line;
  variable CHAR : character;
  variable DATA_1, DATA_2 :
          std_logic_vector(7 downto 0);
  file STIM_IN : text is in
                "stim_in.txt";
begin
  while not endfile(STIM_IN) loop
    readline(STIM_IN, L_IN);
    hread(L_IN, DATA_1);
    W_VALUE_1 <= DATA_1;
    read(L_IN, CHAR);
    hread(L_IN, DATA_2);
    W_VALUE_2 <= DATA_2;
    wait for PERIOD;
  end loop;
  wait;
end process STIMULI;
```

```
00 A1
FF 01
FF 00
11 55
0F 01
1F 05
AA F3
```

- **STIMULI process**

  - File access is limited to only one line at a certain time
  - Only variables are allowed for the parameters of the read functions
  - The function hread(...) is defined in the IEEE.std_logic_textio package; it reads hex values and transforms them into a binary vector

- **Stimuli file 'stim_in.txt'**

  - Each line contains two hex values to stimulate the inputs of the ADDER module

After having instantiated the entity ADDER, a stimuli process is needed that provides the test patterns. Different from previous examples, the stimuli are read from the file 'stim_in.txt'. Some example content is shown below the process code. The first hex value of each line is the stimulus for the port VALUE_1 (2 hex values -> 8 bits); the second hex value is for the port VALUE_2. Each line will be used as input vector for a duration of PERIOD.

The signals W_VALUE_1 and W_VALUE_2 are initialized with the all-zeros vector. After one clock cycle a loop is started where it is checked, whether the stimuli file STIM_IN still contains data. If so, the following statements will be executed; otherwise they will be skipped and the process will suspend at the last '**wait**' statement of this process.

Reading the file works as follows: first one line L_IN is read from the file STIM_IN by the '**readline**' command. Afterwards, three different values, an 8-bit standard logic vector, followed by a single character and another 8-bit vector, are extracted from this line L_IN. The data type is selected by the data type of the variable used in the READ procedure. HREAD is also a kind of read command, which transforms the value read from hexadecimal to '**std_logic_vector**' automatically. HREAD is contained in the STD_LOGIC_TEXTIO package.

After the values from the file are stored in the variables, they have to be assigned to the signals that are connected to the input ports of the DUT. After finishing one line, the process waits for one PERIOD before checking again, whether the stimuli file STIM_IN still contains some data.

Example (4/4)

```
RESPONSE : process(W_RESULT)
  variable L_OUT : line;
  variable CHAR_SPACE : character := ' ';
  file STIM_OUT : text is out
                  "stim_out.txt";
begin
  write(L_OUT, now);
  write(L_OUT, CHAR_SPACE);
  write(L_OUT, W_RESULT);
  write(L_OUT, CHAR_SPACE);
  hwrite(L_OUT, W_RESULT);
  write(L_OUT, CHAR_SPACE);
  write(L_OUT, W_OVERFLOW);
  writeline(STIM_OUT, L_OUT);
end process RESPONSE;
```

```
  0 NS UUUUUUUU 00 U
  0 NS XXXXXXXX 00 X
  0 NS 00000000 00 0
 20 NS 10100001 A1 0
 40 NS 00000000 00 1
 60 NS 11111111 FF 0
 80 NS 01100110 66 0
100 NS 00010000 10 0
120 NS 00100100 24 0
140 NS 10011101 9D 1
```

- **Response process of the testbench**

  - 'NOW' is a function returning the current simulation time

  - Several write commands assemble a line

  - Writeline saves this line in the file

  - The function hwrite(...) is defined in the IEEE.std_logic_textio package; it transforms a binary vector to a hex value and stores it in the line

- **Response file 'stim_out.txt'**

  - 4 columns containing:
    - Simulation time
    - 8-bit result value (binary and hex)
    - Overflow bit

The file output is just the inverse of the file input presented before: a line has to be composed and written to the file when finished. The RESPONSE process stores the current simulation time, the RESULT as '**std_logic_vector**' and in hexadecimal format and the OVERFLOW signal. The process is activated whenever an event occurs at W_RESULT (sensitivity list). This is the reason why three lines are written to the file at 0 NS. First, W_RESULT is uninitialized because no initial value is specified explicitly in the signal definition. So W_RESULT consists of 'U's only, which HWRITE transforms to '0'. The 'X's in the second line occur because the overloaded operator returns 'X' (unknown) when undefined values are added. 'X' and 'U' are treated just same, i.e. the result is also 0.

4.3.2   File Declaration: VHDL'87 versus VHDL'93

```
procedure READ_STIM (
             STIM_FILE : in string;
                  ••• );
   file FILE_IN : text is in STIM_FILE;
   variable STIM_LINE : line ;
•••
end READ_STIM

procedure WRITE_RESP ( RESP_FILE : in string;
                  ••• );
   file FILE_OUT : text is out RESP_FILE;
   variable RESP_LINE : line ;
•••
end WRITE_RESP
```

```
STIM: process
   file STIM_FILE  : text is "INPUT.TXT";
   variable STIM_LINE : line ;
begin
   readline(STIM_FILE, STIM_LINE);
•••
   file_close(STIM_FILE);
   file_open(STIM_FILE,"INPUT.TXT",
                     WRITE_MODE);
•••
   writeline(STIM_FILE, STIM_LINE);
end process STIM;
```

- **VHDL'87**

  - Mode determines if file is readable or writeable

  - Procedure elaborated when called =>
    Files also opened and closed with entering and exiting procedure

  - Now the same file can be written and read afterwards.

- **VHDL'93**

  - Default is READ_MODE

  - Files can be closed and opened with procedure calls

  - Procedures are declared implicit with file declaration

The file declaration in VHDL'87 is not compatible with that of VHDL'93. In VHDL'87 the file was declared with mode 'in' or mode 'out' and could therefore only be read or written. To circumvent the drawback, one had to write the whole reading and writing processes into two separated procedures. So the files could be opened by calling the corresponding procedure and were closed automatically when the procedure was exited. With this, the same file could be written and read afterwards in the same simulation.

In VHDL'93 the modes are called WRITE_MODE and READ_MODE. When a file is declared, the procedures FILE_CLOSE and FILE_OPEN are declared implicit with it. These procedures cannot be found in the predifined package 'textio' but have to be implemented in the simulator! So in VHDL'93 it is possible to write and read the same file in the same simulation by using these procedures.

4.4   Simulation Flow

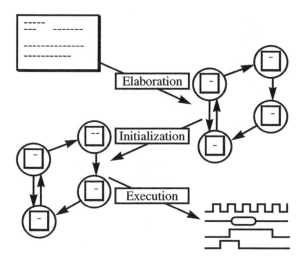

- **Design elaboration**
  - Specified elements are created
- **Signal initialization**
  - Starting values are assigned
- **Simulation is executed on command**

4.4.1   Elaboration

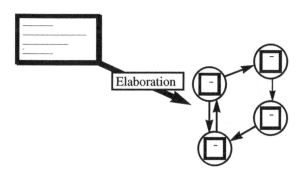

- **During elaboration design elements are created**
- **All design objects are elaborated before the simulation**
- **Except 'for loop'- variables and objects, which are defined in subprograms**

4.4.2   Initialization

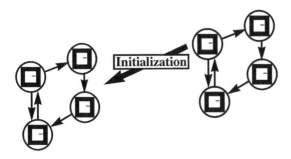

```
type std_ulogic is ('u','x','0'.....)
                 -- First value is 'u' !!!

signal clock: std_ulogic := '0';
signal reset: std_ulogic;
```

- **Initial values:**
  - Start values from declaration

    OR

  - First value from type definition
    (type'left)

- **Every process is executed until it
  is suspended**
  - ... without signal values being
    updated

4.4.3   Execution

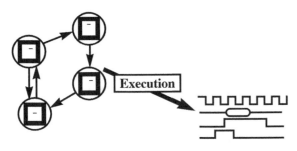

- **Simulation is actually executed**
- **Signal values are evaluated**

The simulation of a VHDL model operates in three phases. First, the simulation model is created in the elaboration phase. The processes and concurrent statements of the whole design are combined in a communication model. This model lists which processes can be activated by which processes, i.e. some sort of netlist is created. All objects are converted to an executable form residing in the simulator memory. Loop variables and subprograms are the only exception as they are elaborated dynamically during the execution of the simulation. The initial values of all signals are assigned in the initialization phase. Either the initial value specified in the signal declaration or the first value in the type definition (='data type'**left**') is used. In the case of the type STD_ULOGIC based types this is a 'u' for uninitialized. Hence the designer can deduce from a 'u' in the simulation waveform that a value has never been assigned to the corresponding signal. Signal values do not return to 'u' except when a 'u' is directly assigned. At the end of the initialization phase every process is executed once until it is suspended. The signal values, however, are not updated. The actual simulation of the design behaviour takes place in the execution phase. By means of testbench processes, the VHDL model is provided with stimuli. The individual signals of the model can then be viewed and checked in the waveform window (stimuli and responses of the model). The actual responses can be compared automatically with the expected values by adequate VHDL statements as well.

For instance, one can compare actual and expected responses at time OCCURRING_TIME by an assertion in an '**if**' statement:

```
if now=OCCURRING_TIME then
  assert EXPECTED_RESPONSE=RECEIVED_RESPONSE
  report "unexpected behaviour" severity error;
end if;
```

4.5   Process Execution

```
architecture A of E is
begin

  P1 : process
  begin
    -- sequential statements
  end process P1;

    -- C2: concurrent statements

  P2 : process
  begin
    -- sequential statements
  end process P2;

    -- C1: concurrent statements

end A;
```

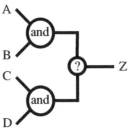

4.5.1   Concurrent vs. Sequential Execution

```
architecture CONCURRENT of MULTIPLE is
  signal A, B, C, D : std_ulogic;
  signal Z : std_logic
begin
  Z <= A and B;
  Z <= C and D;
end CONCURRENT;
```

```
architecture SEQUENTIAL of MULTIPLE is
  signal Z, A, B, C, D : std_ulogic;
begin
  process (A, B, C, D)
  begin
    Z <= A and B;
    Z <= C and D;
  end process;
end SEQUENTIAL;
```

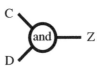

4.5.2 Signal Update

- **Signals have a past value, a current value and a future value**
    - Future value is used within the simulator core only
    - Past value ≠ current value: event
- **Signal values are updated at the end of a process execution:
  the old current value of a signal is overwritten by the future value**
- **Several process calls at one single moment of the simulation are possible**

An architecture can contain processes and concurrent statements that are all active in parallel. The connection of the parallel parts is established via signals and sensitivity lists. Concurrent statements can be interpreted as functionally equivalent processes with a sensitivity list containing all those values that are going to be read in this process. If, for example, the process P1 was triggered, e.g. by a clock edge, its statements are executed one after another. In this way, it is possible to execute parts of the code only after an active edge has occurred.

Let us assume that a couple of signals were modified. The changes will not take effect until the process execution has finished. According to the schematic, these updated values will trigger C1 and P1, which will trigger P1 and C2 in turn, and so on. The execution of the statements continues until a stable state is reached, i.e. no events are generated any more. If the same two signal assignments appear in the VHDL code, once as a concurrent statement in the architecture and once in a process, the result will differ substantially. In the first case, two parallel signal assignments are actually made to the signal. This is only allowed for resolved types, for which a resolution functions is present to decide which value is actually driven. In the second case, the first assignment is executed and its result is stored. Afterwards, this result is overwritten by another assignment, so that only the last signal assignment is carried out.

The signal update mechanism is essential for a VHDL simulator. Signals possess a past, a current and a future value within the simulator's signal management functions. Signal assignments in a process always assign the value to the future value of the signal. The future value is copied to the current value in the signal update phase after the process execution is finished, i.e. the process is suspended.

4.5.3   Delta Cycles (1)

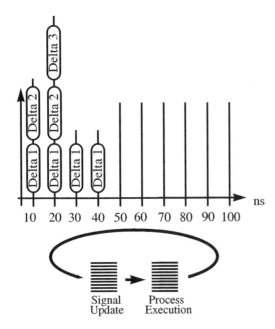

- **One moment of simulation**
- **One loop cycle = 'delta cycle'**
- **Delta time is orthogonal to simulation time**
- **Signals are updated**
- **All processes are initiated**
  - Signal assignments are stored
- **New signal assignments**
  - To execute further processes

4.5.4   Delta Cycles (2)

- **Several delta cycles at any moment of the simulation**

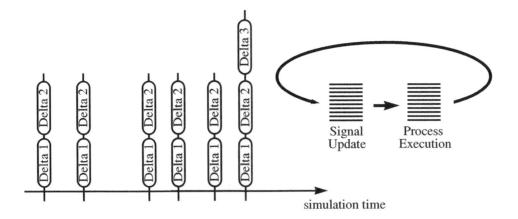

4.5.5   Delta Cycles: Example

library IEEE;
use IEEE.Std_Logic_1164.all;
 	
entity DELTA is
  port (A, B : in std_ulogic;
        Y, Z : out std_ulogic);
end DELTA;
	architecture EXAMPLE of DELTA is
	  signal X : std_ulogic;
	begin
	  process (A, B, X) begin
	    Y <= A;
	    X <= B;
	    Z <= X;
	  end process;
	end EXAMPLE;

```
Event on B (first delta cycle)
   future value of
      Y receives the current value of A (no change)
      X receives the current value of B (new value)
      Z receives the current value of X (no change)

   signal update

Event on X (second delta cycle)
   future value of
      Y receives the current value of A (no change)
      X receives the current value of B (no change)
      Z receives the current value of X (new value)

   signal update

No further events on A, B, X
```

A simulation cycle always consists of a signal update and a process execution phase. Several of these so-called delta cycles may have to be carried out in order to achieve a stable state of the system. The number of delta cycles has no effect on the time in the simulated time frame! It just affects the time that is necessary to carry out the simulation. The delta cycles are lined up orthogonally to the simulation time.

At the beginning, all signals are updated and a list of all processes that are triggered by the signal changes is created. All the processes of this list are executed one after another in delta cycle 1. When the execution is finished, the signal updates will be carried out and a new process list will be created. This continues until the process list remains empty, which means that no further processes are triggered by the signal events. Now, statements that induce a real-time step ('**wait for** ...', '... **after** ...') are carried out and the simulation time advances for the specified amount of time.

Let us assume that the value of signal B changes. In the example, the process is triggered by this event on B and is activated for the first time. The future value of X is given the current value of B. At the end of the process, the future value of X is transferred to its current value. This change of value of X results in an event that calls the process for the second time. Now, the current value of X is written to the future value of Z (B and X remain the same). During the signal update phase only Z's value changes, which is not listed in the sensitivity list, i.e. the process will not be called again. The signals X and Z are set to the value from B in this way.

This example is for demonstrative purposes only. The intermediate signal X conceals the functionality of the process and would not be used in practice. Generally, variables, which are not subject to the update mechanism, should be used instead.

4.5.6 Process Behaviour

```
process (A, B)        process
begin                 begin
  if (A=B) then         if (A=B) then
    Z <= '1';             Z <= '1';
  else                  else
    Z <= '0';             Z <= '0';
  end if;               end if;
end process;          wait on A, B;
                      end process;
```

- **The process is an endless loop**
- **It is stopped by a wait statement**
- **The sensitivity list is equivalent to a wait statement**
- **A process with a sensitivity list must not contain any wait statements**

4.5.7 Postponed Processes

```
postponed process
begin
  Z <=  '0' ;   -- wrong
  wait for 0 ns;
  Z <=  '1' ;   -- wrong
  wait on A, B; -- wrong
end process;
```

```
postponed process (A, B)
begin
  if (A=B) then
    Z <=   '1'  after 5 ns;
  else
    Z <=   '0'  after 4 ns;
  end if;
end process;
```

- **Processes that are executed in the last delta cycle of a certain moment**
- **The following are not permitted:**
  - Wait statements of the time 0
  - Signal assignments without delay (for 0 ns)

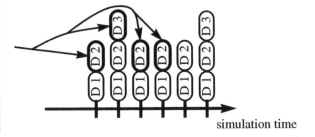

simulation time

'93 Postponed processes are a new feature of VHDL'93

Basically, a process has to be considered as an endless loop. The continuous process execution can be interrupted via wait statements. The use of a sensitivity list is equivalent to a WAIT ON statement. If a sensitivity list is present, WAIT statements must not appear in the process.

Postponed processes are always carried out in the last delta cycle. This means that this process can access already stable signals at this point of simulation time. In postponed processes WAIT statements with 0 ns and signal assignments without delay are not permitted.

Note that postponed processes can only be used in simulation, not in synthesis.

4.6 Delay Models

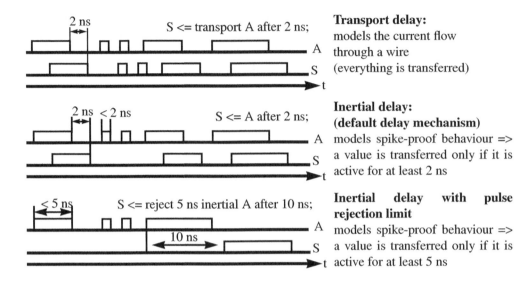

Transport delay:
models the current flow
through a wire
(everything is transferred)

Inertial delay:
(default delay mechanism)
models spike-proof behaviour =>
a value is transferred only if it is
active for at least 2 ns

Inertial delay with pulse rejection limit
models spike-proof behaviour =>
a value is transferred only if it is
active for at least 5 ns

There are two different delay models in VHDL: transport and inertial, which is used per default.

In the transport delay model, everything is transferred via the signal, as can be seen in the upper example, where signal A is an exact copy of signal S, delayed by 2 ns. Transport delay models signal transfers by wire with pure propagation delay; thus spikes are not filtered out.

When using inertial delay, signal transitions are only transferred when the new value remains constant for a minimum amount of time; thus spikes are suppressed.

'S <= A after 2 ns' filters out all spikes of less than 2 ns and delays signal values that remain constant for a longer period of time for 2 ns.

'S <= reject 5 ns inertial A after 10 ns' requires a minimum pulse width of 5 ns and copies all other signal values from A to S with 10 ns delay.

Inertial delay is characteristic of switching circuits. Spikes that are shorter than the necessary specific switching time of the circuit have no effect on the succeeding switch and will not be transmitted.

4.6.1   Projected Output Waveforms (LRM)

- **Transport and inertial delay:**

  - (1) All old transactions that are projected to occur at or after the time at which the earliest new transaction is projected to occur are deleted from the projected output waveform.

  - (2) The new transactions are then appended to the projected output waveform in the order of their projected occurrence.

- **For inertial delay, the projected output waveform is further modified:**

  - (3) All of the new transactions are marked.

  - (4) An old transaction is marked if the time at which it is projected to occur is less than the time at which the first new transaction is projected to occur minus the pulse rejection limit.

  - (5) For each remaining unmarked, old transaction, the old transaction is marked if it immediately precedes a marked transaction and its value component is the same as that of the marked transaction

  - (6) The transaction that determines the current value of the driver is marked.

  - (7) All unmarked transactions (all of which are old transactions) are deleted from the projected output waveform.

The definition of the delay mechanism is quoted from the VHDL language reference manual. In conclusion, all signal assignments can be brought into the following format:

T <= reject TIME_1 inertial VALUE after TIME_2;
The following assignments are equivalent:

T <=   VALUE after TIME_1; -- (default inertial delay)
T <=   inertial VALUE after TIME_1;
T <= reject TIME_1 inertial VALUE after TIME_1;
Also equivalent are:

T <= transport   VALUE after TIME_1;
T <= reject 0 ns inertial VALUE after TIME_1;

This is because a pulse rejection limit of 0 ns makes all transactions marked (step 3), and thus none of the transactions will be deleted in step 7. Consequently steps 3 to 7 have no effect and the delay model is actually equivalent to transport delay.

Furthermore 'T <= VALUE' is just a shortcut for 'T <= VALUE after 0 ns'.

4.6.2   Transport Delay (1)

```
signal S : integer := 0;              signal S : integer := 0;
process                               process
begin                                 begin
      S <= transport 1 after 1 ns;          S <= transport 2 after 2 ns;
      S <= transport 2 after 2 ns;          S <= transport 1 after 1 ns;
      wait;                                 wait;
end process;                          end process;
```

S ──| (1, 1 ns) | S ──| (2, 2 ns) | Timei-1

   S <= transport 1 after 1 ns;   S <= transport 2 after 2 ns;

S ──| (1, 1 ns) | (2, 2 ns) | (cf. 2)   S ──| (1, 1 ns) | Timei (cf. 1)

   S <= transport 2 after 2 ns;   S <= transport 1 after 1 ns;

 A signal driver manages value/time pairs
It is not possible to assign a new value for $Time_i < Time_{i-1}$

Within a signal driver, the actual values are always associated with an activation time. The initial value/time (0, 0 ns) pair for the integer signal of the example is left out in the figures as this pair remains unaffected at any time.

Whenever a signal assignments leads to a new pair, it must be decided whether or not the time in the value/time pair is chronologically after the time of the last list entry. The first signal assignment is the simplest as it is just appended to the list. The same applies to pairs that occur later on in time (left example; step 2). Otherwise the new value/time pair will be inserted chronologically after the pair with the next previous time specification, and all succeeding pairs will be deleted (right example; step 1).

It is not possible to insert a new value/time pair before an already existing one without deleting all succeeding pairs!

4.6.3 Transport Delay (2)

```
signal S : integer := 0;              signal S : integer := 0;
process                               process
begin                                 begin
  S <= transport 1 after 1 ns,          S <= transport 1 after 1 ns,
               3 after 3 ns,                          3 after 3 ns,
               5 after 5 ns;                          5 after 5 ns;
  S <= transport 4 after 4 ns;          S <= transport 4 after 6 ns;
wait;                                 wait;
end process;                          end process;
```

S —| (1, 1 ns) | (3, 3 ns) | (5, 5 ns) |

S <= transport 1 after 1 ns, 3 after 3 ns, 5 after 5 ns;

S —| (1, 1 ns) | (3, 3 ns) | (4, 4 ns) | S —| (1, 1 ns) | (3, 3 ns) | (5, 5 ns) | (4, 6 ns) |

S <= transport 4 after 4ns;   S <= transport 4 after 6 ns;

 New pairs are either appended to the list or overwrite the remaining elements

After the first signal assignment the driver of S contains three value/time pairs.

The signal assignment occurring after 4 ns (left example: 'S <= transport 4 after 4 ns') is prior to the last assignment that was specified before. Thus the last entry is overwritten: in step 1, the last list element is deleted; in step 2, the new pair is added. If the list had been longer then the following list entries would have been deleted too.

In the second example ('S <= transport 4 after 6 ns'), the pair is attached to the list, because the time entry of this pair follows chronologically the time entry of the last list element (nothing to do in step 1, only step 2). The time entry t_i of the additional value/time pair decides whether the list is overwritten and the following entries have to be deleted ($t_{i-1} >= t_i$), or whether the pair will be attached to the list ($t_{i-1} < t_i$).

4.6.4 Inertial Delay (1)

```
signal S :          signal S :          signal S :           signal S :
   integer := 0;       integer := 0;       integer := 0;        integer := 0;
process             process             process              process
begin               begin               begin                begin
   S <= 1 after 1 ns;  S <= 1;             S <= 2 after 2 ns;   S <= 1 after 2 ns;
   S <= 2 after 2 ns;  S <= 2;             S <= 1 after 1 ns;   S <= 1 after 1 ns;
   wait;               wait;               wait;                wait;
end process;        end process;        end process;         end process;
```

S ──| (1, 1 ns) | S ──| (1, 0 ns) | S ──| (2, 2 ns) | S ──| (1, 2 ns) |

S <= 1 after 1 ns;   S <= 1;   S <= 2 after 2 ns;   S <= 1 after 2 ns;

S ──| (2, 2ns) | S ──| (2, 0 ns) | S ──| (1, 1 ns) | S ──| (1, 1 ns) |

S <= 2 after 2 ns;   S <= 2;   S <= 1 after 1 ns;   S <= 1 after 1 ns;

```
S <= 1;
-- equivalent to
S <= 1 after 0
ns;
```

 The last assignment to a signal in a process takes effect

In the left example, the pulse rejection limit of the signal assignment 'S <= 2 after 2 ns' equals 2 ns. Therefore all transactions are marked whose recurrence time is smaller than 0 ns (2 ns minus pulse rejection time; step 4). Accordingly the pair (1, 1 ns) is not marked, and is deleted in the final step (step 7).

The time in the new value/time pair in the three right-side examples is at most as big as the time of the pair in the list; thus the old entry is overwritten by the new one (step 1 deletes, step 2 adds a new pair), independent of rejection limit values.

4.6.5 Inertial Delay (2)

```
signal S : integer := 0;
process
begin
    S <= 1 after 1 ns, 3 after 3 ns, 5 after 5 ns;
    S <= 3 after 4 ns, 4 after 5 ns;
    wait;
end process;
```

S ——| (1, 1 ns) | (3, 3 ns) | (5, 5 ns) | Starting waveform in ascending order

S <= 1 after 1 ns, 3 after 3 ns, 5 after 5 ns;

```
signal S : integer := 0;
process
begin
    S <= 1 after 1 ns, 2 after 2 ns, 3 after 3 ns, 5 after 5 ns;
    S <= 3 after 4 ns, 4 after 5 ns;
    wait;
end process;
```

S ——| (3, 3ns) | (3, 4 ns) | (4, 5 ns) | Resulting waveform in ascending order

S <= 3 after 4 ns, 4 after 5 ns;

After the first signal assignment 'S <= 1 after 1 ns, 3 after 3 ns, 5 after 5 ns;' the list contains three value/time pairs.

The second signal assignment 'S <= 3 after 4 ns, 4 after 5 ns;' deletes the last entry from the list because 4 ns <= 5 ns (step 1) and appends two entries (step 2). Then all new transactions (step 3) and also (3, 3 ns) will be marked, because this transaction is a direct predecessor of a marked transaction and it has the same value as this marked transaction, namely 3 (step 5). The unmarked entries will be deleted, namely the pair (1, 1 ns) and (2, 2 ns) in the second case respectively (step 7).

4.6.6 Inertial Delay (3)

```
signal S : integer := 0;
process
begin
  S <= 2 after 3 ns, 2 after 12 ns, 12 after 13 ns, 5 after 20 ns,
      8 after 42 ns;
  S <= reject 15 ns inertial 12 after 20 ns, 18 after 41 ns;
  wait;
end process;
```

S — | (2, 3 ns) | (2, 12 ns) | (12, 13 ns) | (5, 20 ns) | (8, 42 ns) |

S — | (2, 3 ns) | (2, 12 ns) | (12, 13 ns) |

S — | (2, 3 ns) | (2, 12 ns) | (12, 13 ns) | (12, 20 ns) | (18, 41 ns) |

S — | (2, 3 ns) | (2, 12 ns) | (12, 13 ns) | (12, 20 ns) | (18, 41 ns) |

S — | (2, 3 ns) | (2, 12 ns) | (12, 13 ns) | (12, 20 ns) | (18, 41 ns) |

S — | (2, 3 ns) | (12, 13 ns) | (12, 20 ns) | (18, 41 ns) |

The signal assignment 'S <= 2 after 3 ns, 2 after 12 ns, 12 after 13 ns, 5 after 20 ns, 8 after 42 ns;' builds the first list. The second signal assignment 'S <= reject 15 ns inertial 12 after 20 ns, 18 after 41 ns;' modifies this list in the following way:

step 1: all pairs with time values greater than or equal to 20 ns will be removed;
step 2: the new pairs will be attached;
step 3: all new transactions will be marked (light grey);
step 4: old transactions with a time value smaller than the time value of the first new transaction (20 ns) minus the reject limit (15 ns), i.e. 5 ns, will be marked (dark grey);
step 5: still-unmarked transactions will be marked (grey) if they are direct predecessor of a marked transaction and contain the same value as the already-marked transaction;
step 6: the current value/time pair will be marked; as this pair has to be marked anyway, it is not displayed in the list;
step 7: all unmarked transactions will be deleted.

5   Project Management

5.1   File Organization

- **Primary and secondary design units can be split into several files**

- **Advantages of**
  - Several Packages
    - Modularization and reuse aspects (IEEE, corporate, project packages)
    - Separation of synthesizable from simulation only VHDL
  - Package / Package body separation
    - No recompilation of the design hierarchy if body (implementation) changed
  - Entity / Architecture separation
    - System design (top level, structural) independent of implementation
    - Several modelling alternatives (e.g. behavioural, RTL) possible
  - Several top level configurations
    - Adjust design to goal of simulation
    - Comparison of alternative architectures

5.2   Design Components

- **Five basic design units, divided into two groups:**

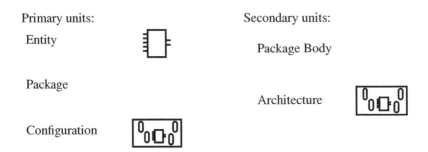

Primary units:

Entity

Package

Configuration

Secondary units:

Package Body

Architecture

- **Each design unit has to be analysed and stored in a library**
- **Packages may be split into header (declarations) and main part**

5.2.1 Libraries

- **Container for compiled design units**
  - Entities, architectures,
  - Packages, package bodies,
  - Configurations
- **Mapped to a directory on the filesystem**
  - Platform independency
  - Setup file/options setting
- **Different libraries in one design project possible**

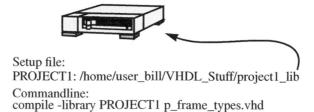

Setup file:
PROJECT1: /home/user_bill/VHDL_Stuff/project1_lib
Commandline:
compile -library PROJECT1 p_frame_types.vhd

VHDL offers several possibilities for implementing hierarchy. The language introduces the main hierarchy into the design, with the philosophy of entity/architecture pairs and their instantiation as components. This leads to a strict separation of interface and implementation. With the help of packages, libraries and concise naming conventions, it is possible to manage huge designs with plenty of files. Switching between the different implementations during simulation is done with the configuration mechanism.

All parts of a VHDL design have to be analysed/compiled before they can be used for simulation or synthesis. In total, five different so-called design units exist: entity/architecture, package/package body and configuration. A file must contain at least one design unit to be accepted by the compiler.

After compilation, the design units are stored in a so-called 'library'. The purpose of the library mechanism is platform independence, i.e. every VHDL tool has to map the logical library name to a physical directory. If the target library is not specified when compiling a VHDL file, the design units are compiled into the default library '**work**'. It is often mapped to the start-up directory of the software by default. Special setup files or option settings are needed to specify alternatives.

In the example above, the logical library name PROJECT1 is mapped to the physical directory '/home/user_bill/VHDL_Stuff/project1_lib' in the setup files for the simulator and synthesis tool. This library must be named as target when VHDL files are compiled, i.e. the command will look like 'compile -library project1 p_frame_types.vhd'. Within another VHDL file the library PROJECT1 has to be made visible with the LIBRARY statement if elements of the P_FRAME_TYPES package are to be used.

5.2.2   The LIBRARY Statement

```
library EXAMPLE;
use EXAMPLE.PKG.all;

entity A is
  . . .
end A;

library EXAMPLE;
use EXAMPLE.PKG.all;

entity B is
  . . .
end B;

architecture BEH of A is
  . . .
end BEH;
```

```
architecture BEH of B is
  . . .
end BEH;
```

- **Occurrence**
  - In front of any design unit
    (entity, architecture, package, ...)
  - Valid for the next unit, only
- **Secondary units 'inherit' library declarations**
- **Libraries WORK and STD are always known by default**
- **Does not declare any VHDL design units/objects**
- **Refers to existing libraries**
- **Easier design management and preparation**
- **May cause visibility problems**

5.2.3   The USE Statement

```
library EXAMPLE;
library OTHER_1;
library OTHER_2;

use EXAMPLE.PKG_1.CONST_A,
    EXAMPLE.PKG_1.CONST_B;

use EXAMPLE.PKG_2.all;

use EXAMPLE.ENTITY_1;

architecture BEH of ENTITY_1 is
   use OTHER_1.all;
   signal A : integer;
begin
   A <= OTHER_2.PKG.CONST_A;
end BEH;
```

- **Occurrence**
  - In front of any design unit
  - Valid for the next unit only
  - May appear in declarative parts if all items
    of an object are made visible
- **Secondary units 'inherit' use clauses**
- **Library must be known**
- **Grants access to individual items**
  - Design units (e.g. entities)
  - Objects from packages (e.g. constants)
  - 'all' accesses all objects
- **Elements of STANDARD package are always accessible by default**
- **Complete 'logical pathname' needed if 'use' is omitted**

5.3   Name Spaces

```
package PKG is
  constant C : integer := 1;
end PKG;

use work.PKG.all;
entity ENT is
end ENT;
architecture RTL of ENT is
  signal C : integer := 8;
begin
  -- only signal C is visible
  C <= 24;
  process
    variable C : integer := 9;
  begin
    -- only variable C is
    -- visible
    C := 42;
    for C in 0 to 5 loop
    -- only loop parameter C
    -- is visible
    ENT.C <= C; -- selected name
    end loop;
    ENT.C <= work.PKG.C;
  end process;
end RTL;
```

- **Multiple objects of same names are allowed:**
  - Without selected names: local name overrides
  - Assignment with complete selected names: ENT.C <= 12;
- **Declarations in ...**
  - a package are visible in all design units that use this package
  - an entity declarative part is visible in all the architectures of this entity
  - an architecture is visible for all processes of this architecture
  - a process is visible only inside this process
  - a loop statement (loop parameter) or a subprogram is visible only inside these objects.

Library statements may only be placed in front of VHDL design units and are valid for the immediately following unit only. Secondary design units, however, inherit library declarations that apply to their primary counterparts. Thus a library clause need not be repeated in front of an architecture or package body, even when they are placed in separate files (cf. 'architecture BEH of B'). The libraries WORK and STD are visible by default and need not be declared via library statements. Libraries can be used advantageously to separate the object code of different design projects.

A library statement alone does not give access to the design units and objects contained in this library. An additional use clause is necessary for this purpose. Most of the rules concerning its location and consequences are equivalent to the library statement and consequently both statements appear conjunctively most of the time. A use clause makes individual elements of a library visible within a design unit. It is even possible to select specific objects from a package. Usually, however, the keyword '**all**' is used to make all its declarations available to the user. The keyword '**all**' is also applicable to complete library contents. While the library statement is always necessary, objects can be accessed via their 'selected name' instead of a use clause. Then the complete logical path consisting of the names of the library, design unit and object must be specified.

Visibility problems may arise when libraries and packages are used because objects with identical names and parameter lists can be defined in several locations. An illegal redeclaration error will be reported if objects with the same name and parameter lists are present within one VHDL file. If non-distinguishable objects are referenced during compilation, none of the eligible objects is used and an error message is generated, even if the objects are identical.

5.3.1   Packages

- **Packages contain VHDL objects that may be shared by many design units**
  - (Sub-)type declarations
  - Constants
  - Subprograms
  - Components
- **Package contents must be made available via use clauses**
- **Implementation details can be hidden in a package body**
- **Package body**
  - Visible only within a package
  - Always linked to a package
  - May contain all declarations/definitions that are legal for a package
  - Holds definition of previously declared constants and subprograms

5.3.2   Package Syntax

Package declaration: Package body declaration:

```
package IDENTIFIER is
   -- declaration of
   -- types and subtypes
   -- subprograms
   -- constants, signals and shared
   --                      variables
   -- files
   -- aliases
   -- components
end [ package ] [ IDENTIFIER ];
```

```
package body IDENTIFIER is
   -- definition of previously declared
   -- constants
   -- subprograms
   -- declaration/definition of
   -- additional types and subtypes
   -- subprograms
   -- constants, signals and shared
   --                         variables
   -- files
   -- aliases
   -- components
end [ package body ] [ IDENTIFIER ];
```

 Only the package content is visible, NOT the body

 Subprogram definitions cannot be placed in a package

 The keywords 'package' / 'package body' may be repeated after the keyword 'end'

5.3.3   Package Example

```
package PKG is                    library STD;          -- VHDL default
   type T1 is ...                 library WORK;         -- VHDL default
   type T2 is ...                 use STD.standard.all; -- VHDL default
   constant C : integer;          use work.PKG.all;
   procedure P1 (...);
end PKG;                          entity EXAMPLE is
                                  end EXAMPLE;
package body PKG is
   type T3 is ...                 architecture BEH of EXAMPLE is
                                     signal S1 : T1;
   C := 17;                          signal S2 : T2;
   procedure P1 (...) is             signal S3 : T3; -- error: T3 not declared
     . . .
   end P1;                        begin
   procedure P2 (...) is
     . . .                          P1 (...);
   end P2;                          P2 (...);         -- error: P2 not declared
end PKG;
                                  end BEH;
```

- **Signals or procedures that are declared in the package body cannot be accessed**

- **A specific new data type may be defined in only one of the referenced packages**

- **Deferred constants: actual value assignment is package body**

Packages are the only language mechanism to share objects among different design units. Usually, they are designed to provide standard solutions for specific problems,e.g. data types and corresponding subprograms such as type conversion functions for a certain bus protocol, procedures and components (macros) for signal processing purposes, etc. A body is strictly needed if subprograms are to be placed in packages, because only the declaration of functions and procedures may be placed in the package itself. A package body is not needed if no subprograms or deferred constants are used. Note that only objects declared in a package can be referenced via use statements.

The libraries WORK and STD and the STANDARD package are available by default. Thus the corresponding VHDL statements are not needed. If a package body exists, it should be placed in a separate file. Otherwise it would not be possible to compile the body separately. Only the package content can be made visible with use statements, so changes to constant declarations or subprogram bodies can be made in the package body without implying a recompilation of the complete design. Only the package body has to be recompiled then. A package body is not necessary if no subprograms or deferred constants are declared. In this example the type T3 and the procedure P2 are declared in the package body only. This leads to an error during compilation because these two items are not visible in the architecture.

5.4   Design Reuse

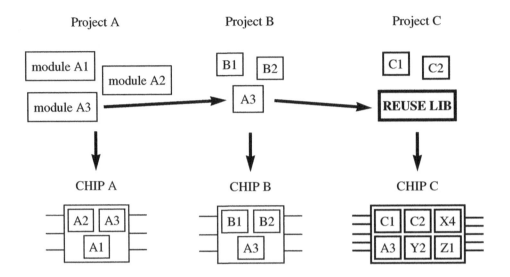

5.4.1   Why Reuse?

- **Continuous growth of complexity (approx. 60% per year)**
- **Limited increase of designer productivity (approx. 20% per year)**

  => Gap between technology and product capabilities

- **Reuse:**
  - Readily available solutions for specific problems
    (micro controllers, bus interfaces, signal processors, etc.)
  - Reduced amount of verification effort
  - Prerequisite for System-on-a-Chip (SoC)

5.4.2 Design for Reuse

- **Traditional approach: copy, paste and modify**
  - Difficult to maintain
  - Risk of bug propagation
- **Reuse concepts**
  - System-specific constant definition in packages
  - Standard data types at interface
  - Internal use of problem-specific data types for runtime error checking
  - Subprograms for common features:
    easy scalability because of unconstrained formal parameters
    flexibility because of embedding in architectures
  - Self-contained modules for complex functions
- **General requirements**
  - Technology independence
  - Tool independence (simulation, synthesis)
  - Parameterization with constants and generics
  - Detailed documentation

Reuse means to fall back on existing problem solutions. Every design engineer will try to apply previous VHDL code to the current situation. This is fairly simple because all details of the implementation are already known and consequently the code can be easily changed.

Reuse of previously designed modules on a bigger scale has become a necessity since the designer productivity cannot keep pace with the advances in the field of technology. Currently, the complexity of integrated circuits increases at a rate of approximately 60 % per year whereas the designer productivity increases by just 20 %. The only way to fill this gap is to reduce the design effort by reusing existing solutions.

Old designs, however, cannot simply be collected in a reuse library to provide the desired standard solutions. In order for developers who are not familiar with the internals to be able to use the parts of the library, the documentation must be extremely detailed. Additionally, the code must be written with reusability in mind, because modifications might consume more time than a complete redesign. This means that the VHDL must not rely on short-term settings such as technology or tool features. Possible applications have to be covered via parameterizable behaviour, i.e. the code itself need not be modified. Thus simple structures and standard solutions have the biggest reuse potential.

5.4.3   Bad Example

```
library IEEE;
use IEEE.std_logic_1164.all;
-- synopsys packages
use IEEE.std_logic_arith.all;
use IEEE.std_logic_unsigned.all;
entity ZERO_COUNT is
  port(DATA_IN:in std_logic_vector(7 downto 0);
       CNT, ONES : out
             std_logic_vector (3 downto 0));
end ZERO_COUNT;
architecture RTL of ZERO_COUNT is
begin
  CNT_PROC : process(DATA_IN)
    variable CNT_TEMP : integer range 0 to 8;
  begin
    CNT_TEMP := 0;
    for I in 0 to 7 loop
      if DATA_IN(I) = '0' then
        CNT_TEMP := CNT_TEMP + 1;
      end if;
    end loop;
    CNT<= conv_std_logic_vector(CNT_TEMP,4);
    ONES<= 8-conv_std_logic_vector(CNT_TEMP,4);
  end process;
end RTL;
```

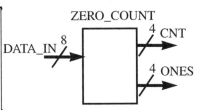

- **Use of Synopsys packages**
  - not standardized (quasi-standard)
  - might not be available in other tools
- **Hard coded values (vector ranges)**
  - not usable in applications with different bus width

5.4.4   Good Example (1/2)

```
library IEEE;
use IEEE.std_logic_1164.all; use IEEE.numeric_std.all;
package BITCOUNT is
  procedure COUNT(VECTOR: in std_logic_vector;
       VALUE: in std_logic;
       signal RESULT: out std_logic_vector);
end BITCOUNT;
package body BITCOUNT is
  procedure COUNT(VECTOR: in std_logic_vector;
       VALUE: in std_logic;
       signal RESULT: out std_logic_vector) is
    variable COUNT: integer;
    variable MAXVALUE:
       unsigned(RESULT'length-1 downto 0);
  begin
    COUNT := 0; MAXVALUE := (others => '1');
    for I in VECTOR'range loop
      if VECTOR(I) = VALUE then
        COUNT := COUNT + 1;
      end if;
    end loop;
    if COUNT > MAXVALUE then
      RESULT <= (others => '1');
    else
      RESULT <= std_logic_vector(to_unsigned(
             COUNT, RESULT'length));
    end if;
  end COUNT;
end BITCOUNT;
```

- **Standardized packages only**
- **Counter functionality implemented as subprogram**
  - Synchronous/combinational circuit may be used
  - Flexibility because of unconstrained formal parameters
- **Hardcoded ranges replaced by VHDL attributes**
- **Note the overflow handling in case the output vector is too small**

5.4.5   Good Example (2/2)

```
library IEEE;
use IEEE.std_logic_1164.all;
use WORK.BITCOUNT.all;

entity ZERO_COUNT is
  generic(D_WIDTH   : integer := 8;
          C_WIDTH   : integer := 4;
          COUNT_1S: integer range 0 to 1 := 1);
  port(DATA_IN : in
          std_logic_vector(D_WIDTH-1 downto 0);
       CNT, ONES : out
          std_logic_vector(C_WIDTH-1 downto 0));
end ZERO_COUNT;

architecture RTL of ZERO_COUNT is
begin
  COUNT(DATA_IN, '0', CNT);

  ONES <= (others => '0');
  CNT_ONES: if COUNT_1S=1 generate
    COUNT(DATA_IN, '1', ONES);
  end generate CNT_ONES;
end RTL;
```

- **Parameterized interface via generics**
- **Additional generic to control module behaviour**
- **if ... generate statement to avoid unnecessary hardware overhead**

The difference in design philosophy will be demonstrated with an example module that has to count the number of '0' and '1' elements in a bit vector.

The first version is a straightforward implementation of the specification. Synopsys packages are used for bit vector arithmetic based on '**std_logic_vector**'. Although these packages are frequently used in industry, they are not standardized. Because the vector widths from the actual task are hard-coded, it is not possible to place an identical module in a different environment.

The counting of specific values within a vector is a very basic function that should be implemented as a subprogram. This subprogram should be placed in a package in order to make it easily accessible. Subprograms may use unconstrained formal parameters, which allows for parameterizability without much of additional effort.

In order to fulfil the requirements, an entity/architecture pair must be created that shows the specified behaviour. The new entity has generic parameters that may be used to define port width. Their default values allow a drop in replacement of the old design without the necessity for a generic map. While the first two parameters are used to set the data width, the third parameter COUNT_1S affects the behaviour of the module. It allows one to turn off the counting of '1' elements. The '**if ... generate**' construct is used to reduce the amount of hardware that gets synthesized.

VHDL-AMS
TUTORIAL

6   VHDL-AMS

6.1   Overview and Introduction

- **What is VHDL-AMS?**

  - VHDL-AMS = Very High Speed Integrated Circuit Hardware Description Language for Analogue and Mixed Signals


```
VHDL-AMS =

IEEE VHDL 1076-1993
        +
IEEE VHDL 1076.1-1999
```

- **VHDL-AMS = Digital Hardware Description Language (VHDL) + Analogue and Mixed Signal Extensions (AMS)**

The aim of this part of the book is to give a general understanding of how modelling and simulation of analogue and mixed-signal systems work. The tutorial is based on the information in the unproved draft of the VHDL-AMS Language Reference Manual. At this point of time, the IEEE Language Reference Manual as well as a simulator are not yet available, so the examples could not be tested in a simulator.

VHDL-AMS consists of the digital part, which is defined in the IEEE Standards 1076 and 1076-1993, and the analogue and mixed-signal extensions, which are defined in the IEEE Extension 1076.1-1999. The definition as an IEEE Standard means that the language can be used by different tool vendors. The language definition does not define the whole internal operation of the simulator in the analogue domain. This means, that the simulation results can be different with tools from different vendors, even if the same models are used. The reason is that continuous functions cannot be computed exactly by a computer. In all cases, rounding and iterative as well as numerical algorithms are inevitable, and allow an approximate result only.

6.1.1   Current Design Flow

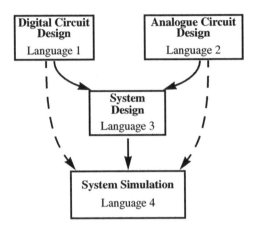

- **Different languages**
- **Many tools**
- **No general automatic translation between languages**
- **Translation is time-intensive**
- **Risk of translation errors**
- **System simulation is difficult**

The design of a modern integrated circuit can consist of an analogue part and a digital part. General considerations are done on the system level.

Currently, no uniform language exists that can be used for the different descriptions of the design parts.

Each design level can have its own description language and a corresponding simulator. Only a simulation for the design parts that are covered by the corresponding tools is possible.

This means that at least three different simulator tools and languages must be used, with only a weak possibility of combining the models for a design that has a digital and an analogue part and a system level description. The interfaces between the models are of special interest for the system designer because for the verification of a system not only the parts themselves but also the interface interconnections have to be validated.

6.1.2 IC Design with VHDL-AMS

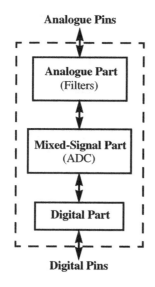

Analogue Pins

Analogue Part
(Filters)

Mixed-Signal Part
(ADC)

Digital Part

Digital Pins

- **Mixed-signal design with filter, ADC and digital part**
- **Digital part: VHDL description**
- **Analogue part: AMS description**
- **Simulation of whole circuit possible**
- **One language for the whole design**
- **Designers create system model**
- **System simulation for**
  - System verification
  - Verification of the interaction of components with the system

With the new language, it should be possible to exchange and combine models from different domains without manually translating them. Also, it should be possible to combine models from different vendors.

Instead of different models in various description and modelling languages, all parts of a design can now be described in VHDL-AMS. The design can then be simulated in parts or as a whole.

One example of a VHDL-AMS application is the design of integrated circuits that contain digital and analogue parts (mixed-signal chips). As integration density grows, it is no longer necessary to split the digital and analogue parts onto different chips, so only one language is needed to simulate the whole design and the interaction between its parts. When VHDL-AMS is used for the design of all parts of the chip, no translation between the models has to be done.

6.1.3   Application Fields in System Design

Example: Automobile

- **Simulation of different domains with one simulator**

- **Basis: System models of different parts**

- **Interaction between domains**

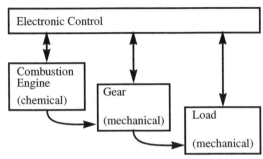

The electrical part itself is only a part of the entire system. An automotive model, for example, also consists of mechanical and chemical parts. Instead of building up a prototype, it can be much faster and cheaper to simulate the system or parts of it.

Like on the circuit level, VHDL-AMS aims to provide a language to simulate all the different domains. For the electrical part, system models from the circuit designers can be used.

6.1.4 Discrete System–Continuous System (1)

Discrete

- **State change:**
  - Discontinuous
  - At countable moments

Continuous

- **State change:**
  - Steady
  - Every moment

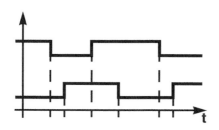

6.1.5 Discrete System–Continuous System (2)

Discrete

- **Assignments**
- **Events**
- **Bits**
- **Difference equations**

Continuous

- **Equations**
- **Internal time steps**
- **Real numbers**
- **Differential equations**
- **Nonlinear equations**

```
process (B,D)
begin
  A <= B;
  C <= B + D;
end process;

E <= F + G;
```

```
procedural
begin
  A := B'dot;
  C := B * B;
end procedural;

E == F + G;
```

6.1.6   Discrete System–Continuous System (3)

Discrete
- Isolated computations
- Delta cycles
- Timesteps

- Fast computation
- High abstraction level
- No continuous signals

Continuous
- Matrix inversion
- Numeric integration
- Linearizing

- Slow computation
- Modelling of physical laws
- No frequency limit

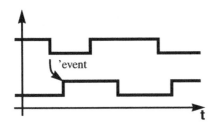

$$u = A^{-1}*b$$

Discrete (digital) systems change their states unsteadily at countable moments, in contrast to the state changes of continuous (analogue) systems. Analogue systems change their states steadily. Consequently, an exact analogue simulation between any two moments would take an infinite number of calculation steps. The balance between the accuracy of the results and calculation effort, the degree of abstraction, is a major problem in the simulation of analogue signals. Mixed-signal simulation can expand the degree of abstraction by transferring parts of a system into a digital model.

Discrete systems are described by events and processes. They can form a set of difference equations. Analogue systems are in general described by a set of nonlinear differential equations. In the electrical domain, they correspond to ideal analogue circuit elements, such as resistors, capacitors or operational amplifiers.

To compute a discrete time step in a digital system, only the variables that are explicitly modelled need be considered. To compute an analogue time step, all variables forming the analogue system have to be considered. For the solution of the analogue model, linearization, numerical integration and the solution of a linear equation system is necessary.

The simulation of digital systems is usually faster than the computation of analogue models. That means that every simulation is a compromise between high precision and costly computation times in the analogue domain and low precision and short computation times in the digital domain.

6.1.7   Simulation Cycle (1)

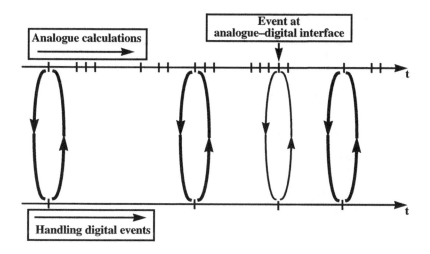

A set of computations of the analogue equations is executed between the digital evaluation points. The digital evaluation points can consist of several delta cycles. The time step of the analogue simulator is determined by the internal algorithm of the simulator, which means it cannot be defined by the user.

It is possible to specify the maximum period of time that may elapse between two evaluations of the value of a quantity; see Section 6.2.5.

6.1.8   Simulation Cycle (2)

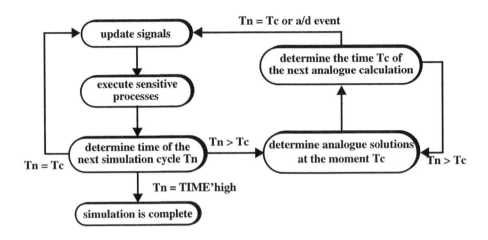

The simulation starts with the initialization phase, where the initial values of the signals are computed and the processes are executed until they suspend. The initial analogue equation system is determined using the initial equations from the break statements (see Section 6.2.15). The simulation cycle itself starts with a computation of analogue solution points. This continues until the next digital event is scheduled or an event occurs at the analogue–digital interface. To compute a digital evaluation point, signals are updated. After that, processes are executed. If the time for the next digital evaluation **Tn** is equal to **Tc**, the digital simulator is called again (delta cycle). If **Tn** is not equal to **Tc**, the analogue solver is called, and the next cycle begins. This continues until the end of the simulation is reached (**Tn = TIME'high**).

6.1.9   Analogue–Digital Coupling

- **Two different time steps in analogue and digital parts**
- **Synchronization necessary**
- **Small time steps with synchronization at every time step is very time-consuming**
- **Better: synchronization only when necessary by rolling back in the analogue part**

The analogue and digital solvers use different time steps. This reduces the simulation time, but a mechanism is necessary to exchange data between the analogue and digital parts at the correct time. This problem arises because the analogue solver cannot anticipate when a synchronization point will occur, which means when a threshold will be crossed. So the time when the synchronization point is computed by the analogue solver might be some time after the actual synchronization point. To compute the synchronization point, the analogue simulator has to roll back and compute the analogue network again at the actual synchronization point. After that, the digital solver may be called, which itself might send back signals to the analogue solver.

6.2 New VHDL-AMS Language Elements

Analogue modelling elements

- **Quantity**
- **Terminal**
- **Nature**
- **Tolerance**
- **Spectrum + noise**

Connectivity statements

- **Sequential break statement**
- **Concurrent break statement**
- **Attributes**

Attributes

- **AD interaction**
- **Differential operators**
- **Other attributes**

Statements

- **Simultaneous statements**
- **Simultaneous procedural statement**

The new language elements give the possibility of writing analogue models; this means describing a physical fact as a set of mathematical equations. The results of these equations describe the behaviour of the model at a certain simulation time or at a certain operation frequency, depending on the value of the signal '**DOMAIN**'.

The predefined signal '**DOMAIN**' can have the values '**QUIESCENT_DOMAIN**', '**TIME_DOMAIN**' or '**FREQUENCY_DOMAIN**'. Because '**DOMAIN**' is an unresolved data type, and the solver kernel drives the signal, it is not permitted to have a driver for the '**DOMAIN**' signal in the model.

Parts of the analogue results can be used to trigger events, that affect other parts of a mixed signal design. The coupling of an analogue model and a digital part of the design is done by the different versions of the break statement and some attributes of analogue terms. To describe a analogue model in VHDL-AMS, equations are written in simultaneous or procedural statements. The term 'Object' has a special meaning in VHDL and VHDL-AMS. There are only six classes of objects: constants, signals, variables, files, terminals and quantities. So there are two new objects introduced in VHDL-AMS: terminals and quantities. Natures are bound to terminals. They describe a specific physical field. Natures define some aspects of physical facts that belong together.

Due to the well-known fact that no analogue solver is able to calculate exact results from (nonlinear) equations, a tolerance has to be introduced. This allows the solver to interrupt calculation if the error is smaller than a given tolerance.

Uncertainties or other influences on the analogue model can be described by noise simulation.

6.2.1 Natures

nature	across	through
electrical	voltage	current
thermal	temperature	heat flow rate
mechanical	velocity	power

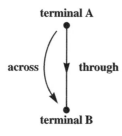

- **Across:** potential difference between two terminals
- **Through:** flux through the connection of two terminals
- **Across** and **through** form a branch
- **More than one connection possible between two terminals**

To model a part of the characteristics of a physical object, the nature of this object has to be declared. A nature can describe every possible physical scenario where a potential difference in an object occurs. It can also describe a flux between two points of potential difference in this object. In general, a nature description covers a special field of physics, i.e. physical aspects that belong together.

Examples:

- thermal issues like heat and heat flow, thermal capacity of an object, thermal resistance;
- electrical issues like electrical networks with voltages and currents;
- pneumatic issues like pressure;
- mechanical tasks.

Terminals belong to their nature. The nature declares its across type and through type. A reference for the across type of the nature is also declared.

6.2.2 Types of Natures

```
subtype VOLTAGE is
  real tolerance "voltage";
subtype CURRENT is
  real tolerance "current"
nature ELECTRICAL is
  VOLTAGE across
  CURRENT through
  GROUND reference;
```

- **Scalar natures**

  - Across and through aspect of type floating point
  - Reference is a terminal identifier

```
nature ELECTRICAL_VECTOR is
  array (NATURAL range <>)
        of ELECTRICAL;
```

```
nature ELECTRICAL_BUS is
  record
     STROBE : ELECTRICAL;
     DATABUS: ELECTRICAL_VECTOR
  end record;

nature THERMAL is
  record
     ELJUNCTION :ELECTRICAL;
     THJUNCTION :THERMAL;-- illegal
  end record;
```

- **Composite natures**

  - Array: consists of identical elements
  - Record: elements must have the same simple nature

There are two types of natures: scalar natures and composite natures.

A scalar nature is defined by the 'across type', the 'through type' and the reference terminal. Each type or subtype can have a tolerance, which is a string expression that denotes a tolerance group. The across type defines the physical potential; the through type defines the flux. The reference declaration is a terminal identifier; the across and through types are called branch types of the nature. All potential differences that occur in the model and belong to the denoted nature are related to the reference potential, e.g. **GROUND** for electrical systems.

A composite nature is either an array of one scalar nature or a record of several natures of the same base nature. It is used to bundle natures of the same type that belong together. Then, groups of terminals (buses) can be defined, which have a single (terminal) name. A composite terminal is bound to a composite nature.

6.2.3 Terminals

```
entity EXAMPLE is
  port(terminal INP, OUTP: ELECTRICAL;
       terminal T : THERMAL;
       terminal B : ELECTRICAL_BUS);
end entity EXAMPLE;

architecture BHV of EXAMPLE is
  terminal K1, K2, K3: ELECTRICAL;
  ...
  begin
    ...
end architecture BHV;
```

- **Connection point (port)**
- **Physical characteristics**
- **Bound to terminal nature**
- **Internal nodes in architectures**
- **Terminals together with branch quantities describe a netlist**

 Terminals are not directed

A terminal denotes a fixed point in the structure of the physical model and defines the nature of this point. In a physical interpretation, every terminal is assigned a potential.

It can be used for the description of ports (interface terminal). In this case, the terminals are connected with branch quantities, which are defined in the architecture of the module that is one hierarchy step above.

It also denotes internal points of an architecture belonging to an entity that models a physical object. Here the terminals are connected internally. A terminal can be a node of a network in the electrical domain. See Section 6.2.5.

Together with a terminal declaration, its reference and its contribution quantity are declared; see Section 6.2.11

6.2.4 Quantities

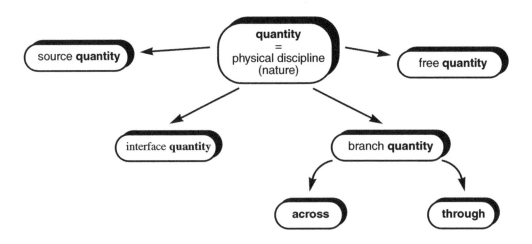

A quantity represents a physical magnitude. It can describe the direction of a flux and the flux type (its nature), and it can connect terminals and can build a branch of a netlist. It can also denote a physical characteristic such as the capacity of a capacitor or the resistance of a wire. This is called a free quantity. A source can be described by a quantity too.

It can have aspects that model the type of the quantity:

An across aspect describes the potential difference between two points. Each quantity that is used in this aspect is an across quantity. In electrical systems the across quantities describe the voltages in a network.

The through aspect describes a flux between two terminals. The quantities used for this are called through quantities. In electrical models the current fluxes are modelled as through quantities.

The terminal aspect denotes the terminals concerned. Usually two terminal names are given here. If the second terminal is omitted, the reference terminal of the nature of the first terminal is used instead (electrical: **GROUND**). If the terminals have composite natures then the lengths of the arrays or records must be the same. Each nature at a distinct place in the record or array of one terminal must have an equivalent counterpart at the nature bound to the other terminal.

The source aspect is either a spectrum, which describes magnitude and phase of a source, or a noise expression.

A branch quantity must have either an across aspect or a through aspect or both. It also must have a terminal aspect.

Another kind of quantity is an interface quantity; see Section 6.2.6.

6.2.5 Branch Quantity

```
package ELECTRICAL_SYSTEM is
  subtype VOLTAGE is real;
  subtype CURRENT is real;
  nature ELECTRICAL is
    VOLTAGE across
    CURRENT through
  ...
end package ELECTRICAL_SYSTEM;
```

- **nature** electrical
  package electrical_system
  library IEEE.Disciplines

```
architecture ARC of ENTITY_1 is
  quantity V1 across
        IA, IB through K1 to K2;
  quantity V2 across K2 to K3;
  ...
begin
  ...
end architecture ARC;
```

- **In architecture declaration part**
- **Directional (between two terminals)**

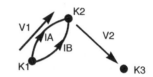

```
limit quantity_list : type_mark
     with real_expression;
```

- **Step limit specification**

```
limit V1 : VOLTAGE with 0.1
```

All natures and subtypes of a special physical field should be declared in packages.

In the example package **ELECTRICAL_SYSTEM** the subtypes **VOLTAGE** and **CURRENT** are declared, which have both the type **real**. A tolerance aspect could also be defined here. The most important line of this example is the declaration of the nature **ELECTRICAL**. Here the across and through types of the terminals of every model that uses this package (and nature) are declared. These types are called branch types of the nature.

K1, **K2**, **K3** are of nature **ELECTRICAL**. There could be an entity that defines those terminals as ports (**terminal K1,K2,K3 : ELECTRICAL;**), or they could be internal nodes of the netlist, which are defined in the declarative part of the architecture.

It is possible to specify the maximum period of time that may elapse between two evaluations of the value of a quantity.

The type_mark of the step limit specification must be the same as the type_mark of the quantity. For quantity_list, the reserved words 'all' or 'others' can be used. Like in the VHDL 'case' statement, the term '**all**' denotes all quantities that are listed in the declarative part of the design bloc;, '**others**' denotes the quantities that do not have yet a step limit specification and are also listed in the declarative part.

Each quantity can have only one step limit.

In the example, **V1** has at least 10 analogue solution points in the simulation time interval $\Delta t=1$.

6.2.6 Interface Quantity

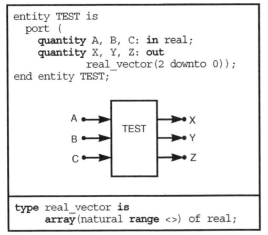

```
entity TEST is
  port (
    quantity A, B, C: in real;
    quantity X, Y, Z: out
            real_vector(2 downto 0));
end entity TEST;
```

- **Directed signal flow**

- **Input- / output signal in the portlist of a entity, otherwise in the architecture**

- **Node assignment (input, output) and data type**

- **Data type: real**

```
type real_vector is
     array(natural range <>) of real;
```

- **Vector presentation: real_vector**

⚠ Directed signal flow

In contrast to a terminal, the interface quantity is a directed connection port between entities. Possible modes are '**in**' and '**out**'. An interface quantity belongs to a type of port interface declarations. Port interface declarations appear in the port clause of the entity header.

Port interface declarations can be quantity declarations, signal declarations or terminal declarations.

Interface quantities can be used in signal flow diagrams, where directed signals (quantities) between two hierarchy levels are needed.

6.2.7 Tolerance

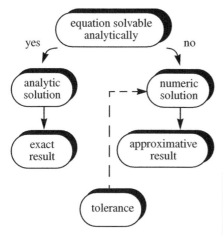

- **In general differential equations have no analytic solution**

- **Tolerance value determines the quality of the solution**

- **Every quantity and every equation belong to a tolerance group**

- **Tolerance group defined by the user**

- **Tolerance is string expression**

```
quantity cur:real tolerance "current";
X == Y'Dot tolerance "low_voltage";
```

The language itself does not define how tolerances are used and what they do exactly. It is left to the tool how the tolerance characteristics are calculated. This enables the writer of the model to change the behaviour of the solver by specifying the tolerance group for the components of his model.

The tolerance group for a quantity can be determined in the subtype of the quantity or at the quantity declaration. It can also be defined in the nature declaration for a terminal. Each through aspect or across aspect can have a tolerance aspect where the tolerance group of the branch quantity is declared.

If tolerances overlap or tolerance groups for a quantity are redeclared, the tolerance for a quantity is determined as follows:

If a quantity has a tolerance aspect itself then this tolerance group is used. If no tolerance is declared in the quantity declaration then the tolerance group of the (sub-)types of the used quantities or terminals are used.

Simultaneous statements can also have a tolerance aspect. This aspect overrides all other previously declared tolerances.

In general, subsequently declared tolerances have priority.

6.2.8   Frequency and Noise

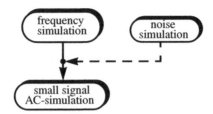

```
architecture FREQ of I_SOURCE is
  quantity SPEC: CURRENT
              spectrum MAG, PHASE;
  quantity THNS: CURRENT
        noise sqrt(4.0*CONST/TEMP);
  quantity I through P to M;
      ...
begin
  I == AMPL * sin (2.0*PI*FREQU*NOW) +
                    SPEC + THNS;
end architecture FREQ;
```

- **Frequency simulation**

  - Spectral source: magnitude + phase
  - Predefined word: SPECTRUM

- **Noise simulation**

  - Support in the frequency domain
  - Noise source: magnitude spectrum
  - Predefined word: NOISE

In the example both possibilities for source quantities are listed.

The calculation of frequency and noise behaviour is done in a small signal model. This is created by calculating a quiescent point from the characteristic expressions of the model. Then the characteristic equations concerned are linearized around the quiescent point.

For a given frequency, the frequency domain value for each quantity is determined.

Noise calculation is done in a similar manner: for a given frequency, the noise value is determined. For noise calculations, power considerations are used.

All calculations are done with complex values.

6.2.9   Analogue–Digital Interface

- **Analogue signal Q crosses a threshold E**
  - Event for digital part
  - Attribute: Q'above(E)

- **If value of Q-E is sufficiently larger than 0.0:**
  Q'above(E) is TRUE;
  if sufficiently smaller: FALSE;
  else: Q'above(E)'delayed

- **Expression E need not be a static name**

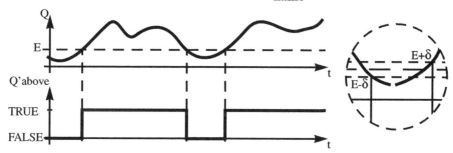

Analogue-to-digital coupling is done by the attribute **'above(E)**.

The term sufficiently larger implies that there is a hysteresis in signal change. The result of **Q'above(E)** stays **FALSE** as long as the quantity **Q** has not reached the upper boundary of **E**, which is **E+δ**.

Q'above(E) stays **TRUE** as long as the quantity **Q** is bigger than **E-δ**, which is the lower boundary of **E**. The size of δ is not defined by the language. It is implementation-dependent and could be treated like a tolerance.

Due to the fact that the result type of **Q'above(E)** is a (digital) boolean signal, an event is generated at every signal change. The digital part of the design will react on this event if a concurrent statement reads this signal or if the sensitivity list of a process contains this signal, or if an equivalent wait statement in a process without sensitivity list is triggered.

The calculation of the hysteresis is done by a **'delayed** attribute, see Section 6.2.12. The default delay is 0, so the delayed quantity stays at the same value as long as the result of **Q'above(E)** does not change.

6.2.10 Attributes for Natures and Terminals

Attribute	Description	Result Type
N'across	Across type of N	Across type of N
N'through	Through type of N	Through type of N
T'reference	Across quantity between T and its reference terminal, see Section 6.2.11	Across type of the nature of T
T'contribution	Contribution quantity of terminal T, see Section 6.2.11	Through type of the nature of T
T'tolerance	Get tolerance group of T	String

The attributes for natures can be used to get information about the elements of the nature. Usually the types used in the nature declaration are subtypes.

Example: If **N** is of nature **ELECTRICAL**, its across type **N'across** is **VOLTAGE**, which is a subtype of type **real**. Its through type **N'through** is **CURRENT**, which is also a subtype of type **real**.

The argument **T** of **T'tolerance** may be a floating point type or subtype.

6.2.11 Attributes for Terminals

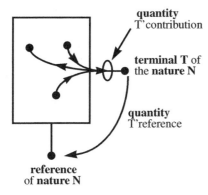

* **T'reference**

    * Represents an across quantity
    * Voltage between a terminal and a reference node (i.e. ground)
    * From terminal plus to terminal minus

* **T'contribution**

    * Represents a through quantity
    * Value is equal to the sum of all through quantities connected to the terminal

The attributes for the terminals give information about connected branch quantities.

The plus terminal of **T'reference** is always **T**; the minus terminal is the reference of the nature of this terminal. The reference is defined in the corresponding nature of the terminal.

The contribution quantity returned by **T'contribution** has the through type of the nature of terminal **T**. It is the (signed) sum of all through quantities that are connected to this terminal.

6.2.12 Attributes for Quantities

Attribute	Description	Result Type
Q'tolerance	Tolerance	String
Q'dot	Derivative of time	Same as Q
Q'integ	Time integral	Same as Q
Q'delayed[(TI)]	Time-delayed quantity	Same as Q
Q'above(E)	See Section 6.2.9	Boolean
Q'ltf(NUM,DEN)	Laplace transfer function	Base type of Q
Q'zoh(T [,INIT_DELAY])	Zero-order hold	Base type of Q
Q'ztf(NUM,DEN,T[, INIT_DELAY])	Z-domain transfer function	Same as Q
Q'slew[(MAX_RISING_SLOPE [,MAX_FALLING_SLOPE])]	Maximal slew rate of a quantity; see Section 6.2.13	Base type of Q

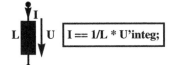

Parameters:

TI:	Type real, default is 0.0
E:	Expression of the same type as Q
NUM:	Type REAL_VECTOR, contains numerator coefficients
DEN:	Type REAL_VECTOR, contains denominator coefficients
INIT_DELAY:	Type REAL, first sample after INIT_DELAY

At **Q'tolerance**, only a scalar quantity is allowed.

6.2.13 Attributes for Signals

Attribute	Description	Result Type
S'ramp[(TRISE[,TFALL])]	Follows signal with a ramp	Base type of S
S'slew[(RISING_SLOPE[,FALLING_SLOPE])]	Follows signal with a slope	Base type of S

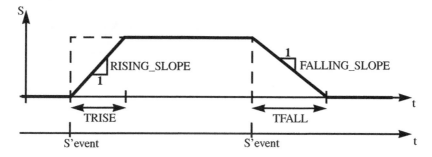

S'ramp is a quantity that follows the signal **S** (dashed line). The rise time is given by the parameter **TRISE** and the fall time by the parameter **TFALL**.

S'slew is a quantity that follows the signal **S**. The slope for rising and falling signals is defined by the parameters **RISING_SLOPE** and **FALLING_SLOPE**.

The signal **S** must be of type floating point.

6.2.14 Example: Simple Diode Model

```
entity DIODE is
  port (terminal A : electrical;
        terminal C : electrical);
end entity DIODE;

architecture EQ of DIODE is
  quantity VD across ID,IC through A to C;
  quantity QC: real;
  constant VT : voltage := 0.026;
  constant IS0 : real := 1.0e-14;
  constant TAU : real := 1.0e-15;
  constant RD : real :=0.0;
  begin
    ID == IS0 * (exp((VD-RD*ID)/VT)-1);
    QC == TAU*ID tolerance "charge";
    IC == QC'dot;
end architecture EQ;
```

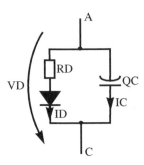

In the simple diode model some of the above-mentioned features of VHDL-AMS are implemented. In the entity of the diode model, two terminals with the nature **ELECTRICAL** are declared. These are the electrical ports to the outside of the model. With the help of these ports, a netlist with this diode as an instance can be modelled. The behaviour of the diode is described in the architecture, which belongs to the entity above. Several quantities are defined:

A branch quantity, which connects the two terminals 'A' and 'C' with its terminal aspect. Its through aspect defines two currents '**ID**' and '**IC**'. Its across aspect denotes the voltage between the terminals.

A free quantity, which denotes the charge of a capacitor, is also defined.

The electrical behaviour is modelled in several equations, so-called simultaneous statements; see Section 6.2.17.

Each simultaneous statement (as well as each quantity) belongs to a certain tolerance group, which is denoted by a string expression. The quantity on the left-hand side of the statement gets its tolerance group from the quantity on the right-hand side. Another possibility is to set the tolerance group explicitly in the statement: **QC == TAU*ID tolerance "charge";**

6.2.15 Concurrent Break Statement

```
[label:] break [break_list]
[on sensitivity_list] [when condition];
```

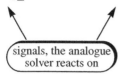

signals, the analogue
solver reacts on

Equivalent process statement:

```
[label:] process
begin
  break [break_list] [when condition]
  wait [on sensitivity_list] | [on name];
end process;
```

- **Represents a process containing a break statement**
- **Models discontinuities**
- **Handling like sequential break**
- **Sensitivity_list (digital event)**
  - Event triggers break
  - Restarts analogue calculations
- **Condition**
  - Expression triggers break
  - Restarts analogue calculations
- **Break_list**
  - New initial values or equations for analogue solver

The break statement will be needed if there is a discontinuity in the model. A discontinuity can be a physical circumstance, e.g. a bouncing ball reaching the ground, or an event from the digital part of the model that affects the analogue part. In both cases, the analogue solver has to be reinitialized and calculates new solutions, or the equations have to be adapted to the new physical facts.

The concurrent break statement has an equivalent description as a sequential break statement in a process. For the VHDL designer the sequential break in a process is easier to understand:

The wait statement of the process reacts on its sensitivity list and allows execution of the process. The sensitivity list of the wait statement is either the sensitivity list of the break statement or the names of the signals, quantities, etc. in the condition of the concurrent wait statement. This means: Whenever a signal in the sensitivity list changes, the process is executed. A break will be triggered if the condition of the break statement is TRUE.

Name denotes signals that appear in the condition clause of the break statement.

6.2.16 Sequential Break Statement

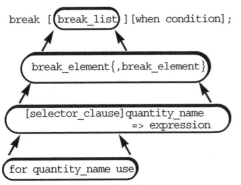

- **Discontinuity of an equation => reset of quantity value can be necessary**

- **Break_elements: quantities are replaced by the expressions**

- **Selector_clause: affected quantity must be of the form Q'dot or Q'integ**

- **Without conditions: quantities are initialized at simulation start time**

Initialization of analogue solver with condition:

Initialization of analogue solver without condition:

`Q == C * V;`
`I == Q'dot;`
break for `Q` **use** `V => INIT`
`        `**when** `INIT /= real'low;`
	break `A => 0.0;`
	
	break `X => 1.5, Y => 0.0, Z => 20;`

`I == C * V'dot;` **break** `V => INIT` **when** `INIT /= real'low;`	

If a break statement is executed, its break list is evaluated. If a selector clause exists, the quantities (derivatives or integrals) denoted in the selector clause are affected by the discontinuities. This means that each equation with an integral or derivative of a quantity listed in the selector clause is reinitialized by the rules declared in the break list. If no explicit selector clause exists, the quantity_name(s) of the break list acts as selector clause. All quantities with the accordant name are replaced by the expression statement(s) of the break list. The analogue solver uses the expression(s) as initial values for a recalculation of the equations.

The impact on the examples (Initialization with condition) is as follows:

Whenever 'INIT' changes its value and is not equal to **real'low**, the charge 'Q' of the capacitor is recalculated by $Q == C*INIT$.

Then the new value (because the selector clause says: **for Q use...**) is used to recalculate the current by $I == Q'dot$.

If the derivatives or integrals are directly accessible, the selector clause is not necessary. The wait statement for the second example would be:

wait for V use V => INIT when INIT /= real'low;

In this case the equation is $I == V'dot$. The quantity is accessible and a derivative, so the quantity in the selector clause is redundant.

6.2.17 Simultaneous Statements

Example DIODE model:

```
ID == IS0 * (exp((VD-RD*ID)/VT)-1);
QC == TAU*ID tolerance "charge";
IC == QC'dot;
```

Simultaneous Statements

- **Set of differential and algebraic equations (DAEs)**

- **Describe a continuous system**

- **Discontinuities or initialization done by break statements**

- **Basis for non-digital systems**

- **Based on natures (electrical, mechanical, thermal)**

There are several simultaneous statements:

The 'simple simultaneous statement' is an expression, usually denoting an equation. It can have a tolerance aspect. The 'simultaneous if statement' chooses different simple simultaneous statement parts depending on the condition of the if statement. The 'simultaneous case statement' chooses different simple simultaneous statements, depending on the condition of the case statement. The 'simultaneous procedural statement' will be used if it is necessary to handle statements sequentially. This means that the equations written in the body of the simultaneous procedural statement are handled in the order in which they appear. The evaluation of a 'simultaneous null statement' has no effect.

All simultaneous statements are concurrent, which means that the order in which they appear in the source code is not important for the calculation of any result.

6.2.18 Simultaneous Procedural Statement

```
procedural [is]
  procedural_declarative_part;
begin
  procedural_statement_part;
end procedural;
```

- **In the architecture**
- **Statement_part handled sequentially**
- **Declarative_part:**
  constants, variables, attributes, ...

```
architecture SIMPLE of DAC is
begin
  procedural
    variable CONV: real = 0.0;
  begin
    for I in D_VECTOR'right to
            D_VECTOR'left loop
      if D_VECTOR(I) = '1' then
        CONV := real(2**i) + CONV;
      end if;
    end loop;
    ANALOG := CONV;
  end procedural;
end architecture SIMPLE;
```

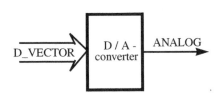

 Statements in simultaneous procedural statements are processed sequentially

The simultaneous procedural statement is used for calculations over several lines of code that have to be handled sequentially. This is suitable for large equation systems, for loops or recursions. The simultaneous procedural statement is the analogue counterpart of the (digital) process statement. It can be interrupted by a break statement or a wait statement.

Important: The statements in a procedural are the same as in digital VHDL; the break statement as sequential statement is an additional option.

The assignments of quantities are done by the ':=' operator.

The whole statement is part of the analogue equation set and is processed simultaneously.

6.2.19 Simultaneous If/Case Statement

```
if condition use
  {simultaneous statement;}
{[elsif condition use
  {simultaneous statement;}]}
[else
  simultaneous statement;]
end use;
```

- **Used as in digital VHDL**
- **Piecewise-defined signals**
- **Intergradations**

```
if VIN < VLOW use
  VOUT == MAX;
elsif VIN < V0 use
  VOUT == SLOPE1 * VIN;
elsif VIN < VHIGH use
  VOUT == 0.0;
else
  VOUT == SLOPE * (VIN - VHIGH);
end use;
```

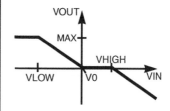

```
case expression use
  when choices =>
    {simultaneous statement;}
  [when {choices} =>
    {simultaneous statement;}]
end case;
```

Simultaneous '**if**' statements, as well as simultaneous '**case**' statements, can be used for describing conditions in physical models. Elements such as a limiter or the reaction of the model on switched signals (digital) can be modelled this way.

Like the '**if**' statement and the '**case**' statement in digital VHDL, the analogue counterparts follow the same rules:

If a condition of an '**if**' or '**elsif**' is '**TRUE**', the statements in following sequence are executed in the order the '**if**' and '**elsif**' appear.

The choices of the '**case**' expression must be exhaustive and mutually exclusive. Like in digital VHDL, a '**when OTHERS use ...**' statement is possible to fulfil this requirement.

6.3   Modelling

6.3.1   Analogue Modelling Modes

Signal flow   **Network**

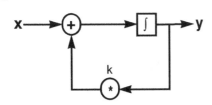   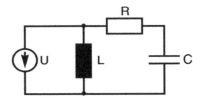

- **Modelling of transfer functions**   · **Modelling of a system of nonlinear**
- **Signal flow is directed**   **differential equations**
- **No implicit feedback on the previous**   · **Network is undirected**
  system components   · **Feedback between components**
- **Non-conservative system**   · **Conservative system**

Analogue systems can be modelled as signal flow graphs or networks. Normally, signal flow descriptions are used on the system level, whereas network descriptions are used when a detailed model is necessary. Most linear networks can be transformed into a signal flow description. This can reduce the simulation time, especially when the network does not contain many reactive elements. Signal flows have a flow direction; networks have no flow direction. The direction of the current is used to define the sign of the current variable only.

6.3.2 Networks

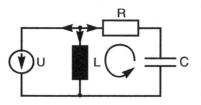

- **Based on Kirchhoff's laws**
  - Kirchhoff's current law
  - Kirchhoff's voltage law
- **Based on a nature (e.g. electrical)**
  - Through quantities
  - Across quantities
- **Modelling of a set of differential equations**
- **Simulator has to solve a matrix**
- **Algorithms for linearizing and numeric integration necessary**
- **Relatively high simulation time**
- **No signal flow direction**

Networks are the most flexible and detailed form for modelling. The mathematical foundations, Kirchhoff's current and voltage laws, allow application in different domains, such as the electrical and mechanical domains. Networks allow implicit feedback and the computation of continuous signals. This detailed simulation needs a lot of simulation time. The simulation time increases with the number of variables and the number of connections between the nodes.

6.3.3   VHDL-AMS vs. SPICE

SPICE

- **Modelling of elements**
- **Behavioural modelling difficult**
- **Low flexibility**
- **VHDL-AMS models usually cannot be converted**
- **Computation time mostly independent of modelling style**
- **Nodes**

VHDL-AMS

- **Modelling of differential equations**
- **Easy behavioural modelling**
- **Higher flexibility**
- **Spice models can be converted into VHDL-AMS**
- **Computation times depend on modelling style**
- **Code is often longer**

`r.rl N1 N2 = 5`	`terminal N1, N2;`
	`quantity CUR through VLT across N1 to N2;`
	`CUR == VLT / 5;`

VHDL-AMS is, in a way, the successor of the SPICE-syntax. VHDL-AMS includes the modelling of the SPICE syntax, so SPICE models can be converted automatically into VHDL-AMS. The modelling in VHDL-AMS, however, is much more flexible, because all relations inside a branch that can be expressed in an equation can be used. To solve these equation systems, the existing solution algorithms have to be extended. The example shows a resistor model in SPICE and VHDL-AMS.

6.3.4 DAEs

- **Extended description of the systems by:**

  algebraic equations
  differential equations ==> **DAEs** (Differential and Algebraic Equations)

- **Representation: $\underline{F}(d\underline{X}/dt, \underline{X}, t) == \underline{0}$**
  - $\underline{F}$:= vector of expressions
  - $\underline{X}$:= vector of unknowns
  - t := time
  - [number of equations] = [number of unknowns] --> solution possible

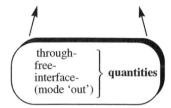

When modelling network equations, the user has to make sure that the system is solvable. The most important condition is that the number of (independent) equations equals the number of unknowns. Also, the system should have exactly one solution point. In some cases, several solutions are possible. This is a problem because the user cannot predict which solution will be found by the simulator. The last problem is the finding of the solution when nonlinear equations are included. Especially when these nonlinear equations are non-monotonous, the iterative solution algorithm might be unable to find the solution.

In all these cases the user has to modify the equations so that the simulator can find a solution.

6.3.5 Signal Flows

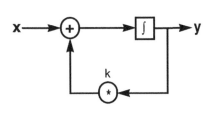

- **Only through quantities**
- **Kirchhoff's laws do not apply:**
  - Energy may scale:
  - Non-conservative system
- **Modelling of nonlinear differential equations**
- **Signal flow is directed**
- **No backlash on the previous system components**
- **No solution of system matrix necessary**
- **Simulation is relatively fast**

Signal flow charts represent a description in the Laplace level. Normally they are used to model a system where the transfer function is given. They can be an effective way to describe the behaviour of a system.

VHDL WORKSHOP

1 Introduction

This VHDL teaching program is divided into several exercises. By writing typical VHDL programs, you learn how to use this hardware description language. In the beginning you are guided in a step-by-step manner; later on when you are used to the language and the tools you will solve the tasks on your own. We are referring to the VHDL'87 standard, because the VHDL'93 is not yet supported by all tool manufacturers.

1.1 Structure of the Exercises

The tasks are divided into different sections:

- **Synopsis**: In this section you learn about the goal of the task and the function of the model within the whole design.
- **Behaviour**: This section tells you more about the function of the model.
- **Data Types**: In this section the types to be used in the current exercise are described.
- **To Do**: Here is the precise description of your job to solve the task.
- **Implementation**: Here you find a list of VHDL code that represents a possible implementation.

1.2 Style Guide

In VHDL it is very important to have a consistent naming. The following naming conventions should be followed within this workshop:

File name:	**mydesign.vhd**	for the VHDL file
Entity name:	**MYDESIGN** **TB_MYDESIGN**	for the model for the test bench
Architecture name:	**RTL** **TEST**	for RTL code for the architecture of the test bench
Configuration name:	**CFG_TB_MYDESIGN**	for the configuration of the test bench
Type definition name:	**T_<TYPE_NAME>**	a leading T_ ...

1.3 Design Structure

The goal of this course is the design of a camera control system. Its main focus is to demonstrate the application of the hardware description language VHDL in a real-world setting. Of course, the problem has been heavily simplified, but it is powerful enough to point out all main concepts of the language to the beginner. After completing the course you should feel comfortable writing VHDL code on your own.

The camera control system has to generate the appropriate signals for the lens shutter and the film transportation motor. It also generates the input signals for a small 7-segment display showing either the current exposure time or the total number of pictures taken so far. The user controls the camera operation via several keys.

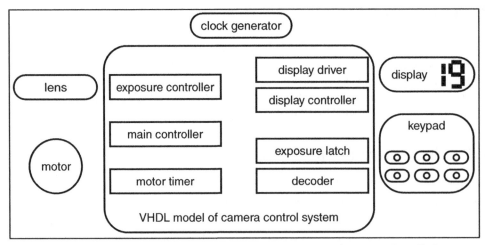

The central control system that is to be developed during this course is split into seven modules, as shown in the above figure:

- A decoder (**decoder**) is used to preprocess the signals from the input device for the controller.
- The exposure latch (**exp_ff**) stores the selected exposure time.
- A timer for the film transport (**motor_timer**) is used to detect errors during film transportation, e.g. if the film is torn apart.
- The exposure controller (**exp_ctrl**) opens the lens shutter for the selected exposure time and counts the number pictures that have been taken.
- The photo controller (**main_ctrl**) is the central control unit for the camera control system.
- A specialized display controller (**disp_ctrl**) selects the appropriate data for the 7-segment display.
- The display driver (**disp_drv**), finally, converts the internal data signals into a format suitable for the output device.

The clock frequency of the camera control is 8192 Hz. It allows for exposure times according to the following formula: 2^{-i} seconds (for $i = 0..9$). You need this information later on in order to implement the required times. The camera control system has to:

- determine the exposure time,
- take a (sequence of) picture(s),
- generate the exposure control signal,
- generate a control signal for the servo that transports the film,
- detect the end of the film and tears in the film while transporting the film.

2   VHDL Working Environment

In order to follow the exercises, you will need an editor to enter the code. It is advisable to use an editor with a VHDL language mode, as this facilitates the detection of typographic errors in VHDL keywords. The notorious Emacs disposes of a powerful VHDL macro set with templates for most language constructs, special copy-and-paste functions for signal lists, and much more.

As the VHDL simulators cannot deal with ASCII text immediately, your designs need to be compiled into a machine-readable format first. After the proper behaviour has been verified, a synthesis tool is used to map the RTL description to a network of gates. In addition to the software package, you will also need a library containing a description of the properties of all available cells.

The goal of this pre-exercise is to get used to the simulation and synthesis tools, and to learn the basic commands of the tools used. As there are a great variety of tools, we can give only very generally descriptions of the tasks to do. This exercise does not require any specific VHDL knowledge. In order to get used to the tools, refer to the corresponding user manuals of the software tools used and proceed through the following steps.

2.1   Directory Structure

First, you will need a directory where you can store the VHDL source code files. In the following, we assume that ~/workshop is the base directory for this project. It is advisable to separate the VHDL sources from their derived files, i.e. we will create a subdirectory ~/workshop/WORK for the analysed objects.

2.2   Working Environment

The simulation and synthesis software can have their own setup files, especially if you are using tools from different producers. The principles for initializing the software are quite often similar. Consult your software documentation for detailed information.

2.2.1   Simulation Setup

Normally a setup file has to be created. You can do this either by hand with an editor (save the file in the current, it is the ~/workshop directory) or within a menu of the software used.

Example:

`TIMEBASE = NS`	Defines the time scale (nanoseconds) for the simulation.
`WORK    >    DEFAULT` `DEFAULT :    ./WORK`	The VHDL library WORK is mapped to the logical library DEFAULT. The physical path for this library is ./WORK, i.e. the analysed files will be stored there (~user/workshop/WORK).
`USE = .`	List of directories where the simulator searches for the VHDL source code.

2.2.2   Synthesis Setup

Normally a setup file has to be created. You can do this either by hand with an editor (save the file in the current, it is the ~/workshop directory) or within a menu of the software used. If you use a framework, perhaps only one setup file for simulation and synthesis is needed.

Example:

`search_path = search_path + { . }`	Adds current directory to the search path.
`define_design_lib work -path` `  ./WORK`	Defines library for the analysed files (~user/workshop/WORK).

`link_path      = { vendorlib.db }`
`target_library = { vendorlib.db }`
`symbol_library = { vendorlib.sdb }`
`link_library   = { vendorlib.db }`
	Define the link, target, and symbol library of the target library.

2.3   VHDL Code

The design flow that will be followed throughout the exercises will be demonstrated at the example of a simple AND-gate. Create a file named and_gate.vhd in your VHDL sources directory (~/workshop) and enter the following code:

```
library IEEE;
use IEEE.std_logic_1164.all;

entity AND_GATE is
port (A,B : in  std_logic;
      Z   : out std_logic);
end AND_GATE;

architecture RTL of AND_GATE is
begin
   Z <= A and B;
end RTL;
```

2.4 VHDL Compiler

Before you will be able to simulate the design, you have to compile your ASCII sources. A so-called analyser (sometimes also called "compiler", "reader", ...) is used for this purpose. The resulting files are stored in the default library, which is mapped to the directory ./WORK in the simulation setup file. If you need to compile your sources into a different library, refer to the corresponding user manual. Of course, the other library has to be mapped to a physical directory as well.

Remember that the VHDL design units have to be analysed in a certain order. You will have to observe the following rules in order to avoid compilation errors (sometimes the software will do this for you):

- **Main units have to be analysed before side- or subunits**
    - entity before architecture
    - package before package body

- **Units that others refer to have to be analysed first**
    - package before entity/architecture
    - entity/architecture before configuration

The referenced standard package std_logic_1164 is already available in compiled format, i.e. you just have to analyse the entity AND_GATE before its RTL architecture. As the entity description is located in front of the architecture definition in the source code, just compile this file and you will be ready to simulate the design.

2.5 VHDL Simulator

In order to verify the proper behaviour of your VHDL code, you will also need to create testbenches that stimulate your design. The testbench for the AND gate contains the instantiation of the device under test (DUT) and a simple stimulus process that assigns all possible signal combinations to the component inputs.

Create the file tb_and_gate.vhd and enter the following VHDL code:

```
library IEEE;                          STIMULI : process
use IEEE.std_logic_1164.all;           begin
                                           W_A <= '0';
entity TB_AND_GATE is                      W_B <= '0';
end TB_AND_GATE;                           wait for 10 ns;

                                           W_A <= '1';
                                           wait for 10 ns;

architecture TEST of TB_AND_GATE is        W_B <= '1';
    component AND_GATE                      wait for 10 ns;
        port (A, B : in  std_logic;
              Z    : out std_logic);       W_B <= '0';
    end component;                          wait for 10 ns;

    signal W_A, W_B, W_Z : std_logic;          wait;
begin                                      end process STIMULI;
                                       end TEST;
    DUT : AND_GATE
        port map(A => W_A,             configuration CFG_TB_AND_GATE of
                 B => W_B,                                 TB_AND_GATE is
                 Z => W_Z);                for TEST
                                           end for;
                                       end CFG_TB_AND_GATE;
```

Prior to simulation you will also have to compile the file, i.e. run the VHDL analyser (e.g. 'myanalyser and_gate.vhd'; or you have to select a menu entry, e.g. 'analyse').

Now you are ready to invoke the VHDL simulator if this has not already been done. If it is not done automatically, you have to choose the object to simulate and specify additional simulation parameters. Remember that the configuration is the only VHDL object that can be simulated. Some tools require no (top-) configuration as they build up a default configuration on their own. In this case you can select the top entity for simulation (here it would be TB_AND_GATE). In the other case select CFG_TB_AND_GATE and press OK to open the simulation control window. The next points describe features that are common to most simulation tools:

- The source code currently simulated is shown in a window. Normally you can change the content of this window by moving up and down in the design hierarchy.

- In another window some status information (current hierarchy level, current simulation time, etc.) is given and there are a couple of shortcut buttons for the most commonly used commands.

- Sometimes there is a command interface to the simulator, e.g. a command line at the very bottom of the display.

- Normally you can move your design hierarchy using commands or a design hierarchy browser. The design hierarchy is mostly presented like a file system (UNIX: '/' denotes the root of the hierarchy, '..' the previous level). In this example, the first hierarchy level contains your testbench (/TB_AND_GATE) and the referenced packages (/STD_LOGIC_1164 and /STANDARD), which is always loaded.

- In order to view the data in a waveform display, you will have to invoke the waveform display tool. Sometimes this is done automatically when you start the simulation.

Make sure that all signals of your testbench are being traced during simulation (refer to the user manual of the simulation software used).

- **Simulation Control**
  - The actual simulation cycle is started with the a 'run' command (or button). If no additional options are given, the simulator normally stops when no signals need to be updated anymore. In this example, the simulator will stop after 40 ns.
    Optionally, you may specify a maximum run time, e.g. 'run 100' to display the signal values for 100 ns.
  - If you have, for example, a clocked design and want to simulate just one clock cycle at a time, it is convenient to enter the clock period as an argument of the 'run' command. Perhaps you have to fix the simulation step width in a menu entry.
  - You may stop the simulation cycle either by setting breakpoints or with a manual interrupt. Of course, the simulation will also be stopped if an VHDL assertion with the appropriate severity level is violated or if a runtime error occurs.
  - There exist two breakpoint variants: the 'Stop at' function halts the execution when the corresponding VHDL code line is reached. Note, however, that in this case probably not all signals carry their new values for the current time step. The 'Event Bkpt.' function enables you to interrupt the simulation whenever the selected signal changes its value.
  - Once the simulation is stopped, you can normally proceed stepwise via a 'step' and/or 'next' command.
  - Normally the simulation tool creates a history (file) of the commands you entered. So you can repeat your simulation by loading this history.

2.6   VHDL Synthesis

After you have verified the function of your model with the simulator, you can run the synthesis tool. Again you have to analyse the VHDL source code. This is normally done automatically when you read in your VHDL file.

- Read the file "and_gate.vhd" (via File -> Read). Go through the tool messages to check whether your design is conform to the synthesis subset supported by your synthesis tool. In general only a subset of the 1076-VHDL standards is supported. This subset is now (end of 1999) standardized but not so far supported by the tools.

In future tasks/exercises we will define our own packages. The synthesis tool requires that packages are read (analysed) before they are used or referenced. The most frequent errors with the synthesis are missing not read (analysed) packages!

- Sometimes you can examine your design after you have read in the source file. This representation is called generic netlist. (Translation of the VHDL code in a set of tool specific symbolic gates).
- Most tools are optimizing for area if no specific synthesis constraints are set. Use the defaults constraint settings and start the design optimization (the actual synthesis; refer to your user manual).

- You will now get a netlist that is optimized for the selected target library (see Section 2.2.2: Synthesis Setup).

- Examine the gate-level implementation. Normally commands for zooming in and out, features for highlighting special paths, analysis functions and report generators are available.

  The report of the area (ASIC) needed or percent of available resources (FPGA) used, the maximum clock frequency possible and sometimes an estimation of the power consumption are interesting reports.

3 Exercises

3.1 STEP 1: A Multiplexer

3.1.1 Synopsis

Your first task is to write the VHDL description of a multiplexer. The camera display will either show the number of pictures that have already been taken or the current exposure time. The following figure shows a schematic of the multiplexer:

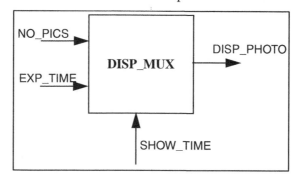

- **Behaviour:**

  The multiplexer output will be equal to its EXP_TIME input when the control signal SHOW_TIME is '1'. Else, DISP_PHOTO be set to NO_PICS.

- **Data types:**

  As EXP_TIME and NO_PICS hold whole-numbered values, **integer** is the natural data type for the data signals. **Bit** might be the natural choice for the SHOW_TIME control signal as it holds only two reasonable values. However, you should use **std_ulogic** instead, as multivalued logic is especially suited to model actual hardware.

- **To do:**
  - Create a VHDL model of the multiplexer.
  - Use your VHDL compiler to find and eliminate all syntax errors.
  - Create a testbench to verify the proper behaviour.
  - Compile the testbench.
  - Run the simulation. Trace the signal values in a waveform display for verification.
  - Synthesize the model using your favourite synthesis tool.

3.1.2 Implementation

Implementation of the multiplexer:

```
library ieee;
use ieee.std_logic_1164.all;




entity DISP_MUX is
  port(EXP_TIME    : in  integer;
       NO_PICS     : in  integer;
       SHOW_TIME   : in  std_ulogic;
       DISP_PHOTO  : out integer);
end DISP_MUX;

architecture RTL of DISP_MUX is
begin


  process(SHOW_TIME, NO_PICS, EXP_TIME)
  begin

    if SHOW_TIME = '1' then
      DISP_PHOTO <= EXP_TIME;
    else
      DISP_PHOTO <= NO_PICS;
    end if;
  end process;
end RTL;
```

- **As the std_ulogic data type is used for the control signal SHOW, the std_logic_1164 package needs to be referenced. It is located in the IEEE library.**

- **Interface definition according to the specification.**

- **As the VHDL code will be synthesized, the architecture is called RTL.**

- **The multiplexing algorithm is implemented as a process with sensitivity list. All signals that are read in the process have to be listed in order to obtain the same behaviour on RT and gate levels.**

- **An if construct always results in a multiplexer.**

Testbench for the DISP_MUX module:

```
library ieee;
use ieee.std_logic_1164.all;

entity TB_DISP_MUX is
end TB_DISP_MUX;



architecture TEST of TB_DISP_MUX is
  component DISP_MUX
    port(EXP_TIME    : in integer;
         NO_PICS     : in integer;
         SHOW_TIME   : in std_ulogic;
         DISP_PHOTO  : out integer);
  end component;

  signal W_EXP_TIME    : integer    := 0;
  signal W_NO_PICS     : integer    := 0;
  signal W_SHOW_TIME   : std_ulogic := '0';
  signal W_DISP_PHOTO  : integer;
```

- **The testbench is always the top level of the hierarchy, i.e. it does not have an interface to other modules.**

- **The device under test (DUT) has to be declared before it can be used in the architecture.**

- **The signals that are connected to the DUT need to be declared as well. All signals acting as DUT stimulus are also initialized.**

Testbench for the DISP_MUX module:

```
begin                -- architecture
  DUT : DISP_MUX
    port map (
      EXP_TIME    => W_EXP_TIME,
      NO_PICS     => W_NO_PICS,
      SHOW_TIME   => W_SHOW_TIME,
      DISP_PHOTO  => W_DISP_PHOTO);

  STIMULI : process
  begin
    wait for 30 ns;
    W_NO_PICS   <= 2;
    W_EXP_TIME  <= 64;
    wait for 20 ns;
    W_NO_PICS <= 10;
    wait for 20 ns;
    W_SHOW_TIME <= '1';
    wait for 20 ns;
    W_NO_PICS <= 20;
    wait for 20 ns;
    W_SHOW_TIME <= '0';
    wait for 20 ns;
    wait;
  end process;
end TEST;

configuration CFG_TB_DISP_MUX of
                TB_DISP_MUX is
  for TEST
  end for;
end CFG_TB_DISP_MUX;
```

- **Instantiation of the DUT.**

- **Stimulus process.**

- **Plain wait statement: Stop process execution**

- **The default configuration may be used for the testbench as the component name of the DUT matches the entity name.**

3.1.3 Results

The waveform display shows that DISP_PHOTO always holds the current value of the selected input port. Changes to this value are transferred to the output immediately whereas modifications to the other port do not affect the output. Thus the multiplexer behaves as specified. When inspecting the synthesized result, note that the bus width for the data signals is 32 bits. This is because their data type was specified as integer without any range restrictions. Generally, omitting the range specification will result in a waste of resources. This is one of the reasons for a redesign of the multiplexer as the next step.

3.2 STEP 2: Extending the Multiplexer

3.2.1 Synopsis

As the module will be used to multiplex single-digit values later on, the bus widths need to be adjusted. This is easily done by specifying a range for all data signals that are of type integer.

Additionally, error conditions will also be signaled to the user via the camera display. Therefore an additional control input named ERROR is needed. The following figure shows the updated schematic:

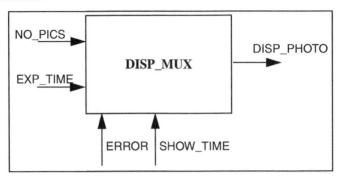

- **Behaviour:**

  DISP_PHOTO will be set to '10' when the ERROR signal is active. Otherwise, the multiplexer behaviour will not be changed, i.e. the output will be equal to the EXP_TIME input when the control signal SHOW_TIME is 1. Else, DISP_PHOTO will be set to NO_PICS.

- **Data types:**

  All data signals (NO_PICS, EXP_TIME, DISP_PHOTO) will be of type **integer** with a range of valid values from 0 to 10. The new control signal ERROR will be of type **std_ulogic**, like the SHOW_TIME signal.

- **To do:**
  - Modify the existing multiplexer model.
  - Compile your design.
  - Modify the testbench according to the changes of the DISP_MUX interface and create new stimuli to verify the proper behaviour.
  - Compile the testbench.
  - Run the simulation.
  - Synthesize the model.

3.2.2 Implementation

Modified DISP_MUX module:

```
library ieee;
use ieee.std_logic_1164.all;

entity DISP_MUX is
  port(EXP_TIME    : in  integer
                          range 0 to 10;
       NO_PICS     : in  integer
                          range 0 to 10;
       SHOW_TIME   : in  std_ulogic;
       ERROR       : in  std_ulogic;
       DISP_PHOTO  : out integer
                          range 0 to 10);
end DISP_MUX;

architecture RTL of DISP_MUX is
begin
  process (SHOW_TIME, NO_PICS, EXP_TIME,
           ERROR)
  begin
    if SHOW = '0' then
      DISP_PHOTO <= NO_PICS;
    else
      DISP_PHOTO <= EXP_TIME;
    end if;

    if ERROR = '1' then
      DISP_PHOTO <= 10;
    end if;
  end process;
end RTL;
```

- **Data signals restricted to 4 bits (0–10).**
- **New ERROR signal.**

- **The ERROR signal is read during process execution, i.e. it must be added to the sensitivity list.**

- **As the ERROR signal is checked last, all previous signal assignments will be overwritten.**

3.3 STEP 3: A 7-Segment Display Driver

3.3.1 Synopsis

As the data has to appear on a 7-segment display it is not sufficient just to multiplex the incoming signals. The information also has to be transformed from a binary representation into a vector of seven driver signals, one per display element. In order to enhance the readability of the VHDL code, constants should be used to represent the various numbers, i.e.

```
constant SEG_8 : std_ulogic_vector(6 downto 0):= "1111111";
```

The package P_DISPLAY contains the definitions SEG_0 to SEG_9. They define which segment to drive for which number. The additional definition SEG_E can be used if an error occurs, and should be assigned to the number 10.

The new design will be called DISP_DRV and provides basically the same functionality as the DISP_MUX module. The main difference is that the output signal is now called DISPLAY and its width is now seven bits in order to drive the 7-segment display. The former output port DISPLAY_PHOTO will be used as an internal signal from now on. This is necessary because the input signals cannot be multiplexed directly to the new output signal DISPLAY since they are of a different data type.

The following figure shows the block diagram of the new design:

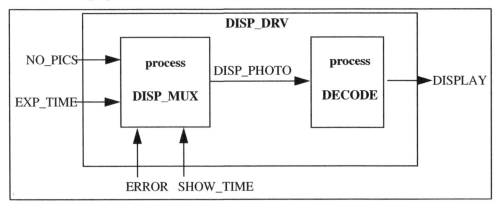

- **Behaviour:**

    The DISP_MUX process is the same as in the previous exercise. Additionally, you have to write a decoder process that maps the integer values of DISP_PHOTO to their corresponding DISPLAY values.

- **Data types:**

    A (large) VHDL design is usually developed by a team. Therefore it is reasonable to define common data types for common signals. This is done by defining one package, which is then referenced by all designers. In our case the two signals NO_PICS and EXP_TIME will be of type **T_DIGITS**. The output signal DISPLAY will be of type **T_DISPLAY**. These data types are defined in the package P_DISPLAY, together with the constants for the 7-segment display.

- **To do:**

    - Copy the previous design DISP_MUX to DISP_DRV.
    - Adapt the module interface (port names and data types) and add the internal DISP_PHOTO signal.
    - Add a new process to map the integer values to display driver signals.
    - Generate a testbench for the new design. It may be easiest to copy the old testbench and to adapt it to the new interface. The stimulus generation need not be changed as the functionality of the multiplexer has not been changed.

        It is error-prone to verify the decoder process via the waveform display. The DISPLAY_DIGIT procedure from the P_DISPLAY package allows you to display the seven segments graphically in a text file. Use the concurrent statement DISPLAY_DIGIT(DISPLAY) in your testbench to update the file contents whenever the DISPLAY signal changes.

    - Compile all source files (packages first!) and run the simulation.
    - Synthesize the design.

3.3.2   Implementation

The display driver code:

```
library ieee;
use ieee.std_logic_1164.all;
use work.P_DISPLAY.all;


entity DISP_DRV is
  port(ERROR      : in  std_ulogic;
       SHOW_TIME  : in  std_ulogic;
       NO_PICS    : in  T_DIGITS;
       EXP_TIME   : in  T_DIGITS;
       DISPLAY    : out T_DISPLAY);
end DISP_DRV;

architecture RTL of DISP_DRV is
  signal DISP_PHOTO : T_DIGITS;
begin


  DISP_MUX:process (SHOW_TIME, ERROR,
                    EXP_TIME, NO_PICS)
  begin


    if ERROR = '1' then
      DISP_PHOTO <= 10;
    elsif SHOW_TIME = '0' then
      DISP_PHOTO <= NO_PICS;
    else
      DISP_PHOTO <= EXP_TIME;
    end if;
  end process DISP_MUX;

  DECODE: process (DISP_PHOTO)
  begin
    case DISP_PHOTO is
      when 0     => DISPLAY <= SEG_0;
      when 1     => DISPLAY <= SEG_1;
      when 2     => DISPLAY <= SEG_2;
      when 3     => DISPLAY <= SEG_3;
      when 4     => DISPLAY <= SEG_4;
      when 5     => DISPLAY <= SEG_5;
      when 6     => DISPLAY <= SEG_6;
      when 7     => DISPLAY <= SEG_7;
      when 8     => DISPLAY <= SEG_8;
      when 9     => DISPLAY <= SEG_9;
      when others => DISPLAY <= SEG_E;
    end case;
  end process DECODE;
end RTL;
```

- **Include the declarations from the P_DISPLAY package. The library WORK is always known and need not be declared.**

- **User-defined data types are now used for the data ports.**

- **An internal signal is needed to link the two processes together.**

- **The process label is used to enhance readability, as two processes are present in this architecture.**

- **Instead of a separate if statement (as in the previous example) an if-elsif-else construct is used here.**

- **The decoder is activated whenever the multiplexer changes its output.**

- **As there does not exist a priority for the different values of DISP_PHOTO, a case statement is used to map the integer value to the bit vector.**

- **Only the values 0–9 will be displayed as digits. In all other cases the user will get an 'E'rror.**

3.4   STEP 4: A Three Digit 7-Segment Display Driver

3.4.1   Synopsis

In the final version, DISP_DRV has to drive a 7-segment display with three digits. Other than that, the design need not be modified. The most convenient way to handle the data within the design is to define a new type, i.e. an array of three integer, respectively bit vector, values. As user-defined types are already used, it is only necessary to change the definition of T_DIGITS, respectively T_DISPLAY.

It is one of the main advantages of using project-specific packages in bigger projects that the interface of the different modules is easily changed by modifying the type definition. Of course, it is also necessary to change the VHDL code accordingly. The multiplex process is already almost finished as the control signals have not changed. It is just the assignment of 10 in case of an error that must be augmented to be an array of '10's that is assigned.

The mapping functionality itself is also correct. The decoder process, however, needs to be modified as all three integer values have to be mapped to their corresponding vector representation. The easiest solution is to place the case statement that performs the actual decoding within a loop that processes one digit per iteration.

- **Behaviour:**

  The basic behaviour remains unchanged.

- **Data types:**

  The names of the data types of the signals remain the same. It is just the definition of the **T_DIGITS** and **T_DISPLAY** types that has to be changed to an array type.

- **To do:**

  - Edit the P_DISPLAY package so that T_DIGITS and T_DISPLAY are arrays of type integer and std_ulogic_vector, respectively. The length of the arrays will be 3. Do not forget to include the range specification for the array elements!

  - Adjust the two processes of the DISP_DRV architecture so that they cope with the new data types.

  - Modify the stimuli generation in the testbench to verify the correct behaviour.

  - Compile all source files and run the simulation.

  - Synthesize the design.

3.4.2   Implementation

The modified display driver code:

```
...
DISP_MUX:process (SHOW_TIME, ERROR,
                  EXP_TIME, NO_PICS)
begin
  if ERR = '1' then
    DISP_PHOTO <= (10, 10, 10);
  elsif SHOW_TIME = '0' then
    DISP_PHOTO <= NO_PICS;
  else
    DISP_PHOTO <= EXP_TIME;
  end if;
end process DISP_MUX;

DECODE: process (DISP_PHOTO)
begin
  for I in T_DISPLAY'range loop
    case DISP_PHOTO(I) is
      when 0       => DISPLAY(I) <= SEG_0;
      when 1       => DISPLAY(I) <= SEG_1;
      when 2       => DISPLAY(I) <= SEG_2;
      when 3       => DISPLAY(I) <= SEG_3;
      when 4       => DISPLAY(I) <= SEG_4;
      when 5       => DISPLAY(I) <= SEG_5;
      when 6       => DISPLAY(I) <= SEG_6;
      when 7       => DISPLAY(I) <= SEG_7;
      when 8       => DISPLAY(I) <= SEG_8;
      when 9       => DISPLAY(I) <= SEG_9;
      when others => DISPLAY(I) <= SEG_E;
    end case;
  end loop;
end process DECODE;
```

- **Entity and declarative part of the architecture remain unchanged.**

- **As data types have to match, an array of 3 integer values is needed for the assignment to DISP_PHOTO, i.e. the single integer value has been replaced by an aggregate construct.**

- **The loop variable I is implicitly declared by the for statement.**

- **The 'range signal attribute is used for the loop range for better reusability.**

3.5   STEP 5: A Decoder

3.5.1   Synopsis

The camera has a different button for each exposure time, i.e. the data signals from the keypad are transferred via a 10-bit data bus. If a button is pressed, the corresponding wire is set to 1.

The exposure times are calculated according to the following formula:
time(button) = $2^{(-button)}$, for button=0..9 (time in seconds).

The result (1/1 s, 1/2 s, 1/4 s, ..., 1/512 s) will be shown on the 7-segment display. Thus another decoder is needed. We will not introduce any new VHDL concepts in this exercise but suggest that you try out different implementations and observe their impact on the synthesis result.

The block diagram of the new module is rather simple:

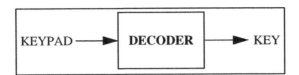

- **Behaviour:**

    As already mentioned, the functionality of this module is fairly simple. The denominator of the following calculation will be coded in a suitable form for the 7-segment display:

    $2^{\wedge}(\text{-button}) = 1 / (2^{\wedge}(\text{button})) = 1/1, 1/2, 1/4, 1/8, ..., 1/512$ (button = 0..9)

    It is up to you to decide about the behaviour when more than one button is pressed. There are basically two options: either the buttons have a certain priority or the user input is ignored.

- **Data types:**

    The input data is generated by an external keypad and consists of 10 wires, one per button. Thus a **std_ulogic_vector** is used for the KEYPAD signal. The decoded values will be processed by the display logic, i.e. **T_DIGITS** is the most suitable data type.

- **To do:**

    - Create new files for the decoder entity and its architectures if you want to try out different implementations. Remember that synthesis tools ignore the VHDL configuration and use the most recent architecture.

    - Generate a testbench for the new design and add stimuli that cover "illegal" user input (more than one button pressed simultaneously).

    - Compile the VHDL code (package->entity->architectures->configurations).

    - Simulate the configurations and look out for differences in the behaviour.

    - Synthesize the architectures and find out about their area and maximum delay from input to output.

3.5.2 Implementation

The decoder entity:

```
library ieee;
use ieee.std_logic_1164.all;
use work.P_DISPLAY.all;

entity DECODER is
  port (KEYPAD : in  std_ulogic_vector
                             (9 downto 0);
        KEY    : out T_DIGITS);
end DECODER;
```

- **The use clause is only valid for the very next following design unit. However, it applies automatically to any secondary units, i.e. these statements need not to be repeated in the architecture files.**

The decoder architecture based on a case structure:

```
architecture RTL_CASE of DECODER is
begin
  process(KEYPAD)
  begin
    case KEYPAD is
      when "1000000000" => KEY <= (5,1,2);
      when "0100000000" => KEY <= (2,5,6);
      when "0010000000" => KEY <= (1,2,8);
      when "0001000000" => KEY <= (0,6,4);
      when "0000100000" => KEY <= (0,3,2);
      when "0000010000" => KEY <= (0,1,6);
      when "0000001000" => KEY <= (0,0,8);
      when "0000000100" => KEY <= (0,0,4);
      when "0000000010" => KEY <= (0,0,2);
      when "0000000001" => KEY <= (0,0,1);
      when others        => KEY <= (0,0,0);
    end case;
  end process;
end RTL_CASE;
```

- **The input signal is a vector numbered 9 down to 0. Thus the signal that refers to button 9 is the leftmost signal of the data bus.**

- **The input is decoded only if a single button is pressed. All other inputs are ignored.**

The decoder architecture based on a if-elsif structure:

```
architecture RTL_IF of DECODER is
begin
  process(KEYPAD)
  begin
    if    KEYPAD(0) = '1' then
      KEY <= (0,0,1);
    elsif KEYPAD(1) = '1' then
      KEY <= (0,0,2);
    elsif KEYPAD(2) = '1' then
      KEY <= (0,0,4);
    elsif KEYPAD(3) = '1' then
      KEY <= (0,0,8);
    elsif KEYPAD(4) = '1' then
      KEY <= (0,1,6);
    elsif KEYPAD(5) = '1' then
      KEY <= (0,3,2);
    elsif KEYPAD(6) = '1' then
      KEY <= (0,6,4);
    elsif KEYPAD(7) = '1' then
      KEY <= (1,2,8);
    elsif KEYPAD(8) = '1' then
      KEY <= (2,5,6);
    elsif KEYPAD(9) = '1' then
      KEY <= (5,1,2);
    else
      KEY <= (0,0,0);
    end if;
  end process;
end RTL_IF;
```

- **A different name is used for this architecture, which makes it possible to select the implementation via the VHDL configuration mechanism.**

- **This implementation defines a priority for the buttons. The display value is generated as soon as a '1' is detected in the incoming signal. (0,0,0) appears only if none of the keys is pressed.**

- **It is also possible to compare the entire KEYPAD signal with fixed values (if KEYPAD= "1000000000" ...) In this case, both architectures would show the same behaviour in simulation. The synthesis result will also be the same if the compiler is able to detect that the conditions do not overlap.**

The configuration for the decoder unit:

```
configuration CFG_TB_DECODER of
                        TB_DECODER is
  for TEST
    for all : DECODER
      use entity work.DECODER(RTL_CASE);
      -- use entity work.DECODER(RTL_IF);
    end for;
  end for;
end CFG_TB_DECODER;
```

- **The configuration creates a simulatable object and may be placed in a separate file.**

- **Here the default configuration has been replaced with the VHDL code to switch between the two alternatives.**

3.6   STEP 6: A Register

3.6.1   Synopsis

When an exposure time is selected by the user it has to be stored. Edge-triggered flip flops are used for this purpose. The contents of the register are updated only with the rising edge of the clock signal. In this way, differences in the path delay become irrelevant as long as the maximum delay is shorter than the clock period.

In addition to the clock signal, a second enabling condition is needed in this case. Valid exposure times will be stored until another exposure time is selected. Only legal button combinations are mapped to display values other than (0,0,0) by the decoder, i.e. it is sufficient to exclude this value triple from being stored.

The reset input signal is necessary to be able to bring the chip into a defined state, e.g. after power-up.

The complete interface of the register is shown in the following figure:

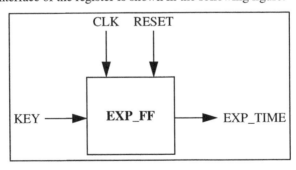

- **Behaviour:**

    The reset will be implemented asynchronously, i.e. a process with sensitivity list is the only viable option in this case. The following template for clocked processes has to be used:

```
if RESET
   ...
elsif RISING_CLOCK_EDGE
   ...
```

After a rising clock edge has been detected, it must be checked whether a key was pressed. If yes, the new exposure time is stored in the register.

- **Data types:**

  The exposure latch is used to store the exposure time, i.e. **T_DIGITS** is the appropriate type for the data signals. CLK and RESET are single-bit control signals and will therefore be of type **std_ulogic**.

- **To do:**

  - Write a new file with the VHDL description of the exposure latch.
  - Write a testbench to verify the design. The periodic clock signal generation should be placed in a separate stimuli process!
  - Compile and simulate the design.
  - Synthesize the module.

3.6.2 Implementation

The exposure latch code:

```
library ieee;
use ieee.std_logic_1164.all;
use work.P_DISPLAY.all;

entity EXP_FF is
port(CLK          : in  std_ulogic;
     RESET        : in  std_ulogic;
     KEY          : in  T_DIGITS;
     EXP_TIME     : out T_DIGITS);
end EXP_FF;

architecture RTL of EXP_FF is
begin
  process(CLK, RESET)
  begin
    if (RESET = '1') then
      EXP_TIME <= (0,0,1);

    elsif (CLK'event and CLK = '1') then



      if (KEY /= (0,0,0)) then
        EXP_TIME <= KEY;
      end if;
    end if;
  end process;
end RTL;
```

- **As the reset signal is evaluated asynchronously, it has to be included in the sensitivity list.**

- **The following code is executed after each rising clock edge.**

- **The decoder output is set to (0,0,0) if no or several keys are pressed. Other values signal a valid exposure time that has to be stored.**

3.7 STEP 9: A State Machine for the Display

3.7.1 Synopsis

In order to control the 7-segment display, a simple state machine is necessary. In addition to the buttons for the desired exposure time, another special button is present on the camera panel that allows the user to switch between the current exposure time and the number of pictures that have already been taken.

If one of the exposure time buttons is pressed, the display will have to show the corresponding exposure time immediately. Otherwise, the display should toggle between exposure time and number of pictures whenever the SWITCH button is pressed.

The figure below shows the module interface:

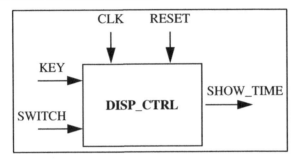

- **Behaviour:**

  Valid selections of a new exposure time are signaled by KEY values other than (0, 0, 0). Illegal combinations are filtered out by the keypad decoder module. Thus SHOW_TIME has to be set to '1' if KEY is not equal to (0,0,0).

  The SWITCH signal cannot be used directly to toggle the display as the button will be pressed down for much longer than the clock period. If the signal level is used for the decision, the display will flicker as it switches between picture count and exposure time every 100 microseconds. Therefore a register is needed that stores the last value of the SWITCH signal.

  The button has just been pressed when the SWITCH signal is '1' and has been '0' during the last clock cycle. Then the SHOW_TIME signal is inverted. Due to the fact that signals declared as out cannot be read by processes within the entity, an additional display state signal is also needed.

- **Data types:**

  All control signals will be of type **std_ulogic**, as usual. Thus only the KEY signal has a different data type, namely **T_DIGITS** from the P_DISPLAY package.

- **To do:**
    - Write a new file with the VHDL description of the display controller.
    - Write the corresponding testbench.
    - Compile and simulate the design.
    - Synthesize the module.

3.7.2   Implementation

The VHDL code for the display controller:

```
library ieee;
use ieee.std_logic_1164.all;
use work.P_DISPLAY.all;

entity DISP_CTRL is
  port (CLK        : in   std_ulogic;
        RESET      : in   std_ulogic;
        SWITCH     : in   std_ulogic;
        KEY        : in   T_DIGITS;
        SHOW_TIME  : out  std_ulogic);
end DISP_CTRL;

architecture RTL of DISP_CTRL is
  signal SHOW_STATE: std_ulogic;
begin
  SHOW_TIME <= SHOW_STATE;



  process (CLK, RESET)
    variable LAST_SWITCH: std_ulogic;
  begin
    if (RESET = '1') then
      LAST_SWITCH := '0';
      SHOW_STATE   <= '0';



    elsif (CLK'event and CLK = '1') then
      if KEY /= (0,0,0) then
        SHOW_STATE <= '1';
      else
        if LAST_SWITCH = '0' and
           SWITCH = '1' then
          SHOW_STATE <= not(SHOW_STATE);
        end if;
      end if;

      LAST_SWITCH := SWITCH;
    end if;      -- end of clocked process
  end process;
end RTL;
```

- **The internal SHOW_STATE signal is connected directly to the SHOW_TIME port. In this way the signal can be read by the processes of the entity.**

- **Variables that might be read before they are updated infer flip flops that have to be reset as well.**

- **If an exposure time is selected, the display will show that time value.**

- **Else, we have to wait for a rising edge of the SWITCH signal.**

- **The current level of the SWITCH signal is stored for comparison in the next clock cycle.**

3.8   STEP 7: A Timer

3.8.1   Synopsis

After a picture has been taken, the film is transported forward automatically. In order to detect malfunction, e.g. end of film or a torn film, a transport supervision module needs to be implemented. If the servo motor has not finished the film transport after 2 seconds, an error signal is generated.

The timeout function is generated with the help of a counter. As the clock frequency is 8192 Hz, 2 seconds correspond to a maximum value of 16383 (=14 bits). The CLK and RESET signals are needed for the flip flops again.

The start of the film transport is signalled via the MOTOR_GO signal. It is set to '1' when the transportation begins. When the servo motor has finished, the MOTOR_READY signal is set to '1'. An error is reported via the MOTOR_ERROR signal in the same way, i.e. it is set to '1' if the MOTOR_READY pulse has not occurred in time. The signals are active for the duration of one clock period only, in order to make an edge detection dispensable.

The interface of the module is depicted in the following figure:

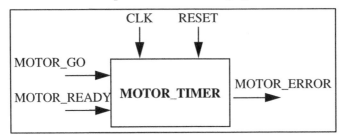

- **Behaviour:**

  Usually, the reset strategy is defined for the complete design. As an asynchronous reset was used in the first clocked module, we have to use the same template for clocked processes as before.

  The timeout counter is started whenever a '1' is detected on the MOTOR_GO signal. The counter is stopped either if the MOTOR_READY signal is set to '1' or if the counter reaches its maximum value. In the last case, the MOTOR_ERROR is set to '1' for one clock cycle.

- **Data types:**

  The module processes and generates control signals only. They are of type **std_ulogic**, as usual. The counter is most easily implemented by a counter variable of type **integer**.

- **To do:**

  - Create a new VHDL file for the MOTOR_TIMER module.
  - Write a testbench to verify the design. The clock period is approximately 122.07 μs, in case you want to use realistic time values for the stimuli generation.

- Compile and simulate the design.
- How many flip flops are generated? Synthesize the design and compare your answer with the synthesis result.

3.8.2 Implementation

The VHDL code for the motor timeout supervision:

```vhdl
library ieee;
use ieee.std_logic_1164.all;

entity MOTOR_TIMER is
  port(CLK         : in  std_ulogic;
       RESET       : in  std_ulogic;
       MOTOR_GO    : in  std_ulogic;
       MOTOR_READY : in  std_ulogic;
       MOTOR_ERROR : out std_ulogic);
end MOTOR_TIMER;

architecture RTL of MOTOR_TIMER is
begin
  process (CLK, RESET)
    variable COUNTER : integer
                        range 0 to 16383;
    variable COUNT   : std_ulogic;
  begin
    if (RESET = '1') then
      COUNTER     := 0;
      COUNT       := '0';
      MOTOR_ERROR <= '0';

    elsif (CLK'event and CLK = '1') then
      MOTOR_ERROR <= '0';

      if MOTOR_GO = '1' then
        COUNT   := '1';
        COUNTER := 0;
      end if;

      if MOTOR_READY = '1' then
        COUNT   := '0';
      end if;

      if COUNT = '1' then
        if COUNTER /= 16383 then
          COUNTER := COUNTER + 1;

        else
          MOTOR_ERROR <= '1';
          COUNT := '0';
        end if;
      end if;     -- if COUNTING
    end if;       -- end of clocked process
  end process;
end RTL;
```

- Only std_ulogic and the predefined integer data type are used in this module.

- Variables are declared within a process. The COUNT flag is used to signal whether the module is actually counting.

- An error should be an exception, i.e. the MOTOR_ERROR signal is set to '0' as default.

- The counter is reset to 0 and the COUNT flag is set when the film transport begins.

- The counter has to be stopped when the motor has finished.

- If we are actually counting...

- The counter is incremented as long as the timeout condition is not fulfilled.

- Else, the counter is stopped and the error is reported.

- For the sake of clarity, the corresponding condition is added as comment after the end of if statements that span many lines

3.9   STEP 8: A BCD Counter

3.9.1   Synopsis

The desired exposure time and the number of pictures are stored in BCD (Binary Coded Decimal) format. This means that every decimal digit is coded by its binary value. Therefore two times 4 bits are needed to represent the decimal number '15'. If a binary representation were used, 4 bits would be enough.

While this representation is convenient for the display driver modules, it makes it a lot harder to do the actual counting. A procedure will be designed that implements a single-digit BCD adder with carry. A complete BCD counter is then generated by calling this procedure for each digit of the counter range.

The start of a new exposure is signalled via TIMER_GO. It is not necessary to detect a rising edge, as this signal is active for the duration of one clock period only. When the start signal arrives, the lens shutter has to be opened. The lens shutter remains open as long as the EXPOSE signal is set to '1'. The picture count (NO_PICS) will be incremented whenever a new picture is taken, i.e. whenever a rising edge of the EXPOSE signal is detected. Additional TIMER_GO signals during the actual exposure of the new picture have to be ignored.

The exposure timer is a bit tricky as only the display values (EXP_TIME) are available as input. It is therefore necessary to map the BCD values to counter limits. Of course, it would be possible to use a single counter. However, it is probably more comprehensible to split the task between two counters as all exposure times are a multiple of 1/512 second. At a clock frequency of 8192 Hz this equals 16 clock cycles. These time steps will be counted by a second counter and will be compared with the counter limits from the mapper.

Have a look at the module interface before you start to design:

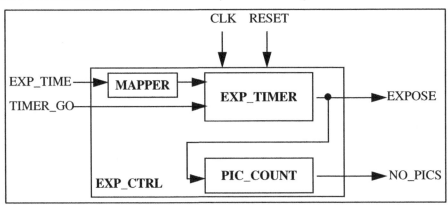

- **Behaviour:**

    A procedure to increment a BCD digit is needed. The digit itself and a carry flag are needed as parameters for this purpose.

    Based on this procedure, a counter for the number of pictures is to be implemented. The value will be incremented whenever a rising edge of the EXPOSE signal occurs.

A combinational process maps the exposure time to the equivalent number of 1/512 s timesteps.

The exposure timer will be realized with another process, and consists of two counters. The first counter will generate the 1/512 s timebase, i.e. a pulse is to be generated every 16th clock cycle. This pulse is used to count the number of timesteps, and the counter value will be compared with the limit that results from the selected exposure time.

It is good design practice in synchronous designs to keep the number of clock domains, i.e. the number of different clock signals for the flip flops as small as possible. This avoids problems during synthesis of the design. Therefore the CLK signal will be used for all registers!

- **Data types:**

  The control signals CLK, REST, TIMER_GO and EXPOSE will be of type **std_ulogic**, as usual. The data signals EXP_TIME and NO_PICS are of the **T_DIGITS** type that is defined in the P_DISPLAY package. An **integer** variable may be used for the binary counter of the exposure timer.

- **To do:**

  - Create the new VHDL file.
  - Write a testbench to verify the design. Use assertions to check the exposure times during the simulation run.
  - Compile and simulate the design.
  - Compare the number of flip flops that you would expect with the synthesis result again.

3.9.2 Implementation

The VHDL code for the exposure controller:

```
library ieee;
use ieee.std_logic_1164.all;
use work.P_DISPLAY.all;

entity EXP_CTRL is
  port(CLK      : in      std_ulogic;
       RESET    : in      std_ulogic;
       TIMER_GO : in      std_ulogic;
       EXP_TIME : in      T_DIGITS;
       EXPOSE   : buffer std_ulogic;
       NO_PICS  : buffer T_DIGITS);
end EXP_CTRL;
```

- **The EXPOSE and NO_PICS signals are generated by this module, but are also read by processes of this entity. Therefore the port mode buffer is used, which allows the signal to be used as input as well. This does not indicate that a buffer cell should be placed on these ports during synthesis!**

The VHDL code for the exposure controller:

```vhdl
architecture RTL of EXP_CTRL is
  signal LIMIT: integer range 0 to 511;



  procedure INC_DIGIT (
    DIGIT        : inout integer;
    CARRY        : inout std_ulogic) is



  begin
    if CARRY = '1' then


      if DIGIT /= 9 then
        DIGIT := DIGIT + 1;
        CARRY := '0';


      else
        DIGIT := 0;
      end if;              -- OVERFLOW
    end if;                -- CARRY = '1'
  end INC_DIGIT;

begin                      -- architecture
  MAPPER: process (CLK, RESET)
  begin
    if RESET='1' then
      LIMIT <= 0;
    elsif (CLK'event and CLK = '1') then
      if EXPOSE = '0' then
        if    EXP_TIME = (5,1,2) then
          LIMIT <=   0;
        elsif EXP_TIME = (2,5,6) then
          LIMIT <=   1;
        elsif EXP_TIME = (1,2,8) then
          LIMIT <=   3;
        elsif EXP_TIME = (0,6,4) then
          LIMIT <=   7;
        elsif EXP_TIME = (0,3,2) then
          LIMIT <=  15;
        elsif EXP_TIME = (0,1,6) then
          LIMIT <=  31;
        elsif EXP_TIME = (0,0,8) then
          LIMIT <=  63;
        elsif EXP_TIME = (0,0,4) then
          LIMIT <= 127;
        elsif EXP_TIME = (0,0,2) then
          LIMIT <= 255;
        elsif EXP_TIME = (0,0,1) then
          LIMIT <= 511;
        end if;
      end if;
    end if;
  end process MAPPER;
```

- **The LIMIT signal will hold the result of the mapping from the exposure time to the number of 1/512 s timesteps.**

- **This procedure implements a single BCD digit increment algorithm. The digit itself and the carry bit are modified "in place", i.e. they have to be of mode inout.**

- **As the carry bit will be added, the operation is carried out only if the carry bit is '1'.**

- **As long as no overflow occurs, a 1 is added to the digit value and the carry bit is reset to 0.**

- **Else, the result would be 10, i.e. the carry bit remains set and the digit value is set to 0.**

- **Abnormal exposure time values will be ignored.**

- **The mapping algorithm is executed whenever the exposure time changes. If a new picture is currently taken (EXPOSE='1') then the exposure time should not be allowed to change. Remember that all signals that might be read in a pure combinational process must be placed in the sensitivity list.**

The VHDL code for the exposure controller:

```
EXP_TIMER: process (CLK, RESET)
  variable COUNT_16: integer
                          range 0 to 15;
  variable TIMER:    integer
                          range 0 to 511;
begin
  if RESET = '1' then
    COUNT_16 := 0;
    TIMER    := 0;
    EXPOSE   <= '0';

  elsif (CLK'event and CLK = '1') then
    if EXPOSE = '1' then

      if COUNT_16 /= 15 then
        COUNT_16 := COUNT_16 + 1;
      else
        COUNT_16 := 0;
        if TIMER = LIMIT then
          EXPOSE <= '0';
        else
          TIMER := TIMER + 1;
        end if;
      end if;
    elsif TIMER_GO = '1' then
      EXPOSE   <= '1';
      COUNT_16 := 0;
      TIMER    := 0;
    end if;
  end if;
end process EXP_TIMER;
PIC_COUNT: process(CLK, RESET)
  variable LAST_EXPOSE: std_ulogic;
  variable CARRY:       std_ulogic;
  variable DIGIT:       integer;

begin
  if RESET = '1' then
    LAST_EXPOSE := '0';
    NO_PICS     <= (0, 0, 0);


  elsif CLK'event and CLK = '1' then
    if EXPOSE      = '1' and
       LAST_EXPOSE = '0' then
      CARRY := '1';
      for I in T_DIGITS'low
             to T_DIGITS'high loop
        DIGIT := NO_PICS(I);
        INC_DIGIT(DIGIT, CARRY);
        NO_PICS(I) <= DIGIT;
      end loop;
    end if;

    LAST_EXPOSE := EXPOSE;
  end if;
end process PIC_COUNT;
end RTL;
```

- The counter of the exposure time is split into 2 parts: a divider by 16 in order to get the 1/512 s timebase and a counter for the number of 1/512 s intervals.

- If the exposure timer is currently active...

- Wait for the end of another 1/512 s interval.

- Restart the timebase counter.

- If the counter limit is reached, the exposure is terminated, else the counter is incremented.

- Otherwise, if no picture is currently being taken, the exposure timer waits for the GO signal.

- In order to detect a rising edge of the EXPOSE signal, the current value must be compared with the last one.

- The CARRY and DIGIT variables are just temporary variables for the BCD counter and do not infer flip flops. Therefore a range specification and a reset value are not necessary.

- If a rising edge of the EXPOSE signal is detected, the picture counter is incremented. The CARRY bit must be set to '1' as initial value for the least significant digit.

- Finally, the current value of the EXPOSE signal is stored for later comparison.

3.10 STEP 9: A State Machine for the Main Controller

3.10.1 Synopsis

A main control unit is needed to coordinate the actions of the different modules. The interface of the module is depicted in the following figure:

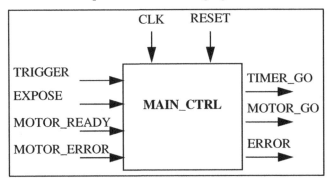

When the trigger button is pressed, the shutter will be opened, and will stay open for the selected exposure time. This is done by setting the TIMER_GO signal one period to high, so the exposure controller opens the shutter for the selected exposure time. After the exposure time has passed, the film has to be transported. So the motor needs a signal to start the transport. Therefore MOTOR_GO is set to high for one period.

Now two things can happen: the motor has successfully transported the film, which is signalled by the MOTOR_READY signal. In this case a new photo can be made by the camera and the TRIGGER signal has to be examined again. Alternatively, an error occurred while transporting the film. In this case the MOTOR_ERROR signal is set and the ERROR output signal has to be set, so the display indicates this case. When the cause of the error is removed (e.g. a new film is inserted) this has to be signalled by the user by pressing the reset button.

- **Behaviour:**

   The current architecture will contain only one finite state machine. For that, a combinational process, a clocked process and the concurrent output assignments are needed. In the clocked process the next state will be stored as the current state with every rising clock edge. Here the flip flops of the state machine are generated.

   In the combinational process the next state will be evaluated in a case statement depending of the current state and the input values of TRIGGER, EXPOSE, MOTOR_READY and MOTOR_ERROR.

   The output values are evaluated and assigned to the outputs in concurrent signal assignments. The expressions in this assignment depend only on the current state. So a Moore machine has to be implemented!

- **Data types:**

  The main controller deals purely with control signals, i.e. only **std_ulogic** is used for the entity ports. Additionally, an internal signal is necessary to store the current controller state. You should define your **own enumeration type** for this purpose that holds all possible states of the finite state machine.

- **To do:**

  - Create the new VHDL file.

  - Write a testbench to verify the design. Use assertions to check the exposure times during the simulation run.

  - Compile and simulate the design.

  - Compare the number of flip flops that you would expect with the synthesis result.

3.10.2 Implementation

The VHDL code for the camera controller:

```vhdl
library ieee;
use ieee.std_logic_1164.all;

entity MAIN_CTRL is
  port(CLK         : in  std_ulogic;
       RESET       : in  std_ulogic;
       TRIGGER     : in  std_ulogic;
       EXPOSE      : in  std_ulogic;
       MOTOR_READY : in  std_ulogic;
       MOTOR_ERROR : in  std_ulogic;
       ERROR       : out std_ulogic;
       TIMER_GO    : out std_ulogic;
       MOTOR_GO    : out std_ulogic);
end MAIN_CTRL;

architecture RTL of MAIN_CTRL is
  type T_STATE is (IDLE, TAKE_PIC, DELAY,
    WAIT_EXP_TIME, FILM_TRANSPORT,
    WAIT_TRANSPORT, BROKEN);
  signal STATE:      T_STATE;
  signal NEXT_STATE: T_STATE;

begin
  process (STATE, TRIGGER, EXPOSE,
           MOTOR_ERROR, MOTOR_READY)
  begin

    NEXT_STATE <= STATE;

    case STATE is
      when IDLE =>
        if TRIGGER = '1' then
          NEXT_STATE <= TAKE_PIC;
        end if;

      when TAKE_PIC =>
        NEXT_STATE <= DELAY;
```

- **The new data type for the FSM states is not used anywhere else. Therefore its definition is not placed in a separate package but in the architecture where it is actually used.**

  Though the declaration of a new enumeration type for the possible states is probably the easiest way to implement a FSM, it is not always the best choice. Look up the tutorial to find out about alternatives.

- **The calculation of the next state is placed in a separate combinational process.**

- **The default action is to keep the current state.**

- **While in IDLE state the camera waits for the user to press the trigger.**

- **TAKE_PIC starts the exposure controller.**

  The exposure controller needs 1 clock cycle to start the actual exposure.

The VHDL code for the camera controller:

```
        when DELAY =>
          NEXT_STATE <= WAIT_EXP_TIME;

        when WAIT_EXP_TIME =>
          if EXPOSE = '0' then
            NEXT_STATE <= FILM_TRANSPORT;
          end if;

        when FILM_TRANSPORT =>
          NEXT_STATE <= WAIT_TRANSPORT;

        when WAIT_TRANSPORT =>
          if MOTOR_ERROR = '1' then
            NEXT_STATE <= BROKEN;
          elsif MOTOR_READY = '1' then
            NEXT_STATE <= IDLE;
          end if;

        when others =>
          NULL;
      end case;
  end process;

  process (CLK, RESET)
  begin
    if (RESET = '1') then
      STATE <= IDLE;
    elsif (CLK'event and CLK = '1') then
      STATE <= NEXT_STATE;
    end if;      -- end of clocked process
  end process;

  with STATE select
    TIMER_GO <= '1' when TAKE_PIC,
                '0' when others;

  with STATE select
    MOTOR_GO <= '1' when FILM_TRANSPORT,
                '0' when others;

  with STATE select
    ERROR    <= '1' when BROKEN,
                '0' when others;
end RTL;
```

- The end of the exposure is reached when the shutter is closed again.
  The next task is to move on the film.

- While waiting for the end of the film transport, two events may occur: either the motor supervision module reports an error, then something is broken, or the motor terminates normally, then we are ready to take the next picture.

- All other states are ignored, i.e. the controller will stay in the **BROKEN** state forever.

- The registers that store the state information are modelled with a second process. The next state information replaces the current state data with every rising clock edge and thus triggers the next state calculation provided that the state has changed.

- The output signals depend upon the current state and are generated with concurrent statements. This is possible because the FSM stays in the **TAKE_PIC** and the **FILM_TRANSPORT** states for one clock cycle, only.

3.11 STEP 10: The Camera

3.11.1 Synopsis

Now all submodules must be merged into one design, the complete camera controller. So all modules have to be connected on a new level of hierarchy. This is called structural modelling. Structural modelling means the use (instantiation) and wiring of components, resulting in a net list. VHDL provides the following means for structural modelling:

- Component declaration
- Component instantiation
- Component configuration

Before you can use an object in VHDL, you have to declare it. As in VHDL'87 only components can be instantiated, these have to be declared first. This is done in the declarative part of an architecture or within a package, which then has to be referenced.

The actual instantiation is the integration and wiring of the component. The component configuration determines which entity has to be used for a specific component instantiation. If the name of the component instantiated and the name of the entity to be used are identical (mandatory for synthesis!) then no specific component configuration has to be given.

The interface of the top module is shown in the following figure:

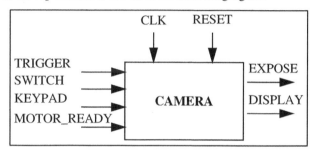

- **To do:**
  - Create the new VHDL file.
  - Write a testbench to verify the design. Use assertions to check the exposure times during the simulation run.
  - Compile and simulate the design.
  - Compare the number of flip flops that you would expect with the synthesis result.

3.11.2 Implementation

Part of the VHDL code of the camera:

```
library ieee;
use ieee.std_logic_1164.all;
use work.P_DISPLAY.all;
entity CAMERA is
  port( CLK     : in  std_ulogic;
        RESET   : in  std_ulogic;
        TRIGGER : in  std_ulogic;
        SWITCH  : in  std_ulogic;
        KEYPAD  : in  std_ulogic_vector
                            (9 downto 0);
        MOTOR_READY : in      std_ulogic;
        EXPOSE  : buffer std_ulogic;
        DISPLAY : out T_DISPLAY);
end CAMERA;
```

- **The top entity contains the ports that will be later connected to pads. So these pads can be connected with the corresponding wires in the camera.**

Part of the VHDL code of the camera:

```
architecture STRUCT of CAMERA is

  component DISP_DRV
    port(•••);
  end component;
  component DECODER
    port (•••);
  end component;
  component EXP_FF
    port(•••);
  end component;
  component DISP_CTRL
    port(•••);
  end component;
  component MOTOR_TIMER
    port(•••);
  end component;
  component EXP_CTRL
    port(•••);
  end component;
  component MAIN_CTRL
    port(•••);
  end component;

  signal W_KEY         : T_DIGITS;
  signal W_NO_PICS     : T_DIGITS;
  signal W_EXP_TIME    : T_DIGITS;
  signal W_SHOW_TIME   : std_ulogic;
  signal W_TIMER_GO    : std_ulogic;
  signal W_MOTOR_GO    : std_ulogic;
  signal W_MOTOR_ERROR : std_ulogic;
  signal W_ERROR       : std_ulogic;

begin
  U_DISP_DRV   : DISP_DRV  port map(•••);
  U_DECODER    : DECODER   port map(•••);
  U_EXP_FF     : EXP_FF    port map(•••);
  U_DISP_CTRL  : DISP_CTRL port map(•••);
  U_MOTOR_TIMER : MOTOR_TIMER port map(•••);
  U_EXP_CTRL   : EXP_CTRL  port map(•••);
  U_MAIN_CTRL  : MAIN_CTRL port map(•••);
end STRUCT;


configuration CFG_CAMERA of CAMERA is
  for STRUCT
    for all : DECODER
      use entity work.DECODER(RTL_CASE);
    end for;
  end for;
end CFG_CAMERA;
```

- As this is the top architecture, all entities modelled so far have to be included. Therefore they are declared as components in the architecture.

- All internal signals have to be declared.

- Here all the components are instantiated and connected to the appropriate signals.

- As there are two architectures for the decoder, a configuration is written. This configuration selects the architecture RTL_CASE.

REFERENCE

1 Design Entities and Configurations

1.1 Entity

. . .
 ENTITY e IS
   ● ● ●
 BEGIN
   ● ● ●
 END e ;
	...
	 ARCHITECTURE a OF e IS
	   ...
	 BEGIN
	   ...
	 END a ;
		...
		 CONFIGURATION c
		   OF e IS
		   ...
		   ...
		 END

...
 PACKAGE pkg IS
   ...
   ...
 END pkg ;
	entity_declaration ::=
	   entity identifier **is**
	     entity_header
	     entity_declarative_part
	   [**begin**
	     entity_statement_part]
	   end [**entity**] [*entity*_simple_name] ;
		...
		 PACKAGE BODY pck
		   IS
		   ...
		   ...
		 END pck ;

...
 b: BLOCK IS
   ...
 BEGIN
   ...
 END BLOCK b ;
	FUNCTION f (...)
	   RETURN r IS
	   ...
	 BEGIN
	   ...
	 END f ;
		PROCEDURE p (...) IS
		   ...
		 BEGIN
		   ...
		 END p ;
			p : PROCESS
			   ...
			 BEGIN
			   ...
			 END PROCESS p ;

1.1.1 Further Definitions

identifier ::=   basic_identifier | extended_identifier

entity_header ::=   [*formal*_generic_clause]
                    [*formal*_port_clause]

entity_declarative_part ::=   { entity_declarative_item }

entity_statement_part ::=   { entity_statement }

simple_name ::=   identifier

1.1.2 Examples

ENTITY testbench **IS** **END** testbench;	Example of a testbench that possesses neither inputs nor outputs.

ENTITY fulladder **IS**
   PORT (X,Y,Cin   : **IN** Bit;
         Cout, Sum : **OUT** Bit);
 END fulladder;
	Entity for a 2-Bit fulladder. *X,Y* and *Cin* are Bit-type inputs. *Cout* and *Sum* are Bit-type outputs.

```ENTITY big_example IS```
   ```GENERIC (m : Positive);```
   ```PORT (```
     ```b1,b2 : IN Bit;```
     ```b3   : OUT Bit_Vector(1 to m));```
   ```TYPE byte IS ARRAY(1 TO 8) OF Bit;```
   ```USE work.timing_library.all;```
   ```CONSTANT tsetup : Time := 12 ns;```
 	
   ```PROCEDURE init```
     ```(SIGNAL b4: OUT byte) IS```
   ```BEGIN```
     ```b4 <= (OTHERS => '1')```
         ```AFTER delay;```
   ```END init;```
 	
 ```BEGIN```
   ```ASSERT b4'DELAYED'STABLE(5 ns)```
     ```REPORT "Error occured!"```
     ```SEVERITY Error;```
   ```passive_procedure(b2,delay);```
 ```END big_example;```
	Entity with several features:
	 Definition of a parameter *m*.
	 b1 and *b2* are inputs (Bits), *b3* is an output vector with the width *m*.
	 Definition of type *byte* as a bitvector.
	 Integrating the objects from the package *timing_library*. Definition and initialization of a constant *tsetup*.
	
	 Definition of procedure *init* with signal transfer. Seizing of b4 with several '1' is carried out only after *delay*.
	
	 Instructions within the entity:
	 If the condition that is to be checked is not fulfilled, an error is reported.
	 Error is the severity level. A passive *procedure* (signal assignments in the entity are not allowed!) with *b4* and *delay* as transfer values is called.

1.2 Architecture

...
 ENTITY e IS
 ...
 BEGIN
 ...
 END e ;
	...
	 ARCHITECTURE a OF e IS
	   ●●●
	 BEGIN
	   ●●●
	 END a ;
			...
			 CONFIGURATION c
			   OF e IS
			 ...
			 ...
			 END

...
 PACKAGE pkg IS
 ...
 ...
 END pkg ;
	architecture_body ::=
	 architecture identifier **of** *entity*_name **is**
	   architecture_declarative_part
	 begin
	   architecture_statement_part
	 end [**architectur**]
	 [*architecture*_simple_name] ;
			..
			 PACKAGE BODY
			   pck IS
			 ...
			 END pck ;

... b: BLOCK IS ... BEGIN ... END BLOCK b ;	FUNCTION f (...) RETURN r IS ... BEGIN ... END f ;	PROCEDURE p (...) IS ... BEGIN ... END p ;	p : PROCESS ... BEGIN ... END PROCESS p ;

1.2.1 Further Definitions

identifier ::=
    basic_identifier | extended_identifier

name ::=
    simple_name
    | operator_symbol
    | selected_name
    | indexed_name
    | slice_name
    | attribute_name

architecture_declarative_part ::=
    { block_declarative_item }

architecture_statement_part ::=
    { concurrent_statement }

simple_name ::= identifier

1.2.2 Examples

```ARCHITECTURE arch OF box IS BEGIN END arch;```	Example of an empty architecture of the entity *box*.
```ARCHITECTURE rtl OF fulladder IS SIGNAL A,B: Bit; BEGIN A <= X XOR Y; B <= A AND Cin; Sum <= A XOR Cin; Cout <= B OR (X AND Y); END rtl;```	Example of an architecture of the entity *fulladder*. A and B are the necessary internal signals. In the architecture body there are several concurrent instructions that describe the function of the fulladder.
```ARCHITECTURE rtl1 OF entity1 IS CONSTANT delay: Time :=5 ns; SIGNAL S: Bit; BEGIN S2 <= czbit(S) AFTER 3 ns; S <= S1 AFTER delay; END rtl1;```	Example of two different architectures for the entity *entity1*. *rtl1*: Definition of the required constant delay and the internal signal *S*. Two concurrent signal assignments with time delays and the function *czbit* being called.

``
ARCHITECTURE rtl2 OF entity1 IS
    SIGNAL S: Bit :='1';
 	
    PROCEDURE proc(SIGNAL A: IN Bit
       SIGNAL B: INOUT Bit) IS
    BEGIN
       B <= NOT B WHEN A ='1' ELSE B;
    END proc;
 	
BEGIN
    P1: proc(S1,S);
    P2: S2 <= czbit(S) AFTER 2 ns;
    P3: PROCESS(S)
       VARIABLE V :Bit;
    BEGIN
       V := S;
    END PROCESS P3;
END rtl2;
``
	rtl2:
	Definition and initialization of the internal signal *S*.
	
	Definition of the procedure *proc* with a signal transfer from *A* and *B*.
	Conditional signal assignment to *B*.
	
	Three concurrent instructions named *P1*, *P2* and *P3*.
	P1 is a procedure call.
	P2 assigns a signal by calling a function.
	
	P3 is a process during which the variable *V* is declared and then given the value of *S* by assignment.

1.3 Configuration

... ENTITY e IS ... BEGIN ... END e ;	... ARCHITECTURE a OF e IS ... BEGIN ... END a ;	. . . CONFIGURATION c OF e IS ••• ••• END

...
PACKAGE pkg IS
...
...
...
END pkg ;
	configuration_declaration ::=
	
	configuration identifier **of**
	    *entity*_name **is**
	    configuration_declarative_part
	    block_configuration
	end [**configuration**]
	    [*configuration*_simple_name] ;
		..
		PACKAGE BODY pck
		    IS
		...
		...
		...
		END pck ;

... b: BLOCK IS ... BEGIN ... END BLOCK b ;	FUNCTION f (...) RETURN r IS ... BEGIN ... END f ;	PROCEDURE p (...) IS p : PROCESS ... ... BEGIN BEGIN ... ... END p ; END PROCESS p ;

1.3.1 Further Definitions

identifier ::=
  basic_identifier | extended_identifier

name ::=
  simple_name
  | operator_symbol
  | selected_name
  | indexed_name
  | slice_name
  | attribute_name

configuration_declarative_part ::= { configuration_declarative_item }

block_configuration ::=
  for block_specification
    {use_clause}
    {configuration_item}
  end for;

simple_name ::= identifier

1.3.2 Examples

```CONFIGURATION cfg OF testbench IS```
```   FOR arch_of_testbench```
```   END FOR;```
```END cfg;```
	Example of a default configuration of a testbench that uses the corresponding analysed object for the architecture *arch_of_testbench*.

```LIBRARY vendor, mylib;```
```CONFIGURATION cfg_of_ex OF example IS```
```   USE mylib.ALL;```
```   FOR structural```
```   FOR ALU1: ALU```
```   USE ENTITY mylib.alu_ver_2(beh);```
```   END FOR;```
```   FOR mux1, mux2, mux3: MUX```
```   USE ENTITY vendor.mux12345(rtl);```
```   END FOR;```
```   FOR ALL: add```
```   END FOR;```
```   END FOR;```
```END cfg_of_ex;```
	The libraries *vendor* and *mylib* are published.
	For the entity *example* the whole content of the library *mylib* is published, and in its architecture *structural* the entity *alu_ver_2* is used with the architecture *beh* from the library *mylib* for the instance *ALU* with the label *ALU1*.
	For the instantiations of *MUX*, labelled *mux1*, *mux2* and *mux3*, the entity *mux12345* with the architecture *rtl* from the library *vendor* is used.
	For all instances of *add* the defaults are used.

2 Subprograms and Packages

2.1 Subprogram Declaration

... ENTITY e IS ___ ••• BEGIN ... END e ;	... ARCHITECTURE a OF e IS ___ ••• BEGIN ... END a ;	... CONFIGURATION c OF e IS ... ... END

...
PACKAGE pkg IS
___ •••
___ •••
___ •••
END pkg ;
	subprogram_declaration ::=
	
	       subprogram_specification ;
		...
		PACKAGE BODY pck
		       IS
		___ •••
		___ •••
		___ •••
		END pck ;

... b: BLOCK IS ___ ••• BEGIN ... END BLOCK b ;	FUNCTION f (...) RETURN r IS ___ ••• BEGIN ... END f ;	PROCEDURE p (...) IS ___ ••• BEGIN ... END p ;	p : PROCESS ___ ••• BEGIN ... END PROCESS p ;

2.1.1 Further Definitions

subprogram_specification ::=
   procedure designator [(formal_parameter_list)]
   | [**pure** | **impure**] **function** designator [(formal_parameter_list)]
     return type_mark

2.1.2 Comment

- A pure function always returns the same value when called different times with the
  same actual parameters. Impure functions can return different values when called
  several times with the same actual parameters. This is the case when, for example, a
  impure function reads in a text file, whose content changes during simulation.

2.1.3 Examples

`PROCEDURE thank_you;`	Simple declaration of the procedure *thank_you* without transfer values

PROCEDURE test (A : Bit);	Declaration of the procedure *test* with the transfer value *A*.
FUNCTION convert (B : Bit) **RETURN** fuzzy_bit;	Declaration of the function *convert* with the transfer value *B* and the result type *fuzzy_bit*.

PROCEDURE regist(
    SIGNAL D : **IN** Bit;
    SIGNAL CK : **IN** Bit;
    SIGNAL Q : **OUT** Bit);
	Declaration of the procedure *regist* with the signals *D*, *CK* and *Q* being transferred.

PROCEDURE p(
    VARIABLE COL : **INOUT** color;
    CONSTANT C   : **IN**   choice);
	Declaration of the procedure *p* with the variable *COL* and the constant *C* being transferred.

2.2 Subprogram Body

... ENTITY e IS ● ● ● BEGIN ... END e ;	... ARCHITECTURE a OF e IS ● ● ● BEGIN ... END a ;		... CONFIGURATION c OF e IS ... ... END

...
PACKAGE pkg IS
...
...
...
END pkg ;
	subprogram_body ::=
	
	subprogram_specification **is**
	    subprogram_declarative_part
	begin
	    subprogram_statement_part
	end [subprogram_kind] [designator] ;
			...
			PACKAGE BODY pck
			IS
			● ● ●
			● ● ●
			● ● ●
			END pck ;

...
b: BLOCK IS
● ● ●
BEGIN
...
END BLOCK b ;
	FUNCTION f (...)
	    RETURN r IS
	● ● ●
	BEGIN
	● ● ●
	END f ;
		PROCEDURE p
		    (...) IS
		● ● ●
		BEGIN
		● ● ●
		END p ;
			p : PROCESS
			● ● ●
			BEGIN
			...
			END PROCESS p ;

2.2.1 Further Definitions

subprogram_specification ::=
  procedure designator [(formal_parameter_list)]
  | [**pure** | **impure**] **function** designator [(formal_parameter_list)] **return** type_mark

subprogram_declarative_part ::=
  { subprogram_declarative_item }

subprogram_statement_part ::=
  { sequential_statement }

subprogram_kind ::= **procedure** | **function**

designator ::= identifier | operator_symbol

2.2.2 Comment

- The declaration of a subprogram is optional. The subprogram specification can act as the declaration.

- *Shared variables* must not be declared in subprograms.

- A 'foreign subprogram' is a subprogram with the attribute **FOREIGN**. The value of the attribute (a string) can contain implementation-specific information for linking the external program (see the example below).

- A pure function must not contain a reference to an explicitly declared file object.

- A pure function must not be the parent of an impure function.

2.2.3 Examples

```PROCEDURE thank_you IS BEGIN ASSERT false REPORT "Thank You !" SEVERITY note; END thank_you;```	Definition of the procedure *thank_you*. If the condition *false* is not fulfilled 'Thank You !' is reported as *note* in the severity level.
```PROCEDURE regist(SIGNAL D : IN Bit; SIGNAL CK : IN Bit; SIGNAL Q : OUT Bit) IS BEGIN LOOP WAIT ON CK; IF CK = '1' THEN Q <= D AFTER 1 ns; END IF; END LOOP; END regist;```	Definition of the procedure *regist* with the transfer values of the signals *D*, *CK* and *Q*. Within the endless loop (LOOP) a register is declared that takes on the value of input *D* from output *Q* at the positive clock-edge with a delay of 1 ns.

FUNCTION exfunc **RETURN INTEGER;**
ATTRIBUTE FOREIGN OF
    exfunc **FUNCTION IS**
    "C:modellib.so.0.1
     ELAB:model_elab";
	The external function *exfunc* is declared.
	
	The attribute *FOREIGN* of *exfunc* gets (simulator-) program-specific information.

FUNCTION convert(B : Bit)
        RETURN fuzzy_bit **IS**
    VARIABLE v : fuzzy_bit;
BEGIN
    IF B = '1' **THEN**
        v := High;
    ELSE
        v := Low;
    END IF;
    RETURN v;
END convert;
	Definition of the function *convert* with the transfer value *B* and the result type *fuzzy_bit*.
	
	In the If loop the variable *v* is assigned the value High or Low, depending on the value of *B*.
	
	v is transferred as transfer value.

PROCEDURE p(
    VARIABLE COL : **INOUT** color;
    CONSTANT C   : **IN** choice) **IS**
    SUBTYPE primary_color **IS**
        color **RANGE** yellow **TO** red;
    VARIABLE X, Y, Z : primary_color;
BEGIN
...
END p;
	Definition of the procedure *p;*
	transfer values of the variable *COL* and the constant *C*.
	
	The subtype *primary_color* is declared from the type *colour* with a range of *yellow* to *red* (from the enumeration type *colour*). The variables *X*, *Y* and *Z* are declared.

2.3 Overloading

2.3.1 Subprogram Overloading

Subprograms which have the same name but different behaviour are declared as usual. This applies to both procedures and functions. According to the following criteria, it has to be possible to choose exactly *one* procedure or function (resolution of overloading):

- Number of arguments
- Argument types
- Names of arguments (in the case of an argument transfer by explicitly naming it 'named association' [=> see Examples])
- Type of return value

If in a function call several variants are valid, the local variant (e.g. in the architecture's declarative part) hides the variant that ranks higher in hierarchy (e.g. from a package). By giving the complete subprogram name and hierarchy, one can still access any desired variant (Qualified Expression).

2.3.2 Overloading Operators

Operators are different from simple functions in two ways:

- The name or the symbol of an operator is not a normal designator but a string, and therefore in declaration it stands in inverted commas.

- In a common operator call the operands are placed before or after the operator (unary operators only afterwards) and not in round brackets placed after the operator. However, it is also possible to call operators with the syntax of normal function calls (=>see Examples).

It is important to consider the handling of operators as strings when declaring overloaded operators. Apart from that, the overloading of operators is not different from that of functions and procedures.

2.3.3 Examples

In these examples only the declarations and calls of the overloaded subprograms are shown. Of course a subprogram definition has to be written for every declaration.

```PROCEDURE write (F : INOUT Text; value : Integer); PROCEDURE write (F : INOUT Text; value : String); write (sys_error, "Unexpected out- put"); write (sys_output, 12);```	Two procedures *write* are declared, with the transfer value *value* being declared once as integer and once as string. In the procedure call the type of the individual second transfer value determines which procedure is to be used.
```PROCEDURE check (setup : Time; SIGNAL D : Data; SIGNAL C : Clock); PROCEDURE check (hold : Time; SIGNAL C : Clock; SIGNAL D : Data); check (setup => 10 ns, D => D_Bus, C => Clk_1); check (hold => 5 ns, D => D_Bus, C => Clk_2); check (15 ns, D_Bus, Clk);```	Two procedures *check* are declared. They differ in the name of the first transfer value as well as in the sequence of definition of the two signals *C* and *D*. With the first two procedure calls the name of the first transfer value determines which procedure is to be used. If types *Data* and *Clock* are identical to each other, the third call is not unique and therefore is forbidden.

`TYPE mvl IS ('0', '1', 'Z', 'X');`
`FUNCTION "AND" (L, R : mvl) RETURN mvl;`
`FUNCTION "OR" (L, R : mvl) RETURN mvl;`
`FUNCTION "NOT" (R : mvl) RETURN mvl;`
`SIGNAL Q, R, S : mvl;`
	According to the definition of the type *mvl* the standard operators *AND*, *OR* and *NOT are* overloaded. Type *mvl* is used as transfer and result value.

`Q <= 'X' OR '1';`
`R <= "OR"('0', 'Z');`
`S <= (Q AND R) OR NOT S;`
	The signal assignments to *Q*, *R* and *S* show the use of overloaded operators. The second call is interesting as in it the operator is called explicitly as a function.

2.4 Resolution Function

2.4.1 Definition

A resolution function determines a signal's value if this signal receives assignments from more than one source at a time. This is necessary if the following concurrent assignments to the **unresolved** signal Z exist.

Examples:

Z <= A;

Z <= B;

If there is no resolution function for Z it is not clear which value Z receives if A='0' and B='1'. In the signal declaration signal and resolution function are linked. It is also possible to declare a subtype that links a type to a resolution function.

2.4.2 Example

`FUNCTION wired_or (inputs : Bit_vector)`
`      RETURN Bit IS`
`   CONSTANT floatvalue : Bit := '0';`
`BEGIN`
`   IF inputs'Length = 0 THEN`
`      RETURN floatvalue;`
`   ELSE`
`      FOR i IN inputs'RANGE LOOP`
`         IF inputs(i) = '1' THEN`
`            RETURN '1';`
`         END IF;`
`      END LOOP;`
`      RETURN '0';`
`   END IF;`
`END;`
	A *resolution function* is declared that resolves multiple signal assignments according to the principle of the *wired_or*.
	The constant *floatvalue* is declared as *Bit* and initialized with '0'.
	
	If there is no source driving a signal (*inputs' length* =0) the value of *floatvalue*, i.e. '0' is transferred
	
	If one of the inputs drives a '1' the value '1' and otherwise the value '0' is transferred.

2.5 Package Declaration

... ENTITY e IS ... BEGIN ... END e ;	... ARCHITECTURE a OF e IS ... BEGIN ... END a ;	CONFIGURATION c OF e IS ... ... END
... **PACKAGE pkg IS** ●●● ●●● ●●● **END pkg ;**	package declaration ::= **package** identifier **is** package_declarative_part **end** [**package**] [*package*_simple_name] ;	.. PACKAGE BODY pck IS ... ... END pck ;
... b: BLOCK IS ... BEGIN ... END BLOCK b ;	FUNCTION f (...) RETURN r IS ... BEGIN ... END f ;	PROCEDURE p (...) IS ... BEGIN ... END p ;	p : PROCESS ... BEGIN ... END PROCESS p ;

2.5.1 Further Definitions

identifier ::=
  basic_identifier | extended_identifier

package_declarative_part ::=
  { package_declarative_item }

simple_name ::= identifier

2.5.2 Examples

| ```
PACKAGE tristate IS
   TYPE Tri IS ('0', '1', 'Z', 'E');
   FUNCTION BitVal (Value : Tri)
      RETURN Bit;
   FUNCTION TriVal (Value : Bit)
      RETURN Tri;
   TYPE TriVector IS ARRAY
      (NATURAL RANGE <>) OF Tri;
   FUNCTION Resolve (Sources : TriVector)
      RETURN Tri;
END tristate;
``` | Declaration of the package *tristate* in which the enumeration type *Tri* and three functions (*BitVal*, *TriVal*, *Resolve*) with the corresponding transfer values and result types are declared. <br> Apart from that, a type *TriVector* is declared as a vector of the type *Tri* and the maximum length (*NATURAL RANGE <>*). |
|---|---|
```

| ```
PACKAGE pck IS
   CONSTANT CINT : integer;
END pck;
``` | Declaration of the package *pck* in which the integer constant *CINT* is declared. |
| ```
PACKAGE pck_2 IS
   USE work.parts.all;

   SIGNAL S : resol_bit BUS := '1';
   DISCONNECT S AFTER 2 ns;
   COMPONENT latch
      GENERIC (C : Natural);
      PORT (
         A : IN  Bit;
         B : OUT Bit_vector (1 TO C));
   END COMPONENT;
   COMPONENT clock
      PORT (CK : OUT Bit);
   END COMPONENT;
END pck_2;
``` | The objects from the library *parts* are integrated.<br>The signal *S* is declared as a *guarded signal* (BUS) and initialized with the value 1.<br>The driver(s) for the signal *S* is/are not separated immediately after *S* has been deactivated but only 2 ns afterwards.<br>The two components *latch* and *clock* with the corresponding in- and outputs are declared. The component *latch* also contains a Generic *N*. |

2.6 Package Body

...	...	...
ENTITY e IS ... BEGIN ... END e ;	ARCHITECTURE a OF e IS ... BEGIN ... END a ;	CONFIGURATION c OF e IS ... ... END

...
PACKAGE pkg IS
 	
...
 	
...
 	
...
END pkg ;
	package_body ::=
	
	package body *package*_simple_name **is**
	   package_body_declarative_part
	end [**package body**]
	   [*package*_simple_name] ;
		..
		PACKAGE BODY pck
		      IS
		●●●
		●●●
		●●●
		END pck ;

... b: BLOCK IS ... BEGIN ... END BLOCK b ;	FUNCTION f (...) RETURN r IS ... BEGIN ... END f ;	PROCEDURE p (...) IS ... BEGIN ... END p ;	p : PROCESS ... BEGIN ... END PROCESS p ;

2.6.1 Further Definitions

simple_name ::= identifier

package_body_declarative_part ::=   { package_body_declarative_item }

2.6.2 Examples

<pre>PACKAGE BODY pck_1 IS
   FUNCTION G (A, B : Bit)
              RETURN Bit IS
   BEGIN
      RETURN NOT (A XOR B);
   END;
 	
   FUNCTION F (S1, S2 : Bit)
              RETURN Bit IS
      VARIABLE V : Bit;
   BEGIN
      V := S1 NAND S2;
      RETURN G(V, S2);
   END;
END pck_1;</pre>
	Definition of the package body *pck_1* in which the two functions *G* and *F* are declared.
	
	In the function *G* the value of the equation *A XOR B* is returned as a result (as Bit).
	
	In the function *F* a variable *V* is declared as Bit which then receives the value from *S1 NAND S2*. The function *F* delivers the bit value from the function call *G(V, S2)* as a result value.

<pre>PACKAGE BODY tristate IS
   FUNCTION BitVal (Value : Tri)
                 RETURN Bit IS
   CONSTANT Bits : Bit_Vector := "0100";
   BEGIN
      RETURN Bits(Tri'Pos(Value))
   END;
 	
   FUNCTION TriVal (Value : Bit)
                 RETURN Tri IS
      VARIABLE V : Tri := 'Z';
   BEGIN
      FOR i IN Sources'Range LOOP
         IF Sources(i) /= 'Z' THEN
            IF V = 'Z' THEN
               V := Sources(i);
            ELSE
               RETURN 'E';
            END IF;
         END IF;
      END LOOP;
      RETURN V;
   END;
END tristate;</pre>
	Definition of the package body *tristate* in which the two functions *BitVal* and *TriVal* are declared.
	
	In the function *BitVal* a constant *Bits* is declared and initialized with the value "0100". As a result, the value of the bit in the position *Tri'Pos(Value)* of *Bits* is returned.
	
	In the function *TriVal* a variable *V* of the type *Tri* is declared and initialized with the value *Z*.
	
	In **LOOP** either the value of *Source(i)* is transferred to *V* or *E* is returned as a result value, depending on the individual value of *Source(i)* and *V*. In the first case *V* is returned as a result value afterwards.

`USE work.pck_0.all;`
 	
`PACKAGE BODY pck IS`
`   CONSTANT cint : integer := f(6);`
`END pck;`
	The objects from the library *pck_0* are integrated. In the package body the constant *cint*, which has to be declared in the package header, is declared as integer and initialized with the result value from function call f(6) (deferred constant).

2.7 Conformance Rules

2.7.1 Definition

Should the syntax rules require or allow the multiple specification of a subprogram, the following variations are permitted:

- One numeric variable can only be replaced by another numeric variable if both variables possess the same value.

- A simple name can only be replaced by a selected name (in which the simple name serves as a selector) if in both specifications the direction of the simple name is determined by the same declaration.

Two specifications for one subprogram are *conform* if – irrespective of comments and the variations mentioned above – both specifications are made up of the same sequence of lexical elements and corresponding lexical elements have the same meaning. The specification of a impure function is never conform to that of a pure function

2.7.2 Examples

`PROCEDURE p (x, y : integer);`
`PROCEDURE p (x : integer ; y : integer);`
`PROCEDURE p (x, y : IN integer);`
	The specifications for the procedure *p* are not conform as they are not made up of the same sequence of lexical elements.

3 Types

3.1 Scalar Types

3.1.1 Definitions

scalar_type_definition ::=
   enumeration_type_definition
   | integer_type_definition
   | floating_type_definition
   | physical_type_definition

3.1.2 Examples

```TYPE distance IS RANGE 0 TO 1E16```
``` UNITS```
```   -- base unit :```
```   A -- Angström```
```   -- metric units :```
```   nm = 10 A;   -- Nanometer```
```   um = 1000 nm; -- Micrometer```
```   mm = 1000 um; -- Millimeter```
```   cm = 10 mm;   -- Centimeter```
```   m   = 1000 mm; -- Meter```
```   km = 1000 m;   -- Kilometer```
``` END UNITS;```
 	
```TYPE time IS RANGE -1E18 TO 1E18```
``` UNITS```
```   fs;   --Femtosecond```
```   ps   = 1000 fs; -- Picosecond```
```   ns   = 1000 ps; -- Nanosecond```
```   us   = 1000 ns; -- Microsecond```
```   ms   = 1000 us; -- Millisecond```
```   sec = 1000 ms; -- Second```
```   min = 60 sec; -- Minute```
``` END UNITS```
	With physical types a real type is defined first. Afterwards the basic unit and its derivative units are declared.
	
	As examples the definitions of the units of length *(distance)* and the units of time *(time)* are shown here.
	
	The physical unit *time* is a predefined type.

```TYPE byte_length_integer IS```
```   RANGE 0 TO 255;```
```TYPE word_index IS```
```   RANGE 31 DOWNTO 0;```
```TYPE my_real IS```
```   RANGE 0.0 TO 9.99;```
```SUBTYPE high_bit_low IS```
```   byte_length_integer```
```   RANGE 0 TO 127;```
	Integer types are generated by stating integral numbers in the range declaration (RANGE). The range can be declared rising (TO) or falling (DOWNTO).
	Real types are created through realistic range declarations.
	Subtypes can be declared by stating the base type and the selected range.

`TYPE Bit IS ('0', '1');`
 	
`TYPE switch_level IS`
`    ('0', '1', 'X');`
 	
`TYPE states IS`
`    (out, sleeping, working);`
 	
`TYPE colors IS`
`    (red, green, blue);`
	Different types are declared. Types *Bit* and *switch_level* are declared as enumeration types through characters and can only have the values *0* or *1* and *X*. One has to distinguish between these values *0* and *1* and the integer values *0* and *1*. These two characters are then overloaded.
	Types *states* and *colours* are declared as enumeration types by self explanatory element names.

3.2 Compound Types

3.2.1 Definitions

composite_type_definition ::=
    array_type_definition
    | record_type_definition

3.2.2 Examples

`TYPE my_word IS` `    ARRAY (0 TO 31) OF bit;`	*mt_word* is declared as a bit vector of the width 32, with the indices increasing from left to right.

`TYPE data_in IS`
`    ARRAY (7 DOWNTO 0)`
`    OF five_level_logic`
	data_in is declared as a vector of the type *five_level_logic* and the width 8, with the indices decreasing from left to right.

`TYPE memory IS`
`    ARRAY (integer RANGE <>)`
`    OF my_word;`
	memory is declared as a vector of the type *my_word* with an arbitrary width (<>). Direction and maximum width are determined by the type *integer*.

`TYPE t IS ARRAY`
`    (positive RANGE min TO max)`
`    OF element;`
	t is declared as a vector of the type *element* with the width 1+(*max-min*) [type *positive*].

`TYPE date IS RECORD`
`   day   : integer RANGE 1 TO 31;`
`   month : month_name;`
`   year  : integer RANGE 0 TO 2100;`
`END RECORD;`
	date is declared as **Record** which consists of the elements *day*, *month* and *year*.

3.3 Access Types

3.3.1 Definitions

access_type_definition ::=
   access subtype_indication

By declaring an access type, an access type is declared that can later be used for declaring an index variable.

incomplete_type_declaration ::=
   type identifier

By giving an incomplete type declaration, it is possible to model recursive structures. The complete type declaration has to be made in the same declarative range.

3.3.2 Examples

`TYPE address IS ACCESS memory;`
 	
`TYPE buffer_ptr IS ACCESS buffer;`
	Access types *address* and *buffer_ptr are declared.* *memory* and *buffer are* target *types.*

`TYPE cell;`
 	
`TYPE link IS ACCESS cell;`
 	
`TYPE cell IS`
`   RECORD`
`      value : integer;`
`      succ  : link;`
`      pred  : link;`
`   END RECORD;`
	A recursive structure is created. At first type *cell* is declared incompletely. As a consequence the access type *link* is declared on the type *cell*.
	Afterwards type *cell* is declared completely as *Record*. The elements *succ* and *pred* are declared as index types. By doing so an interlinked list can be created in which every element receives an index to both its predecessor and its successor.

3.4 File Types

3.4.1 Definitions

file_type_definition ::=
  file of type_mark

3.4.2 Examples

TYPE string_file **IS FILE OF** string **TYPE** natural_file **IS FILE OF** natural	Two file types *string_file* and *natural_file* are declared. They are to contain elements of the type *string* and *natural*.

TYPE ft **IS FILE OF** tm;
 	
PROCEDURE read (
    f   : **IN** ft;
    value : **OUT** tm;
    length : **OUT** natural);
PROCEDURE write (
    f   : **OUT** ft;
    value : **IN** tm);
FUNCTION endfile (f : **IN** ft)
    RETURN boolean;
	A file type *ft* with elements of the type *tm* is declared.
	
	In the procedure *read* the next value is to be read from a file.
	
	In the procedure *write* a value is to be attached to a file.
	The function *endfile* checks whether the end of a file has been reached.

4 Declarations

4.1 Type Declarations

... ENTITY e IS ──── ••• BEGIN ... END e ;	... ARCHITECTURE a OF e IS ──── ••• BEGIN ... END a ;	... CONFIGURATION c OF e IS ... ... END
... PACKAGE pkg IS ──── ••• ──── ••• END pkg ;	type declaration ::= full_type_declaration | incomplete_type_declaration	... PACKAGE BODY pck IS ──── ••• ──── ••• END pck ;

... b: BLOCK IS ──── ••• BEGIN ... END BLOCK b ;	FUNCTION f (...) RETURN r IS ──── ••• BEGIN ... END f ;	PROCEDURE p (...) IS ──── ••• BEGIN ... END p ;	p : PROCESS ──── ••• BEGIN ... END PROCESS p ;

4.1.1 Further Definitions

full_type_declaration ::= **type** identifier **is** type_definition ;

incomplete_type_declaration ::= **type** identifier ;

4.1.2 Examples

`TYPE A IS RANGE 1 TO 10;` `TYPE B IS RANGE 1 TO 10;`	Two integer types *A* and *B*, *both of which have a range of 1 to 10, are declared.*

`TYPE capacitance IS RANGE 0 TO 1E16`
`   UNITS`
`      fF; -- Femtofarad`
`      pF = 1000 fF;   -- Picofarad`
`      nF = 1000 pF;   -- Nanofarad`
`      uF = 1000 nF;   -- Microfarad`
`   END UNITS;`
	The physical type *capacitance* is declared as a real type with a range of 0 to 1E16. Afterwards a base unit and units derived from it are declared.

`TYPE cell;`
 	
`TYPE link IS ACCESS cell;`
 	
`TYPE cell IS`
` RECORD`
`  value : integer;`
`  succ : link;`
`  pred : link;`
` END RECORD;`
	A recursive structure is created. At first type *cell* is declared incompletely. As a consequence the access type *link* is declared on the type *cell*.
	Afterwards type *cell* is declared completely as *Record*. The elements *succ* and *pred* are declared as index types. By doing so an interlinked list can be created in which every element receives an index to both its predecessor and its successor.

`TYPE boolean IS (false, true);`
 	
`TYPE bit IS ('0', '1');`
 	
`TYPE string IS`
` ARRAY (positive RANGE <>)`
` OF character;`
`TYPE bit_vector IS`
` ARRAY (natural RANGE <>)`
` OF bit;`
	These are examples of standard predefined types. *boolean*, *bit* and *character* are enumeration types.
	
	string and *bit_vector* are arrays that can have any width (RANGE <>) with the maximum width being determined by the corresponding type (*positive*, *natural*).

4.2 Subtype Declarations

... ENTITY e IS ___ ●●● BEGIN ... END e ;	... ARCHITECTURE a OF e IS ___ ●●● BEGIN ... END a ;	... CONFIGURATION c OF e IS ... END
... PACKAGE pkg IS ___ ●●● ___ ●●● END pkg ;	subtype_declaration ::= **subtype** identifier **is** subtype_indication ;	... PACKAGE BODY pck IS ___ ●●● ___ ●●● END pck ;
... b: BLOCK IS ___ ●●● BEGIN ... END BLOCK b ;	FUNCTION f (...) RETURN r IS ___ ●●● BEGIN ... END f ;	PROCEDURE p (...) IS ___ ●●● BEGIN ... END p ; p : PROCESS ___ ●●● BEGIN ... END PROCESS p ;

4.2.1 Further Definitions

identifier ::=
   basic_identifier | extended_identifier

subtype_indication ::=
   [*resolution_function_*name] type_mark [constraint]

4.2.2 Examples

`SUBTYPE natural IS integer`
    `RANGE 0 TO integer'high;`
 	
`SUBTYPE positive IS integer`
    `RANGE 1 TO integer'high;`
	These are standard predefined subtypes. *natural* is an *integer* type that is restricted to the range of 0 to the maximum *integer* value. *positive* is an *integer* type that is restricted to the range of 1 to the maximum *integer* value.

`SUBTYPE primary_color IS color`
    `RANGE yellow TO blue;`
`SUBTYPE same_color IS primary_color;`
 	
`SUBTYPE address_integer IS integer`
    `RANGE 0 TO 127;`
`SUBTYPE human_size IS real`
    `RANGE 0.50 TO 2.50;`
 	
`SUBTYPE byte IS bit_vector (7 DOWNTO 0);`
`SUBTYPE name IS string (1 TO 31);`
`SUBTYPE color_10 IS colors (1 TO 10);`
	These are common examples such as subtypes that are created from basic types by means of range constraints.
	
	The ranges of *integer* and *real* subtypes are declared with the keyword *RANGE*.
	
	The ranges of *character*, *string* and *enumeration* subtypes are declared by explicitly stating a certain section.

`SUBTYPE sbit IS wiredX zbit;`
`SUBTYPE xbit IS wiredX zbit`
    `RANGE 'X' TO '1';`
	The two subtypes *sbit* and *xbit* are declared as subtypes of *zbit* and a resolution function *wiredX* is assigned to both of them. The resolution function makes sure that in a multiple assignment to a signal only definite values are assigned.

4.3 Constant Declarations

...	...	...
ENTITY e IS _____ ••• BEGIN ... END e ;	ARCHITECTURE a OF e IS _____ ••• BEGIN ... END a ;	CONFIGURATION c OF e IS ... ... END
... PACKAGE pkg IS _____ ••• _____ ••• END pkg ;	constant_declaration ::= **constant** identifier_list : subtype_indication [:= expression] ;	... PACKAGE BODY pck IS _____ ••• _____ ••• END pck ;

...	FUNCTION f (...)	PROCEDURE p (...) IS	p : PROCESS
b: BLOCK IS _____ ••• BEGIN ... END BLOCK b ;	RETURN r IS _____ ••• BEGIN ... END f ;	_____ ••• BEGIN ... END p ;	_____ ••• BEGIN ... END PROCESS p ;

4.3.1 Further Definitions

identifier_list ::= identifier {, identifier }

subtype_indication ::=
    [*resolution_function*_name] type_mark [constraint]

expression ::=
    relation { **and** relation }
  | relation { **or** relation }
  | relation { **xor** relation }
  | relation [**nand** relation]
  | relation [**nor** relation]

4.3.2 Examples

`CONSTANT` cte : integer := 5; `CONSTANT` Vdd, Vcc : bit := '1'; `CONSTANT` min_setup_time : time := 5 ns;	The constant *cte* is of the type *integer* and has the value 5. The constants *Vdd* and *Vcc* are of the type *bit* and have the value '1'. The constant *min_setup_time* is of the physical type *time* and has the value 5 ns.

`CONSTANT name : string := "Dupond";`
 	
`CONSTANT address :`
`   bit_vector := "00110110";`
 	
`CONSTANT mask :`
`   bit_vector(1 TO 3) := "0101";`
 	
`CONSTANT bittab : bit_vector(1 TO 9)`
`   := (1 TO 3 => '0', 7 | 9 => 'Z',`
`      OTHERS => '1');`
 	
`CONSTANT tab : table_type(0 TO 4)`
`   := (2, 3, 4, -2, 0);`
	The constant *name* contains the string *"Dupond"*.
	The bit vector *address* has the constant value "00110110".
	The constant *mask* is declared as a subtype of *bit_vector* with the value "0101".
	The constant *bittab* is declared as a subtype of *bit_vector* with the value "000111Z1Z".
	The constant *tab* is declared as a subtype of *table_type* with the individual elements being assigned the constant values 2, 3, 4, -2 and 0.

`PACKAGE P IS`
`   CONSTANT deferred : integer;`
`END P;`
 	
`PACKAGE BODY P IS`
`   CONSTANT deferred :`
`                integer := 200;`
`END P;`
	An incomplete declaration of a constant may only be contained in the package declaration. The complete declaration of the constant has to be contained in the package body.

4.4 Signal Declarations

... ENTITY e IS **•••** BEGIN ... END e ;	... ARCHITECTURE a OF e IS **•••** BEGIN ... END a ;		... CONFIGURATION c OF e IS ... ... END

...
PACKAGE pkg IS
•••
•••
END pkg ;
	signal_declaration ::=
	
	signal identifier_list : subtype_indication
	    [signal_kind] [:= expression] ;
			...
			PACKAGE BODY pck
			       IS
			...
			...
			END pck ;

... b: BLOCK IS **•••** BEGIN ... END BLOCK b ;	FUNCTION f (...) RETURN r IS ... BEGIN ... END f ;	PROCEDURE p (...) IS ... BEGIN ... END p ;	p : PROCESS ... BEGIN ... END PROCESS p ;

4.4.1 Further Definitions

identifier_list ::= identifier { , identifier }

subtype_indication ::=
  [*resolution_function*_name] type_mark [constraint]

signal_kind ::=
  register | **bus**

expression ::=
  relation { **and** relation }
  | relation { **or** relation }
  | relation { **xor** relation }
  | relation [**nand** relation]
  | relation [**nor** relation]

The signals declared with **REGISTER** or **BUS** are 'guarded signals'. 'Guarded signals' have to be 'resolved signals'. Guarded signal assignments have the following meaning for 'guarded signals':

```
IF guard_expression THEN
      sig_name <= sig_waveform ;
ELSE
      sig_name <= NULL ;
END IF ;
```

The assignment of **NULL** to the signal *sig_name* means that the driver of this signal assignment is switched off. This has the following consequences for the 'resolved signal':

- If not all drivers were switched off, the resulting signal is only determined by the drivers that were not switched off.

- If all drivers were switched off, the last available signal value is kept in case of the signal declaration **REGISTER**.

- If all drivers were switched off, the default value stated in the 'resolution function' is used in case of the signal declaration **BUS**.

The signal driver is switched off immediately, i.e. without delay, after the *guard_expression* has taken on the value *false* except if an explicit delay time was planned to be given to the signal by the disconnection statement after it was declared as a controlled signal. An extensive example on this can be found in the Section 5.3 on Disconnection Specification.

4.4.2 Examples

SIGNAL clk_1, clk_2: time;	The signals *clk_1* and *clk_2* of the physical type *time* are declared.

SIGNAL address_bus:
    resolved_bit_vector
    BUS:= "10011001";
	The signal *address_bus* is declared as a guarded signal (BUS) of the type *resolved_bit_vector* and initialized with the value "10011001".

``SIGNAL resolved_s:
        resolution_function
        zbit REGISTER;```
	The signal *resolved_s* is declared as a guarded signal (REGISTER) of the type *zbit*. In addition, the signal is also assigned a resolution function *resolution_function*.

``SIGNAL address: bit8
          := "00110110";
SIGNAL bittab:
    bit_vector(1 TO 9)
    := (1 TO 3 => '0', 7 |
       9 => 'Z', OTHERS => '1');
SIGNAL tab:
    table_type(0 TO 4)
    := (2, 3, 4, -2, 0);```
	The signal *address* of the type *bit8* is declared and initialized with the value "00110110". The signal *bittab* is declared by the type *bit_vector* and initialized with the value "000111Z1Z". The signal *tab* is declared by the type *table_type* and initialized with the values 2, 3, 4, -2 and 0.

4.5 Variable Declarations

...	...	...
ENTITY e IS _____ ●●●	ARCHITECTURE a OF e IS _____ ●●●	CONFIGURATION c OF e IS
BEGIN	BEGIN	...
...	...	...
END e ;	END a ;	END

...
PACKAGE pkg IS
_____ ●●●
_____ ●●●
END pkg ;
	variable_declaration ::=
	
	    [**shared**] **variable** identifier_list :
	    subtype_indication [:= expression] ;
		...
		PACKAGE BODY pck
		        IS
		_____ ●●●
		_____ ●●●
		END pck ;

... b: BLOCK IS _____ ●●● BEGIN ... END BLOCK b ;	FUNCTION f (...) RETURN r IS _____ ●●● BEGIN ... END f ;	PROCEDURE p (...) IS _____ ●●● BEGIN ... END p ;	p : PROCESS _____ ●●● BEGIN ... END PROCESS p ;

4.5.1 Further Definitions

identifier_list ::= identifier { , identifier }

subtype_indication ::=
    [*resolution_function*_name] type_mark [constraint]

expression ::=
  relation { **and** relation }
  | relation { **or** relation }
  | relation { **xor** relation }
  | relation [**nand** relation]
  | relation [**nor** relation]

4.5.2 Comment

- Shared variables declarations are allowed only in the declarative part of entities, architectures, packages, package bodies and blocks. Shared variables declarations must not be used in processes and subprograms.

- More than one process can access shared variables. If several processes access a given shared variable in the same simulation cycle, the sequence of accesses is not prescribed. It is not the actual value of the variable after the simulation cycle, nor are the different values of the variable read within the simulation cycle deterministic. See the example below.

4.5.3 Examples

`VARIABLE count : positive;`	The variable *count* of the type *positive* is declared.

`VARIABLE index : integer`
`    RANGE 0 TO 99 := 0;`
`VARIABLE memory : bit_matrix`
`    (0 TO 7, 0 TO 1023);`
	The variables *index* and *memory* are declared as subtypes of the types *integer* and *bit_matrix*.

`ARCHITECTURE beh OF sv_example IS`
`    SHARED VARIABLE counter : integer`
`                    RANGE 0 TO 1 := 0;`
`BEGIN`
`    p1: PROCESS`
`    BEGIN`
`        counter := counter + 1;`
`        wait;`
`    END PROCESS p1;`
`    p2: PROCESS`
`    BEGIN`
`        counter := counter - 1;`
`        wait;`
`    END PROCESS p2;`
`END ARCHITECTURE beh;`
	An example of the non-deterministic nature of using *shared variables*:
	
	A *shared variable* that is manipulated by two processes is declared in the architecture.
	It is not prescribed whether
	- first p1 increments counter by one (counter = 1) and then p2 decrements counter by one (counter = 0)
	- first p2 tries to decrement counter by one, which would lead to an error because of the subtype violation

```VARIABLE address_bus : bit8```
```   := "00110110";```
 	
```VARIABLE integer_address :```
```   integer := 2**nb_bit - 1;```
 	
```VARIABLE bittab : bit_vector(1 TO 9)```
```   := (1 TO 3 => '0', 7 | 9 => 'Z',```
```   OTHERS => '1');```
 	
```VARIABLE tab : table_type(0 TO 4)```
```   := (2, 3, 4, -2, 0);```
	address_bus is declared as a variable of the type *bit8* and initialized with the value "00110110".
	integer_address is declared as a variable of the type *integer* and initialized with (2**nb_bit-1).
	The variable *bittab* is declared as a subtype of the type *bit_vector* and initialized with "000111Z1Z".
	The variable *tab* is declared as a subtype of the type *table_type* and initialized with the values 2, 3, 4, -2 and 0.

4.6 File Declarations

... ENTITY e IS ●●● BEGIN ... END e ;	... ARCHITECTURE a OF e IS ●●● BEGIN ... END a ;	... CONFIGURATION c OF e IS ... ... END
... PACKAGE pkg IS ●●● ●●● END pkg ;	file_declaration ::= **file** identifier_list : subtype_indidcation [file_open_information] ;	... PACKAGE BODY pck IS ●●● ●●● END pck ;
... b: BLOCK IS ●●● BEGIN ... END BLOCK b ;	FUNCTION f (...) RETURN r IS ●●● BEGIN ... END f ;	PROCEDURE p (...) IS / p : PROCESS ●●● / ●●● BEGIN / BEGIN ... / ... END p ; / END PROCESS p ;

4.6.1 Further Definitions

identifier_list ::= identifier { , identifier }

subtype_indication ::=
  [*resolution_function*_name] type_mark [constraint]

file_open_information ::=
  [**open** *file_open_kind*_expression] is file_logical_name

4.6.2 Comments

- File declarations are incompatible between VHDL'87 and VHDL'93!

- The standard does not define what happens if more than one logical file accesses the same physical file, specifically for different access modes.

4.6.3 Examples

VHDL'87

`FILE simulation_output : my_file_type` `    IS OUT "/home/usr2/sim.res";`	*simulation_output* is declared as a (virtual) output file of the type *my_file_type* with the physical path and name /home/usr2/sim.res.
`FILE rom_content : rom_file_type` `    IS IN "rom2048.txt";`	*rom_content* is declared as a (virtual) input file of the type *rom_file_type* with the physical name "rom2048.txt".

`FILE input : text IS IN "std_input";`
 	
`FILE output : text IS OUT "std_output";`
	input and *output* are predefined files of the type *text* with the physical names *std_input* and *std_output*.

`FILE sim_output : my_file_type` `    OUT "/home/usr3/sim.trc";`	*sim_output* is declared as a (virtual) output file (mode **IN** is default) of the type *my_file_type* with the physical path and name /home/usr3/sim.trc.

VHDL'93

`FILE nowhere : my_file_type;`	*nowhere* is declared as (virtual) file of type *my_file_type,* but without explicitly opening it.
`FILE simulation_input : my_file_type` `    IS "/home/usr2/sim.res";`	*simulation_input* is declared as (virtual) file of type *my_file_type* with the physical path and name /home/usr2/sim.in. At elaboration, FILE_OPEN (simulation_input, "/home/usr2/sim.res") is called implicit with the default READ_MODE.

`FILE simulation_output : my_file_type`
`    OPEN WRITE_MODE IS`
`    "/home/usr2/sim.res";`
	simulation_output is declared as (virtual) output file of type *my_file_type* with the physical path and name /home/usr2/sim.res.

4.7 Interface Declarations

Interface declarations define interface objects of a precisely defined type.

Interface objects are interface constants, interface signals, interface variables and interface files.

interface_list ::=   interface_element { ; interface_element }

interface_element ::=   interface_declaration

interface_declaration ::=
   interface_constant_declaration
   | interface_signal_declaration
   | interface_variable_declaration
   | interface_file_declaration

interface_constant_declaration ::=
   [**constant**] identifier_list : [**in**] subtype_indication [:= *static_expression*]

interface_signal_declaration ::=
   [**signal**] identifier_list : [mode] subtype_indication [**BUS**] [:= *static_expression*]
   -- subtype_indication may not be a file or access type.

interface_variable_declaration ::=
   [**variable**] identifier_list : [mode] subtype_indication [:= *static_expression*]

interface_file_declaration ::=   **file** identifier_list subtype_indication
   -- subtype_indication have to indicate a subtype of a file type.

4.8 Alias Declarations

... ENTITY e IS **•••** BEGIN ... END e ;	... ARCHITECTURE a OF e IS **•••** BEGIN ... END a ;		... CONFIGURATION c OF e IS ... ... END

...
 PACKAGE pkg IS
 •••
 •••
 END pkg ;
	alias_declaration ::=
	
	 alias alias_designator
	   [: subtype_indication] **is**
	     name [signature];
			...
			 PACKAGE BODY pck
			 IS
			 •••
			 •••
			 END pck ;

... b: BLOCK IS **•••** BEGIN ... END BLOCK b ;	FUNCTION f (...) RETURN r IS **•••** BEGIN ... END f ;	PROCEDURE p (...) IS **•••** BEGIN ... END p ;	p : PROCESS **•••** BEGIN ... END PROCESS p ;

4.8.1 Further Definitions

alias_designator ::= identifier | character_literal | operator_symbol

subtype_indication ::=
  [*resolution_function*_name] type_mark [constraint]

name ::=
  simple_name
  | operator_symbol
  | selected_name
  | indexed_name
  | slice_name
  | attribute_name

signature ::= [[type_mark { , type_mark }] [**return** type_mark]]

4.8.2 Additional Information

Alias can be used for all named entities except labels, loop parameters and generate parameters. An alias for an object (constant, variable, signal, file) is an object alias. All others are non-object aliases. The alias of an overloadable object is itself overloadable.

The following rules apply to object aliases:

1. Signatures are not allowed.

2. The name in an alias declaration has to be a static name (see Section 6.1). If the subtype indication is present, it has to match the basetype of the name in the alias declaration. This type must not be a multi dimensional array type. The following rules apply:

- If the subtype indication is absent or it denotes an unconstrained array type:

  - If the alias designator denotes a slice of an object then the subtype of the object is viewed as if it were of the subtype specified by the slice.

  - Otherwise the object has the same type as implied by the name.

- If the subtype indication denotes a constrained array type then the object is of this subtype. Moreover, the subtype must have matching elements for each element of the type denoted by the name.

- If the subtype indication denotes a scalar type then the object is of this subtype. Moreover, the bounds and direction must be the same.

3. The same applies to attribute references, where the prefix of the attribute name denotes the alias.

4. A reference of a object alias is automatically a reference to the original object (also applies to slices of arrays).

The following rules apply to non-object aliases:

1. Subtype indications are not allowed.

2. If the name denotes a subprogram (including a operator) or a enumeration literal then a signature is required. The signature has to match the parameter and result type profile (2.3) of exactly one subprogram or enumeration literals denoted by the name.

3. If the name denotes a enumeration type then the alias declaration implies further aliases for every enumeration literal (alias_designator = enumeration_literal; name = enumeration_type.enumeration_literal).

4. The equivalent applies to an alias of an physical type.

5. If the name denotes a type then the alias declaration implies further aliases for defined operators of this type and if needed for corresponding values and units. Every implicit operator alias declaration has a signature that exactly matches one of the parameter and result type profiles (Section 2.3) of the original operator.

4.8.3 Examples

| ```
CONSTANT tc : time := 2.5 ns;
ALIAS delay : time IS tc;
``` | Because of the alias declaration, the constant *tc* can now also be addressed via the name *delay*. |
| ```
VARIABLE real_number :
   bit_vector(0 TO 31);

ALIAS sign : bit IS real_number(0);

ALIAS mantissa : bit_vector(0 TO 23)
   IS real_number(8 TO 31);

ALIAS exponent : bit_vector(1 TO 7)
   IS real_number(1 TO 7);
``` | Here the variable *real_number* is aliased differently. Via *sign*, the MSB of *real_number* can be addressed. With *mantissa*, the elements 8 to 31 of *real_number* are addressed, with the indices ranging from 0 to 23. With *exponent*, the elements 1 to 7 of *real_number* are addressed, with the indices ranging from 1 to 7 as well. |
| ```
ALIAS std_bit IS STD.STANDARD.BIT;

-- ALIAS '0' IS STD.STANDARD.'0'
--      [RETURN STD.STANDARD.BIT];
-- ALIAS '1' IS STD.STANDARD.'1';
--      [RETURN STD.STANDARD.BIT];
-- ALIAS "and" IS STD.STANDARD."and";
-- [STD.STANDARD.BIT, STD.STANDARD.BIT
--      RETURN STD.STANDARD.BIT];
-- ALIAS "or" IS STD.STANDARD."or";
-- [STD.STANDARD.BIT, STD.STANDARD.BIT
--      RETURN STD.STANDARD.BIT];
-- ●●●
``` | The predefined type *BIT* of the automatically visible package *STANDARD* of the library *STD* is aliased to *std_bit*.<br><br>With this further alias declarations for the values of the enumeration type and the predefined operators are implied. These are shown as comments. |
| ```
VARIABLE vector : bit_vector(0 TO 7);
ALIAS reverse_vector :
   bit_vector(vector'length DOWNTO 1)
   IS vector;
``` | Through the alias, the variable *vector* can now be addressed via the name *reverse_vector*, with the indices ranging from 8 to 1. |

4.9 Attribute Declarations

... ENTITY e IS _____ ●●● BEGIN ... END e ;	... ARCHITECTURE a OF e IS _____ ●●● BEGIN ... END a ;	... CONFIGURATION c OF e IS ... ... END
... PACKAGE pkg IS _____ ●●● _____ ●●● END pkg ;	attribute_declaration ::= **attribute** identifier : type_mark ;	... PACKAGE BODY pck IS ... ... END pck ;
... b: BLOCK IS _____ ●●● BEGIN ... END BLOCK b ;	FUNCTION f (...) RETURN r IS _____ ●●● BEGIN ... END f ;	PROCEDURE p (...) IS _____ ●●● BEGIN ... END p ; p : PROCESS _____ ●●● BEGIN ... END PROCESS p ;

Attributes can be used to poll the characteristics of objects (e.g. signals). In many cases this allows a shorter and more elegant VHDL description to be created. The most important attributes are predefined ones. In order to be able to use one's own attributes, one has to write a corresponding function, which then provides the attribute's value at any given time. For further information see Section 5.1 on Attribute Specification.

4.9.1 Further Definitions

identifier ::=   basic_identifier | extended_identifier

type_mark ::=   *type*_name
                    | *subtype*_name

4.9.2 Examples

`ATTRIBUTE cap_value: cap;`	*cap_value* is declared as an attribute of the type *cap*.

`TYPE coordinate IS RECORD`
    `x, y : integer;`
 `END RECORD;`
 `TYPE positive IS integer`
    `RANGE 1 TO integer'high;`
 `ATTRIBUTE location: coordinate;`
 `ATTRIBUTE pin_no: positive;`
	Two different attributes are declared.
	
	 location is of the type *coordinate*, which is a Record type.
	 pin_no is of the type *positive*, which is a subtype of *integer*.

`SUBTYPE pin_natural IS natural`
   `RANGE 1 TO 24;`
`ATTRIBUTE pin_number:`
   `pin_natural;`
	The attribute *pin_number* declared here is of the subtype *pin_natural*.

`SIGNAL a1: bit_vector(3 DOWNTO 0);`
`PROCESS (a)`
`BEGIN`
  `z<= "0000";`
  `FOR i in 0 TO 3 LOOP`
    `IF (a = i) THEN`
      `z(i) <= '1';`
    `END IF;`
  `END LOOP;`
`END PROCESS;`
	By using predefined attributes, the loop instruction can be written in a different way as well:
	
	`FOR i IN a1'LOW TO a1'HIGH`
	`FOR i IN a1'RIGHT TO a1'LEFT`
	`FOR i IN a1'REVERSE_RANGE`
	`FOR i IN a1'RANGE`

4.10 Component Declarations

...
ENTITY e IS
...
BEGIN
...
END e ;
	...
	ARCHITECTURE a OF e IS
	   •••
	BEGIN
	...
	END a ;
			...
			CONFIGURATION c
			   OF e IS
			...
			...
			END

...
PACKAGE pkg IS
•••
•••
END pkg ;
	component_declaration ::=
	
	`component` identifier [`is`]
	   [*local*_generic_clause]
	   [*local*_port_clause]
	`end component` ;
			...
			PACKAGE BODY pck
			   IS
			...
			...
			END pck ;

...
b: BLOCK IS
   •••
BEGIN
...
END BLOCK b ;
	FUNCTION f (...)
	   RETURN r IS
	...
	BEGIN
	...
	END f ;
		PROCEDURE p (...) IS
		...
		BEGIN
		...
		END p ;
			p : PROCESS
			...
			BEGIN
			...
			END PROCESS p ;

4.10.1 Further Definitions

identifier ::=   basic_identifier | extended_identifier

generic_clause ::= `generic` (generic_list) ;

port_clause ::= `port` (port_list) ;

4.10.2 Examples

```COMPONENT adder_8_bit```
```PORT (a, b : IN bit_vector(1 TO 8);```
```   cin : IN bit;```
```   sum : OUT bit_vector(1 TO 8);```
```   cout : OUT bit);```
```END COMPONENT;```
	The component *adder_8_bit* declared here has the inputs *a*, *b* and *cin* and the outputs *sum* and *cout*.

```COMPONENT adder_n_bit```
```GENERIC (n : positive);```
```PORT (a, b : IN bit_vector(1 TO n);```
```   cin : IN bit;```
```   sum : OUT bit_vector(1 TO n);```
```   cout : OUT bit);```
```END COMPONENT;```
	The component *adder_n_bit* declared here is parameterized via the generic n.
	
	The widths of the input vectors *a* and *b* and that of the output vector *sum* are determined by the value of the generic *n*.

4.11 Group Template Declarations

... ENTITY e IS ••• BEGIN ... END e ;	... ARCHITECTURE a OF e IS ••• BEGIN ... END a ;		... CONFIGURATION c OF e IS ... END
... PACKAGE pkg IS ••• ••• END pkg ;	group_template_declaration ::= **group** identifier **is** (entity_class_entry_list) ;		... PACKAGE BODY pck IS ••• ••• END pck ;
... b: BLOCK IS ••• BEGIN ... END BLOCK b ;	FUNCTION f (...) RETURN r IS ••• BEGIN ... END f ;	PROCEDURE p (...) IS ••• BEGIN ... END p ;	p : PROCESS ••• BEGIN ... END PROCESS p ;

4.11.1 Further Definitions

entity_class_entry_list ::=
    entity_class_entry { , entity_class_entry }

entity_class_entry ::=
    entity_class [<>]

4.11.2 Examples

`GROUP pin2pin IS (SIGNAL, SIGNAL);`	Groups of this type consist of two signals.
`GROUP pin_set IS (SIGNAL <>);`	Groups of this type consist of any number of signals.
`GROUP file_groups IS (FILE <>);`	Groups of this type consist of any number of files.
`GROUP gog IS (GROUP <>);`	Groups of this type consist of any number of groups.

4.12 Group Declaration

...	...	...	
ENTITY e IS ••• BEGIN ... END e ;	ARCHITECTURE a OF e IS ••• BEGIN ... END a ;	CONFIGURATION c OF e IS ••• ••• END	
... PACKAGE pkg IS ••• ••• END pkg ;	group_declaration ::= **group** identifier : group_template_name (group_constituent_list) ;	... PACKAGE BODY pck IS ••• ••• END pck ;	
... b: BLOCK IS ••• BEGIN ... END BLOCK b ;	FUNCTION f (...) RETURN r IS ••• BEGIN ... END f ;	PROCEDURE p (...) IS ••• BEGIN ... END p ;	p : PROCESS ••• BEGIN ... END PROCESS p ;

4.12.1 Further Definitions

group_constituent_list::=
   group_constituent { , group_constituent }

group_constituent ::=
   name | character_literal

4.12.2 Examples

GROUP pinpair1 : pin2pin (clk, q1); **GROUP** pinpair2 : pin2pin (clk, q2);	Groups of type *pin2pin* are declared.
GROUP clocked : gog (pinpair1, pinpair2);	A group of the former declared groups.
GROUP path **IS** (**SIGNAL**, **SIGNAL**); **GROUP** a_to_s : path (a,s); **ATTRIBUTE** propagation_delay : time; **ATTRIBUTE** propagation_delay **OF** a_to_s : **GROUP IS** 250 ns;	The group template *path* is declared. The group *a_to_s* is declared. The attribute *propagation_delay* is declared. The attribute *propagation_delay* is assigned to *a_to_s* and is given the value of 250 ns.

GROUP pin_set **IS** (**SIGNAL** <>);
GROUP paths **IS** (**GROUPS** <>);
 	
GROUP sources : pin_set (inp1, inp2);
GROUP targets : pin_set (outp1, outp2);
GROUP ins_to_outs :
    paths (sources, targets);
 	
ATTRIBUTE propagation_delay : time;
 	
ATTRIBUTE propagation_delay **OF**
    ins_to_outs : **GROUP IS** delay;
	The group template *pin_set* is declared.
	The group template *paths* is declared.
	
	The group of signals *sources* and *targets* are declared.
	The group of groups *ins_to_outs* is declared.
	
	The attribute *propagation_delay* is declared.
	The attribute *propagation_delay* is assigned to *ins_to_outs* and is given the value of *delay*.

5 Specification

5.1 Attribute Specification

... ENTITY e IS _____ ••• BEGIN ... END e ;	... ARCHITECTURE a OF e IS _____ ••• BEGIN ... END a ;	... CONFIGURATION c OF e IS _____ ••• _____ ••• END
... PACKAGE pkg IS _____ ••• _____ ••• END pkg ;	attribute_specification ::= **attribute** attribute_designator **of** entity_specification **is** expression ;	.. PACKAGE BODY pck IS ... ... END pck ;

... b: BLOCK IS _____ ••• BEGIN ... END BLOCK b ;	FUNCTION f (...) RETURN r IS _____ ••• BEGIN ... END f ;	PROCEDURE p (...) IS _____ ••• BEGIN ... END p ;	p : PROCESS _____ ••• BEGIN ... END PROCESS p ;

5.1.1 Further Definitions

attribute_designator ::= *attribute*_simple_name

entity_specification ::=   entity_name_list : entity_class

expression ::=   relation { **and** relation }
                | relation { **or** relation }
                | relation { **xor** relation }
                | relation [**nand** relation]
                | relation [**nor** relation]

5.1.2 Examples

| ```
ATTRIBUTE pin_number OF cin :
    SIGNAL IS 10;
ATTRIBUTE pin_number OF cout :
    SIGNAL IS 5;
``` | Values for the attribute *pin_number* are determined. For the signal *cin* the attribute value is *10* and for the signal *cout* it is *5*. |
|---|---|
| ```
ATTRIBUTE instance_location OF
    adder_1: LABEL IS (10, 15);
ATTRIBUTE instance_location OF
    OTHERS: LABEL IS (25, 65);
``` | For the label *adder_1* the value of the attribute *instance_location* is *(10,15)*; for all other labels it is *(25,65)*. |

`ATTRIBUTE author OF add_entity :`
`        ENTITY IS "Martin";`
`ATTRIBUTE is_generic OF cmos_nand :`
`        COMPONENT IS false;`
`ATTRIBUTE date OF rtl :`
`        ARCHITECTURE IS (11, aug, 95);`
`ATTRIBUTE safety OF arithm_conv :`
`        PROCEDURE IS bug;`
`ATTRIBUTE confidentiality`
`        OF cmos_pkg:`
`        PACKAGE IS restrictive ;`
	The attribute *author* of the entity *add_entity* is seized by the string *Martin*. The attribute *is_generic* of the component *cmos_nand* is seized by the value *false*. The attribute *date* of the architecture *rtl* is seized by the Record *(14,Aug,95)*. The attribute *safety* of the procedure *arithm_conv* is seized by the value *bug*. The attribute *confidentiality* of the package *cmos_pkg* is seized by the value *restrictive*.

`SIGNAL a1: bit_vector(3 DOWNTO 0);`
`PROCESS (a)`
`BEGIN`
`    z<= "0000" :`
`    FOR i in 0 TO 3 LOOP`
`        IF (a = i) THEN`
`            z(i) <= '1';`
`        END IF;`
`    END LOOP;`
`END PROCESS;`
	By using predefined attributes, the loop instruction can be written in a different way as well:
	
	`FOR i IN a1'LOW TO a1'HIGH`
	`FOR i IN a1'RIGHT TO a1'LEFT`
	`FOR i IN a1'REVERSE_RANGE`
	`FOR i IN a1'RANGE`

5.2 Configuration Specification

... ENTITY e IS ... BEGIN ... END e ;	... ARCHITECTURE a OF e IS ●●● BEGIN ... END a ;	... CONFIGURATION c OF e IS ... ... END

...
PACKAGE pkg IS
...
...
END pkg ;
	configuration_specification ::=
	
	for component_specification
	        binding_indication ;
		...
		PACKAGE BODY pck
		        IS
		...
		...
		END pck ;

... b: BLOCK IS ●●● BEGIN ... END BLOCK b ;	FUNCTION f (...) RETURN r IS ... BEGIN ... END f ;	PROCEDURE p (...) IS ... BEGIN ... END p ;	p : PROCESS ... BEGIN ... END PROCESS p ;

5.2.1 Further Definitions

component_specification ::=
   instantiation_list : *component*_name

binding_indication ::=
   [**use** entity_aspect]
   [generic_map_aspect]
   [port_map_aspect]

5.2.2 Comment

- In the generic map aspect an actual must be an expression or the reserved word **OPEN**.

- In the port map aspect an actual must be a signal, an expression or the reserved word **OPEN**.
  (In VHDL'87 only signals could be connected with input ports; in VHDL'93 globally static values can be used.)

5.2.3 Examples

`FOR c1, c2, c3 : add_comp USE` `ENTITY work.add_1(behaviour);`	For the components *add_comp* of the labels *c1*, *c2* and *c3* the behavioural description *add_1* from the default library (*work*) is to be used.
`FOR OTHERS : add_comp USE` `CONFIGURATION work.add_configuration;`	In all other labels (**OTHERS**) the description *add_configuration* from the default library (*work*) is to be used for the components *add_comp*.
`FOR ALL : register_comp USE OPEN;`	All components *register_comp* that are used are not to be linked.

`FOR c(1 TO 5) : nand2_comp USE`
   `ENTITY nand(arc)`
      `GENERIC MAP (N => 2)`
      `PORT MAP (I(1) => a,`
               `I(2) => b,`
               `O => s);`
 	
`FOR c(6) : nand2_comp USE`
   `CONFIGURATION`
      `my_lib.nand2_configuration`
   `PORT MAP (a, b, s);`
	For the components *nand2_comp* of the labels *c(1)* to *c(5)* the entity *nand* with the generic *N=2* and the corresponding in-/output concatenation (**PORT MAP**) is to be used.
	For the component *nand2_comp* of the label *c(6)* the configuration *nand2_configuration* from the library *my_lib* is to be used with the corresponding in-/output concatenation (**PORT MAP**)

5.3 Disconnection Specification

... ENTITY e IS ●●● BEGIN ... END e ;	... ARCHITECTURE a OF e IS ●●● BEGIN ... END a ;	... CONFIGURATION c OF e IS ... ... END
... PACKAGE pkg IS ●●● ●●● END pkg ;	disconnection_specification ::= **disconnect** guarded_signal_specification **after** *time*_expression ;	... PACKAGE BODY pck IS ... ... END pck ;
... b: BLOCK IS ●●● BEGIN ... END BLOCK b ;	FUNCTION f (...) RETURN r IS ... BEGIN ... END f ;	PROCEDURE p (...) IS ... BEGIN ... END p ;	p : PROCESS ... BEGIN ... END PROCESS p ;

5.3.1 Further Definitions

guarded_signal_specification ::=   *guarded*_signal_list : type_mark

expression ::=   relation { **and** relation }
              | relation { **or** relation }
              | relation { **xor** relation }
              | relation [**nand** relation]
              | relation [**nor** relation]

5.3.2 Examples

SIGNAL a: resolved_type **REGISTER;** **DISCONNECT** a: resolved_type **AFTER** 1 ns;	*a* is declared as a guarded signal of the type **REGISTER**. If during simulation a driver for the signal *a* is deactivated, this happens with a delay of 1 ns.

SIGNAL sig1, sig2, sig3:
   resolved_bit **REGISTER;**
DISCONNECT sig1 :
   resolved_bit **AFTER** 5 ns;
DISCONNECT OTHERS:
   resolved_bit **AFTER** 8 ns;
	sig1, *sig2* and *sig3* are declared as guarded signals of the type **REGISTER**. During simulation the drivers for *sig1* are switched off with a delay of 5 ns and those of the other signals with a delay of 8 ns.

| ```
CONSTANT delay: time := 5 ns;
SIGNAL bus_a, bus_b : res_bus BUS;
DISCONNECT ALL: res_bus AFTER delay;
``` | *bus_a* and *bus_b* are declared as guarded signals of the type **BUS**. During simulation the drivers for both signals are switched off with a delay of 5 ns. |
| ```
PACKAGE fourval IS
   TYPE mvl4 IS ('X','0','1','Z');
   TYPE mvl4_vector IS ARRAY
     (natural RANGE <>) OF mvl4;
   FUNCTION resolved (a: mvl4_vector)
     RETURN mvl4;
   SUBTYPE mvl4_r IS resolved mvl4;
END fourval;

PACKAGE BODY fourval IS
   FUNCTION resolved (a: mvl4_vector)
     RETURN mvl4 IS
     VARIABLE result : mvl4 := 'Z';
   BEGIN
     ...
     RETURN result;
   END resolved;
END fourval;

USE work.fourval.ALL;
ENTITY mux_2_1 IS
   PORT (
     in_sig  : IN mvl4_vector (1 TO 2);
     choice  : IN integer;
     out_sig : OUT mvl4_r BUS);
END mux_2_1;

ARCHITECTURE with_guards OF mux_2_1 IS
   DISCONNECT out_sig : mvl4_r
     AFTER 25 ns;
BEGIN
   choice_1 : BLOCK (choice = 1)
   BEGIN
     out_sig <= GUARDED in_sig(1)
                      AFTER 20 ns;
   END BLOCK;
   choice_2 : BLOCK (choice = 2)
   BEGIN
     out_sig <= GUARDED in_sig(2)
                      AFTER 18 ns;
   END BLOCK;
END with_guards;
``` | In the **PACKAGE** *fourval* a four valued logic *mvl4* and a corresponding vector are defined.

The function *resolved* is declared. Consequently a 'resolved signal' can be derived as a **SUBTYPE**.

In the **PACKAGE BODY** the function *resolved* is described.

If the input signal *choice* changes to *1*, the signal driver of the first block is activated and passes the first input signal on to the output after 20 ns. If *choice* changes to *2*, the second block passes the second input signal on the output after 18 ns. As the first signal driver switches off only after 25 ns, both drivers are active simultaneously for 7 ns. The resulting signal is determined by the 'resolution function' of the output signal. If *choice* changes to a value other than *1* or *2*, the last active driver switches off after 25 ns and the output signal changes to its default value (in this case 'Z'), as it is declared as a **BUS**. If it were declared as a **REGISTER**, the last signal value would be kept. |

6 Names

6.1 Name

6.1.1 Definition

name ::=
   simple_name
   | operator_symbol
   selected_name
   indexed_name
   slice_name
   | attribute_name

6.2 Simple Names

6.2.1 Definition

simple_name ::=   identifier

With a simple name, different objects in VHDL code can be addressed and manipulated.

6.3 Selected Names

6.3.1 Definitions

selected_name ::=
   prefix . suffix

prefix ::=
   name
   | function_call

suffix ::=
   simple_name
   | character_literal
   operator_symbol
   | **all**

6.3.2 Examples

`instruction.opcode`	The element *opcode* of the Record *instruction* is addressed.
`ptr.`**`ALL`**	All elements (**ALL**) to which the index *ptr* points are addressed.
`ttl.SN74LS221`	The design unit *SN74LS221* from the library *ttl* is addressed.
`cmos.`**`ALL`**	All design units from the library *cmos* are addressed.
`measurements.voltage`	The entity *voltage* from the package *measurements* is addressed.
`standard.`**`ALL`**	All entities from the package *standard* are addressed.
`p.data`	The entity *data*, which is defined in the process *p*, is addressed.

6.4 Indexed Names

6.4.1 Definition

indexed_name ::=   prefix (expression { , expression })

6.4.2 Examples

`register_array(5)`	The 5th element of the array *register_array* is addressed.
`memory_cell(1024, 7)`	The elements with the indices *(1024,7)* of the two dimensional array *memory_cell* are addressed.

6.5 Range Names

6.5.1 Definition

slice_name ::=   prefix (discrete_range)

6.5.2 Examples

| ```
SIGNAL    r15  : bit_vector(0 TO 31);
CONSTANT data : bit_vector(31 DOWNTO 0);

r15(0 TO 7);
data(24 DOWNTO 1);
data(24 TO 25);
``` | Different slices are addressed. The first slice addresses the range *0* to *7* of *r15*. The second slice addresses the range *24* to *1* of *data*. The third slice is invalid, as the direction of indication in the declaration is opposed to that in the slice. |

6.6 Attribute Names

6.6.1 Definitions

attribute_name ::=
    prefix [signature] ' attribute_designator [(expression)

6.6.2 Examples

`register'left(1)`	The left element of the first dimension of the one- or multi dimensional array *register* is addressed.
`output'fanout`	The attribute *fanout* provides the number of signals driven by *output*.
`clk'delayed(5 ns)`	The signal *clk*, delayed by 5 ns, is addressed.
| ```
SIGNAL a1: bit_vector(3 DOWNTO 0);

PROCESS (a)
BEGIN
   z<= "0000" :
   FOR i in 0 TO 3 LOOP
      IF (a = i) THEN
         z(i) <= '1';
      END IF;
   END LOOP;
END PROCESS;
``` | By using predefined attributes the loop instruction can be written in a different way as well:<br><br>`FOR i IN a1'LOW TO a1'HIGH`<br>`FOR i IN a1'RIGHT TO a1'LEFT`<br>`FOR i IN a1'REVERSE_RANGE`<br>`FOR i IN a1'RANGE` |

7 Expressions

7.1 Expression

7.1.1 Definitions

Each expression is equal to an equation that forms a rule for the calculation of a value.

expression ::=
   relation { **and** relation }
   | relation { **or** relation }
   | relation { **xor** relation }
   | relation { **nand** relation }
   | relation { **nor** relation }

relation ::=
   shift_expression [relational_operator shift_expression]

shift_expression ::=
   simple_expression [shift_operator simple_expression]

simple_expression ::=
   [sign] term { adding_operator term }

7.2 Logic Operators

7.2.1 Definition

The logic operators **AND**, **OR**, **NAND**, **NOR**, **XOR**, **XNOR** and **NOT** are defined for the predefined data types *bit* and *boolean*. They can also be used for one dimensional array types (*Array*) whose elements are of the type *bit* or *boolean*. If the operators **AND**, **OR**, **NAND**, **NOR**, **XOR** and **XNOR** are to be used in this last case, the following has to be taken into consideration:

1. Both arrays have to have the same length.
2. The operation is carried out with the corresponding elements of both arrays.
3. The result is a array that has the same field depth as the left operand.

Basically the same is valid for the operator **NOT**; however, the operation is carried out with every individual element of the array. All binary logic operators have the lowest priority. The unary operator **NOT** has top priority.

7.2.2 Truth table

A	B	A **AND** B	A	B	A **OR** B	A	B	A **XOR** B		
F	F	F	F	F	F	F	F	F		
T	F	F	T	F	T	T	F	T		
F	T	F	F	T	T	F	T	T		
T	T	T	T	T	T	T	T	F		
A	B	A **NAND** B	A	B	A **NOR** B	A	B	A **XNOR** B	A	**NOT** A
F	F	T	F	F	T	F	F	T	F	T
T	F	T	T	F	F	T	F	F	T	F
F	T	T	F	T	F	F	T	F		
T	T	F	T	T	F	T	T	T		

T stands for true (type *boolean*), '1' (type *bit*).

F stands for false (type *boolean*), '0' (type *bit*).

7.3 Relational Operators

7.3.1 Definition

Comparing operators are used to compare operands according to their equality, inequality and size.

The operands always have to be of the same type.

The result of the operation is of the predefined type *boolean*.

7.3.2 Comment

- The comparison of discrete array types is done by comparing the 'left' values of the arrays. Vectors for example are aligned to the left and then compared.
  ("110" < "1000" results in false, as only the first three bits are relevant.)

7.3.3 Overview

Operator	Operation	Operand type	Result type
=	Equality	any	boolean
/=	Inequality	any	boolean
< <= > >=	Comparison	any scalar type or a array type	boolean

7.4 Shift Operators

7.4.1 Definition

The shift operators are defined for any one dimensional arrays with elements of type **BIT** or **BOOLEAN**.

The operators are defined as follows, where L is the left operand and R the right operand:

- **L sll R**: Shift L logically left (R≥0), respectively right (R<0), by R index positions. The foremost (R≥0), respectively the last (R<0), elements drop out and T'LEFT is inserted. T is the type of the elements of the array.

- **L srl R**: Shift L logically right (R≥0), respectively left (R<0), by R index positions. The last (R≥0), respectively the foremost (R<0), elements drop out and T'LEFT is inserted. T is the type of the elements of the array.

- **L sla R**: Shift L arithmetically left (R≥0), respectively right (R<0), by R index positions. The foremost (R≥0), respectively the last (R<0), elements drop out and L'RIGHT (R≥0), respectively L'LEFT (R<0), is inserted. It is the last (R≥0), respectively the foremost (R<0), value of L that is inserted.

- **L sra R**: Shift L arithmetically right (R≥0), respectively left (R<0), by R index positions. The last (R≥0), respectively the foremost (R<0), elements drop out and L'LEFT (R≥0), respectively L'RIGHT (R<0), is inserted. It is the foremost (R≥0), respectively the last (R<0), value of L that is inserted.

- **L rol R**: Rotate L logically left (R≥0), respectively right (R<0), by R index positions. The foremost (R≥0), respectively the last (R<0), values are inserted in front of (R≥0), respectively behind (R<0).

- **L ror R**: Rotate L logically right (R≥0), respectively left (R<0), by R index positions. The last (R≥0), respectively the foremost (R<0), values are inserted behind (R≥0), respectively in front (R<0).

7.4.2 Overview

Operator	Operation	Operand type (left)	Operand type (right)	result type
sll	Shift Left Logical	Any one dimensional array type with elements of the type BIT or BOOLEAN	INTEGER	Type of the left operand
srl	Shift Right Logical	Any one dimensional array type with elements of the type BIT or BOOLEAN	INTEGER	Type of the left operand

Operator	Operation	Operand type (left)	Operand type (right)	result type
sla	Shift Left Arithmetic	Any onedimensional array type with elements of the type BIT or BOOLEAN	INTEGER	Type of the left operand
sra	Shift Right Arithmetic	Any one dimensional array type with elements of the type BIT or BOOLEAN	INTEGER	Type of the left operand
rol	Rotate Left Logical	Any one dimensional array type with elements of the type BIT or BOOLEAN	INTEGER	Type of the left operand
ror	Rotate Right Logical	Any one dimensional array type with elements of the type BIT or BOOLEAN	INTEGER	Type of the left operand

7.5 Adding Operators

7.5.1 Definition

The addition operators + and - are predefined in their known meaning for every numerical type. The concatenation operator & is predefined for any one dimensional array type.

7.5.2 Overview

Operator	Operation	Operand type (left)	Operand type (right)	Result type
+	Addition	any numerical type	same type	same type
-	Subtraction	any numerical type	same type	same type
&	Chaining (Concate-nation)	any array type	same array type	same array type
		any array type	element type	same array type
		element type	any array type	same array type
		element type	element type	any array type

7.5.3 Additional Information

The prefixes + and - are predefined for any numerical type.

According to the priority rules for expressions, a prefix operand must not follow multiplication operators, the exponentiation operator ** or the operators **ABS** and **NOT**.

The following expressions are syntactically wrong:

A / +B   A ** -B

Expressions of the following forms, however, are permitted:

A / (+B)   A ** (-B)

7.6 Multiplying Operators

7.6.1 Definition

The multiplying operators * and / are predefined for every integer- and floating point type. Further the operators * and / are predefined for any physical type. The operators **MOD** and **REM** are predefined for any integer type.The result of every operation is of the same type as the operands (which are also of the same type). Exceptions are the * and / operators used with a physical type. Normally the result type is the physical type.

7.6.2 Overview

Operator	Operation	Operand type (left)	Operand type (right)	Result type
*	Multiplication	any integer type	same type	same type
		any floating point type	same type	same type
/	Division	any integer type	same type	same type
		any floating point type	same type	same type
MOD	Modulo	any integer type	same type	same type
REM	Remainder	any integer type	same type	same type
*	Multiplication	any physical type	integer	same as left operand
		any physical type	real	same as left operand
		integer	any physical type	same as right operand
		real	any physical type	same as right operand

Operator	Operation	Operand type (left)	Operand type (right)	Result type
		any physical type	integer	same as left operand
/	Division	any physical type	real	same as left operand
		any physical type	same type	universal integer

7.7 Miscellaneous Operators

7.7.1 Definition

The unary operator **ABS** is predefined for any numerical type.

The exponentiation operator ** is predefined for any integer- or floating-point type. The right operand (= exponent) is always of the predefined type *integer*.

7.7.2 The Operator ABS

Operator	Operation	Operand type	Result type
ABS	absolute value	any numerical type	same type

7.7.3 The Operator **

Exponentiation with negative exponents is only possible if the left operand is a floating point type.

Operator	Operation	Operand type (left)	Operand type (right)	Result type
		any integer type	*integer*	same type as left operand
**	exponentiation	any floating point type	*integer*	same type as left operand

7.8 Literals

7.8.1 Definitions

literal ::=
   numeric_literal
   | enumeration_literal
   | string_literal
   | bit_string_literal
   | **null**

numeric_literal ::=
   abstract_literal
   | physical_literal

7.8.2 Examples

3.14159_26536	A literal of the type *universal_real* (abstract type).
5280	A literal of the type *universal_integer* (abstract type).
10.7 ns	A literal of a physical type
O"4777"	A literal of the type *bit_string*.
"54LS281"	A literal of the type *string*.
""	A *string* literal which represents an empty array.

7.9 Aggregates

7.9.1 Definitions

aggregate ::=   (element_association { , element_association })

element_association ::=   [choices =>] expression

choices ::=   choice { | choice }

choice ::=
   simple_expression
   | discrete_range
   | *element*_simple_name
   | **others**

7.9.2 Examples

`(a_bit, b_bit, c_bit, d_bit)`	This aggregate has width 4.
`(7 => '1', 5 DOWNTO 1 => '1', 6 => b_bit, OTHERS => '0')`	With this aggregate it is possible to assign different values to the individual elements of an array.
`(OTHERS => (OTHERS => '0'));`	With this aggregate it is possible to assign the value *0* to all individual elements of a two dimensional array.

7.10 Function Call

7.10.1 Definitions

function_call ::=
  *function*_name [(actual_parameter_part)]

actual_parameter_part ::=
  *parameter*_association_list

7.10.2 Examples

`exnor_out <= exnor(in1, in2);`	With this function call *exnor_out* receives the return value of the function *exnor*.

`x2 <= exnor (`
`    a => in1(2 DOWNTO 0),`
`    b => in2(2 DOWNTO 0));`
	x2 receives the return value of the function *exnor*. Here the transfer parameters *a* and *b* have the values of the stated vector ranges.

`i <= bit_to_integer(bit_a =>` `    in(8)) + count_ones(in2);`	i receives the sum of the return values of the two functions *bit_to_integer* and *count_ones*.

7.11 Qualified Expression

7.11.1 Definitions

qualified_expression ::=
  type_mark ' (expression)
  | type_mark ' aggregate

7.11.2 Example

| ```
w  <=  (a=b)  =  (c=d);
x  <=  (a=b)  =  mvl4'(c=d);
y  <=  (a=b)  =  bit'(c=d);
z  <=  (a=b)  =  boolean'(c=d);
``` | The type of the individual return value is explicitly selected by the qualified expressions. Thus the corresponding '=' function is selected as well. |
| ```
CASE vec_type'(A & B) is
   WHEN "00" => VALUE <= 0;
   WHEN "01" => VALUE <= 1;
   WHEN "10" => VALUE <= 2;
   WHEN "11" => VALUE <= 3;
   WHEN OTHERS => VALUE <= 9;
END CASE;
``` | The qualified expression merges two single-bit types to a vector with the (sub-) type vec_type. The value of this newly formed vector is examined in the case assignment |

7.12 Type Conversion

7.12.1 Definitions

type_conversion ::=   type_mark (expression)

7.12.2 Examples

`integer(float_varibale)`	The *float_variable* is turned into an integer type by rounding up/down.
`real(integer_variable)`	The *integer_variable* is turned into the type *real*.

7.13 Allocator

7.13.1 Definition

allocator ::=   **new** subtype_indication
             | **new** qualified_expression

7.13.2 Examples

| ```
NEW node
NEW node'(15 ns, NULL)
NEW node'(delay => 5 ns,
          \next\ => stack)
``` | Memory is allocated for the type *node*.<br>In the first example the default value of the type *node* is used for initialization, in the second example the values stated in brackets are used. |
```

`NEW bit_vector'("01100010")`	By initializing it with *"01100010"*, the width of the allocated object is determined to be 8.
`NEW string(1 TO 10)`	The size of the allocated memory range is restricted by the determination of the string width (10).

7.14 Static Expression

7.14.1 Definition

There are two categories of static expressions.

An expression is called *locally static* if every operator in the expression is an implicit defined operator, if both operands and results are scalar and every primary in the expression is a *locally static primary*; *locally static primaries* are:

1. Variables of any type other then type **TIME**.
2. Constants that are explicitly declared by a constant declaration and initialized by a locally static expression (**NOT** (deferred) constants).
3. An alias whose aliased name is a locally static name.
4. Function calls whose names represent a predefined operator and whose current parameters are locally static expressions.
5. Predefined attributes that are values, other than **'PATH_NAME**, and whose prefix is either a locally static subtype or is an object name that is of a locally static subtype.
6. Predefined attributes, except '**LAST_EVENT**, '**LAST_ACTIVE**, '**LAST_VALUE**, '**DRIVING** and '**DIRIVNG_VALUE**, of locally static subtypes, which are functions and whose actual parameters are locally statics.
7. User defined attributes whose values are defined by locally static expressions.
8. Qualified expression whose results are locally static subtypes and whose operands are locally static expressions.
9. A type conversion whose expression is a locally static expression.
10. Locally static expression enclosed in parentheses.

An expression is called *global static* (not dynamically elaborated) if every function in the expression is a pure function and every primary in the expression is a *global static primary*; *global static primaries* are:

1. Literals of type **TIME**.
2. Locally static primaries.
3. Generic constants.
4. Generic parameters.
5. Constants, including (deferred) constants.
6. Aliases whose aliased names are a globally static primaries.
7. Array aggregates of global static subtypes whose elements consist only of global static expressions and whose elements have only globally static ranges.
8. Record aggregates, if all elements are globally static expressions.

9. Function calls whose names represent pure functions and whose actual parameters are global static expressions.
10. Predefined attributes that are values and whose prefix is either a globally static subtype or is an object or function call that is of a globally static subtype.
11. Predefined attributes that are functions other than 'EVENT, 'ACTIVE, 'LAST_EVENT, 'LAST_ACTIVE, 'LAST_VALUE, 'DRIVING or 'DRIVING_VALUE, whose prefix is either a globally static subtype or is an object or function call that is of a globally static subtype, and whose actual parameter (if any) is a globally static expression.
12. User defined attributes whose values are defined by global static expressions.
13. Qualified expressions whose operand is a global static expression.
14. Type conversion whose expression is a globally static expression.
15. Allocators of the first form (see Section 7.13) whose subtype indication denotes a globally static subtype.
16. Allocators of the second form whose qualified expression is a globally static expression.
17. Global static expressions enclosed in parentheses.
18. Subelements or slices of a globally static primary, provided that any index expressions are globally static expressions and any discrete ranges used in slice names are globally static discrete ranges.

7.14.2 Comments

- On text places where only "static" is used, locally or globally static can be inserted.

- The rules for locally and globally static expressions imply that a constant or a generic may be initialized with a non-static expression; the constant itself may be a locally or globally static. Only interface constants, variables and signal declarations require static initialization expressions.

7.15 Universal Expression

7.15.1 Definition

A universal expression is an expression whose results are either of the type *universal integer* or *universal real*.

7.15.2 Overview

Operator	Operation	Left Operand type	Right Operand type	Result type
*	Multiplication	universal_real	universal_integer	universal_real
		universal_integer	universal_real	universal_real
/	Division	universal_real	universal_integer	universal_real

8 Sequential Statements

8.1 Wait

... ENTITY e IS ... BEGIN ... END e ;	... ARCHITECTURE a OF e IS ... BEGIN ... END a ;	... CONFIGURATION c OF e IS ... ... END
... PACKAGE pkg IS ... ... END pkg ;	wait_statement ::= [label :] **wait** [sensitivity_clause] [condition_clause] [timeout_clause] ;	... PACKAGE BODY pck IS ... ... END pck ;

... b: BLOCK IS ... BEGIN ... END BLOCK b ;	FUNCTION f (...) RETURN r IS ... BEGIN •• • END f ;	PROCEDURE p (...) IS ... BEGIN •• • END p ;	p : PROCESS ... BEGIN •• • END PROCESS p ;

8.1.1 Further Definitions

label ::= identifier

sensitivity_clause ::=
  on sensitivity_list

condition_clause ::=
  until condition

timeout_clause ::=
  for *time*_expression

8.1.2 Comments

- The WAIT statement must not be used within a function or procedure that itself is called within a function.

- The WAIT statement must not be called by a process that possesses a sensitivity list.

- In general, the WAIT statement is "sensitive" to all signals used within the statement, except when a sensitivity list is used (as in a WAIT ON statement; see the last example).

- In a postponed process the condition in a WAIT statement may already be false at the actual time (last delta cycle) when the process execution is resumed.

8.1.3 Examples

`WAIT;`	The process is permanently interrupted.
`WAIT FOR 5 ns;`	The process is interrupted for 5 ns.
`WAIT ON sig_1, sig_2;`	The process is interrupted until the value of one of the two signals changes.
`WAIT UNTIL clock = '1';`	The process is interrupted until the value of *clock* is 1.
`WAIT UNTIL data=good FOR 25 ns;`	The process is interrupted until the value of *data* = *good* or 25 ns have passed.

`WAIT ON sig_1, sig_2, sig_3`
`    UNTIL clock = '1'`
`    FOR 25 ns;`
	Initially one waits for the signals sig_1, sig_2 and sig_3 to change; if clock is 1, the process is resumed; otherwise, not; the process is suspended for at most 25 ns.

8.2 Assertion

... ENTITY e IS ... BEGIN ... END e ;	... ARCHITECTURE a OF e IS ... BEGIN ... END a ;		... CONFIGURATION c OF e IS ... ... END

...
PACKAGE pkg IS
...
...
END pkg ;
	assertion_statement ::=
	
	    [label :] assertion ;
			...
			PACKAGE BODY pck
			    IS
			...
			...
			END pck ;

...
b: BLOCK IS
...
BEGIN
...
END BLOCK b ;
	FUNCTION f (...)
	    RETURN r IS
	...
	BEGIN
	    ●●●
	END f ;
		PROCEDURE p (...) IS
		...
		BEGIN
		    ●●●
		END p ;
			p : PROCESS
			...
			BEGIN
			    ●●●
			END PROCESS p ;

8.2.1 Further Definitions

assertion ::=
  assert condition
  [**report** expression]
  [**severity** expression]

condition ::= *boolean*_expression

expression ::=
  relation { **and** relation }
  | relation { **or** relation }
  | relation { **xor** relation }
  | relation [**nand** relation]
  | relation [**nor** relation]

8.2.2 Comments

- The **REPORT** expression has to be of type string.

- In the absence of the **REPORT** clause, the default string "Assertion Violation". will be used.

- The **SEVERITY** expression has be of type severity_level. Possible values are: note, warning, error, failure.

- In the absence of the **SEVERITY** clause, the default error will be used.

8.2.3 Examples

ASSERT signal_reset = '1';	It is checked whether *signal_reset* is not equal to *1*.
ASSERT variable_reset = '1' **REPORT** "Reset is active !";	If *variable_reset* is not equal to *1*, the report "Reset is active" is given.
ASSERT reset = '1' OR set = '1' **REPORT** "Reset and Set simultaneously active !" **SEVERITY** failure;	If the condition that is to be verified is not fulfilled an error is reported and measures in accordance with the severity level are taken.

ASSERT data = 0
REPORT "Datum ist gleich " &
      integer_to_string(data)
      & " !"
SEVERITY note;
	If *data* is not equal to *0*, a severity note containing the current value of *data* is given.

ASSERT false **REPORT** "End of simulation!" **SEVERITY** failure;	This assertion automatically (false) stops (severity_level=failure) the simulation at the time evaluated

8.3 Report

... ENTITY e IS ... BEGIN ... END e ;	... ARCHITECTURE a OF e IS ... BEGIN ... END a ;	... CONFIGURATION c OF e IS ... ... END
... PACKAGE pkg IS ... ... END pkg ;	report_statement ::= [label :] **report** expression [**severity** expression] ;	... PACKAGE BODY pck IS ... ... END pck ;

... b: BLOCK IS ... BEGIN ... END BLOCK b ;	FUNCTION f (...) RETURN r IS ... BEGIN ●●● END f ;	PROCEDURE p (...) IS ... BEGIN ●●● END p ;	p : PROCESS ... BEGIN ●●● END PROCESS p ;

8.3.1 Comments

• The **REPORT** expression has to be of type string.

• The **SEVERITY** expression has be of type severity_level. Possible values are: note, warning, error, failure.

• In the absence of the **SEVERITY** clause, the default note will be used.

8.3.2 Examples

REPORT "End of simulaion!" **SEVERITY** failure ;	This assertion stops (severity_level=failure) the simulation at the time evaluated
REPORT "Entering process clkdiv";	This entering of process *clkdiv* will be reported.

8.4 Signal Assignment

... ENTITY e IS ... BEGIN ... END e ;	... ARCHITECTURE a OF e IS ... BEGIN ... END a ;		... CONFIGURATION c OF e IS ... ... END
... PACKAGE pkg IS ... ... END pkg ;	signal_assignment_statement ::= target <= [delay_mechanism] waveform ;		... PACKAGE BODY pck IS ... ... END pck ;
... b: BLOCK IS ... BEGIN ... END BLOCK b ;	FUNCTION f (...) RETURN r IS ... BEGIN ●●● END f ;	PROCEDURE p (...) IS ... BEGIN ●●● END p ;	p : PROCESS ... BEGIN ●●● END PROCESS p ;

8.4.1 Further Definitions

delay_mechanism ::=
  transport
    | [**reject** *time*_expression] **inertial**
target ::=
  name
  | aggregate
waveform ::=
  waveform_element { , waveform_element }
  | **unaffected**

8.4.2 Comments

- The keyword **UNAFFECTED** is allowed only in concurrent signal assignments.
- The default delay mechanism is **INERTIAL**.
- With **TRANSPORT** all pulses are transmitted.
- With **INERTIAL** only those pulses are transmitted which width is greater than the given limit. This limit is given by the value following **REJECT** or the first time value in the waveform.
- The value after **REJECT** must not be greater than the first time value of the waveform.

8.4.3 Examples

`A <= B AFTER 5 ns;`	The value of *B* is assigned to signal A after 5 ns. In the first example the inertial delay model is used, in the second example the transport delay model is used.
`A <= TRANSPORT B AFTER 5 ns;`	

`data <= 2 AFTER 1 ns,`
`        4 AFTER 3 ns,`
`       10 AFTER 8 ns;`
	A waveform is assigned to signal *data*, according to which *data* receives the value *2* after 1 ns, the value *4* after 3 ns and the value *10* after 8 ns.

`A <= my_function(data, 4) AFTER 5 ns;`	Signal *A* is assigned the result of the function *my_function* by the inertial delay model In the first example this happens after 5 ns; in the second and third examples this happens after a time that is determined by the constant delay. In the third example the value *0* is transferred to A 2 ns after the preceding assignment.
`A <= my_function(data, 4) AFTER delay;`	
`A <= my_function(data, 4) AFTER delay,` `     0 AFTER delay + 2 ns;`	

`ouptut <= input AFTER 6 ns;`
`output <= INERTIAL input AFTER 6 ns;`
`output <= REJECT 6 ns INERTIAL`
`          input AFTER 6 ns;`
	These assignments are equivalent. The value of *input* is driven to *output* with a delay of 6 ns. Pulses smaller 6 ns are suppressed.

`output1 <= REJECT 3 ns INERTIAL`
`           input1 AFTER 6 ns;`
`output2 <= REJECT 3 ns INERTIAL`
`           input2 AFTER 6 ns,`
`           NOT input2 AFTER 12 ns;`
	Here the pulse rejection limit is smaller than the first time expression in the waveform. All pulses smaller than 3 ns are suppressed.

`output1 <= TRANSPORT input1 AFTER 6 ns;`
`output2 <= TRANSPORT input2 AFTER 6 ns,`
`           NOT input2 AFTER 12 ns;`
 	
`output3 <= REJECT 0 ns INERTIAL`
`           input1 AFTER 6 ns;`
`output4 <= REJECT 0 ns INERTIAL`
`           input2 AFTER 6 ns,`
`           NOT input2 AFTER 12 ns;`
	The signal assignments to *output1* and *ouput2* are equivalent to those of *ouput3* and *output4*.
	
	No pulses are suppressed.

VHDL'87	
``sig2   <= input AFTER 3 ns;
output <= TRANSPORT sig2 AFTER 9 ns;``` VHDL'93 ```output <= REJECT 3 ns INERTIAL
input AFTER 12 ns;```	In VHDL'87 one had to choose the above assignments. Both variants are equivalent.

8.5 Variable Assignment

... ENTITY e IS ... BEGIN ... END e ;	... ARCHITECTURE a OF e IS ... BEGIN ... END a ;	... CONFIGURATION c OF e IS ... ... END
... PACKAGE pkg IS ... ... END pkg ;	variable_assignment_statement ::= [label :] target := expression ;	... PACKAGE BODY pck IS ... ... END pck ;

...
b: BLOCK IS
 	
...
BEGIN
 	
...
END BLOCK b ;
	FUNCTION f (...)
	  RETURN r IS
	...
	
	BEGIN
	  •••
	END f ;
		PROCEDURE p (...) IS
		...
		
		BEGIN
		  •••
		END p ;
			p : PROCESS
			...
			
			BEGIN
			  •••
			END PROCESS p ;

8.5.1 Further Definitions

label ::= identifier

target ::=   name
              | aggregate

expression ::=   relation { **and** relation }
                  | relation { **or** relation }
                  | relation { **xor** relation }
                  | relation [**nand** relation]
                  | relation [**nor** relation]

8.5.2 Examples

`var := 0;`	*var* receives the value *0*.
`a := my_function (data, 4);`	*a* receives the result of the function *my_function* as a new value.

`var_int := my_function(data, 4) +`
`          4 * a_function(var_int) -`
`          2 ** data;`
	var_int receives the result of the right equation as its value.

`str_a := "Mein Name ist " &` `    get_name & ", und Ihrer?";`	*str_a* is assigned a string that consists of three interlinked parts.

8.6 Procedure Call

... ENTITY e IS ... BEGIN ... END e ;	... ARCHITECTURE a OF e IS ... BEGIN ... END a ;		... CONFIGURATION c OF e IS ... ... END
... PACKAGE pkg IS ... ... END pkg ;	procedure_call_statement ::= [label :] procedure_call ;		.. PACKAGE BODY pck IS ... ... END pck ;
... b: BLOCK IS ... BEGIN ... END BLOCK b ;	FUNCTION f (...) RETURN r IS ... BEGIN ___●●● END f ;	PROCEDURE p (...) IS ... BEGIN ___●●● END p ;	p : PROCESS ... BEGIN ___●●● END PROCESS p ;

8.6.1 Further Definitions

label ::= identifier

procedure_call ::= *procedure*_name [(actual_parameter_part)]

8.6.2 Examples

`a_proc;`	The procedure *a_proc* is called; it does not have any parameters.
`my_proc(sig_1, sig_2, var_3);`	The procedure *my_proc* is called, with the formal parameters *sig_1*, *sig_2*, *var_3*.
`another_proc(var_1, var_2, q => const_3);`	The procedure *my_proc* is called, with the formal parameters *var_1*, *var_2* and *q*.
`register_proc(ck => clock, d => reg_in, q => reg_out);`	The procedure *register_proc* is called, with the formal parameters *ck*, *d*, *q*, which are explicitly assigned by names.

8.7 IF

... ENTITY e IS ... BEGIN ... END e ;	... ARCHITECTURE a OF e IS ... BEGIN ... END a ;		... CONFIGURATION c OF e IS ... ... END
... PACKAGE pkg IS ... ... END pkg ;	if_statement ::= [*if*_label :] **if** condition **then** sequence_of_statements { **elsif** condition **then** sequence_of_statements } [**else** sequence_of_statements] **end if** [*if*_label] ;		... PACKAGE BODY pck IS ... ... END pck ;
... b: BLOCK IS ... BEGIN ... END BLOCK b ;	FUNCTION f (...) RETURN r IS ... BEGIN ●●● END f ;	PROCEDURE p (...) IS ... BEGIN ●●● END p ;	p : PROCESS ... BEGIN ●●● END PROCESS p ;

8.7.1 Further Definitions

label ::= identifier

condition ::= *boolean*_expression

sequence_of_statements ::=
  { sequential_statement }

8.7.2 Examples

```IF a = '1' THEN b := '0'; END IF;```	If *a* has the value *1* then *b* is assigned the value *0*.
```IF a > 0 THEN b := a; ELSE b := ABS(a + 1); END IF;```	If the value of *a* is bigger than *0* then *b* is assigned the value of *a*, otherwise that of **ABS** (a + *1*).
```IF val >= 5 AND val < 10 THEN int := 7; ELSIF val < 5 THEN int := val + func(val + 2); ELSIF val < 15 THEN int := func(val); ELSE int := 0; END IF;```	This is an example of a complete **IF ELSIF** loop. The conditions are checked one after the other. When the first match is found the relevant actions are carried out and the **IF** loop is left.

8.8 CASE

... ENTITY e IS ... BEGIN ... END e ;	... ARCHITECTURE a OF e IS ... BEGIN ... END a ;	... CONFIGURATION c OF e IS ... ... END

...
 PACKAGE pkg IS
 ...
 ...
 ...
 END pkg ;
	case_statement ::=
	 [*case*_label :]
	    case expression **is**
	      case_statement_alternative
	      { case_statement_alternative }
	    end case [*case*_label];
		..
		 PACKAGE BODY pck
		     IS
		 ...
		 ...
		 ...
		 END pck ;

...
 b: BLOCK IS
 ...
 BEGIN
 ...
 END BLOCK b ;
	FUNCTION f (...)
	    RETURN r IS
	 ...
	 BEGIN
	    •••
	 END f ;
		PROCEDURE p (...) IS
		 ...
		 BEGIN
		    •••
		 END p ;
			p : PROCESS
			 ...
			 BEGIN
			    •••
			 END PROCESS p ;

8.8.1 Further Definitions

label ::= identifier

expression ::=
   relation { **and** relation }
   | relation { **or** relation }
   | relation { **xor** relation }
   | relation [**nand** relation]
   | relation [**nor** relation]

case_statement_alternative ::=
   when choices =>
   sequence_of_statements

8.8.2 Examples

| ```
CASE a IS
    WHEN '0' => s <= "0000" AFTER 2 ns;
    WHEN '1' => s <= "1111" AFTER 2 ns;
END CASE;
``` | The value of bit *a* is checked. If it is *0* then *s* is assigned the value *0000* after 2 ns; otherwise it is assigned the value *1111*, also after 2 ns. |
|---|---|
```

```CASE int_value IS WHEN 0 => int := 5; WHEN 1│2│8 => int := int_value; WHEN 3 TO 7 => int := int_value+5; WHEN 9 => NULL; WHEN OTHERS => int := 0; END CASE;```	The value of the integer *int_value* is checked. If it is *0* then *int* is assigned the value *5*; if it is *1, 2* or *8, int* is assigned the value of *int_value*; if it is between *3* and *7, int* is assigned the value *int_value 5*; if it is *9*, no action is carried out. For all other values of *int_value, int* is assigned the value *0*.
```CASE two_bit'(a_enable & b_enable) IS WHEN "00" => s <= zero AFTER 1 ns; WHEN "10" => s <= a AFTER 1 ns; WHEN "01" => s <= b AFTER 2 ns; WHEN "11" => s <= one AFTER 1 ns; END CASE;```	Depending on the value of the expression *two_bit'(a_enable & b_enable)*, *s* is assigned the corresponding value after a certain delay.

8.9 LOOP

... ENTITY e IS ... BEGIN ... END e ;	... ARCHITECTURE a OF e IS ... BEGIN ... END a ;		... CONFIGURATION c OF e IS ... ... END
... PACKAGE pkg IS ... ... END pkg ;	loop_statement ::= [*loop*_label :] [iteration_scheme] **loop** sequence_of_statements **end loop** [*loop*_label] ;		... PACKAGE BODY pck IS ... ... END pck ;
... b: BLOCK IS ... BEGIN ... END BLOCK b ;	FUNCTION f (...) RETURN r IS ... BEGIN ••• END f ;	PROCEDURE p (...) IS ... BEGIN ••• END p ;	p : PROCESS ... BEGIN ••• END PROCESS p ;

8.9.1 Further Definitions

label ::= identifier

iteration_scheme ::=
  while condition
  | **for** *loop*_parameter_specification

sequence_of_statements ::=
  { sequential_statement }

8.9.2 Examples

```LOOP WAIT UNTIL clock = '1'; q <= d AFTER 1 ns; END LOOP;```	This is an endless loop in which the signal *q* is assigned the value of *d* 1 ns after the condition *clock = '1'* has been fulfilled.
```lbl: FOR i IN 0 TO 5 LOOP var := var + 5; END LOOP;```	This loop, which has a label, is run six times. In each pass the value of var is raised by 5.
```PROCESS (a) BEGIN z<= "0000"; FOR i in 0 TO 3 LOOP IF (a = i) THEN z(i) <= '1'; END IF; END LOOP; END PROCESS;```	By using predefined attributes, the loop instruction can be written in a different way as well: ```FOR i IN a1'LOW TO a1'HIGH FOR i IN a1'RIGHT TO a1'LEFT FOR i IN a1'REVERSE_RANGE FOR i IN a1'RANGE```
```FOR i IN 10 DOWNTO 2 LOOP FOR j IN 0 TO i LOOP table(i, j) := i + j - 7; END LOOP; END LOOP;```	These are two examples of chained **FOR** loops that are needed to calculate the values of the elements of a two dimensional array.
```lbl_1: FOR i IN 10 DOWNTO 2 LOOP lbl_2 : FOR j IN 0 TO i LOOP EXIT lbl_2 WHEN i = j; table (i, j) := i + j - 7; END LOOP lbl_2; END LOOP lbl_1;```	In the second example each of the **FOR** loops has its own label. With the **EXIT** statement, the inner loop is left if *i = j*.

8.10 NEXT

... ENTITY e IS ... BEGIN ... END e ;	... ARCHITECTURE a OF e IS ... BEGIN ... END a ;	... CONFIGURATION c OF e IS ... ... END
... PACKAGE pkg IS ... ... END pkg ;	next_statement ::= [label :] **next** [*loop*_label] [**when** condition] ;	... PACKAGE BODY pck IS ... ... END pck ;

...
 b: BLOCK IS
 ...
 BEGIN
 ...
 END BLOCK b ;
	FUNCTION f (...)
	     RETURN r IS
	 ...
	 BEGIN
	     ●●●
	 END f ;
		PROCEDURE p (...) IS
		 ...
		 BEGIN
		     ●●●
		 END p ;
			p : PROCESS
			 ...
			 BEGIN
			     ●●●
			 END PROCESS p ;

8.10.1 Further Definitions

label ::= identifier

condition ::= *boolean*_expression

8.10.2 Examples

| ```
WHILE value > 0 LOOP
   NEXT WHEN value = 3;
   tab(value) := value REM 2;
   value := value / 2;
END LOOP;
``` <br><br> ```
WHILE value > 0 LOOP
   IF value = 3 THEN
      NEXT;
   END IF;
   tab(value) := value REM 2;
   value := value / 2;
END LOOP;
``` | In both examples the statements following the **NEXT** statement are ignored if *value = 3*. <br><br> In the first example this is achieved by a conditional **NEXT** statement, whereas in the second example an unconditional **NEXT** statement has been integrated into an **IF** loop. |
|---|---|

``
lbl_1:
   FOR i IN 10 DOWNTO 2 LOOP
   lbl_2 :
      FOR j IN 0 TO i LOOP
         NEXT lbl_2 WHEN i = j;
         table (i, j) := i + j - 7;
      END LOOP lbl_2;
   END LOOP lbl_1;
``
	These are two examples of chained **FOR** loops that are needed to calculate the values of the elements of a two dimensional array.
	
	In the first example the succeeding statements for the inner loop are ignored if $i = j$.

``
lbl_1:
   FOR i IN 10 DOWNTO 2 LOOP
      lbl_2 :
      FOR j IN 0 TO i LOOP
         NEXT lbl_1 WHEN i = j;
         table (i, j) := i + j - 7;
      END LOOP lbl_2;
   END LOOP lbl_1;
``
	In the second example the process is continued with the next passage of the external loop if $i = j$.

8.11 EXIT

...	...	...
ENTITY e IS ... BEGIN ... END e ;	ARCHITECTURE a OF e IS ... BEGIN ... END a ;	CONFIGURATION c OF e IS ... ... END
... PACKAGE pkg IS ... ... END pkg ;	exit_statement ::= [label :] **exit** [*loop*_label] [**when** condition] ;	... PACKAGE BODY pck IS ... ... END pck ;

...
b: BLOCK IS
...
BEGIN
...
END BLOCK b ;
	FUNCTION f (...)
	    RETURN r IS
	...
	BEGIN
	    ●●●
	END f ;
		PROCEDURE p (...) IS
		...
		BEGIN
		    ●●●
		END p ;
			p : PROCESS
			...
			BEGIN
			    ●●●
			END PROCESS p ;

8.11.1 Further Definitions

label ::= identifier

condition ::= *boolean*_expression

8.11.2 Examples

| ```
LOOP
    EXIT WHEN value = 0;
    tab( value ) := value REM 2;
    value := value / 2;
END LOOP;
``` | In both cases the loops are left with the **EXIT** statement if *value = 0*. |
| ```
LOOP
    IF value = 0 THEN
        EXIT;
    END IF;
    tab(value) := value REM 2;
    value := value / 2;
END LOOP;
``` | In the first example this is achieved by a conditional **NEXT** statement, whereas in the second example an unconditional **NEXT** statement has been integrated into an **IF** loop. |
| ```
lbl_1:
  FOR i IN 10 DOWNTO 2 LOOP
    lbl_2 :
      FOR j IN 0 TO i LOOP
        EXIT lbl_2 WHEN i = j;
        table (i, j) := i + j - 7;
      END LOOP lbl_2;
  END LOOP lbl_1;
``` | These are two examples of chained **FOR** loops that are need to calculate the values of the elements of a two dimensional array. |
| ```
lbl_1:
  FOR i IN 10 DOWNTO 2 LOOP
    lbl_2 :
      FOR j IN 0 TO i LOOP
        EXIT lbl_1 WHEN i = j;
        table (i, j) := i + j - 7;
      END LOOP lbl_2;
  END LOOP lbl_1;
``` | In the first example the inner loop is left if $i = j$.<br>In the second example the outer loop is left if $i = j$. |

8.12 RETURN

... ENTITY e IS ... BEGIN ... END e ;	... ARCHITECTURE a OF e IS ... BEGIN ... END a ;	... CONFIGURATION c OF e IS ... ... END
... PACKAGE pkg IS ... ... END pkg ;	return_statement ::= [label :] **return** [expression] ;	... PACKAGE BODY pck IS ... ... END pck ;

...
b: BLOCK IS
...
BEGIN
...
END BLOCK b ;
	FUNCTION f (...)
	    RETURN r IS
	...
	BEGIN
	    •••
	END f ;
		PROCEDURE p (...) IS
		...
		BEGIN
		    •••
		END p ;
			p : PROCESS
			...
			BEGIN
			...
			END PROCESS p ;

8.12.1 Further Definitions

label ::= identifier

expression ::=
    relation { **and** relation }
    | relation { **or** relation }
    | relation { **xor** relation }
    | relation [**nand** relation]
    | relation [**nor** relation]

A function body must contain a **RETURN** statement.

8.12.2 Examples

RETURN;	No value is returned.
RETURN value;	The return value is that of *value*.
RETURN my_function(data, 5 pF);	The return value is the result of the function *my_function*.
RETURN a + b + 5 ns;	The return value is the sum *a + b + 5 ns*.
RETURN "author name: " & name;	The return value is a chained string.

8.13 NULL

... ENTITY e IS ... BEGIN ... END e ;	... ARCHITECTURE a OF e IS ... BEGIN ... END a ;		... CONFIGURATION c OF e IS ... ... END
... PACKAGE pkg IS ... ... END pkg ;	null_statement ::= [label :] **null** ;		...PACKAGE BODY pck IS ... ... END pck ;

...
b: BLOCK IS
...
BEGIN
...
END BLOCK b ;
	FUNCTION f (...)
	    RETURN r IS
	...
	BEGIN
	    •••
	END f ;
		PROCEDURE p (...) IS
		...
		BEGIN
		    •••
		END p ;
			p : PROCESS
			...
			BEGIN
			    •••
			END PROCESS p ;

8.13.1 Example

NULL;	The **NULL** statement explicitly prevents any action from being carried out.

9 Concurrent statements

9.1 Block

... ENTITY e IS ... BEGIN ... END e ;	... ARCHITECTURE a OF e IS ... BEGIN **•••** END a ;	... CONFIGURATION c OF e IS ... ... END

...
PACKAGE pkg IS
...
...
END pkg ;
	block_statement ::=
	*block*_label : **block** [(*guard*_expression)] [**is**]
	    block_header
	    block_declarative_part
	begin
	    block_statement_part
	end block [*block*_label] ;
		...
		PACKAGE BODY pck
		  IS
		...
		...
		END pck ;

. . . **b: BLOCK IS** **•••** **BEGIN** **•••** **END BLOCK b ;**	FUNCTION f (...) RETURN r IS ... BEGIN ... END f ;	PROCEDURE p (...) IS ... BEGIN ... END p ;	p : PROCESS ... BEGIN ... END PROCESS p ;

9.1.1 Further Definitions

label ::= identifier

expression ::=   relation { **and** relation }
                | relation { **or** relation }
                | relation { **xor** relation }
                | relation [**nand** relation]
                | relation [**nor** relation]

block_header ::=   [generic_clause
                    [generic_map_aspect ;]]
                    [port_clause
                    [port_map_aspect ;]]

block_declarative_part ::=   { block_declarative_item }

block_statement_part ::=   { concurrent_statement }

9.1.2 Examples

``
b : BLOCK BEGIN
   s <= '1' AFTER 2 ns;
END BLOCK b;
``
	This simple block has a label and a delayed signal assignment in the statement part.

| ```
c: BLOCK
   SIGNAL int : bit_vector(1 TO 3);
BEGIN
   s <= int AFTER 5 ns;
END BLOCK c;
``` | This block has an additional header in which the signal *int* is declared. |
| ```
latch : BLOCK (clock = '1')
BEGIN
   latch_output <= GUARDED latch_input
                   AFTER 1 ns;
END BLOCK latch;
``` | In this block a controlled signal assignment is used. If the condition *clock = '1'* is not fulfilled then the signal assignment is not carried out. |
| ```
lbl : BLOCK
   PORT (a, b : INOUT bit);
   PORT MAP (a => s1, b => s2);
BEGIN
   b <= a AFTER 1 ns;
   a <= b AFTER 1 ns;
END BLOCK lbl;
``` | This block has separate in- and outputs, which are linked to the overriding signals by the PORT MAP. |

9.2 Process

...	...	...
ENTITY e IS ... BEGIN ●●● END e ;	ARCHITECTURE a OF e IS ... BEGIN ●●● END a ;	CONFIGURATION c OF e IS ... ... END

...
 	
PACKAGE pkg IS
 	
...
 	
...
 	
END pkg ;
	process_statement ::=
	[*process*_label :] [**postponed**] **process**
	    [(sensitivity_list)]
	        process_declarative_part
	begin
	    process_statement_part
	end [**postponed**] **process** [*process*_label];
		...
		
		PACKAGE BODY pck
		        IS
		
		...
		
		END pck ;

...	FUNCTION f (...)	PROCEDURE p (...) IS	p : PROCESS
b: BLOCK IS ... BEGIN ●●● END BLOCK b ;	RETURN r IS ... BEGIN ... END f ;	... BEGIN ... END p ;	●●● BEGIN ●●● END PROCESS p ;
```

9.2.1 Further Definitions

label ::= identifier

sensitivity_list ::= *signal*_name { , *signal*_name }

process_declarative_part ::=   { process_declarative_item }

process_statement_part ::=   { sequential_statement }

9.2.2 Comments

- Alternatively, for a sensitivity list, after the keyword **PROCESS** the following wait statement can be used at the end of the process: **WAIT ON** sensitivity_list;

- A process may only have a sensitivity list or one respective several WAIT statements.

- A **PROCESS** statement within the statement part of an **ENTITY** has to be a passive **PROCESS** statement.

- A process with the keyword **POSTPONED** is called "postponed process". This process will always (given there is only one postponed process) be executed in the last delta cycle of a simulation cycle. This implies that only signal assignments with a delay greater than 0 are allowed (otherwise other processes would be executed in subsequent delta cycles).

9.2.3 Examples

```PROCESS```
```BEGIN```
   ```IF (clock='1') THEN```
      ```q <= d AFTER 2 ns;```
   ```END IF;```
   ```WAIT ON clock;```
```END PROCESS;```
	This process describes a flip flop.
	
	The positive clock-edge is detected by the **WAIT** statement and by checking the condition *clock* = '1'. 2 ns after the clock-edge the value of input *d* is on output *q*.

```reg: PROCESS (clock)```
```BEGIN```
   ```IF clock = '1' THEN```
      ```q <= d AFTER 1 ns;```
   ```END IF;```
```END PROCESS reg;```
	This named process also describes a flip flop. The positive clock-edge is detected by the sensitivity list and by checking the condition *clock* = '1'. 1 ns after the clock-edge the value of input *d* is on output *q*.

```POSTPONED PROCESS (testsig)```
```BEGIN```
  ```ASSERT testsig=expected_value```
  ```REPORT "testsig differs from" &```
      ```& "expected value!"```
  ```SEVERITY error;```
```END POSTPONED PROCESS;```
	A postponed process is defined to assert the value of a signal.

`passive:` **`PROCESS`**
`BEGIN`
    `WAIT ON` `clock;`
    `IF` `clock = '1'` **`THEN`**
        `ASSERT` `reset = '1';`
        `REPORT` `"reset is active!";`
        `SEVERITY` `warning;`
    `END IF;`
`END PROCESS` `passive;`
	This is an example of a passive process.
	
	With the positive clock-edge only the condition *reset = '1'* is checked and a warning given if necessary.

`PROCESS`
    `VARIABLE` `v1,v2 : integer := 1;`
`BEGIN`
    `sig_1 <= v1` **`AFTER`** `1 ns;`
    `WAIT UNTIL` `sig_2 = 0;`
    `v2 := v2 * 2;`
    `v1 := v2 + 4;`
    `sig_1 <= v1` **`AFTER`** `1 ns;`
    `WAIT ON` `sig_1, sig_2;`
    `FOR` `i` **`IN`** `1` **`TO`** `3` **`LOOP`**
        `v1 := v1 + v2;`
    `END LOOP;`
`END PROCESS;`
	This process contains two **`WAIT`** statements.
	
	The first **`WAIT`** statement interrupts the process until *sig_2 = 0* whereas the second **`WAIT`** statement causes a change of one of the two signals *sig_1* or *sig_2* to be waited for.

9.3 Concurrent Procedure Call

...	...	...
ENTITY e IS ... BEGIN __•••__ END e ;	ARCHITECTURE a OF e IS ... BEGIN __•••__ END a ;	CONFIGURATION c OF e IS ... ... END
... PACKAGE pkg IS ... ... END pkg ;	concurrent_procedure_call ::= [label :] [**postponed**] procedure_call ;	... PACKAGE BODY pck IS ... ... END pck ;

...	FUNCTION f (...)	PROCEDURE p (...) IS	p : PROCESS
b: BLOCK IS ... BEGIN __•••__ END BLOCK b ;	RETURN r IS ... BEGIN ... END f ;	... BEGIN ... END p ;	... BEGIN ... END PROCESS p ;

9.3.1 Further Definitions

procedure_call ::=
    *procedure*_name [(actual_parameter_part)]

9.3.2 Comment

- For any concurrent procedure call statement, there is an equivalent process statement.

- The equivalent process statement of a concurrent procedure call statement including the keyword **POSTPONED** is a postponed process.

- A concurrent procedure call within the statement part of an **ENTITY** has to be a passive concurrent procedure call.

9.3.3 Examples

`a_proc;`	Procedure call without transfer parameters
`lab: my_proc(sig_1, sig_2, sig_3);`	Named procedure call with transfer parameters which are linked by position.

`register_proc(ck => clock,`
`              d => reg_in,`
`              q => reg_out);`
	Procedure call with transfer parameters that are linked by explicit assignment.

`another_proc(sig_1,`
`             sig_2,`
`             q => sig_3);`
	Procedure call with transfer parameters that are linked either by position or by explicit assignment.

`check_timing(tplh, tphl, clk, d, q);`
`   -- concurrent procedure call`
 	
`PROCESS -- corresponding process`
`BEGIN`
`   check_timing(tplh, tphl, clk, d, q);`
`   WAIT ON clk, d, q;`
`END PROCESS;`
	This example shows that a concurrent procedure call is equal to a process that has a statement part that only contains the procedure call.

9.4 Concurrent Assertion

... ENTITY e IS ... BEGIN ● ● ● END e ;	... ARCHITECTURE a OF e IS ... BEGIN ● ● ● END a ;		... CONFIGURATION c OF e IS ... ... END
... PACKAGE pkg IS ... ... END pkg ;	concurrent_assertion_statement ::= [label :] [**postponed**] assertion		... PACKAGE BODY pck IS ... ... END pck ;
... b: BLOCK IS ... BEGIN ● ● ● END BLOCK b ;	FUNCTION f (...) RETURN r IS ... BEGIN ... END f ;	PROCEDURE p (...) IS ... BEGIN ... END p ;	p : PROCESS ... BEGIN ... END PROCESS p ;

9.4.1 Further Definitions

label ::= identifier

assertion ::=   **assert** condition
                [**report** expression]
                [**severity** expression]

9.4.2 Comment

- For any concurrent assertion statement, there is an equivalent (passive) process statement.

- The equivalent process statement of a concurrent assertion statement including the keyword **POSTPONED** is a postponed process.

- If the concurrent assertion contains a static condition then the assertion will be executed only once at the beginning of the simulation.

9.4.3 Examples

ASSERT reset = '1';	Nothing happens.
ASSERT reset = '1' **REPORT** "Reset is active!";	If reset does not equal '1' then the report is printed in the simulation window.

<table>
<tr>
<td>

```
lbl: ASSERT reset = '1'
     REPORT "Reset is active !"
     SEVERITY warning;
```

</td>
<td>These are three different examples of assertions.</td>
</tr>
<tr>
<td>

```
latch_check: ASSERT reset = '1' OR set = '1'
             REPORT "Reset and Set are" &
                    "active simultaneously!"
             SEVERITY failure;
```

</td>
<td rowspan="2">One condition at a time is checked (**ASSERT**), and if it is not fulfilled then a report is given (**REPORT**). The severity level determines which actions are carried out if the condition that is to be checked is not fulfilled.</td>
</tr>
<tr>
<td>

```
lbl: ASSERT data = 0
     REPORT "Date equals " &
            integer_to_string (data) & "!"
     SEVERITY note;
```

</td>
</tr>
</table>

9.5 Concurrent Signal Assignment

<table>
<tr>
<td>

...
ENTITY e IS
...
BEGIN
...
END e ;

</td>
<td>

...
ARCHITECTURE a OF e IS
...
BEGIN
   ●●●
END a ;

</td>
<td>

...
CONFIGURATION c
   OF e IS
...
...
END

</td>
</tr>
<tr>
<td>

...
PACKAGE pkg IS
...
END pkg ;

</td>
<td>

concurrent_signal_assignment_statement::=
[label :] [**postponed**]
   conditional_signal_assignment
| [label :] [**postponed**]
   selected_signal_assignment

</td>
<td>

...
PACKAGE BODY pck
   IS
...
...
END pck ;

</td>
</tr>
<tr>
<td>

...
b: BLOCK IS
...
BEGIN
   ●●●
END BLOCK b ;

</td>
<td>

FUNCTION f (...)
   RETURN r IS
   ...
BEGIN
   ...
END f ;

</td>
<td>

PROCEDURE p (...) IS
...
BEGIN
   ...
END p ;

</td>
<td>

p : PROCESS
...
BEGIN
   ...
END PROCESS p ;

</td>
</tr>
</table>

9.5.1 Further Definitions

conditional_signal_assignment ::=   target <= options conditional_waveforms ;

selected_signal_assignment ::=   **with** expression **select**
               target <= options selected_waveforms ;

9.5.2 Additional Information

- With a conditional signal assignment there is always an equivalent process statement; in general, this is valid for all concurrent assignments.

- The equivalent process statement of a concurrent signal assignment statement including the keyword **POSTPONED** is a postponed process.

- If the conditional signal assignment has the form

```
target <= options waveform_1 WHEN condition_1 ELSE
         waveform_2 WHEN condition_2 ELSE
             •••
         waveform_n-1 WHEN condition_n-1 ELSE
         waveform_n ;
```

then the signal assignment in the corresponding process statement has the form

```
IF condition_1 THEN
  target <= wave_transform_1 ;
ELSIF condition_2 THEN
  target <= wave_transform_2 ;
        •••
ELSIF condition_n-1 THEN
  target <= wave_transform_n-1 ;
ELSE
  target <= wave_transform_n ;
END IF ;
```

If the (conditional) waveform is a simple waveform then the signal assignment in the corresponding process statement has the form

```
target <= wave_transform ;
```

The process statement of the wave_transform of a waveform of the form

```
        waveform_element1, waveform_element1, ..., waveform_elementN
```

has the form

```
  target <= [delay_mechanism] waveform_element1, waveform_element2, ...,
waveform_elementN ;
```

The process statement of the wave_transform of a waveform of the form

```
        UNAFFECTED
```

has the form

```
        NULL ;
```

NULL is here a null statement, not a null transaction!
The waveforms' characteristics and the conditions contained in the signal assignment have to be formulated appropriately so that the IF statement in the corresponding process statement is a permitted statement.

- With a selected signal assignment there is always an equivalent process statement. If the selected signal assignment has the form

```
WITH expression SELECT
  target <= options waveform_1  WHEN choice_list_1 ,
         waveform_2 WHEN choice_list_2 ,
             •••
```

waveform_n-1 **WHEN** choice_list_n-1 ,
waveform_n **WHEN** choice_list_n ;

then the signal assignment in the corresponding process statement has the form

```
CASE expression IS
  WHEN choice_list_1 => target <= wave_transform_1 ;
  WHEN choice_list_2 => target <= wave_transform_2 ;
                    •••
  WHEN choice_list_n-1 => target <= wave_transform_n-1 ;
  WHEN choice_list_n => target <= wave_transform_n ;
END CASE ;
```

For wave_transform look at the previous topic on conditional signal assignment. The characteristics of the selected expression, of the waveforms and the criteria of selection contained in the signal assignment have to be formulated appropriately so that the **CASE** statement in the corresponding process statement is a permitted statement.

• If the option **GUARDED** is contained in the signal assignment then it is a so called controlled assignment. If the target is also controlled then the statement part of the corresponding process statement looks as follows:

```
IF guard THEN
  signal_transform
ELSE
  disconnection_statements
END IF ;
```

If the target is not controlled then the statement part of the corresponding process statement looks as follows:

```
IF guard THEN
  signal_transform
END IF ;
```

It is also possible that neither signal assignment nor target is controlled. If this is the case then the statement part of the corresponding process statement looks as follows:

```
  signal_transform
```

It is not permitted to handle a signal assignment as being not controlled while handling the corresponding target as being controlled!

9.5.3 Examples

`a <= b AFTER 5 ns;`	The value of *b* is assigned to the signal *a* after 5 ns. In the first case the inertial delay model is used and in the second case the transport delay model is used.
`lbl: a <= TRANSPORT b AFTER 5 ns;`	
`c: data_bus <= GUARDED reg_output` `              AFTER 3 ns;`	The controlled signal assignment is only carried out if the corresponding condition in the block declaration is fulfilled.

`a <= '1' AFTER 5 ns WHEN sel = 0 ELSE`
`    '0' AFTER 3 ns,`
`    '1' AFTER 5 ns WHEN sel = 1 ELSE`
`    'X' AFTER 2 ns;`
	If *sel=0* then *a* is assigned the value *1* after 5 ns; if *sel=1* then *a* is assigned the value *0* after 3 ns and the value *1* after 5 ns; otherwise *a* is given the value *X* after 2 ns.

`lmux : WITH muxval SELECT`
`        sig <= TRANSPORT`
`            "001" AFTER 2 ns WHEN 0 ,`
`            "110" AFTER 5 ns WHEN 1 ,`
`            "000" AFTER 5 ns WHEN 2 ,`
`            "111" AFTER 5 ns WHEN 3 ,`
`            "XXX" WHEN OTHERS;`
	In this value assignment to the signal *sig* the value of *muxval* is taken into consideration. If *muxval=0* then *sig* is assigned the value *001*, etc. For this assignment the delay model **TRANSPORT** is used irrespective of the value of *muxval*.

`S <= UNAFFECTED`
`    WHEN input = S'DRIVING_VALUE`
`    ELSE input AFTER delay;`
	S is only driven if the driver value is different from the current value of *S*; otherwise nothing happens.

9.6 Component Instantiation

... ENTITY e IS ... BEGIN ... END e ;	... ARCHITECTURE a OF e IS ... BEGIN ●●● END a ;	... CONFIGURATION c OF e IS ... ... END

...
PACKAGE pkg IS
...
...
...
END pkg ;
	component_instantiation_statement ::=
	*instantiation*_label :
	    instantiated_unit
	        [generic_map_aspect]
	        [port_map_aspect] ;
		...
		PACKAGE BODY pck
		IS
		...
		...
		END pck ;

... b: BLOCK IS ... BEGIN ●●● END BLOCK b ;	FUNCTION f (...) RETURN r IS ... BEGIN ... END f ;	PROCEDURE p (...) IS ... BEGIN ... END p ;	p : PROCESS ... BEGIN ... END PROCESS p ;

9.6.1 Further Definitions

instantiated_unit ::=
    [**component**] *component*_name
    | **entity** *entity*_name [(*architecture*_identifier)]
    | **configuration** *configuration*_name

generic_map_aspect ::=
  generic map (*generic*_association_list)

port_map_aspect ::=
  port map (*port*_association_list)

9.6.2 Comments

- In VHDL'87 it was only possible to instantiate components. In VHDL'93 it is also allowed to instantiate entities and configurations.

- For an instantiation of a component this component must have been declared before.

- For the instantiation of an entity or a configuration these have to be compiled into a library. This library has to be visible when compiling the instantiations.

9.6.3 Examples

`c_1: my_component;`	*my_component* is integrated into the current architecture without a port map.

`c: add_n`
   `GENERIC MAP (8)`
   `PORT MAP (`
      `Vss, a8, b8, sum => s8,`
      `cout => sig);`
	The component *add_n* is instantiated with the generic value *8*. In this process the signal *s8* is linked to the ports *Vss*, *a8*, *b8*, *sum*, and *sig* is linked to the port *cout* of the instantiated component.

`u_myent: ENTITY`
   `work.my_entity(beh)`
   `PORT MAP (I1 => S1 , I2 => S2);`
	The entity *my_entity* is instantiated directly. The signals *I1* and *I2* of *my_entity* are connected with the local signals S1 and S2.

`u_config: CONFIGURATION`
   `work.my_cfg`
   `PORT MAP (I1 => S1 , I2 => S2);`
	The configuration *my_cfg* is instantiated. The signals *I1* and *I2* of the entity linked by the configuration are connected with the local signals S1 and S2.

`the_ram: ram_comp`
   `GENERIC MAP (`
      `nb_data => 8,`
      `nb_addr => 5)`
   `PORT MAP (`
      `cs    => cs,`
      `rw    => rw,`
      `d     => data,`
      `a     => address,`
      `ready => OPEN);`
	When *ram_comp* is instantiated the generics *nb_data* and *nb_addr* are preseized.
	
	The signals are linked to the ports of *ram_comp* by name assignment; the port *ready* is not linked.

```COMPONENT comp PORT (a , b: INOUT bit); c: comp PORT MAP (a => s1, b => s2);```	This example is to clarify the interrelationships <- Component declaration
	<- Component instantiation with linking of ports
```FOR c: comp USE ENTITY x(y) PORT MAP (p1 => a, p2 => b);```	<- Declaration of the configuration (For comp the architecture y of the entity x is to be used.)
```ENTITY x IS PORT (p1, p2: INOUT bit); CONSTANT delay: time:= 1 ms; BEGIN```	<- Entity declaration
``` check_timing(p1, p2, 2 * delay); END x;```	(check_timing is a passive procedure!)
	<- Architecture declaration
```ARCHITECTURE y OF x IS SIGNAL p3: bit; BEGIN p3 <= p1 AFTER delay; p2 <= p3 AFTER delay; b: BLOCK ... BEGIN ... END BLOCK; END y;```	
	This is the code that is equivalent to that above:
```c: BLOCK PORT (a, b: INOUT bit); PORT MAP (a => s1, b => s2); BEGIN```	<- Component block <- local ports <- Port association
``` x: BLOCK PORT (p1, p2: INOUT bit); PORT MAP (p1 => a, p2 => b); CONSTANT delay: time:= 1 ms; SIGNAL p3: bit; BEGIN```	<- Entity block <- formal ports <- Port association <- Agreement within the entity <- Agreement within the architecture
``` check_timing(p1, p2, 2 * delay); p3 <= p1 AFTER delay; p2 <= p3 AFTER delay; b: BLOCK ... BEGIN ... END BLOCK; END BLOCK x; END BLOCK c;```	<- Architecture statements <- internal block hierarchy

9.7 Generate Statement

... ENTITY e IS ... BEGIN ... END e ;	... ARCHITECTURE a OF e IS ... BEGIN ___●●● END a ;	... CONFIGURATION c OF e IS ... ... END

...
PACKAGE pkg IS
...
...
END pkg ;
	generate_statement ::=
	*generate*_label :
	    generation_scheme **generate**
	        [{ block_declarative_item }
	    begin]
	        { concurrent_statement }
	        end generate [*generate*_label] ;
		..
		PACKAGE BODY pck
		    IS
		...
		...
		END pck ;

... b: BLOCK IS ... BEGIN ___●●● END BLOCK b ;	FUNCTION f (...) RETURN r IS ... BEGIN ... END f ;	PROCEDURE p (...) IS ... BEGIN ... END p ;	p : PROCESS ... BEGIN ... END PROCESS p ;

9.7.1 Further Definitions

label ::= identifier

generation_scheme ::=
    for *generate*_parameter_specification
    | **if** condition

block_declarative_item ::=
    subprogram_declaration
    | subprogram_body
    | type_declaration
    | subtype_declaration
    | constant_declaration
    | signal_declaration
    | *shared*_variable_declaration
    | file_declaration
    | alias_declaration
    | component_declaration
    | attribute_declaration
    | attribute_specification
    | configuration_specification
    | disconnection_specification
    | use_clause
    | group_template_declaration
    | group_ declaration

```
concurrent_statement ::=
    block_statement
  | process_statement
  | concurrent_procedure_call_statement
  | concurrent_assertion_statement
  | concurrent_signal_assignment_statement
  | component_instantiation_statement
  | generate_statement
```

9.7.2 Comment

• In VHDL'87 there was no declarative region in a generate assignment.

9.7.3 Examples

```lbl_1: FOR i IN 1 TO 5 GENERATE c1: comp_1 PORT MAP (ck => clock, d => a(i), q => a(i+1)); c2: comp_2 PORT MAP (ck => clock, d => a(i)); END GENERATE;```	This generate statement forms a parallel chain out of the two components *comp_1* and *comp_2* with a length of 5.
```lbl_2: IF n > 0 GENERATE sig_1 <= '1' AFTER 5 ns; sig_2 <= sig_1 AFTER 2 ns; c: my_comp PORT MAP (a, b, c); END GENERATE;```	If the generic *n* is bigger than 0 then the signal assignments take effect and the component *my_comp* is instantiated.
```cadd: FOR i IN 1 TO n GENERATE cb: IF i = 1 GENERATE add_b: add_begin PORT MAP (...); END GENERATE; cm: IF i > 1 AND i < n GENERATE add_m: add_middle PORT MAP (...); END GENERATE; ce: IF i = n GENERATE add_e: add_end PORT MAP (...); END GENERATE; END GENERATE cadd;```	Example of a chained generate statement.

Within the external statement several components are instantiated irrespective of the counter variable *i*. |

```
b: BLOCK
BEGIN

    l1: cell PORT MAP
            (top, bottom,
            a(0), b(0));

    l2: FOR i IN 1 TO 3 GENERATE
        l3: FOR j IN 1 TO 3 GENERATE
        l4: IF i + j > 4 GENERATE
            l5: cell PORT MAP (a(i-1),
                    b(j-1), a(i),b(j));
            END GENERATE;
        END GENERATE;
    END GENERATE;

    l6: FOR i IN 1 TO 3 GENERATE
        l7: FOR j IN 1 TO 3 GENERATE
        l8: IF i + j < 4 GENERATE
            l9: cell PORT MAP (a(i+1),
                    b(j+1), a(i), b(j));
            END GENERATE;
        END GENERATE;
    END GENERATE;

END BLOCK b;
```

Example of the wide range of applications of the generate statement.

In order to make them easier to survey, the chained generate statements at label *l2* were duplicated at label *l6* with an altered **IF** condition.

The generate statement at label *l8* can also be stated within the generate statement at label *l3*.

10 Miscellaneous

10.1 Visibility and Validity Ranges

10.1.1 Declarative Range

Declarative ranges are parts of the description text. Separate, declarative ranges are:

- Entity declarations together with their corresponding architecture bodies
- Configuration declarations
- Subprogram declarations together with the corresponding subprogram body
- Package declarations together with the corresponding package body (if present)
- Record-type declarations
- Component declarations
- Block statements
- Process statements
- Loop statements
- Block configurations
- Component configurations
- Generate statements

10.1.2 Validity Range of a Declaration

A declaration's validity range goes from the beginning of the declaration to the end of the declarative range in which the declaration is made; this range is called the immediate range.

The validity range of the following declarations extends beyond the corresponding declarative range:

- Declarations that are made immediately within a package declaration
- Element declarations within a record-type declaration
- Declarations of formal parameters within subprogram declarations (subprogram specifications if there is no subprogram declaration)
- Declarations of local generics within component declarations
- Declarations of local ports within component declarations
- Declarations of formal generics within entity declarations
- Declarations of formal ports within entity declarations

In general, the validity range also includes the corresponding configuration, declaration and the configurations and declarations contained therein (hierarchy).

10.1.3 Visibility

Elements are either made visible by selection or are directly visible. The visibility rules define the range in which a declared object (identifier!) can be accessed. Moreover, only one declaration can be valid for using the object (overloading). A declaration is made visible by selection in the following positions:

1. For a primary unit in a library: in the suffix's position in a selected name whose prefix qualifies a library.

2. For an architecture that is linked to an entity: in the position of a block specification within the block configuration of an external block whose interface is defined by the current entity.

3. For a declaration within a package declaration: in the suffix's position in a selected name whose prefix qualifies a package.

4. For an element declaration of a given record declaration: in the suffix's position in a selected name whose prefix fits for this type; also in the position of a selection in an assignment by names within an aggregate of that type.

5. For a predefined attribute that fits in a definition range: in the designator's position in an attribute name whose prefix is assigned to a given range.

6. For a user-defined attribute: in the designator's position in an attribute name whose prefix qualifies an entity.

7. For a formal parameter declaration within a given subprogram declaration: in the formal designator's position in a name assignment list within the subprogram call.

8. For the local generic declaration of a given component declaration: in the formal designator's position within a generic name assignment list belonging to the corresponding component instantiation; also in the current designator's position within a generic name assignment list of the corresponding binding indication.

9. For a local port declaration of a given component declaration: in the formal designator's position within a port name assignment list of the corresponding component instantiation; also in the current designator's position in a port name assignment list of the corresponding binding indication.

10. For a local generic declaration of a given entity declaration: in the formal designator's position within a generic name assignment list of the corresponding binding indication.

11. For a formal port declaration of a given entity declaration: in the formal designator's position in a port name assignment list of the corresponding binding indication.

12. For a formal generic declaration or a formal port declaration of a given block statement: at the place of the formal designator in a formal part of a named association element of a corresponding generic or port map aspect.

Eventually, every declaration that stands within the declarative range of any given construct (with the exception of RECORD) is made visible as the suffix of an expanded name with the prefix marking the construct mentioned above.

1. e.g., within a configuration: **USE ENTITY** WORK.tv(SAT1)
                                                     Prefix.Suffix

2. as 1.

3. Rom cell(0) <= ROMBIB.rom_package.constant(0)

4. date.month <= "April"
   date <= (Year => 1997, Day => 9, Month => "April") ;

5. **ASSERT** ack'sTABLE(setup_time)
      REPORT "setup time violation by Ack"
      SEVERITY WARNING

6. **ATTRIBUTE** author **OF** tb_i2c : **ENTITY IS** "Martin Padeffke"

7. **FUNCTION** ksc_fans(Number) **RETURN INTEGER ;**
   ARCHITECTURE einschaltquoten **OF** tv **IS**
   BEGIN

      ...
   pot_viewers <= ksc_fans(football_fans) + ...
   END einschaltquoten ;

8. UUT : bus_monitor
   GENERIC MAP (setup_time => setup, clock_period => clk_period , ...) ;

9. **PORT MAP** (bus => scd, takt => scl, ...) ;

10. , 11. and 12. as 8. respective as 9.

10.1.4 Direct Visibility

Any given declaration is directly visible within its immediate validity range (except for hidden declarations): package declaration can be made directly visible by Use statements.

A declaration is called *hidden* if it is overlapped by a local declaration (see the example).

Exception: overloading – several declarations which that the same identifier exist at the same time and the fitting declaration is selected from the context of the call (Overloading resolution).

lbl_1 : **BLOCK**
  SIGNAL a, b : bit ;
BEGIN
 	
  lbl_2 : **BLOCK**
    SIGNAL b : bit ;
  BEGIN
    a <= b **AFTER** 5 ns ;
    b <= lbl_1.b **AFTER** 10 ns ;
  END BLOCK lbl_2 ;
 	
  b <= a **AFTER** 15 ns ;
END BLOCK lbl_1 ;
	Signal *b* is declared in block *lbl_1* and in block *lbl_2*. If *b* is addressed without any further designation the 'inner' signal is addressed. Otherwise this has to be explicitly designated by placing the corresponding label as a prefix.
	
	Equivalents:
	`<- lbl_1.a <= lbl_2.b` **AFTER** `5 ns;`
	`<- lbl_2.b <= lbl_1.b` **AFTER** `10 ns;`
	
	`<- lbl_1.b <= lbl_1.a` **AFTER** `15 ns;`

10.2 Use Statements

••• ENTITY e IS ___ ••• BEGIN ... END e ;	••• ARCHITECTURE a OF e IS ___ ••• BEGIN ... END a ;	••• CONFIGURATION c OF e IS ••• ••• ••• END
••• PACKAGE pkg IS ___ ••• ___ ••• ___ ••• END pkg ;	use_clause ::= **use** selected_name { , selected_name } ;	••• PACKAGE BODY pck IS ___ ••• ___ ••• ___ ••• END pck ;

... b: BLOCK IS ___ ••• BEGIN ... END BLOCK b ;	FUNCTION f (...) RETURN r IS ___ ••• BEGIN ... END f ;	PROCEDURE p (...) IS ___ ••• BEGIN ... END p ;	p : PROCESS ___ ••• BEGIN ... END PROCESS p ;

10.2.1 Comment

The **USE** statement can also be placed as a context statement in front of every library module such as entity, architecture, package, package body and configuration.

10.2.2 Examples

USE work.**ALL**;	All packages from the default library *work* are integrated.
USE work.my_package.**ALL**;	All elements of the package *my_package* from the library *work* are integrated.
USE work.my_package.my_function;	The function *my_function* from the package *my_package* in the library *work* is integrated.
USE lib_1.pkg_1.**ALL**, lib_1.pkg_2.proc_1, lib_2.pkg_3.**ALL**;	All elements from the packages *pkg_1* and *pkg_3* are integrated; from package *pkg_2* only the procedure *proc_1* is integrated.

10.2.3 Overloading Resolution

Overloading is defined for subprograms, operators and values of enumeration types.

Overloading is the simultaneous visibility of several subprograms, operators or of object values that have the same name and may belong to different enumeration types. The several variants of a subprogram or an operator differ only in the type and number of their arguments and results. VHDL programs recognize from the context (i.e. from the number and types of arguments) which of the visible variants is to be used. If a definite decision is not possible, i.e. if several visible alternative prove to be 'suitable' for the required task, an error is reported.

10.3 Design Units and Their Analysis

●●● ENTITY e IS ... BEGIN ... END e ;	●●● ARCHITECTURE a OF e IS ... BEGIN ... END a ;		●●● CONFIGURATION c OF e IS ... ... END
●●● PACKAGE pkg IS ... END pkg ;	library_clause ::= **library** logical_name_list ;		●●● PACKAGE BODY pck IS ... END pck ;
... b: BLOCK IS ... BEGIN ... END BLOCK b ;	FUNCTION f (...) RETURN r IS ... BEGIN ... END f ;	PROCEDURE p (...) IS ... BEGIN ... END p ;	p : PROCESS ... BEGIN ... END PROCESS p ;

10.3.1 Further Definitions

logical_name_list ::=   logical_name { , logical_name }

10.3.2 Examples

LIBRARY my_library_1, my_library_2;	Several libraries are made public.
LIBRARY my_library; **USE** my_library.my_pack.**ALL**;	After the library *my_library* has been made public all elements from the package *my_pack* are integrated.

The **LIBRARY** statement can be placed as a context statement in front of every library module such as entity, architecture, package, package body and configuration.

11 Elaboration and Simulation

Elaboration is defined for declarations, design hierarchies and statements (including concurrent statements). A construct can only be activated by elaboration. As long as elaboration is not finished the corresponding construct does not exist!

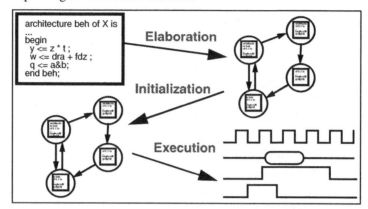

In order to execute a model, it is at first necessary to elaborate the design hierarchy that describes the model. Afterwards the model's nets are initialized and after that model simulation is started. Simulation includes several runs of the simulation cycle. During that simulation, processes are executed and netlist parameters are newly calculated or updated.

11.1 Elaboration of a Blockheader

11.1.1 The Generic Statement

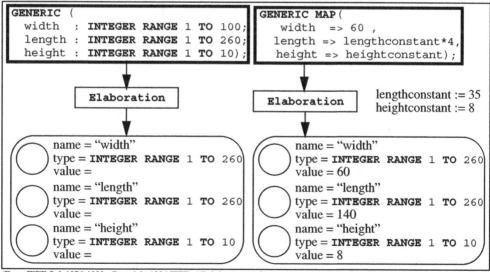

Elaboration of the generic declarations contained in the generic statement is carried out in the given sequence. During that elaboration the generic's subtypes are formed and a generic constant is provided for each of these subtypes. The individual value is only determined when consecutive generic map statements are elaborated. If these map statements are missing, the system uses the corresponding default value of the individual generic constant.

11.1.2 The Generic Map Statement

Here the generic concatenation list is elaborated. It contains an implicitly defined assignment element for every generic constant that is not explicitly assigned.

```
GENERIC (explicit_generic : INTEGER := 9);
```

The part of the implicitly defined assignment element that is to be calculated is the expression contained in the individual selection constant.

The elaboration of the list elements that consist of a formal and a current part is carried out sequentially. While this is done, the formal part of a generic constant is seized with the values that result from the calculation of the individual current driver.

11.1.3 The Port Statement

The system evaluates the port declarations contained in the statement in the given sequence. In the elaboration of a port declaration, first the subtype is determined and then a port is created for this subtype.

11.1.4 The Port Map Statement

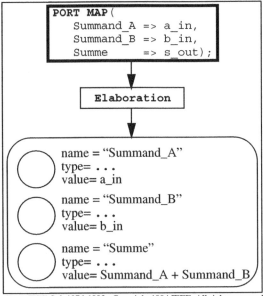

```
PORT MAP (
    Summand_A => a_in,
    Summand_B => b_in,
    Summe     => s_out);
```

Elaboration

name = "Summand_A"
type= . . .
value= a_in

name = "Summand_B"
type= . . .
value= b_in

name = "Summe"
type= . . .
value= Summand_A + Summand_B

Here the system evaluates the port concatenation list. It contains assignment statements that assign the signal specified in the actual expression to the formal expression. This assignment includes a check of the rules and restrictions concerning ports.

A given expression within a port declaration (statement of initialization) is elaborated using the actual values. If in this assignment statement no signal is linked to this port and if this port is an input, it receives a default value if one has been defined for this port.

11.2 Elaboration of a Declaration

Elaborating a declaration corresponds to generating the declared construct. The syntactic rules (above all those concerning the validity range) do not allow a construct to be used before the corresponding declaration has been elaborated.

11.2.1 Subprogram Declaration and Bodies

A subprogram declaration is elaborated by elaborating the corresponding interface -parameter list. By doing so, the subtype of every interface element and thus also the subtype of every formal parameter in the subprogram is determined.

The elaboration of the subprogram body allows the subprogram to be used in following (not in previous!) subprogram calls.

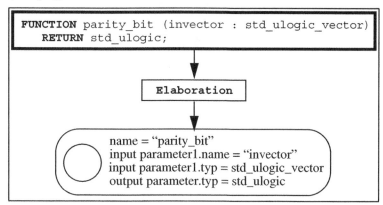

11.2.2 Type Declaration

The system first elaborates the type definition and afterwards generates the type. With a constrained array declaration, however, first the equally valued unconstrained array type is elaborated (i.e. the elements' subtypes are elaborated) and then the subtype that corresponds to the unconstrained array type is elaborated.

The elaboration of an enumeration type generates the corresponding type. With integer-, floating-point- or physical-type definitions the corresponding subtypes are determined. With physical-type definitions the units are generated as well.

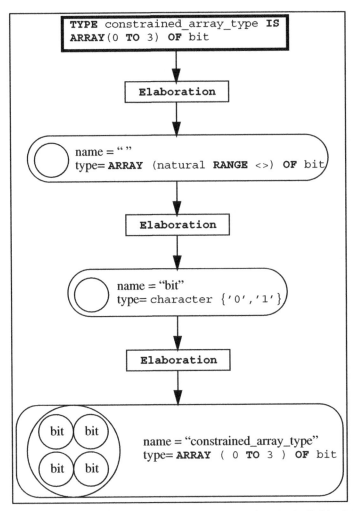

One data set (Record construction) is elaborated by elaborating the individual elements' declarations in the given sequence (similar to array type).

The elaboration of an element declaration consists of determining the subtype. The elaboration of an index declaration is equal to that of the corresponding subtype.

11.2.3 Subtype Declaration

Here the subtype is determined and generated. If the subtype is unconstrained it is similar to the base type. Otherwise, first the limitation is elaborated and afterwards compatibility towards the base type is checked.

A limitation to the value range is elaborated by calculating this value range. In doing so the value limits and the counting direction of the range are defined. A limitation in size is elaborated by calculating the corresponding expression.

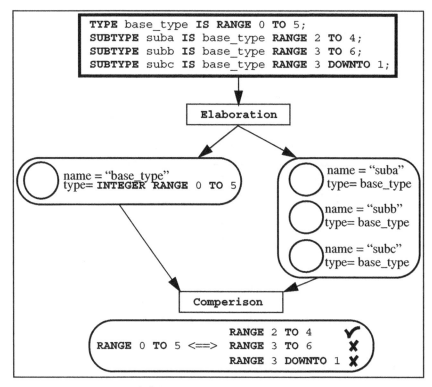

11.2.4 Object Declaration

Here one has to distinguish between file objects and other objects. With file objects, first the subtype is determined and then generated. The logical file name is determined and the corresponding physical file is linked to the new object.

The following procedure is valid for all other types of objects (except for port and generic declarations):

1. The object's subtype is defined.
2. If the object's declaration contains an explicit expression of initialization the value of this expression is calculated. It is then the object's initial value. If this is not the case, the object is given an implicitly defined initial value.
3. The object is generated.
4. The initial value is assigned to the object.

During initialization it is checked whether the subtype belongs to the object's subtype.

With an array object that is signified by an object declaration the first step is to transform the subtype until the object is a constant whose subtype is a type of an unconstrained array.

An error occurs if the name of one of the object's subtypes is used before the corresponding declaration has been elaborated.

If a file elaborated which declaration contains no file open information then first FILE_OPEN is called.

11.2.5 Alias Declaration

The subtype associated with the alias is determined and generated. After that an alternative name is generated.

The creation of an alias for an array object involves a check that the subtype associated with the alias includes a matching element for each element of the named object.

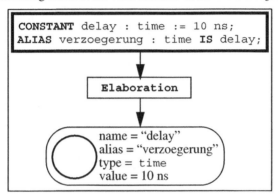

11.2.6 Attribute Declaration

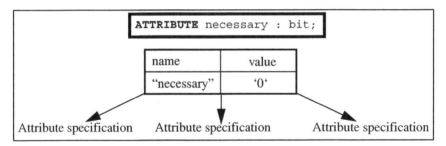

A template is generated with which it is possible to define attributes for the individual elements.

11.2.7 Component Declaration

The system generates a template for generating the component's instants.

11.2.8 Elaboration of a Specification

Here additional information is assigned to a previously declared program part.

11.2.9 Attribute Specification

Elaboration proceeds as follows:

1. An entity's specification is elaborated in order to be able to determine which individual elements are affected by the attribute specification.

2. In order to determine the attribute's value, the expression is evaluated.

3. A new attribute instance is generated and linked to every program element or point affected by it.

4. Each new attribute instance is given the value of the expression.

The assignment described at 4 comprises a test to check whether the value belongs to the attribute's subtype. With a constrained array type's attribute, first the subtype has to undergo an implicit type conversion similar to a statement of assignment. Such a conversion is not necessary for unconstrained array types.

11.2.10 Configuration Specification

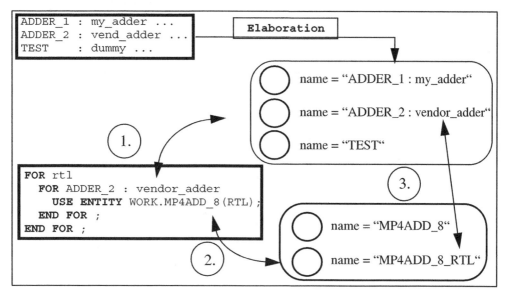

Elaboration proceeds as follows:

1. Component specification is elaborated to determine which instances are affected by the configuration.

2. The binding indication is elaborated in order to identify the entity to which the component instances determined at 1 are linked.

3. The binding information is associated with each component instance influenced to make sure that they can be used to generate further instances later on.

The procedure described here comprises a test to make sure that the entity declaration and the corresponding architecture implied by the binding indications exist within the specified library.

11.2.11 Disconnection Specification

This includes the following steps:

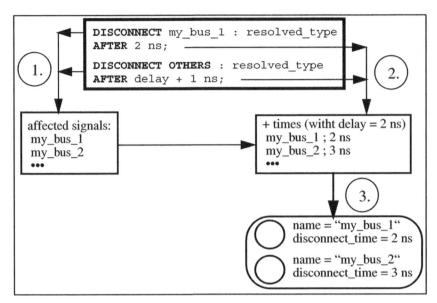

1. The guarded signal specification is elaborated in order to determine which signals are affected by the disconnection specification.

2. The time expression is evaluated in order to determine the disconnection time for the drivers of the signals determined at 1.

3. The disconnection time is associated with every signal affected. It can be used to formulate disconnection statements (in processes for guarded signal seizures).

11.3 Elaboration of a Statement Part

The elaboration rules are valid for all statement parts except these of an architecture with the attribute **FOREIGN**. These are elaborated implementation-dependent.

11.3.1 Block Statements

```
my_block : BLOCK (enable = '1')
PORT (farbe_1, farbe_2, select : std_ulogic;
                        auswahl : std_ulogic BUS);      1.
PORTMAP (farbe_1 => color(0),
        farbe_2 => color(1),
        auswahl => point);
```

```
                    SIGNAL inter : std_ulogic;          2.
```

```
BEGIN
    inter    <= farbe_1 WHEN select = '0' ELSE farbe_2;
    auswahl <= GUARDED inter;                           3.
END BLOCK my_block;
```

The block's beginning, its declarative part and its statement part are elaborated successively:

1. Begin (if present)
2. Declarative part
3. Statement part

A block statement can be elaborated under the control of a configuration declaration. An enclosed block configuration can generate a number of additional implicitly defined specifications which are used when the corresponding block statement is elaborated and which are thus elaborated at the same time.

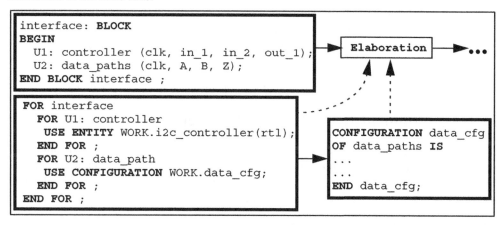

Each of these implicit specifications consists of that configuration's specification that is implied by the component configurations within the block configuration.

11.3.2 Generate Statement

The generate statement is replaced by copies of block statements whose statement part consists of the concurrent statements contained in the generate statement. Each block statement is afterwards elaborated.

With a **FOR** generate statement the individual value range is elaborated. Then a block statement is generated for every value within that range.

(From IEEE Std. 1076-1993. Copyright 1994 IEEE. All rights reserved.)

This statement has the following characteristics:

1. The names of the block statement and of the generate statement are the same.

2. The declarative part contains a constant declaration that declares a constant under the name of the generate parameter. The constant's value is equal to that of the generate parameter; its type is determined by the base type of the generate parameter's value range.

3. The statement part contains a copy of the concurrent statements from the generate statement.

With an **IF** generate statement the logic expression is calculated. If the expression takes on the value 'true' a block statement is generated that has the following characteristics:

1. The same names are valid for both the block and the generate statement.

2. The block's declarative part is empty.

3. The statement part contains a copy of the concurrent statements (see above).

11.3.3 Component Instantiation Statements

The component either has to be fully linked to an entity determined by an entity declaration and an architecture, or it has to be linked to an entity's configuration. Both the implicitly defined block statement, which describes the component's instant, and the block statement, which is also implicit and refers to the entity mentioned above, are elaborated.

11.3.4 Other Concurrent Statements

All other concurrent statements are either process statements or statements for which an equal process statement exists. Elaboration comprises the following steps:

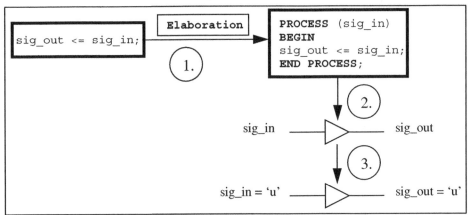

1. The declarative part of the process is elaborated.

2. The drivers required by the process statement are provided.

3. The initial process, which is defined by the default values of scalar signals, is inserted into the corresponding driver.

In the elaboration of all concurrent signal assignment statements and of all concurrent assertion statements an equal process statement is generated and then elaborated.

11.4 Dynamic Elaboration

In order to be able to execute program parts that contain sequential statements, it is necessary to elaborate these program parts as well. This is done while the model is executed.

Here are some examples in which elaboration is carried out dynamically during simulation:

- In order to execute a **FOR** iteration loop it is necessary to elaborate the loop parameters before the statements within the loop can be carried out. Elaboration generates the loop parameters and calculates their value ranges.

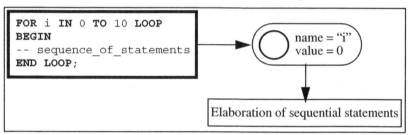

- In order to execute a subprogram call it is at first necessary to elaborate the parameter interface list of the corresponding subprogram declaration. In doing so every interface declaration is elaborated so that the formal parameters can be generated. These are then linked to the actual parameters. Eventually, the declarative part of the corresponding subprogram body is elaborated and the subprogram body's sequence of statements is carried out.

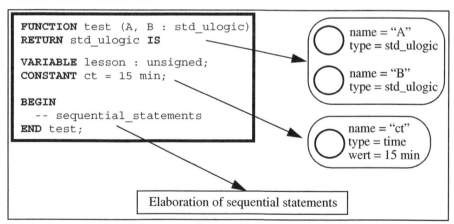

- In order to calculate an index that contains a subtype identification it is necessary to elaborate the subtype determination before the generated instance is assigned.

As a consequence of the rules mentioned above, declarations within a subprogram body's declarative part are elaborated every time the corresponding subprogram is called. If this is the case, the elaboration of a declaration can lead to different results with different characteristics. Thus, for example, the elaboration of one and the same subtype within a subprogram body can lead to subtypes with different characteristics being generated.

```
FUNCTION diff_subtypes (N : INTEGER)
RETURN INTEGER IS

   SUBTYPE my_int IS INTEGER RANGE 0 TO N;
   VARIABLE out_sig : my_int;

BEGIN
...
```

N here is a constant's formal parameter (default for formal parameters of mode IN).
The actual parameter that is linked to N may, however, also be a signal, for example,
=> subtype my_int can change with every function call depending on N!

11.5 Elaboration of a Design Hierarchy

By elaborating a design hierarchy a number of processes that are linked by nets are generated, which can then be executed to simulate the behaviour of the original design (model).

A design hierarchy that is defined by an entity is translated by elaborating a block statement that corresponds to the external block defined by the entity. It is also possible to determine the design hierarchy by means of a configuration. When this is done, a block statement is elaborated corresponding to the external block that is defined within the entity, which is defined by the corresponding configuration part.

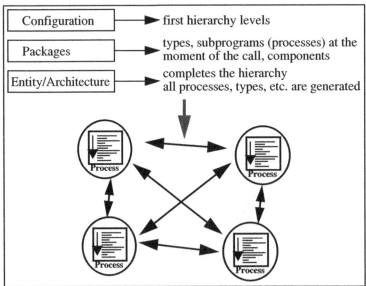

Configuration	► first hierarchy levels
Packages	► types, subprograms (processes) at the moment of the call, components
Entity/Architecture	► completes the hierarchy all processes, types, etc. are generated

Within a block statement, all packages that have not been evaluated and all packages contained therein are elaborated. Initially, the package declaration's declarative part and after that the package body's declarative part are carried out.

11.6 Execution of a Model

A generated *model* is executed by elaborating the user specified *processes*.

Within the design hierarchy the core process:

- monitors and coordinates during simulation the activities of all processes provided by the user;
- has signal values transferred and the values of implicitly defined values, such as S'stable(t), updated;
- registers events and has suitable processes carried out in response to these events; it seizes one variable each with the actual value of every signal that is explicitly declared within the model and provides the variable's value for all calculations using the signal;
- updates the variables' values mentioned above at regular intervals during the simulation cycle,
- seizes each variable with the actual value of every implicitly declared guarded signal and provides one driver and the one variable that contains the actual value for

   S'Stable(t) signals,

   S'Quiet(t) signals,

   S'Transaction signals and

   prefixes S and times t used within the model.

11.6.1 Propagation of Signal Values

As simulation time passes, the signal form within the waveform receives the values of the corresponding drivers. A driver is *active* when it is assigned a new value. A signal is *active* if

- one of the signal sources is active;
- one of the subelements is activated;
- the signal is used in the formal part of an element in a port concatenation list and the actual part is active; or if
- the signal is a subelement of an active resolved signal.

If a compound type signal has a source that is based on another type, every scalar subelement is considered active if the signal source is activated.

The same is valid for ports and for signals linked to them. An implicitly defined signal is active if this signal is updated by the core process. If a signal is not active, it is called *quiet*.

For certain signals the *core process* monitors two different signal values. The *driver value* is the value of a signal that serves as a source for other signals. The effective value is the value determined by calculating the signal relations within an expression. The driver value and the effective value are not identical above all when a resolution function or type conversions are involved. The following table shows the particularities of both signal types:

Signal type	Driver value	Effective value
Scalar signal S	S without a source: Driver value = default value	S is declared by a signal declaration; port of the type *buffer* or an unlinked port of the type *inout*: effective value=driver value
	Driver is source of S, S is unresolved: Driver value = value of the driver	S is a linked port of the type *in* or *input*: effective value of S = effective value of the actual part of the assignment element, Is part is calculated.
	Port is source of S, S is unresolved: Driver value = driver value of the formal part of the element which links S to the port.	S to be an unlinked port of the type *in*: effective value = default value
	S is resolved: driver value = resolved value of S, resolution function is calculated using the driver values of the sources of S as transfer parameters	**Control value and effective value both have the subtype of S**
Compound signal V	Driver value = summary of the driver values of every scalar subelement of V	Effective value = summary of the effective values of every scalar subelement of V

When a signal is updated the core process first calculates the driver value and the effective value, then the variable belonging to the signal is newly seized. If the signal is not derived from an *array type*, the effective value is used. It is checked whether this value belongs to the signal's subtype. The variable that stores the actual value receives the effective value by assignment. If the signal is based on an *array type,* the effective value is transformed implicitly into the signal's subtype (including a consistency test between the signal elements and the elements of the effective value). The result of the type conversion is assigned to the variable mentioned above.

11.6.1.1 Comments

An element of a compound signal can be *quiet* while the signal itself is *active*.

For ports of the type *out* no effective value is specified as they are not allowed to be read.

The rules mentioned above are not valid for implicitly defined signals.

11.6.2 Updating Implicitly Defined Signals

The core process links the values of implicitly defined *guarded signals* to a block statement that contains a guarded expression. At the same time the system updates the implicit signals S'Stable(t), S'Quiet(t) and S'Transaction as well as their drivers.

A guarded signal is changed in its current values only if the corresponding guarded expression is related to the signal and the signal is active. When this is done the expression's value is calculated and assigned to the variable that contains the signal's actual value.

The signals S'Stable(t), S'Quiet(t) and S'Transaction have the following special characteristics:

Characteristic	S'Stable(t)	S'Quiet(t)	S'Transaction
Change current value only if	an event occurs in the current simulation cycle	the signal is activated	the signal is activated
	the driver is activated	the driver is activated	
Update by	assigning the value '**false**' to the corresponding variable; driver is given the form '**true**' after the period t	assigning the value '**false**' to the corresponding variable; driver is given the form '**true**' after the period t	assigning the expression value to the corresponding variable (only **one** assignment is possible within one simulation cycle)
	assigning the driver's current value to the corresponding variable.	assigning the driver's current value to the corresponding variable.	

The current value of an implicit value D *depends on* the current value of another signal E if:

- D is a *guarded signal* and E appears within the *guarded expression* that determines the current value of D;
- D is of the type S'Stable(t), S'Quiet(t) or S'Transaction.

Within a simulation cycle the current value of E is updated **in time before** the current value of D, thus the principle of causality is valid.

11.6.3 The Simulation Cycle

A model is executed by repeatedly executing process statements from the level of model description. One repetition is called a simulation cycle. Within a cycle all signal values are calculated. Depending on that, the system starts executing process statements, i.e., if an event occurs at a signal, all processes that are sensitive to this signal are started. The execution is preceded by an *initialization,* which consists of the following steps:

1. The driver values and the effective values of all *explicitly declared* signals are calculated. The current values receive the effective value and are valid until simulation starts.

2. The value of *implicitly declared* signals of the form S'Stable(t) or S'Quiet(t) is determined to be 'true'. Signals of the type S'Transaction remain undefined.

3. The system seizes the value of implicit *guarded signals* with value of the corresponding *guarded expression.*

4. Each of the model's non-postponed processes is executed individually (until it is suspended).

5. Each of the model's postponed processes is executed individually (until it is suspended).

6. The time for the next simulation cycle is calculated according to 6 below.

The simulation's start is usually assigned the time 0 ns.

The simulation cycle consists of the following parts:

1. If all drivers are inactive, the simulation time is set to the moment at which one driver is activated or an interrupted process is continued. Simulation is ended when simulation time has reached the maximum value.

2. Every activated, *explicitly declared* signal is updated. So-called e*vents* can occur, based on which the system decides which process statements are carried out.

3. All *implicitly declared* signals are updated.

4. Every process that currently influences a certain signal in connection with an event is continued to be executed.

5. All restarted non-postponed processes are continued and executed until an interrupt occurs.

6. The time for the next simulation cycle is calculated by setting it to the earliest of the following times:

*   TIME'High

*   Next time at which a driver becomes active

*   Next time at which a process resumes

If this time equals the current simulation time, a new delta cycle is started.

7. If no new delta cycle starts, all postponed processes, not executed until now, are executed. After this no new delta cycle is allowed. The time for the next simulation cycle is calculated according to 6.

12 Lexical Elements

12.1 Character Set

Definitions	graphic_character ::=
	    basic_graphic_character | lower_case_letter | other_special_character
	
	basic_character ::=
	    basic_graphic_character | format_effector
	
	basic_graphic_character ::=
	    upper_case_letter | digit | special_character | space_character

Specification	(a) upper_case_letter
	  A B C D E F G H I J K L M N O P Q R S T U V W X Y Z
	
	(b) digit
	  0 1 2 3 4 5 6 7 8 9
	
	(c) special_character
	  " # & ' ( ) * + , - . / : ; < = > _ |
	
	(d) space_character
	
	(e) lower_case_letter
	  a b c d e f g h i j k l m n o p q r s t u v w x y z
	
	(f) other_special_character
	  ! $ % @ ? [\ ] ^ ` { } ~
	
	(g) Format effectors (*format_effectors*) are
	
	    • Tab (horizontal and vertical),
	
	    • Carriage return,
	
	    • Line feed and
	
	    • Form feed.

12.2 Delimiters

Specification	(a) delimiter & ' ( ) * + , - . / : ; < = > | (b) compound_delimiter => ** := /= >= <= <>
Comments	Every lexical element has to fit into one line as the end of the line represents a delimiter.

12.3 Identifiers

Definition	identifier ::= basic_identifier | extended_identifier
	basic_identifier ::= *letter* { [underline] *letter_or_digit* }
	letter_or_digit ::= *letter* | digit
	letter ::= upper_case_letter | lower_case_letter
	extended_identifier ::= \graphic_character { graphic_character }\
Comments	A basic identifier must not contain any blanks!
Examples	count x c_out store_next_item \74S05\ \a\\b\

12.4 Abstract Literals

Definition	abstract_literal ::= *decimal_literal* | *based_literal*
	decimal_literal ::= *integer* [. *integer*] [*exponent*]
	based_literal ::= *base* # *based_integer* [. *based_integer*] # [*exponent*]
	base ::= *integer*
	based_integer ::= *extended_digit* { [underline] *extended_digit* }
	extended_digit ::= digit | letter
	exponent ::= E [+] *integer* | E - *integer*
	integer ::= digit { [underline] digit }

Comments	For *integer_literals* the exponent must not be negative. High order zeros are permitted. 'Space' is not permitted as 'space' is a delimiter. _ only serves to improve readability and does not influence the value. permitted base statements: 2,..,16
Examples	Integer figures 12 0 1E6 123_456 Real figures 12.0 0.0 0.4556 3.14159_26 Real figures with an exponent 1.34E-12 1.0E+6 6.023E+24 Integer figures of the value 255 2#1111_1111# 16#FF# 016#0FF# Integer figures of the value 224 16#E#E1 2#1110_0000# Real figures of the value 4095.0 (32-bit IEEE floating-point format) 16#F.FF#E+2 2#1.1111_1111_111#E11

12.5 Character Literals

Definition	character_literal ::= ' graphic_character '
Examples	'A' '*' ' ' ' ' '

12.6 String Literals

Definition	string_literal ::= " { graphic_character } "
Comments	A character string must not extend to the following lines as it is a lexical element. Character strings that do not fit into one line can be divided into two or more character strings and be chained or linked to each other. (see the example). '"' within a character string has to be entered as '""'.

Examples	an error report "setup time too small" an empty character string "" three character strings of the length 1 " ", "a", """" "Characters such as $, % and } may be contained in character string" "first part of a character string," & "which only ends on the next line"

12.7 Bit String Literals

Definition	bit_string_literal ::= *base_specifier* " *bit_value* " base_specifier ::= B | O | X bit_value ::= *extended_digit* { [underline] *extended_digit* } extended_digit ::= digit | letter
Comments	B means binary, O means octal and X means hexadecimal.
Examples	bit_vector(7 downto 0) := B"1111_1111" -- equivalent to "11111111" bit_vector(7 downto 0) := X"FF" -- equivalent to B"1111_1111" bit_vector(8 downto 0) := O"777" -- equivalent to B"111_111_111" bit_vector(11 downto 0) := X"777" -- equivalent to B"0111_0111_0111"

12.8 Comments

Definition	Comments are used to explain VHDL Code.
Examples	**END** ; -- line is no longer worked upon -- an extensive comment can be subdivided into two -- or more successive lines ------- the first two hyphens introduce the comment

12.9 Reserved Words

Specification	ABS ACCESS AFTER ALIAS ALL AND ARCHITECTURE ARRAY ASSERT ATTRIBUTE BEGIN BLOCK BODY BUFFER BUS CASE COMPONENT CONFIGURATION CONSTANT	DISCONNECT DOWNTO ELSE ELSIF END ENTITY EXIT FILE FOR FUNCTION GENERATE GENERIC GROUP GUARDED IF IMPURE IN INERTIAL INOUT IS	LABEL LIBRARY LINKAGE LITERAL LOOP MAP MOD NAND NEW NEXT NOR NOT NULL OF ON OPEN OR OTHERS OUT	PACKAGE PORT POSTPONED PROCEDURE PROCESS PURE RANGE RECORD REGISTER REJECT REM REPORT ROL ROR RETURN SELECT SEVERITY SIGNAL SHARED SLA SLL	SRA SRL SUBTYPE THEN TO TRANSPORT TYPE UNAFFECTED UNITS UNTIL USE VARIABLE WAIT WHEN WHILE WITH XNOR XOR
Comments	A reserved word must not be used as an explicitly declared identifier.				

12.10 Replacing Characters

Definition	A vertical line (|) can be replaced by an exclamation mark (!), which represents an operation character (*delimiter*). The number signs (#) in *based literals* can be replaced by colons (:) if both characters are replaced. Quotation marks (") at the beginning and at the end of character strings can be replaced by percent signs (%). If this is done, both the quotation marks at the beginning and at the end of the character string have to be replaced; if this is the case, however, there must not be any quotation marks within the character string. Every percent sign within the character string then has to be doubled. This doubled percent sign is interpreted as a single percent sign. It is possible to do the same exchange for *bit string literals* if both surrounding quotation marks are replaced.
Example	16#ED# --> 16:ED: O"777" --> O%777% "5 ns rise time" --> %5 ns rise time% "50% of propagation delay time" --> %50%% of propagation delay time%

13 Predefined Attributes

`T'BASE`	Kind	type
	Prefix	any type or subtype T
	Result type	base type of T
	Restrictions	This attribute can only be used as a prefix for the names of other attributes, e.g., T'BASE'LEFT.
`T'LEFT`	Kind	value
	Prefix	any scalar type or subtype T
	Result type	same type as T
	Result	left bound of T
`T'RIGHT`	Kind	value
	Prefix	any scalar type or subtype T
	Result type	same type as T
	Result	right bound of T
`T'HIGH`	Kind	value
	Prefix	any scalar type or subtype T
	Result type	same type as T
	Result	upper bound of T
`T'LOW`	Kind	value
	Prefix	any scalar type or subtype T
	Result type	same type as T
	Result	lower bound of T
`T'ASCENDING`	Kind	value
	Prefix	any scalar type or subtype T
	Result type	boolean
	Result	TRUE if T has an ascending range; FALSE otherwise.
`T'IMAGE(X)`	Kind	function
	Prefix	any scalar type or subtype T
	Parameter	expression whose type is the base type of T
	Result type	string

	Result	the string of the parameter value. Preferably lower case letters are used without additional chars (Exception: Extended Identifier -> \ ; Character Literal -> '). Physical types are represented with the primary unit, except the type time. The current resolution limit of the simulator determine the unit. Numbers of type real are represented up to R number right of the decimal point. Unnecessary zeros are left out. Replacement characters (Section 12.10) are not allowed.
	Restrictions	the type of the parameter has to be of the subtype of the prefix.
T'VALUE(X)	Kind	function
	Prefix	any scalar type or subtype T
	Parameter	expression of type string
	Result type	base type of T
	Result	value of T whose string representation is X. Additional leading and trailing white spaces are allowed and ignored. Numerical types are represented as numbers with any valid base. Physical types are represented with any valid unit. The replacement characters of Section 12.10 are allowed.
	Restrictions	the parameter has to be a valid string representation of a literal of type T.
T'POS(x)	Kind	function
	Prefix	any discrete or physical type or subtype T
	Parameter	expression with a base type of T
	Result type	universal_integer
	Result	position of the parameter value
T'VAL(x)	Kind	function
	Prefix	any discrete or physical type or subtype T
	Parameter	expression of an integer type
	Result type	base type of T
	Result	value of the element whose positional number = X
	Restrictions	an error occurs if the result does not belong to the range T'LOW **to** T'HIGH.

T'SUCC(x)	Kind	function
	Prefix	any discrete or physical type or subtype T
	Parameter	expression whose base type is of the type T
	Result type	base type of T
	Result	value of the element whose positional number = X+1
	Restrictions	An error occurs if X=T'HIGH or if X does not belong to the range T'LOW **to** T'HIGH.
T'PRED(x)	Kind	function
	Prefix	any discrete or physical type or subtype T
	Parameter	expression whose base type is of the type T
	Result type	base type of T
	Result	value of the element whose positional number = X-1
	Restrictions	an error occurs if X=T'LOW or if X does not belong to the range T'LOW **to** T'HIGH.
T'LEFTOF(x)	Kind	function
	Prefix	any discrete or physical type or subtype T
	Parameter	expression whose base type is of the type T
	Result type	base type of T
	Result	value of the element which is to the left of the addressed element.
	Restrictions	an error occurs if X=T'LEFT or if X does not belong to the range T'LOW **to** T'HIGH.
T'RIGHTOF(x)	Kind	function
	Prefix	any discrete or physical type or subtype T
	Parameter	expression whose base type is of the type T
	Result type	base type of T
	Result	value of the element that is to the right of the element that is addressed by X.
	Restrictions	an error occurs if X=T'RIGHT or if X does not belong to the range T'LOW **to** T'HIGH.
A'LEFT[(n)]	Kind	function

	Prefix	any prefix that is suitable as an array object, an alias of it or a conditional array subtype
	Parameter	locally static expression of the type universal_integer whose value must not exceed the dimension of A. If there is no parameter, it defaults to 1.
	Result type	type of the left bound of the Nth index range of A
	Result	left bound of the Nth index range of A
A'RIGHT[(n)]	Kind	function
	Prefix	any prefix that is suitable as an array object, an alias of it or a conditional array subtype
	Parameter	locally static expression of the type universal_integer whose value must not exceed the dimension of A. If there is no parameter, it defaults to 1.
	Result type	type of the right bound of the Nth index range of A
	Result	right bound of the Nth index range of A
A'HIGH[(n)]	Kind	function
	Prefix	any prefix that is suitable as an array object, an alias of it or a conditional array subtype
	Parameter	locally static expression of the type universal_integer whose value must not exceed the dimension of A. If there is no parameter it defaults to 1.
	Result type	type of the upper bound of the Nth index range of A
	Result	upper bound of the Nth index range of A
A'LOW[(n)]	Kind	function
	Prefix	any prefix that is suitable as an array object, an alias of it or a conditional array subtype
	Parameter	locally static expression of the type universal_integer whose value must not exceed the dimension of A. If there is no parameter it defaults to 1.
	Result type	type of the lower bound of the Nth index range of A
	Result	lower bound of the Nth index range of A
A'RANGE[(n)]	Kind	range
	Prefix	any prefix that is suitable as an array object, an alias of it or a conditional array subtype

	Parameter	locally static expression of the type universal_integer whose value must not exceed the dimension of A. If there is no parameter, it defaults to 1.
	Result type	type of the Nth index range of A
	Result	The range A'RIGHT(n) **to** A'LEFT(n) for an increasing or A'RIGHT(n) **downto** A'LEFT(n) for a decreasing direction of the Nth index range of A
A'REVERSE_ **RANGE[(n)]**	Kind	range
	Prefix	any prefix that is suitable as an array object, an alias of it or a conditional array subtype
	Parameter	locally static expression of the type universal_integer whose value must not exceed the dimension of A. If there is no parameter, it defaults to 1.
	Result type	type of the Nth index range of A
	Result	The range A'RIGHT(n) **downto** A'LEFT(n) for an increasing or A'RIGHT(n) **to** A'LEFT(n) for a decreasing direction of the Nth index range of A.
A'LENGTH[(n)]	Kind	value
	Prefix	any prefix that is suitable as an array object, an alias of it or a conditional array subtype
	Parameter	locally static expression of the type universal_integer whose value must not exceed the dimension of A. If there is no parameter, it defaults to 1.
	Result type	universal_integer
	Result	number of values in the Nth index range
A' **ASCENDING[(n)]**	Kind	value
	Prefix	any prefix that is suitable as an array object, an alias of it or a conditional arraysubtype
	Parameter	locally static expression of the type universal_integer whose value must not exceed the dimension of A. If there is no parameter it defaults to 1.
	Result type	boolean
	Result	TRUE if the Nth index range of A is defined with an ascending range; FALSE otherwise.
S'DELAYED[(t)]	Kind	signal

	Prefix	any signal
	Parameter	static expression of the type time that provides a value greater than 0. If t is missing, it defaults to 0.
	Result type	base type of S
	Result	a signal delayed by t time units, equivalent to S
S'STABLE[(t)]	Kind	signal
	Prefix	any signal
	Parameter	static expression of the type time that provides a value greater than 0. If t is missing, it defaults to 0.
	Result type	boolean
	Result	a signal that has the value TRUE if there has been no event at S for t time units; otherwise it has the value FALSE.
S'QUIET[(t)]	Kind	signal
	Prefix	any signal
	Parameter	static expression of the type time that provides a value greater than 0. If t is missing, it defaults to 0.
	Result type	boolean
	Result	a signal that has the value TRUE when S has been quiet for t time units; otherwise it has the value FALSE.
S'TRANSACTION	Kind	signal
	Prefix	any signal
	Result type	bit
	Result	a signal whose value is inverted in each simulation cycle in which the signal S is activated.
	Restrictions	a description must not depend on the initial value of S'TRANSACTION.
S'EVENT	Kind	function
	Prefix	any signal
	Result type	boolean

	Result	a signal that has the value TRUE when there has been an event at S in the current simulation cycle; otherwise it has the value FALSE.
S'ACTIVE	Kind	function
	Prefix	any signal
	Result type	boolean
	Result	a signal that has the value TRUE when S is active in the current simulation cycle; otherwise it has the value FALSE.
S'LAST_EVENT	Kind	function
	Prefix	any signal
	Result type	time
	Result	the amount of time that has passed since the last event occurred on signal S.
S'LAST_ACTIVE	Kind	function
	Prefix	any signal
	Result type	time
	Result	the amount of time that has passed since S was last active.
S'LAST_VALUE	Kind	function
	Prefix	any signal
	Result type	base type of S
	Result	the value of S immediately before the last change.
S'DRIVING	Kind	function
	Prefix	any signal
	Result type	boolean
	Result	S = scalar: FALSE if the current value of the driver of S in the current process is determined by the null transaction; TRUE otherwise. S= composite: TRUE if for every subelement R of S R'DRIVING is TRUE. FALSE otherwise. S = null slice: S'DRIVING=TRUE.

	Restrictions	this attribute is available only from within a process, a concurrent statement with an equivalent process or a subprogram. If S is a port then the port must have the mode inout, out or buffer. If the attribute name appears in a subprogram body then it has to be a declarative item contained within a process statement and S has to be a formal parameter of the given subprogram or of a parent of that subprogram. The formal parameter of the subprogram then has to be of mode inout or out.
S'DRIVING_ VALUE	Kind	function
	Prefix	any signal
	Result type	base type of S
	Result	S = scalar: current value of the driver of S in the current process S= composite: corresponding aggregate. S = null slice: null slice.
	Restrictions	this attribute is available only from within a process, a concurrent statement with an equivalent process or a subprogram. If S is a port then the port must have the mode inout, out or buffer. If the attribute name appears in a subprogram body then it has to be a declarative item contained within a process statement and S has to be a formal parameter of the given subprogram or of a parent of that subprogram. The formal parameter of the subprogram has then to be of mode inout or out. S'DRIVING has to be TRUE at the time S'DRIVING_VALUE is evaluated.
E'SIMPLE_NAME	Kind	value
	Prefix	any named entity (see Section 5.1)
	Result type	string
	Result	the simple name, character literal or operator symbol of the named entity, without leading or trailing whitespace or quotations marks. (Exception: character literal -> ' and extended identifier -> \). Except for extended identifiers lower case characters are used.
E'INSTANCE_	Kind	value

NAME	Prefix	any named entity (see Section 5.1) other then the local ports and generics of a component declaration.
	Result type	string
	Result	the complete hierarchical path including instantiated entities beginning at the current level downto the name object.
E'PATH_NAME	Kind	value
	Prefix	any named entity (see Section 5.1) other then the local ports and generics of a component declaration.
	Result type	string
	Result	the complete hierarchical path excluding instantiated entities beginning at the root level downto the name object.
B'BEHAVIOUR (VHDL'87 only)	Kind	value
	Prefix	any block or entity architecture
	Result type	boolean
	Result	a value which is **TRUE** if the block or respectively the architecture contains no component instantiation; otherwise the value is **FALSE**.
B'STRUCTURE (VHDL'87 only)	Kind	value
	Prefix	any block or entity architecture
	Result type	boolean
	Result	a value thst is **TRUE** if the block or respectively the architecture contains neither a passive process statement nor a concurrent statement with a corresponding process statement; otherwise the value is **FALSE**.

14 Package STANDARD

PACKAGE STANDARD **IS**

```
    -- predefined enumeration types:
    TYPE boolean IS (false, true);
    TYPE bit IS ('0', '1');
    TYPE character IS (
      NUL, SOH, STX, ETX, EOT, ENQ, ACK, BEL, BS, HT, LF, VT, FF, CR,
      SO, SI, DLE, DC1, DC2, DC3, DC4, NAK, SYN, ETB, CAN, EM, SUB, ESC,
      FSP, GSP, RSP, USP, ' ', '!', '"', '#', '$', '%', '&', ''', '(',
      ')', '*', '+', ',', '-', '.', '/', '0', '1', '2', '3', '4', '5',
      '6', '7', '8', '9', ':', ';', '<', '=', '>', '?', '@', 'A', 'B',
      'C', 'D', 'E', 'F', 'G', 'H', 'I', 'J', 'K', 'L', 'M', 'N', 'O',
      'P', 'Q', 'R', 'S', 'T', 'U', 'V', 'W', 'X', 'Y', 'Z', ' [', '"',
      ']', '^', '_', '`', 'a', 'b', 'c', 'd', 'e', 'f', 'g', 'h', 'i',
      'j', 'k', 'l', 'm', 'n', 'o', 'p', 'q', 'r', 's', 't', 'u', 'v',
      'w', 'x', 'y', 'z', '{', '|', '}', '~', DEL, C128, C129, C130,
      C131, C132, C133, C134, C135, C136, C137, C138, C139, C140, C141,
      C142, C143, C144, C145, C146, C147, C148, C149, C150, C151, C152,
      C153, C154, C155, C156, C157, C158, C159, '*', '¡', '¢', '£', '¤',
      '¥', '|', '§', '¨', '©', 'ª', '«', '¬', '†', '®', '¯', '°', '±',
      '²', '³', '´', 'µ', '¶', '•', ',', '¹', '°', '»', '¼', '½', '¾',
      '¿', 'À', 'Á', 'Â', 'Ã', 'Ä', 'Å', 'Æ', 'Ç', 'È', 'É', 'Ê', 'Ì',
      'Í', 'Î', 'Ï', '?', 'Ñ', 'Ò', 'Ó', 'Ô', 'Õ', 'Ö', '✕', 'Ø', 'Ù',
      'Ú', 'Û', 'Ü', 'Y', 'Þ', 'ß', 'à', 'á', 'â', 'ã', 'ä', 'å', 'æ',
      'ç', 'è', 'é', 'ê', 'ì', 'í', 'î', 'ï', 'ð', 'ñ', 'ò', 'ó', 'ô',
      'õ', 'ö', ' ', 'ø', 'ù', 'ú', 'û', 'ü', 'ý', 'þ', 'ÿ');
    TYPE severity_level IS (note, warning, error, failure);

    -- predefined numeric types:
    TYPE integer IS RANGE implementation_defined;
    TYPE real IS RANGE implementation_defined;

    -- predefined type time:
    TYPE time IS RANGE implementation_defined
      UNITS
        fs; -- femtosecond
        ps  = 1000 fs; --picosecond
        ns  = 1000 ps; --nanosecond
        us  = 1000 ns; --microsecond
        ms  = 1000 us; --millisecond
        sec = 1000 ms; --second
        min = 60 sec;  --minute
        hr  = 60 min;  --hour
      END UNITS;
    SUBTYPE delay_length IS time RANGE 0 fs TO TIME'HIGH;
```

```
-- function that returns the current simulation time:
IMPURE FUNCTION now RETURN delay_length;

-- predefined numeric subtypes:
SUBTYPE natural IS integer RANGE 0 TO integer'high;
SUBTYPE positive IS integer RANGE 1 TO integer'high;

-- predefined array types:
TYPE string IS ARRAY (positive RANGE <>) OF character;
TYPE bit_vector IS ARRAY (natural RANGE <>) OF bit;

-- predefined types for opening files:
TYPE file_open_kind IS (READ_MODE, WRITE_MODE, APPEND_MODE);
TYPE file_open_status IS (OPEN_OK, STATUS_ERROR, NAME_ERROR,
 MODE_ERROR);

-- the 'foreign attribute:
ATTRIBUTE foreign: string;

END STANDARD;
```

15 Package TEXTIO

PACKAGE TEXTIO **IS**

```
    -- type definitions for text I/O:
    TYPE line IS ACCESS string;
    TYPE text IS FILE OF string;
    TYPE side IS (right, left);
    SUBTYPE width IS natural;

    -- standard text files:
    -- old VHDL'87 standard
    -- FILE input: text IS IN "std_input";
    -- FILE output: text IS OUT "std_output";

    -- new VHDL'93 standard
    FILE input: text OPEN READ_MODE IS "std_input";
    FILE output: text OPEN WRITE_MODE IS "std_output";

    -- input routines for standard types:
    PROCEDURE readline (f: IN text; l: OUT line);
    PROCEDURE read (l: INOUT line; value: OUT bit; good: OUT boolean);
    PROCEDURE read (l: INOUT line; value: OUT bit);
    PROCEDURE read (l: INOUT line; value: OUT bit_vector;
                   good: OUT boolean);
    PROCEDURE read (l: INOUT line; value: OUT bit_vector);
    PROCEDURE read (l: INOUT line; value: OUT boolean;
                   good: OUT boolean);
    PROCEDURE read (l: INOUT line; value: OUT boolean);
    PROCEDURE read (l: INOUT line; value: OUT character;
                   good: OUT boolean);
    PROCEDURE read (l: INOUT line; value: OUT character);
    PROCEDURE read (l: INOUT line; value: OUT integer;
                   good: OUT boolean);
    PROCEDURE read (l: INOUT line; value: OUT integer);
    PROCEDURE read (l: INOUT line; value: OUT real; good: OUT boolean);
    PROCEDURE read (l: INOUT line; value: OUT real);
    PROCEDURE read (l: INOUT line; value: OUT string;
                   good: OUT boolean);
    PROCEDURE read (l: INOUT line; value: OUT string);
    PROCEDURE read (l: INOUT line; value: OUT time; good: OUT boolean);
    PROCEDURE read (l: INOUT line; value: OUT time);

    -- output routines for standard types:
    PROCEDURE writeline (f: OUT text; l: IN line);
    PROCEDURE write (l: INOUT line; value: IN bit;
                   justified: IN side:= right; field: IN width:= 0);
```

(From IEEE Std. 1076-1993. Copyright 1994 IEEE. All rights reserved.)

```
PROCEDURE write (l: INOUT line; value: IN bit_vector;
                 justified: IN side:= right; field: IN width:= 0);
PROCEDURE write (l: INOUT line; value: IN boolean;
                 justified: IN side:= right; field: IN width:= 0);
PROCEDURE write (l: INOUT line; value: IN character;
                 justified: IN side:= right; field: IN width:= 0);
PROCEDURE write (l: INOUT line; value: IN integer;
                 justified: IN side:= right; field: IN width:= 0);
PROCEDURE write (l: INOUT line; value: IN real;
                 justified: IN side:= right; field: IN width:= 0;
                 digits: IN natural:= 0);
PROCEDURE write (l: INOUT line; value: IN string;
                 justified: IN side:= right; field: IN width:= 0);
PROCEDURE write (l: INOUT line; value: IN time;
                 justified: IN side:= right; field: IN width:= 0;
                 unit: IN time:= ns);

-- file position predicates:
-- FUNCTION endline (l: IN line) RETURN boolean; -- only VHDL'87
FUNCTION endfile (f: IN text) RETURN boolean;

END TEXTIO;
```

16 BNF

abstract_literal ::= decimal_literal | based_literal

access_type_definition ::= **access** subtype_indication

actual_designator ::=
    expression
   | *signal*_name
   | *variable*_name
   | *file*_name
   | **open**

actual_parameter_part ::= *parameter*_association_list

actual_part ::=
    actual_designator
   | *function*_name (actual_designator)
   | type_mark (actual_designator)

adding_operator ::= + | - | &

aggregate ::=
   (element_association { , element_association })

alias_declaration ::=
   alias alias_designator [: subtype_indication] **is** name [signature] ;

alias_designator ::= identifier | character_literal | operator_symbol

allocator ::=
   new subtype_indication
   | **new** qualified_expression

architecture_body ::=
   architecture identifier **of** *entity*_name **is**
      architecture_declarative_part
  begin
       architecture_statement_part
  end **[architecture]** [*architecture*_simple_name] ;

architecture_declarative_part ::=
   { block_declarative_item }

architecture_statement_part ::=
   { concurrent_statement }

array_type_definition ::=
   unconstrained_array_definition | constrained_array_definition

assertion ::=
    assert condition
    [**report** expression]
    [**severity** expression]

assertion_statement ::= [label :] assertion ;

association_element ::=
   [formal_part =>] actual_part

association_list ::=
   association_element { , association_element }

attribute_declaration ::=
   attribute identifier : type_mark ;

attribute_designator ::= *attribute*_simple_name

attribute_name ::=
   prefix [signature] ' attribute_designator [(expression)]

attribute_specification ::=
   attribute attribute_designator **of** entity_specification **is** expression ;

base ::= integer

base_specifier ::= B | O | X

based_integer ::=
   extended_digit { [underline] extended_digit }

based_literal ::=
   base # based_integer [. based_integer] # [exponent]

basic_character ::=
   basic_graphic_character | format_effector

basic_graphic_character ::=
   upper_case_letter | digit | special_character| space_character

basic_identifier ::= letter { [underline] letter_or_digit }

binding_indication ::=
   [**use** entity_aspect]
   [generic_map_aspect]
   [port_map_aspect]

bit_string_literal ::= base_specifier " [bit_value] "

bit_value ::= extended_digit { [underline] extended_digit }

block_configuration ::=
   for block_specification
     { use_clause }
     { configuration_item }
   end for ;

block_declarative_item ::=
     subprogram_declaration
   | subprogram_body
   | type_declaration
   | subtype_declaration
   | constant_declaration
   | signal_declaration
   | *shared*_variable_declaration
   | file_declaration
   | alias_declaration
   | component_declaration
   | attribute_declaration
   | attribute_specification
   | configuration_specification

   | disconnection_specification
   | use_clause
   | group_template_declaration
   | group_ declaration

block_declarative_part ::=
   { block_declarative_item }

block_header ::=
   [generic_clause
   [generic_map_aspect ;]]
   [port_clause
   [port_map_aspect ;]]

block_specification ::=
   *architecture*_name
   | *block_statement*_label
   | *generate_statement*_label [(index_specification)]

block_statement ::=
   *block*_label :
     block [(*guard*_expression)] [**is**]
       block_header
       block_declarative_part
    begin
       block_statement_part
    end block [*block*_label] ;

block_statement_part ::=
   { concurrent_statement }

case_statement ::=
   case expression **is**
       case_statement_alternative
     { case_statement_alternative }
    end case [case_label] ;

case_statement_alternative ::=
   when choices =>
   sequence_of_statements

character_literal ::= ' graphic_character '

choice ::=
   simple_expression
   | discrete_range
   | *element*_simple_name
   | **others**

choices ::= choice { | choice }

component_configuration ::=
   for component_specification
   [binding_indication ;]
   [block_configuration]
  end for ;

component_declaration ::=
   component identifier [**is**]
     [*local*_generic_clause]
     [*local*_port_clause]
   end component [*component*_simple_name] ;

component_instantiation_statement ::=
   *instantiation*_label :
     instantiated_unit
      [generic_map_aspect]
      [port_map_aspect] ;

component_specification ::=
   instantiation_list : *component*_name

composite_type_definition ::=
   array_type_definition
  | record_type_definition

concurrent_assertion_statement ::=
   [label :] [**postponed**] assertion ;

concurrent_procedure_call_statement ::=
   [label :] [**postponed**] procedure_call ;

concurrent_signal_assignment_statement ::=
   [label :] [**postponed**] conditional_signal_assignment
  | [label :] [**postponed**] selected_signal_assignment

concurrent_statement ::=
   block_statement
  | process_statement
  | concurrent_procedure_call_statement
  | concurrent_assertion_statement
  | concurrent_signal_assignment_statement
  | component_instantiation_statement
  | generate_statement

condition ::= *boolean*_expression

condition_clause ::= **until** condition

conditional_signal_assignment ::=
   target <= options conditional_waveforms ;

conditional_waveforms ::=
   { waveform **when** condition **else** }
   waveform [when condition]

configuration_declaration ::=
   configuration identifier **of** *entity*_name **is**
      configuration_declarative_part
     block_configuration
   end [**configuration**] [*configuration*_simple_name] ;

configuration_declarative_item ::=
   use_clause
  | attribute_specification
  | group_ declaration

configuration_declarative_part ::=
  { configuration_declarative_item }

configuration_item ::=
    block_configuration
  | component_configuration

configuration_specification ::=
    for component_specification binding_indication ;

constant_declaration ::=
    constant identifier_list : subtype_indication [:= expression] ;

constrained_array_definition ::=
    array index_constraint **of** *element*_subtype_indication

constraint ::=
    range_constraint
  | index_constraint

context_clause ::= { context_item }

context_item ::=
    library_clause
  | use_clause

decimal_literal ::= integer [. integer] [exponent]

declaration ::=
    type_declaration
  | subtype_declaration
  | object_declaration
  | interface_declaration
  | alias_declaration
  | attribute_declaration
  | component_declaration
  | group_template_declaration
  | group_ declaration
  | entity_declaration
  | configuration_declaration
  | subprogram_declaration
  | package_declaration

delay_mechanism ::=
    transport
      | [**reject** *time*_expression] **inertial**

design_file ::= design_unit { design_unit }

design_unit ::= context_clause library_unit

designator ::= identifier | operator_symbol

direction ::= **to** | **downto**

disconnection_specification ::=
    disconnect guarded_signal_specification **after** *time*_expression ;

discrete_range ::= *discrete*_subtype_indication | range

element_association ::=
[choices =>] expression

element_declaration ::=   identifier_list : element_subtype_definition ;

element_subtype_definition ::= subtype_indication

entity_aspect ::=
  entity *entity*_name [(*architecture*_identifier)]
  | **configuration** *configuration*_name
  | **open**

entity_class ::=
  entity
  | architecture
  | configuration
  | procedure
  | function
  | package
  | type
  | subtype
  | constant
  | signal
  | variable
  | component
  | label
  | literal
  | units
  | group
  | file

entity_class_entry ::= entity_class [<>]

entity_class_entry_list ::=
  entity_class_entry { , entity_class_entry }

entity_declaration ::=
  entity identifier **is**
      entity_header
    entity_declarative_part
  [**begin**
      entity_statement_part]
  end [**entity**] [*entity*_simple_name] ;

entity_declarative_item ::=
  subprogram_declaration
  | subprogram_body
  | type_declaration
  | subtype_declaration
  | constant_declaration
  | signal_declaration
  | *shared*_variable_declaration
  | file_declaration
  | alias_declaration
  | attribute_declaration
  | attribute_specification
  | disconnection_specification
  | use_clause
  | group_template_declaration
  | group_ declaration

entity_declarative_part ::=
   { entity_declarative_item }

entity_designator ::= entity_tag [signature]

entity_header ::=
   [*formal*_generic_clause]
   [*formal*_port_clause]

entity_name_list ::=
   entity_designator { , entity_designator }
  | **others**
    | **all**

entity_specification ::=
   entity_name_list : entity_class

entity_statement ::=
   concurrent_assertion_statement
  | *passive*_concurrent_procedure_call_statement
  | *passive*_process_statement

entity_statement_part ::=
   { entity_statement }

entity_tag ::= simple_name | character_literal | operator_symbol

enumeration_literal ::= identifier | character_literal

enumeration_type_definition ::=
   (enumeration_literal { , enumeration_literal })

exit_statement ::=
   [label :] **exit** [*loop*_label] [**when** condition] ;

exponent ::= E [+] integer | E -integer

expression ::=
   relation { **and** relation }
  | relation { **or** relation }
  | relation { **xor** relation }
  | relation [**nand** relation]
  | relation [**nor** relation]
  | relation { **xnor** relation }

extended_digit ::= digit | letter

extended_identifier ::= \ graphic_character { graphic_character } \

factor ::=
   primary [** primary]
  | **abs** primary
  | **not** primary

file_declaration ::=
   file identifier_list : subtype_indication [file_open_information] ;

file_logical_name ::= *string*_expression

file_open_information ::=
   [**open** *file_open_kind*_expression] **is** file_logical_name

file_type_definition ::=
   file of type_mark

floating_type_definition ::= range_constraint

formal_designator ::=
   *generic*_name
  | *port*_name
  | *parameter*_name

formal_parameter_list ::= *parameter*_interface_list

formal_part ::=
   formal_designator
  | *function*_name (formal_designator)
  | type_mark (formal_designator)

full_type_declaration ::=
   type identifier **is** type_definition ;

function_call ::=
  *function*_name [(actual_parameter_part)]

generate_statement ::=
  *generate*_label :
    generation_scheme **generate**
      [{ block_declarative_item }
    begin]
      { concurrent_statement }
    end generate [*generate*_label] ;

generation_scheme ::=
    for *generate*_parameter_specification
  | **if** condition

generic_clause ::=
   generic (generic_list) ;

generic_list ::= *generic*_interface_list

generic_map_aspect ::=
   generic map (*generic*_association_list)

graphic_character ::=
  basic_graphic_character | lower_case_letter | other_special_character

group_constituent ::= name | character_literal

group_constituent_list ::= group_constituent { , group_constituent }

group_ declaration ::=
   group identifier : *group_ template*_name (group_constituent_list) ;

group_template_declaration ::=
   group identifier **is** (entity_class_entry_list) ;

guarded_signal_specification ::=
  *guarded*_signal_list : type_mark

identifier ::= basic_identifier | extended_identifier

identifier_list ::= identifier { , identifier }

if_statement ::=
    [*if*_label :]
      if condition **then**
            sequence_of_statements
      { **elsif** condition **then**
            sequence_of_statements }
      [**else**
            sequence_of_statements]
      end if [*if*_label] ;

incomplete_type_declaration ::= **type** identifier ;

index_constraint ::= (discrete_range { , discrete_range })

index_specification ::=
    discrete_range
    | *static*_expression

index_subtype_definition ::= type_mark **range** <>

indexed_name ::= prefix (expression { , expression })

instantiated_unit ::=
    [**component**] *component*_name
    | **entity** *entity*_name [(*architecture*_identifier)]
    | **configuration** *configuration*_name

instantiation_list ::=
    *instantiation*_label { , *instantiation*_label }
    | **others**
        | **all**

integer ::= digit { [underline] digit }

integer_type_definition ::= range_constraint

interface_constant_declaration ::=
    [**constant**] identifier_list : [**in**] subtype_indication [:= *static*_expression]

interface_declaration ::=
    interface_constant_declaration
    | interface_signal_declaration
    | interface_variable_declaration
    | interface_file_declaration

interface_element ::= interface_declaration

interface_file_declaration ::=
    file identifier_list : subtype_indication

interface_list ::=
    interface_element { ; interface_element }

interface_signal_declaration ::=
    [**signal**] identifier_list : [mode] subtype_indication [**bus**] [:= *static*_expression]

interface_variable_declaration ::=
    [**variable**] identifier_list : [mode] subtype_indication [:= *static*_expression]

iteration_scheme ::=
    while condition
    | **for** *loop*_parameter_specification

label ::= identifier

letter ::= upper_case_letter | lower_case_letter

letter_or_digit ::= letter | digit

library_clause ::= **library** logical_name_list ;`

library_unit ::=
    primary_unit
   | secondary_unit

literal ::=
    numeric_literal
   | enumeration_literal
   | string_literal
   | bit_string_literal
   | **null**

logical_name ::= identifier

logical_name_list ::= logical_name { , logical_name }

logical_operator ::= **and** | **or** | **nand** | **nor** | **xor** | **xnor**

loop_statement ::=
    [*loop*_label :]
      [iteration_scheme] **loop**
         sequence_of_statements
    end **loop** [*loop*_label] ;

miscellaneous_operator ::= ****** | **abs** | **not**

mode ::= **in** | **out** | **inout** | **buffer** | **linkage**

multiplying_operator ::= ***** | **/** | **mod** | **rem**

name ::=
    simple_name
   | operator_symbol
   | selected_name
   | indexed_name
   | slice_name
   | attribute_name

next_statement ::=
    [label :] **next** [*loop*_label] [**when** condition] ;

null_statement ::= [label :] **null** ;

numeric_literal ::=
    abstract_literal
   | physical_literal

object_declaration ::=
    constant_declaration
   | signal_declaration
   | variable_declaration
   | file_declaration

operator_symbol ::= string_literal

options ::= [**guarded**] [delay_mechanism]

package_body ::=
   package body *package*_simple_name **is**
      package_body_declarative_part
   end [**package_body**] [*package*_simple_name] ;

package_body_declarative_item ::=
    subprogram_declaration
   | subprogram_body
   | type_declaration
   | subtype_declaration
   | constant_declaration
   | *shared*_variable_declaration
   | file_declaration
   | alias_declaration
   | use_clause
   | group_template_declaration
   | group_ declaration

package_body_declarative_part ::=
   { package_body_declarative_item }

package_declaration ::=
   package identifier **is**
      package_declarative_part
   end [**package**] [*package*_simple_name] ;

package_declarative_item ::=
    subprogram_declaration
   | type_declaration
   | subtype_declaration
   | constant_declaration
   | signal_declaration
   | *shared*_variable_declaration
   | file_declaration
   | alias_declaration
   | component_declaration
   | attribute_declaration
   | attribute_specification
   | disconnection_specification
   | use_clause
   | group_template_declaration
   | group_ declaration

package_declarative_part ::=
   { package_declarative_item }

parameter_specification ::=
   identifier **in** discrete_range

physical_literal ::= [abstract_literal] *unit*_name

physical_type_definition ::=
   range_constraint
   units
      base_unit_declaration
    { secondary_unit_declaration }
   end units [*physical_type*_simple_name]

port_clause ::=
   port (port_list) ;

port_list ::= *port*_interface_list

port_map_aspect ::=
   port map (*port*_association_list)

prefix ::=
   name
  | function_call

primary ::=
   name
  | literal
  | aggregate
  | function_call
  | qualified_expression
  | type_conversion
  | allocator
  | (expression)

primary_unit ::=
   entity_declaration
  | configuration_declaration
  | package_declaration

primary_unit_declaration ::= identifier ;

procedure_call ::=
   *procedure*_name [(actual_parameter_part)]

procedure_call_statement ::= [label :] procedure_call ;

process_declarative_item ::=
   subprogram_declaration
  | subprogram_body
  | type_declaration
  | subtype_declaration
  | constant_declaration
  | variable_declaration
  | file_declaration
  | alias_declaration
  | attribute_declaration
  | attribute_specification
  | use_clause
  | group_template_declaration
  | group_ declaration

process_declarative_part ::=
   { process_declarative_item }

process_statement ::=
   [*process*_label :]
    [**postponed**] **process** [(sensitivity_list)] [**is**]
     process_declarative_part
    begin
      process_statement_part
    end [**postponed**] **process** [*process*_label] ;

process_statement_part ::=
   { sequential_statement }

qualified_expression ::=
   type_mark ' (expression)
   | type_mark ' aggregate

range ::=
   *range*_attribute_name
   | simple_expression direction simple_expression

range_constraint ::= **range** range

record_type_definition ::=
   record
       element_declaration
     { element_declaration }
   end record [*record_type*_simple_name]

relation ::=
   shift_expression [relational_operator shift_expression]

relational_operator ::= = | /= | < | <= | > | >=

report_statement ::=
   [label :]
     report expression
      [**severity** expression] ;

return_statement ::=
   [label] **return** [expression] ;

scalar_type_definition ::=
    enumeration_type_definition
    | integer_type_definition
    | floating_type_definition
    | physical_type_definition

secondary_unit ::=
    architecture_body
   | package_body

secondary_unit_declaration ::= identifier = physical_literal ;

selected_name ::= prefix . suffix

selected_signal_assignment ::=
   with expression **select**
     target <= options selected_waveforms ;

selected_waveforms ::=
   { waveform **when** choices , }
   waveform **when** choices

sensitivity_clause ::= **on** sensitivity_list

sensitivity_list ::= *signal*_name { , *signal*_name }

sequence_of_statements ::=
   { sequential_statement }

sequential_statement ::=
    wait_statement
  | assertion_statement
  | report_statement
  | signal_assignment_statement
  | variable_assignment_statement
  | procedure_call_statement
  | if_statement
  | case_statement
  | loop_statement
  | next_statement
  | exit_statement
  | return_statement
  | null_statement

shift_expression ::=
    simple_expression [shift_operator simple_expression]

shift_operator ::= **sll** | **srl** | **sla** | **sra** | **rol** | **ror**

sign ::= + | -

signal_assignment_statement ::=
    [label :] target <= [delay_mechanism] waveform ;

signal_declaration ::=
    signal identifier_list : subtype_indication [signal_kind] [:= expression] ;

signal_kind ::= **register** | **bus**

signal_list ::=
    *signal*_name { , **signal**_name }
  | **others**
    | **all**

signature ::= [[type_mark { , type_mark }] [**return** type_mark]]

simple_expression ::=
    [sign] term { adding_operator term }

simple_name ::= identifier

slice_name ::= prefix (discrete_range)

string_literal ::= " { graphic_character } "

subprogram_body ::=
    subprogram_specification **is**
        subprogram_declarative_part
  begin
        subprogram_statement_part
  end [subprogram_kind] [designator] ;

subprogram_declaration ::=
    subprogram_specification ;

subprogram_declarative_item ::=
    subprogram_declaration
  | subprogram_body
  | type_declaration
  | subtype_declaration

   | constant_declaration
   | variable_declaration
   | file_declaration
   | alias_declaratio
   | attribute_declaration
   | attribute_specification
   | use_clause
   | group_template_declaration
   | group_ declaratio

subprogram_declarative_part ::=
   { subprogram_declarative_item }

subprogram_kind ::= **procedure** | **function**

subprogram_specification ::=
   procedure designator [(formal_parameter_list)]
  | [**pure** | **impure**] **function** designator [(formal_parameter_list)]
   return type_mark

subprogram_statement_part ::=
   { sequential_statement }

subtype_declaration ::=
   subtype identifier **is** subtype_indication ;

subtype_indication ::=
   [*resolution_function*_name] type_mark [constraint]

suffix ::=
   simple_name
   | character_literal
   | operator_symbol
   | **all**

target ::=
   name
   | aggregate

term ::=
   factor { multiplying_operator factor }

timeout_clause ::= **for** *time*_expression

type_conversion ::= type_mark (expression)

type_declaration ::=
   full_type_declaration
   | incomplete_type_declaration

type_definition ::=
   scalar_type_definition
   | composite_type_definition
   | access_type_definition
   | file_type_definition

type_mark ::=
   *type*_name
   | *subtype*_name

unconstrained_array_definition ::=
    array (index_subtype_definition { , index_subtype_definition })
      of *element*_subtype_indication

use_clause ::=
    use selected_name { , selected_name } ;

variable_assignment_statement ::=
    [label :] target := expression ;

variable_declaration ::=
    [**shared**] **variable** identifier_list : subtype_indication [:= expression] ;

wait_statement ::=
    [label :] **wait** [sensitivity_clause] [condition_clause] [timeout_clause] ;

waveform ::=
    waveform_element { , waveform_element }
   | **unaffected**

waveform_element ::=
    *value*_expression [**after** *time*_expression]
   | **null** [**after** *time*_expression]

LITERATURE

[ARM 89]   J. R. Armstrong: "Chip-Level Modeling with VHDL", Prentice Hall, Englewood Cliffs, NJ, 1989

[ARM 93]   J. R. Armstrong, F. G. Gray: "Structured Logic Design with VHDL", Prentice Hall, Englewood Cliffs, NJ, 1993

[ASH 90]   P. J. Ashenden: "The VHDL Cookbook", 1990, via ftp://ftp.cs.adelaide.edu.au/pub/VHDL-Cookbook/ (129.127.8.8) or ftp://bears.ece.ucsb.edu/pub/VHDL/comp.lang.vhdl

[ASH 95]   P. J. Ashenden: "The Designer's Guide to VHDL", Morgan Kaufmann Publishers, 1995

[BAK 93]   L. Baker: "VHDL Programming with Advanced Topics", John Wiley & Sons, New York, 1993

[BER 92]   J.-M. Bergé, A. Fonkoua, S. Maginot: "VHDL Designer´s Reference", Kluwer Academic Publishers, Dordrecht, 1992

[BHA 98]   J. Bhasker: "A VHDL Primer", Prentice Hall, Englewood Cliffs, NJ, 1998

[BHA 98]   J. Bhasker: "A VHDL Synthesis Primer", Star Galaxy Publishing, Allentown, 1998

[BIL 93]   W. Billowitch: IEEE 1164: Helping Designers Share VHDL Models, *IEEE Spectrum*, June 1993, p. 37

[CAM 91]   R. Camposano: "High-Level Synthesis from VHDL", in: *IEEE Design and Test of Computers*, Part 3, 1991

[COE 89]   D. Coelho: "The VHDL Handbook", Kluwer Academic Publishers, Boston, 1989

[COH 99]   B. Cohen: "VHDL Coding Styles and Methodologies", Kluwer Academic Publishers, Boston, 1999; for TOC see http://members.aol.com/vhdlcohen/vhdl

[DAR 90]   J. Darringer, F. Ramming: "Computer Hardware Description Languages and their Applications", North-Holland, Amsterdam, 1990

[GAJ 88]   D. Gajski: Introduction to Silicon Compilation, in: "Silicon Compilation", Addison-Wesley, Reading, MA, 1988

[HAR 91]   R. E. Harr, A. Stanculesco: "Applications of VHDL to Circuit Design", Kluwer Academic Publishers, Boston, 1991

[IEE 88]   The Institute of Electrical and Electronics Engineers: "IEEE Standard VHDL Language Reference Manual (IEEE-1076-1987)", New York, 1988

[IEE 94]   The Institute of Electrical and Electronics Engineers: "IEEE Standard VHDL Language Reference Manual (IEEE-1076-1993)", New York, 1994

[LEU 89]   S. S. Leung, M. A. Shanblatt: "ASIC System Design with VHDL: A Paradigm", Kluwer Academic Publishers, Boston, 1989

[LIS 89]   J. Lis, D. Gajski: VHDL Synthesis Using Structured Modelling, in: "26th Design Automation Conference", 1989

[LIP 89]   R. Lipsett et al.: "An Introduction to VHDL: Hardware Description and Design", Kluwer Academic Publishers, Boston, 1989

[MAZ 92]   S. Mazor, P. Langstraat: "A Guide to VHDL", Kluwer Academic Publishers, Boston, 1992

[MER 92]   J. P. Mermet: "VHDL for Simulation, Synthesis and Formal Proofs", Kluwer International Series in Engineering and Computer Science, Dordrecht, 1992

[MER 93]   J. P. Mermet: "Fundamentals and Standards in Hardware Description Languages", NATO ASI Series, Kluwer Academic Publishers, Dordrecht, 1993

[NAV 93]   Z. Navabi: "VHDL Analysis and Modeling of Digital Systems", McGraw-Hill, New York, 1993

[PER 98]   D. L. Perry: "VHDL", McGraw-Hill, New York, 1998

[RUS 98]   A. Rushton: "VHDL for Logic Synthesis", John Wiley & Sons, Chichester, 1998

[SCH 92]   J. M. Schoen: "Performance and Fault Modeling with VHDL", Prentice Hall, Englewood Cliffs, NJ, 1992

INDEX

Printed and bound by CPI Group (UK) Ltd, Croydon, CR0 4YY

27/10/2024

14580294-0003